THE SILENT PAST

Mysterious and Forgotten Cultures
of the World

BOOKS BY IVAR LISSNER

THE SILENT PAST
Mysterious and Forgotten Cultures of the World

MAN, GOD AND MAGIC

THE CAESARS
Might and Madness

THE LIVING PAST

IVAR LISSNER

THE SILENT PAST

Mysterious and Forgotten Cultures of the World

Translated from the German by

J. MAXWELL BROWNJOHN, M.A. (*Oxon.*)

G. P. PUTNAM'S SONS
NEW YORK

MANUFACTURED IN THE UNITED STATES OF AMERICA

VAN REES PRESS • NEW YORK

A WORD OF THANKS

I SHOULD like to extend my sincere thanks to the archaeologists, scientists and scholars whose advice and suggestions have been of such invaluable assistance to me and who have scrutinized individual sections of this book or shown me over palaces, temples and ruined sites:

PROFESSOR ANTONIO BLANCO FREIJEIRO of Seville University, Director of the Museo del Prado, Madrid, for checking the sections on Tartessus.

PROFESSOR CARL W. BLEGEN, the eminent archaeologist who unearthed the stratum containing Homeric Troy, for taking me over the ruins of Nestor's palace at Pylos.

SOTIRIS DAKARIS, Ephoros Archeotiton at the Museum of Archaeology, Ioannina, for explaining details of the temple precincts and ruins in the Valley of Dramissos and checking the sections dealing with the oracle of Dodona.

DR. HANS-DIETRICH DISSELHOFF, authority on ancient American civilizations and Director of the Museum of Ethnology, Berlin, for much invaluable advice and generous help.

WILLIAM P. FAGG, Deputy Keeper of the Department of Ethnography in the British Museum, for checking the section on Benin.

PROFESSOR DR. MARTIN GUSINDE of Vienna University, Nanzan University, Nagoya, Universidad de Chile and Catholic University, Washington, D. C., ethnologist and expert on prehistoric civilizations, American Indian tribes, especially those of Tierra del Fuego, and many other primitive peoples, who willingly answered all my questions and enlightened me on a number of unsolved problems.

PROFESSOR DR. WILHELM KOPPERS ✝, the distinguished authority on ethnology and prehistory to whom I shall always be indebted for his encouragement and instructive comments.

5
21076

DR. GERDT KUTSCHER of the Ibero-American Library, Berlin, for scrutinizing the sections on the Maya and offering valuable suggestions on the subject of Benin.

PROFESSOR DR. SIEGFRIED LAUFFER of Munich University, for giving me so many valuable hints and checking the sections on Mycenaean civilization and Delphi.

PROFESSOR GIOVANNI LILLIU, Università degli Studi di Cagliari, for personally enlightening me on the culture of ancient Sardinia.

DR. KARL J. NARR, Lecturer in Prehistory at Göttingen University, for looking through the sections on the megalithic cultures.

PROFESSOR DR. ADOLF SCHULTEN ✝, archaeologist and authority on ancient history and geography, particularly that of the Iberian Peninsula, for his many verbal suggestions and interpretations.

PROFESSOR DR. ERNEST SITTIG ✝, who was the first to instruct me on the subject of research into Linear B.

DR. HERBERT TISCHNER, Custodian and Director of the Indo-Oceanic Department of the Museum of Ethnology and Prehistory, Hamburg, for looking through the section on the Sepik culture.

CONCEPCION BLANCO DE TORRECILLAS, Director of the Museo Arqueológico, Cádiz, for granting me access to rare relics of the Tartessus civilization.

CONTENTS

Birds of Passage

HISTORY is imperishable. Unseen and unrecognized, the past lives on in us in its quiet, imperceptible way. Whether lying dormant in the unfathomable sea of the millennia or buried beneath the ground and swathed in a vast winding sheet of earth and stone, "past" civilizations are still with us even though their tangible remains lie hidden and still undiscovered. One and all, the civilizations of the past live on in us, for our lives are rooted deep in the remote, mysterious and ancient civilizations of the past. Once a civilization has existed on earth, its effects are permanent. A memory, a new discovery, a visit to an exhibition—any one of these may suddenly alert us to their mute presence.

Civilization is a word of wide application. It is the sum total of human achievement, of techniques, of methods of building and transportation, of living conditions, of handicrafts and utensils, of written characters, of sciences; it is the moral and religious order of things; it is the behavior of each individual; it embraces all man's spiritual endeavors, his art and morals, his sense of values and his religion.

All human hopes and thoughts are directed toward the eternal and transcendental, for it is man's nature to be more concerned with the mind than the body.

When man made the transition from thinking only of visible things—from "conditioned" thought—to abstract thought, the era of true humanity had arrived. From that moment, no more than six hundred thousand or a million years ago, spirituality has been man's hallmark, his distinguishing feature and his cross. And it has been man's pastime to fight against this cross, to disavow, deride or attempt to destroy it during periods of cultural decline. But matter is not only lifeless: it is not even real. Man alone can infuse it with life and give it the sort of vitality which we shall observe in so many examples of human handiwork—in works by the artists of Benin, for instance. The real bane of our time is not the earth's burgeoning population but the ever-increasing superabundance of inanimate objects and the possessiveness that springs from a sense of personal inadequacy. The greater the number of objects that surround us, the fewer we can infuse with life. Man's intellect has been dulled by

9

a superfluity of mass-produced articles devoid of any breath of life. Only when the West has completely smothered the intellect will it succumb, not before. That is why it is so important to recognize that man's desire for spiritual sustenance will always be stronger than his craving for material objects and to acknowledge that our only means of preserving the world in which we live lies in that realization. Since all spirituality is essentially religious in conception, everything that is good on earth must have its foundation in a belief in God or gods. The same basic belief underlies all civilizations, and to examine them is to receive fresh confirmation of this truth.

Our age yearns for a better knowledge of the buried past. People sense that even the most alien and mysterious civilizations are part of their present existence. It is immensely exciting to spot the truth that lies behind a mystery, to delve beneath the ground and unearth cities, to realize that this was how *they* did things, this was how *they* thought, this was *their* intellectual contribution to *our* life— to realize, in short, that during our brief sojourn on earth we are merely birds of passage.

I believe that in every age man has devoted his greatest efforts to the spiritual aspects of life and that he has always striven to reach beyond sensory perception and grasp the supersensual and divine. Strangely enough, no one has ever denied these attributes to the advanced civilizations of the ancient world, even though the catastrophes that afflict us today are rooted in the shocking and erroneous belief that scientific and technical achievements, social legislation and governmental intervention are the only things that can ameliorate human existence.

I believe that man ought to be alive to the truth contained in the fourth chapter of St. Matthew, namely that he cannot live by bread alone, and that he should insist on his sovereign right to live with complete freedom, spiritually and in the spirit. As Friedrich Schiller said: "Each individual man carries, according to his disposition and determination, a purely ideal man within him"—and the realm of taste is a realm of freedom.

I believe in the self-delusion of the masses and in the spirituality of the individual—even the so-called "savage" who never actually existed at all. We should beware of branding as uncivilized primitive races which in truth possessed a high degree of spiritual culture which we either cannot grasp or do not share.

I believe in the vital force of all civilizations and hold that their life is determined by the untrammeled mind of man, not by nature. I believe in the essential unity of political history and cultural history because I do not recognize the existence anywhere in this world of civilizations which stand alone like isolated trees, unseeded, rootless and sprung from nothing. Either they must have taken seed from some vanished people, some civilization unknown to us, perhaps, but ever present, or their roots have become secretly and subterraneously entwined with those of other civilizations.

I believe that culture springs neither from what we possess nor from what we think but only from what we are. I believe that time is indivisible and that all chronological subdivisions are the work of man; that time is, in fact, an integral, cosmic and divine work of art. I believe that mankind's conception of time is its greatest single error, that in reality there is neither beginning nor end, and that only God can have a truly correct—as it were, oblique—view of time.

Within the true span of our lifetime, therefore, we may have walked the massive walls of Jericho or stood atop the world's oldest tower, four thousand years older than the first Pyramid. We may still remember Tyre, the famous Phoenician island city of twenty-five thousand inhabitants whose man-created water supply helped to make it the most impregnable fortress in the Mediterranean. We may have stoked King Solomon's smelting ovens in the guise of slaves, working in unendurable heat at the desert's edge. With a past as limitless as ours, the eight thousand mysterious towers of the Sardi may seem familiar to us, built though they were in the Bronze-Age spirit of 800 B.C. We may carry within us the wisdom of the Delphic oracle or the truth of Atlantis. A thousand legacies from the distant past are embodied in us. To survey the mysterious caverns, chambers and temples of men who walked the earth long before us is to gain a glimpse of eternal life, because all their achievements, all their art and beliefs are still within us today and are destined to endure forever.

THE SILENT PAST

*Mysterious and Forgotten Cultures
of the World*

THE WALLS OF JERICHO

We have now completed five seasons' excavations. Each year our trenches and squares have got deeper and deeper, and the working levels have to be reached by ever-lengthening staircases cut in the earth down the edges of the area. In several areas we have now reached bedrock, at a depth of some fifty feet from the surface.

—KATHLEEN MARY KENYON, *Digging Up Jericho,*
p. 50, London, 1957

JERICHO was immensely ancient. It was so old that not even the patriarchs Abraham, Isaac and Jacob knew its origins.

Roam the entire world in search of its oldest cities and you will always come back to the Near East, for it was there that man, having lived on earth for about 600,000 years as a nomad, food collector and hunter, first began to set stone on stone and build dwellings and, eventually, cities. Only when the biped Homo had once learned how to sow and reap, capture wild animals and domesticate them, did fixed settlements become practicable.

Very old advanced civilizations have been excavated near the Hwang Ho, Indus and Nile and in the valleys of the Euphrates and Tigris, but what archaeologists have recently unearthed below ground near the Jordan derives immense significance from the fact that it dates the building of fortresses, houses and temples almost as far back as the close of the last Ice Age.

In 600,000 years man has survived four Ice Ages and three warmer interglacial periods. The last Ice Age came to an end about 8000 B.C. Even though the icy masses of the north never penetrated the Near East, the city is still a miracle, for the Ice Age was also a Stone Age in which technical aids were of the most rudimentary kind and man was a nomad. For 600,000 years, the longest homogeneous epoch in human history, tools and utensils were made exclusively of stone, bone and wood. Next came the art of molding clay and loam, then the discovery of casting copper and bronze, and finally the Iron Age.

Jericho was built at a time when man was still ignorant of clay vessels. The people of Jericho lived in a powerful city, yet they were people of the mesolithic or Middle Stone Age (10,000–7500 B.C.), which was followed by the neolithic or Late Stone Age (7500–

4000 B.C.). Jericho is not merely the oldest fortress to be excavated so far; at more than 800 feet below sea level it is also the lowest-lying city in the world. The summers are extremely hot because the area is surrounded by mountains reaching 3,500 feet.

Fifteen miles northeast of Jerusalem and eight miles from where the Jordan flows into the Dead Sea stands the hill of Tell Es-Sultan. In it are buried the remains of many cities superimposed one upon another, the result of a process lasting thousands of years in which new life was forever springing up on the ruins of the past. The site was excavated first by English archaeologists in 1865, then by an Austro-German expedition between 1908 and 1911, and finally by Professor John Garstang of Liverpool University, whose examination of some particularly deep layers convinced him that men had dwelt in houses there in neolithic times. In 1956 further diggings by Kathleen Kenyon revealed the astonishing fact that Jericho had existed as a true town in the pre-ceramic period, i.e. long before 5000 B.C.

It was earlier supposed that men who had ceased to be nomads soon began to make bowls, jugs and other vessels from clay, such articles being much too fragile to be taken on long nomadic treks. Jericho shed a new light on this theory, for men lived there in permanent abodes for thousands of years before they discovered ceramics. Between the nomadic period and the time when clay vessels were first manufactured came an epoch which saw the emergence of thriving towns whose inhabitants made nothing but stone tools and utensils of bone or wood. Jericho's pre-ceramic period goes back some nine or ten thousand years and lasted from about 7800 B.C. to about 5000 B.C. Its ruins lay heaped fifty feet high, each succeeding generation having built upon the debris of its predecessors, but only at the fifty-foot mark do traces of pottery come to light.

The earliest houses were circular in shape and probably resembled beehives or, more precisely, halved eggs. The floors were earthen while the walls were of oval bricks with flat bases and curved sides which still display grooves made by the brickmakers' thumbs. Since the streets of an old city acquire layers of debris and refuse in the course of centuries, the floors of Jericho's houses eventually lay below street level, and one can still make out the steps which led down to them. The latter are known to have been faced with wood, for remnants of charred beams were found everywhere.

The city's earliest period was followed by another period—still

Syria—Jordan

long before 5000 B.C.—which saw the construction of houses with fairly large rectangular rooms whose corners were carefully rounded as if to prevent their collecting dust, as in modern hospitals. These dwellings possessed small store chambers and a number of subsidiary rooms. Cooking was done on a hearth situated in an interior courtyard, and the many layers of ash which were found indicated that meals had been prepared in the same spot for decades or centuries. The walls of the houses, which may even have had two floors, were built of sun-dried bricks which, Mrs. Kenyon tells us, were fitted together with great accuracy. Even today, after eight or nine thousand years, it is difficult to dismantle them or remove individual bricks.

When archaeologists washed the "stuccoed" floors, much as the women of Jericho must have done many thousands of years before, they found to their surprise that these had been polished with great care. The interior walls were also coated with hard stucco and polished to a mirrorlike smoothness. Apparently the people of Jericho appreciated comfort, for their rooms were carpeted with rush mats which, though destroyed by the passage of time, had left their imprint on the floors. It was even possible to see where an ant had once made its way through the carpet!

It is particularly interesting that the bowls, dishes and other receptacles used in the well-appointed houses of so advanced a civilization seem to have been made only of stone. Wood and bone may also have been employed, but nothing of these materials has survived. The people of Jericho still made their tools, which included blades, drills, scrapers and extremely handsome saws, out of flint or obsidian. No large tools were found, yet the builders of such a city must have possessed picks, axes and a range of heavy implements suitable for dealing with balks of timber. Nothing of the sort was found, however, although diggers unearthed flint arrowheads which may have been used in the city's defense as well as for hunting.

Another unsolved riddle is the purpose of some tiny *coups de poing* of green stone which do not seem to be jewelry but may have been used in some form of cult. One house, at any rate, contained a sort of altar or shrine, or so it would appear from the discovery of a small pillar of volcanic rock, a niche and a stone pedestal. The pillar fits the pedestal and both would fit neatly into the niche. Even though they were separated when found in the rubble of the ruined house, they seem to offer support for a theory that the people of Jericho worshiped a god or gods.

The largest chamber to be excavated may also have been employed for religious purposes. In the center of this templelike building stood a basin, and near it two tiny figurines which possibly represented goddesses of fertility. Small female statuettes which served a fertility cult or had some other directly religious significance are already familiar to us from the Aurignacian period. These are the famous "Venus" statuettes found at Willendorf, Lespugue, Brassempouy, Gagarino on the Don, and Malta, northwest of Irkutsk. Some of the European Venus statuettes date back as much as thirty or fifty thousand years.

The city was originally encompassed by a stout wall some sixteen feet high. When the wall collapsed it was rebuilt, and when it collapsed again it was replaced by another, this one over twenty feet high. Mystery surrounds the tower of Jericho, thirty feet in diameter and so solidly built of undressed stone that it now stands there, after excavation, like some massive medieval bastion. The oldest tower in the world, it existed even before Jericho acquired its protective walls. The men who planned and constructed it lived nine thousand or more years ago, and it is about four thousand years older than the oldest Pyramid. Inside the tower a flight of steps built of stone slabs thirty inches long leads up through an opening to the upper platform. Below is a passage faced with stone slabs three feet long, and in this passage archaeologists found twelve skeletons lying close together as though the bodies had been buried in extreme haste. The tower is enclosed by two further rings of stone. Only the outer shell touches the city wall, so the latter must have come into being at a later stage.

The significance of this prehistoric building while it remained unconnected with the wall and had no defensive role is uncertain, but it was probably a cult site or perhaps a temple at whose summit sacrifice was made in honor of gods unknown to us.

Kathleen Kenyon's theory is that the inhabitants of the earliest, conical, houses were forced to defend themselves against people who eventually captured the town and later erected the rectangular houses with the finely polished stucco floors. The victorious newcomers were certainly not nomads, for their well-planned methods of housing construction belonged to a highly developed sedentary culture and presupposed long experience. Miss Kenyon deduces that these experienced architects hailed from existing towns, probably in the neighborhood of Jericho, and brought their knowledge of architecture from there. If this is so, other age-old stone citadels must lie elsewhere, probably in the Jordan valley, still awaiting discovery.

The most important finds made at Jericho were ten human skulls which were dug up, one by one, from beneath some houses. They represent an extraordinary discovery, for through them we are suddenly made aware of man's quest for a higher spirituality, a quest pursued with means and at a period which seem well-nigh fantastic to us today. These skulls were skillfully coated with plaster and their eye sockets had been inlaid with shells with the apparent intention of reproducing the features of the dead as they were in life. Traces can still be seen of the paint with which the people of Jericho tried, with considerable artistic skill, to re-create the complexion and facial expression of their dead. It is yet another example of man's never-ending attempt to conquer death through art.

We are here confronted by the earliest human portraits in the world, for the things that Stone-Age man carved on mammoth's tusk and bone or painted on cave walls in southern France or northwest Spain never aimed at achieving a true likeness. Skeletons with skulls missing were found beneath almost all the houses in Jericho, and the fact that the heads were buried immediately below the floor may point to the existence of a cult devoted to ancestor worship.

It is quite certain that the people of Jericho believed in spiritual powers and in the spiritual activity of their ancestors—perhaps, even, in a life hereafter—for they would never have taken such pains had they not been convinced that the dead and the unseen world of the spirit could communicate with and intervene in the world of the living.

The artistic quality, spiritual exaltation and desire for perpetuity evident in these skulls reveal an almost baffling degree of skill, and the fact that such proficiency existed at a time when the world had been thought to be devoid of towns makes it all the more incredible.

The ruins of Jericho tell a story embracing many thousands of years. The city was overwhelmed and occupied by a succession of invaders, and ultimately newcomers arrived who had already mastered the art of making pottery. They left behind no houses of any

sort, so it is possible that the ancient city had fallen down and that
they settled in the ruins, but they arrived with a well-developed
knowledge of the potter's art. Mountains of broken clay vessels have
been dug up, yet no signs of community life are discernible from this
mysterious period. One discovery made by Professor Garstang was
of particular interest: the remains of three approximately life-sized
limestone statues representing a man, a woman and a child, of which
only the male figure was complete with head. Kathleen Kenyon has
suggested that these figures represent the earliest portrayal of a
"holy family." Carved long before the invention of writing and
thousands of years before the books of the Old Testament came into
being, they seem to offer a first, mute Messianic prophecy and an
indication that, even in the mists of prehistory, people embraced a
religion which may not have been so different from our own
experience.

The next invaders made finer and better-baked clay vessels with
engraved patterns, and for the first time we can distinguish a cultural
relationship between the Jericho people and others whose relics
have been excavated near Sha'ar ha Golan on the river Yarmuk, at
Byblos and in other places. It becomes apparent that by this stage
(about 4750 B.C.) inventions were being introduced into Jericho
from places outside.

Then silence. All signs of human activity disappear, for an intermediate period about which archaeologists can discover nothing. The
next message—a voice from the grave, as it were—does not arrive
until 3200 B.C. The pre-pottery neolithic town builders buried
their dead beneath the floors of their houses, and the potter folk
left virtually no traces of their existence apart from pottery, but the
post-3200 B.C. inhabitants left behind regular graves in the hills
around the city. Professor Kenyon calls this period, whose remains
she has excavated personally, the "proto-urban period." The graves
were usually circular shafts leading downward through the rock into
underground chambers which were sealed by one large stone or
several smaller ones.

In one chamber, which was larger than the rest, no less than 113
human skulls had been carefully arranged so that their empty eye
sockets stared sightlessly toward the center of the grave. The occupants of this grave, which is known as A 94, had been supplied with
clay vessels, bowls, large pitchers and numerous winepots. Archaeo-

logical methods are now so highly developed that it is possible to establish that when the heads were placed in the grave they were already in a skeletal condition. The dead must therefore have been stored somewhere until decomposition was complete and the skulls could be severed from the trunks. The skeletons themselves were carried into the grave and burned in the middle of the chamber, the skulls being arranged around them so that they could "watch" the burning of their own limbs. We know that the skulls were there at the time because they show signs of scorching, whereas the funerary vessels are unmarked by fire and must have been installed subsequently. Two hundred and fifty-one vessels were recovered from A 94. The radiocarbon method of dating, which has been widely used in recent years, reveals that the grave was built about 3260 B.C. Archaeologists think that the occupants of these tombs were nomads.

Eventually, the early Bronze Age arrived. It lasted in Jericho from 2900 until about 2300 B.C. Once again massive walls were built, once again sentries must have stood guard on them, once again the city flourished, and once again the inhabitants of Jericho must, like their forerunners in the very early days, have lived in fear of attack by nomads.

Throughout the whole of recorded human history, culturally advanced peoples who live in fertile, well-watered valleys have always been menaced by parched and famished nomads like those who provide the earliest figures in our Bible. History, as recorded in the Old Testament, goes back to 1700 B.C., the time of the Patriarchs. Archaeologists C. H. Gordon, E. A. Speiser and W. F. Albright have demonstrated that Abraham came from the neighborhood of Harran in northwest Mesopotamia. He left his native land and trekked southward through Palestine and the land of Canaan with his herds and tents. Isaac, Esau and Jacob lived in enmity after Abraham died. In the next generation, Jacob and his twelve sons, like his father and grandfather before him, led a nomad's life. Jacob's son Joseph must have acquired a respected position at the Egyptian court before he and his father and brothers were allowed to settle in the province of Goshen, but under the succeeding Pharaohs and after the fall of the Semitic Hyksos monarchy the Israelites ultimately became serfs until Moses saved his people and extricated the tribes of Jacob from Egypt. Palestine proper was gradually occupied by the Israelites, a process of annexation which is partly attributed to Joshua, Moses' successor.

The Israelites were still seminomads, but they had developed a taste for settled civilization. They marched through fertile plains past towns which were still in the hands of the original Canaanite inhabitants, until ultimately Joshua stood with his people before the walls of Jericho. Once a day for six successive days the Ark of the Covenant was borne around the city to the sound of trumpets. Then, on the seventh day, seven priests circled the city seven times and the walls "fell down flat" to the blaring of trumpets and a "great shout" raised by the besiegers. According to research conducted by the American archaeologist W. F. Albright, the events described in the Book of Joshua took place between 1375 and 1300 B.C., although they were not committed to writing until about 620 B.C.

Jericho was the best-fortified city in the Jordan valley and a place of great strategic importance, for it dominated the passes into the central highlands. Anyone who proposed to capture it had to have precise information about its walls, its military strength and the hazards and difficulties involved. Accordingly, Joshua sent two spies into the city to lodge at the house of the harlot Rahab. When the King of Jericho learned of this and tried to have them arrested, Rahab concealed their presence and swore that although two men had visited her she had had no idea who they were and that, anyway, they had left before the city gates were shut for the night. In reality, she had hidden the spies and later helped them to escape, securing in return a promise that she and her family would be spared if the Israelites captured the city. Rahab was firmly convinced that Jericho was doomed. Bored and irritated by her smug Canaanite compatriots who lived so comfortably within the stout walls of their fortress, she was ripe for treachery.

One more interesting detail emerges from the account in Joshua. Rahab's house was built abutting the city wall. Excavations at Jericho have brought to light just such houses, bounded on one side by the city wall itself.

We do not know why Jericho's walls collapsed. Perhaps its inhabitants were panic-stricken and opened the gates because reports of the besiegers' strength and of Jehovah's support had preceded them, spreading fear and despondency among the Canaanites. Excavations have indicated that houses and city walls were destroyed by earthquakes at different periods. Perhaps one of these earthquakes occurred on the seventh day!

All this happened when Jericho was already immensely old. In its six or seven thousand years of existence it had already seen many cities crumble within its walls, to be replaced by new cities.

If, in about 1300 B.C., the children of Israel chanced to hear of the skulls which men had once tried to preserve for eternity with artistically molded layers of plaster, they may well have assumed that it all happened an unimaginably long time ago and dismissed it as no more than a legend dating from a time when man was not yet man.

Yet the whole fabulous city and its skulls were dug up in our own day. So real and so tangible that no one can doubt their existence, they testify to the amazing spirituality of man in times beyond our ken. Three thousand years separate us from Joshua and the children of Israel who conquered Jericho, but five thousand years separated Joshua from the men who made these first real attempts at human portraiture.

GOOD LIVING IN UGARIT

*From now on it is possible to say that the palace of Ugarit is the
largest and most magnificent among royal residences known to
have existed in the Near East during the second millennium* B.C.

—CLAUDE F. A. SCHAEFFER, *Le Palais Royal d'Ugarit,*
Paris, 1955

THIRTY years ago a hill was opened up to reveal a civilization
which even today exercises a shadowy influence on our attitude
toward life and death, God and the world to come. Behind all our
religious beliefs there stands, latent and almost lost in the remote
reaches of history, a race that inhabited the Biblical lands long before
the Israelites.

Sometimes, like a faint glimmer of light in the gloom of evening,
we catch a glimpse of this mysterious race. At the time the following events occurred the hour was already late and their civilization
had long since passed its prime. The Bible tells us that when Christ
visited the district of Tyre and Sidon he was confronted by an
unfortunate woman whose daughter was mentally ill. The unhappy
mother begged him to help her child, but Jesus remained silent. Still
she persisted, saying: "Lord, help me." It was like the elemental voice
of prayer, the cry from the heart to which the Psalms sometimes
give expression. It was an appeal for help from a heathen world, and
Jesus answered it with the words: "O woman, great is thy faith:
be it even as thou wilt."

This unique story and its moving climax contain a fundamental
truth. They illustrate how boundless a belief in God could and can
still inhabit the heathen breast, that it is age-old, and that a Canaanite
woman was quite capable of such faith.

The race whose civilization was unearthed thirty years ago was
that of the Canaanites, and the woman who confronted Christ in the
Gospels of Matthew and Mark was a latter-day descendant of those
much-maligned seekers after God who lived long before the first
figures in Biblical history. They were the people whom the Greeks
called Phoenicians, the people who ruled over the powerful maritime
cities of Tyre and Sidon. The greatest seafaring race in the ancient
world, they were responsible for founding the city of Carthage in

25

814 B.C. Their greatest son, Hannibal, almost succeeded in conquering Rome during the Punic Wars.

The Phoenicians, who began to roam the seas about 1250 B.C., gained fame as mariners, manufacturers of purple dye, merchants, city builders and, later, as a naval power to be reckoned with.

The extremely interesting culture of this ancient race did not spring into clear focus until recent times. Resident in Syria and Palestine since about 3000 B.C., the Canaanites built upon the ruins of former cities and evolved a way of life and a social order which seemed unbelievably refined to the Israelite herdsmen who followed them. They enjoyed their highly developed culture and continued to look down with contempt from their city walls at the new arrivals from the desert, until they were eventually humbled by the Patriarchs.

That sedentary races in thriving cities should be continually subjugated by invading nomads is the human tragedy and seed of destruction inherent in almost all high cultures. Armed conquest does not, however, always mean victory over a people's culture. For instance, the tough race of hunters known as the Tunguses conquered Peking and the whole of China down to the Yangtze in the twelfth century A.D., yet the Manchu Dynasty founded by their descendants was later vanquished by the insidious refinement of Chinese culture. The Romans conquered Greece, yet in a thousand aspects of cultural life the Greeks triumphed, and the spirit of Greece was ultimately disseminated by the victorious Romans throughout Europe and most of the Near East. In their material as well as their spiritual culture the sedentary Canaanites were undoubtedly superior to the newcomers, and the victorious Israelites were in constant danger—at least until the time of Solomon, who lived circa 950 B.C.—of being bewitched and seduced by the race whom they had subjugated so long before.

Between 3000 and 1200 B.C. the Canaanites' fortifications, domestic architecture, street systems and town planning were true wonders of the contemporary world. In addition, they devised extremely practical sewerage systems, boasted skilled potters and artisans in bronze. Their contribution to the history of ideas is almost inestimable. Greece, Rome and eventually all Europe and half the world owed the Canaanites not only their alphabet but also elements of their religious observances, legends and myths, and the basic principles of town construction.

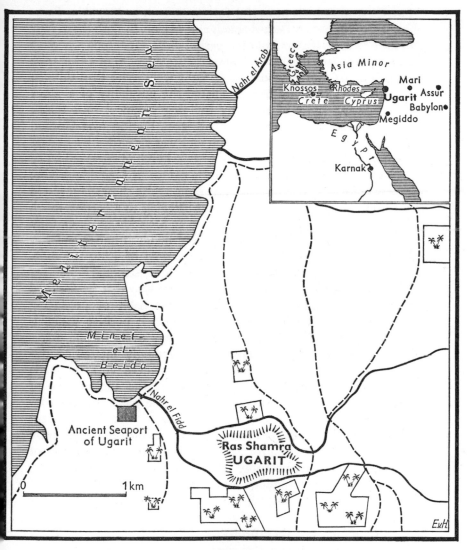

Ugarit, by the shores of the eastern Mediterranean

The Canaanites built powerful fortresses such as Megiddo, Beth-shean, Taanach, Gezer, Beth-shemesh and Hazor. In Beth-shean four Canaanite temples dating from the period circa 1300–1000 B.C. were dug up. At Tanaach diggers unearthed the foundations of a Canaanite royal palace. At Gezer, whose outer walls were more than thirteen feet thick, the Canaanites had eliminated the possibility of a water shortage during times of siege by building a tunnel to a spring situated 130 feet below present ground level. During 1937 Gordon Loud explored the palace at Megiddo and was rewarded by finding beneath its foundation walls a cache of two hundred engraved ivory tablets. One of these plaquettes depicts a prince of Megiddo driving prisoners before his war chariot. The same tablet shows him seated on a throne, drinking from a bowl and listening to a harpist, much as Saul must have listened to David. Also at Megiddo, P. L. O. Guy excavated stables capable of housing three hundred horses and war chariots. These buildings dated from the time of King Solomon. We are told in I Kings: ix, 19, that Solomon constructed "cities for his chariots and cities for his horsemen" and also that he fortified the city of Megiddo. Archaeology's recent habit of producing tangible evidence of Old Testament accounts is positive compensation for the more dangerous aspects of our overscientific era.

In 1929 Claude Schaeffer made an exceedingly interesting discovery. Digging at Ras Shamra on the northern coast of Syria opposite the island of Cyprus, he unearthed the ancient city of Ugarit near the modern town of Latakia. The place had been inhabited for many thousands of years by people whose traces went back to paleolithic times. The lowest layer, in which flint tools were found, lay at a depth of 60 feet. It yielded no pots or receptacles of any kind. These had probably been made of wood or leather, materials which had crumbled away to nothing in the course of thousands of years. At a depth of between 52 and 55 feet Schaeffer found some stone bowls. We do not know what sort of people lived here so long ago, but they probably differed from us very little. It is generally correct to say that the people of the whole world, who have demonstrably belonged to Homo sapiens for at least thirty thousand years and probably far, far longer, are more closely related physically and mentally than we tend to suppose. At Kanjera, northeast of Lake Victoria in East Africa, skulls belonging to sapiens-like men have been found which are no less than three

Stratigraphic drawing of Ugarit, the city excavated by Claude Schaeffer. This plan shows how the layers of an ancient city are superimposed one upon the other. (a) The most recent layer of earth covering the hill of Ugarit. (b) and (c) City and house walls. (d) and (e) The walls of the city between 1415 and 1365 B.C., before it was destroyed by an earthquake. (f), (g) and (h) A burial chamber with funerary gifts for the dead, dating from the period between 1450 and 1365 B.C. (j) Funerary gifts in the Minoan style, imported from Crete between 1900 and 1750 B.C. or made in Ugarit under the guidance of Cretan craftsmen. (k) Layer of earth. (l) Various pieces of jewelry of the period between 2900 and 1900 B.C. (l) and (m) Here, 26 feet beneath the surface of the hill, were found the earliest examples of painted vases in Ugarit.

hundred thousand years old and indicate that neither Peking nor
Neanderthal man was the prototype of the human race.

Between 6000 and 5000 B.C. the inhabitants of Stone-Age Ras
Shamra and Jericho appear to have come into contact, or so similarities between the earliest stone vessels found in both places seem
to indicate. Tools made of quartzite, obsidian and bone lie at depths
of 40 and 50 feet, but even as early as this, man was beginning to
produce painted pottery of amazingly high quality. King Sargon I,
ruler of the Akkadian empire, one of the greatest Semitic statesmen
in world history and the man responsible for uniting the Sumerians
and the Semitic Akkadians, probably passed through the district of
Ugarit about 2300 B.C. and may well have visited the city itself.

Many thousands of years of history and grandeur lie buried
beneath the hill of Ras Shamra. The French archaeologist A. Parrot,
who unearthed the city of Mari beneath Tell Hariri on the middle
reaches of the Euphrates, found a clay tablet among the royal
archives there. A letter from the celebrated lawgiver Hammurabi
(1728–1686 B.C.), who held sway over the whole of Babylonia,
Assyria and Mesopotamia, mentioned that the king of Ugarit had
informed him of his wish to visit the palace of Zimrilim, residence
of the last king of Mari.

We are now in a period whose remains lie some 25 feet below
ground level. Graves of this time yielded bracelets, sewing needles
complete with eyes, necklaces and other articles of adornment made
of bronze. These were traces of Europeans who had either come to
Ugarit from the Balkans, the Danube, the Rhine or the Caucasus or
had exported fine examples of their craftsmanship to the area.
Similar objects have been found throughout these regions.

The mighty land of Egypt established relations with Ugarit, and
it must have been a splendid moment when the stone statuette of
the Egyptian princess Shnumit was borne into the city. In Crete
this was the time of the golden age of Minoan culture. Once again
the soil yields information about the history of commercial relations
between Ugarit and the maritime kingdom of Crete, for fragments
of magnificent Cretan vases have come to light. One grave, for
instance, contained a tiny terracotta bowl no bigger than an eggshell,
undoubtedly imported from Crete between 1900 and 1750 B.C.

What happened after that is hard to tell, for some unidentified
power destroyed the Egyptian statues found in Ugarit. Judging by

their refined tastes and cosmopolitan attitude to life, Ugarit's Semitic inhabitants would never have been responsible for such wanton destruction. The city recovered, however, and the funerary gifts found there display an astonishing variety of artistic styles. People from the island of Cyprus, merchants from Egypt, scholars from Mesopotamia and craftsmen from all over the contemporary world must have congregated within the city's walls.

Ugarit eventually fell prey to the most powerful and competent of Egypt's Pharaohs, Pharaoh Thutmosis III, perhaps the greatest political genius in the pre-Christian Near East. The mummy of this mighty ruler, which has survived, displays a truly royal countenance with a fine aquiline nose, resolute mouth and long occiput. The statue in the Temple of Karnak, too, conveys some measure of the enormous energy which must have animated this man. Thutmosis III needed bases for his campaigns and supply depots for his troops, and his best harbor in the north was Ugarit. The people who lived there about 1500 B.C., Cypriots, Aegeans, Cretans, Egyptians, as well as the natives of Ugarit themselves, all derived benefits from the Egyptian conquest, and under the "pax Aegyptia" the city enjoyed a golden age which produced some truly amazing architecture.

Extensive residential areas were laced by straight streets intersecting at right angles. There were multiroomed houses equipped with baths and elaborate sanitary installations. Rainwater flowed into the city along fine stone canals and there was an admirable drainage system. Walled fountains installed in the courtyards were faced with handsome stone tiles and their central access sheltered by small roofs supported on four legs. Large stone tubs were placed by the fountains to receive water. Living and sleeping quarters were probably situated on the second story, and were approached by stone stairs of considerable width.

If the living lived in comfort, the dead were certainly not neglected. Beneath each house was a burial chamber with a vaulted roof, usually very neatly constructed of stone slabs. A passage led into the interior, and there, beneath their ancestral home, the dead continued to share in the life of the family. They went into eternity provided with costly articles of use and adornment. Indeed, the people of Ugarit buried their dead in truly royal fashion, which is why, unfortunately, almost all the graves have suffered from the depredations of thieves. However, grave robbers normally took

only objects of gold and funerary gifts of obvious value, leaving
behind beautiful pieces of faience, ivory ornaments, alabaster vases
and superb Mycenaean ceramics, most of which originated in workshops on the islands of Rhodes and Cyprus. Many of the Minoan
vases with tapering bases and painted decoration are of unique
beauty. Claude Schaeffer, the discoverer of this amazing city, even
established that the dead were buried with vessels containing brewed
beverages. Great luxury was lavished on the dead in Ugarit, and we
shall later investigate why this implicit belief in an afterlife existed.

The harbor stood on the bay of Minet el Beida. Here, too, the
people of Ugarit had built houses equipped with every amenity, and
here, too, graves of artistic design were found, as well as warehouses
and storerooms of surprisingly modern appearance. In one such
store chamber Schaeffer counted more than eighty earthen jars
which must have contained oil or wine intended either for domestic
use or for export. Some indication of the harbor's large turnover
and commercial activity is provided by a building in which were
stored more than a thousand large jars with handles, mostly of
Cyprian origin and once used to hold perfumed oil which was
exported to Palestine and Egypt.

A highly developed cosmetics industry had grown up in Ugarit.
Fragile phials for scent, ivory rouge boxes, many in the form of
ducks with expressions of comical surprise, and tiny falcons in
bronze with inlaid feathers of gold prove that Egyptian art had
gained a foothold here. Not that the pampered inhabitants of Ugarit
despised Aegean and Minoan craftsmanship. Artists from Crete and
Greece, sculptors, goldsmiths and bronze casters must all have been
patronized in their workshops by the well-dressed, rouged and
powdered matrons of 3,500 years ago. One glazed clay cup found
in a grave in Minet el Beida bears a finely modeled female mask
exemplifying the well-groomed features of the Cretan ladies who
were emulated by the high society of Ugarit. Just over six inches
high, it reposes in the Louvre at Paris and is one of the showpieces
of what is the largest collection of art treasures in the world.

Schaeffer found in the course of his excavations that an earthquake had destroyed the city about the middle of the fourteenth
century B.C. Ruined houses, shattered walls, massive blocks of dis-
placed masonry and widespread evidence of fire can all be clearly
distinguished. Abimilki, King of Tyre, recounted the catastrophe

[1] Male head forming part of the remains of three roughly life-size limestone statues of a man, woman and child excavated by Professor Garstang. In Kathleen Kenyon's opinion, these figures represent the earliest known prehistoric portrayal of a "Holy Family."

[2] Skull sculpture from Jericho modeled around an actual skull. It is roughly 10,000 years old and was probably associated with ancestor worship.

[3] This building was erected in Jericho 7,800 years before Christ's birth. The circular depressions are assumed to have held supporting beams. The people of Jericho were already living in an advanced residential culture by about 2,000 years after the end of the last Ice Age. Theirs is the only city of the period to have been excavated so far.

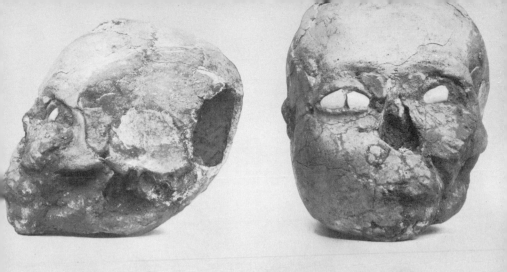

[4] Among the most amazing discoveries made at Jericho were human skulls coated with clay to preserve the features of the departed. The eye sockets were inlaid with shells and the entire sculpture painted to reproduce the natural color of the human face. (Profile and full-face views of the same head.)

[5] The oldest house so far excavated anywhere in the world (photographed from above). It abuts on the city wall (right) and was built between nine and ten thousand years ago. When this house was erected the people of Jericho were still living in the Stone Age. Although they made no pottery, they were already city builders.

[6] Excavated at Ugarit, this small ivory carving of a Canaanite goddess dates from about 1350 B.C. and is now in the Louvre, Paris. The modeling of the face and the artistic coiffure, headband and necklace all reveal that the sculptor either came from Greece or was influenced by early Greek style.

[7] Copper statuette of a deity found by the French archaeologist Claude Schaeffer at Ugarit in 1937. It was made between 1800 and 1600 B.C. The pictures show front and side view of the same figure.

[8] The harbor of Ugarit stood by the sea 4,000 years ago, but in the course of time the bay of Minet el Beida has become silted up. Roughly one half mile farther inland from the port stands the city-mound of Ugarit proper, now called Ras Shamra.

[9] Bronze statuette of the god Baal dating from the 15th or 14th century B.C. The tall coiffure and head are covered with a layer of gold, the body with silver. This rare piece was excavated at Minet el Beida, the ancient harbor of Ugarit, and is now in the Louvre, Paris.

[10] Clay tablet from the central archives of Ugarit. The text is written in the world's oldest alphabet, evolved by the Canaanites about 3,400 years ago. The tablet bears the seal of the royal dynasty.

[11] The clay vessel (*top*) was probably used for mixing wine with water in Ugarit, 1600–1450 B.C. The twin vases (*below*) date from the period 1450–1365 B.C. They too were made out of clay and painted reddish-brown and black.

[12] This fragment from an ivory plaque set into the footboard of the royal bed is one of the finest known examples of Canaanite art. It shows the king of Ugarit menacing a foreign ruler with his sword.

[13] A figurine in reddish terra-cotta portraying a male Phoenician clad in an apron. Just over 5½ inches tall, this very fine piece is more than 3,000 years old and was excavated at Byblos by Maurice Dunand.

[14] Also in reddish terra-cotta, this head with tall hat and chin strap formed the neck of a Phoenician vase. Byblos, where this unusually fine piece was found, was probably inhabited by men with expressive features of this type.

to Pharaoh Amenophis IV in the following words: "The royal city of Ugarit has been destroyed by fire. Half the city was burned; the other half has simply ceased to exist." It is one of the unsolved riddles of history why Ugarit, the Cretan city of Knossos, Troy and other large cities should all have suffered widespread devastation almost simultaneously during the fourteenth century B.C. It seems strange that an earthquake should have struck down such widely scattered places at almost the same time.

Once more Ugarit revived, once more houses and palaces were built and once more the ladies wore splendid robes in the Egyptian and Mycenaean style—more particularly the latter, since the Cretans were by now Ugarit's wealthiest citizens and its arbiters of fashion.

Then, about 1200 B.C., final tragedy struck. Like a tornado, invaders bore down on the fertile land of Syria from the north, from Greece and Asia Minor. These "people from the sea" were armed with unfamiliar weapons of iron, and Ugarit did not withstand their onslaught. The city died with the Bronze Age, and was extinguished forever. The merchants ceased their busy calculations, the scribes laid down their styluses, and their clay tablets were scattered to the winds by the destroyers of their amazing city. The elegant ladies laughed no more, and layer upon layer of earth arose to form the hill which is still in the process of being explored at the present day.

THE WORLD'S FIRST ALPHABET

And Hiram king of Tyre sent his servants unto Solomon; for he had heard that they anointed him king in the room of his father: for Hiram was ever a lover of David. And Solomon sent to Hiram, saying, thou knowest how that David my father could not build an house unto the name of the Lord his God for the wars which were about him on every side, until the Lord put them under the soles of his feet. But now the Lord my God hath given me rest on every side, so that there is neither adversary nor evil occurrent. And, behold, I purpose to build an house unto the name of the Lord my God....

—I KINGS: v, 1-5

NO ARCHAEOLOGIST who proposes to dig up cities and civilizations plies his spade at random. It is far better to delve into books before delving into the ground.

What follows is a splendid example of the fact that ancient pre-Christian literary sources often provide reliable information, that we should not write off as mere fantasy everything that at first sight appears incredible, and that even myths normally contain some truth. We have still to learn that neither man's mental powers nor his basic wisdom have increased appreciably in the course of thousands of years. It is one of the misfortunes of our time that we give complete credence to scientific research but tend to ignore those who have communicated the greatest spiritual truths to mankind, men like Buddha, Confucius, Euripides and Socrates—all of whom, incidentally, lived at about the same period, some 2,500 years ago.

In 485 B.C. a child who was one day to be described as the father of history was born into a respected family in Halicarnassus. Herodotus traveled throughout the contemporary Mediterranean world. A scholar endowed with unusual powers of observation, he was also a man of wide interests and unlimited curiosity. He took the stories he passed on seriously, but was fond of indulging in gentle satire. He paid homage to tradition but was fascinated by novelty. Although he had no expert military knowledge he gave a brilliant description of the great war in which Persia and Greece fought for supremacy of the known world. He was prejudiced against no people or race and believed above all that a man endowed with

34

reason and some knowledge of the past is free to mold his history and his future—that he is by no means merely the plaything of natural forces and blind fate. That was why, unlike later-day prophets of Western decline, Herodotus never attempted to forecast the future of nations, on the principle that no man's future behavior is predictable.

Herodotus tells us in the fifth book of his *Histories* where the Greeks got their written script. The Phoenicians, he writes, came to Greece with King Cadmus, bringing with them many branches of knowledge, among them the art of writing, "which, so I believe, the Hellenes did not possess before."

The world's first historian also believed the Phoenicians to be the inventors of the alphabet from which the Greeks evolved their own sequence of written characters and which has become the alphabet of all European languages. Although his accounts have often been questioned by modern historians, Herodotus has received signal confirmation. What he wrote in the fifth century B.C. has been vindicated in our own, for Claude Schaeffer's excavations between 1929 and the present day have produced concrete evidence of all that Herodotus reported in such detail and with such accuracy thousands of years ago.

While uncovering the city of Ugarit, which was buried beneath the hill of Ras Shamra, Schaeffer identified five separate layers representing five human civilizations ranging from the Stone Age of many thousand years ago to 1100 B.C., when Ugarit disappeared. The fifth layer is the oldest and naturally lies lower than the rest. The first or topmost layer contains the ruins of a city which flourished between 1500 and 1100 B.C. At that level Schaeffer discovered the ruins of a large building with a courtyard at its center surrounded by several sizable rooms and approached through a massive door on the north side. A flight of stairs led upward to the second floor. The palatial building must have been a veritable university devoted to the art of calligraphy, for the scholars of this thriving Canaanite city studied the Akkadian, Sumerian, Hurritic and, most important of all, the proto-Phoenician script used by the ancestors of the Phoenicians—the script, in fact, of the Canaanites. Writing, or the engraving of written characters on clay tablets, was a greater art in those days than it is now, and had to be carefully learned.

Like the archives of Nineveh and Babylon, the library at Ugarit contained clay tablets inscribed on both sides with the characters usually termed cuneiform or "wedge-shaped." One feature of the newly discovered Ugarit script, however, sprang to the eye even before it had been deciphered. The Mesopotamian scripts consisted of several hundred symbols, each of which stood for a whole syllable or word; the Ugarit texts were executed with only 29 or 30 characters. It was at once apparent that the earliest alphabet in the world had been discovered.

In April 1930, one year after the first tablets had been unearthed at Ugarit, the French scholar Virolleaud published texts written in the mysterious script. A brilliant member of Halle University, Professor Hans Bauer, was struck by the thought that a Semitic language similar to Hebrew or Phoenician must be involved. Accordingly, he tried to identify some Semitic words by comparing the juxtaposition of different letters and actually succeeded in discovering the written equivalents of the words "three" and "four" and of several religious names such as Asherat, Ashtart, Baal, El, and Elah.

If this sounds simple, it should be remembered that in this, as in all Semitic languages, vowels are almost always left to be supplied by the reader, so inspired guesswork of this kind demands an extensive knowledge of mythology. STRT stands for the name of the goddess Ashtart or Astarte. Anyone who was not already familiar with this goddess from Egyptian inscriptions would never have realized that STRT meant Astarte. Similarly, the god Baal must be identified from the two letters BL.

Bauer eventually deciphered fourteen out of twenty-eight letters. In nine further cases he went astray, and the remaining five eluded him. The French have done yeoman work in deciphering this script and exploring Canaanite culture in general. After the French scholar Dhorme had succeeded in identifying more of the doubtful letters, Hans Bauer, this time aided by Dhorme's findings, set to work once more and solved the whole mystery with the exception of one letter. Professor Virolleaud began to study large numbers of Canaanite tablets and in 1948 the complete series was at last identified. It dates back to 1400 B.C. and is the world's most ancient alphabet. We shall never know the name of the man who invented it, but he was certainly a Phoenician. As Virolleaud points out, the race that produced such a marvel merits our highest respect and must be allotted a special place in the history of mankind.

The ancient Canaanite alphabet of Ugarit consists of 28 separate letters of which 26 are consonants. The Hebrew alphabet has 23 and the later, classical Phoenician 22. Our own alphabet consists of 26 letters, the Russian of 33. Today, any text written in the Canaanite cuneiform alphabet which has not been destroyed by time can be read with accuracy.

Two kinds of clay tablets have been found, the larger containing legends and myths and the smaller bearing letters, inventories, accounts, instructions, lists of merchandise such as oil, wine and purple, and legal contracts such as of adoption, gift and sale.

It is fascinating to gain a glimpse of life in a city which bequeathed us one of the most ingenious of all human devices but subsequently, some three thousand years ago, was lost to view. For instance, a man named Yasiranu had legally adopted a youth called Ilkuya in

A text written in mankind's oldest alphabet. Written symbols existed in Sumer at an earlier date, but they expressed complete syllables or words. The Canaanites were the first to devise an alphabet as such. The text illustrated here deals with the legal relationship of Yasiranu to his adoptive son Ilkuya. The hatching indicates where the tablets have been damaged.

the presence of the King of Ugarit. It was stipulated in writing that
neither party might sever the relationship without due notice.
Should the adoptive father ever wish to break the bond, he had
to give his adoptive son 100 shekels of silver before sending him on
his way. Should the son take it into his head to leave the father,
on the other hand, he had to raise his hands above his head and walk
out into the street. This reveals the exemplary fashion in which
contracts were drawn up in those days. The raised hands are a
graphic indication that a disloyal son was not permitted to take
anything with him when he left the paternal abode.

We learn of royal gifts, of transactions by barter, sale and purchase. Owners exchanged houses, olive plantations, cattle, donkeys
and sheep. The entire inventory of Queen Ahatmilku's dowry has
survived. It includes four pairs of gold pendants set with precious
stones, gold rings and bracelets, golden cups, bowls and pitchers,
two gold belts, twenty robes of fine Hurritic material and an equal
number of Amurritic, numerous capes and cloaks, seat covers, three
beds inlaid with ivory, gold-plated chairs, basins, jugs, crucibles,
beakers and pitch-burning bronze torches, vessels "filled with sweet
oil," twenty small rouge boxes and a large number of other items.
Queen Ahatmilku appears to have been a wealthy, fastidious and
pampered woman!

Reading of the slave trade, we are told that slaves were sometimes repurchased. In one instance the purchaser could not raise
the necessary 400 silver shekels and arranged an advance of 140
shekels from his principal. However, the purchase price had to be
paid in full upon delivery of the slaves. Since a shekel weighed just
over half an ounce, the slaves cost about fifteen pounds of silver—
not very much by modern standards, although it must be remembered that silver was much rarer and thus more valuable than it
is today. The charger which was sold to the King of Ugarit by the
King of Carchemish's master of horse was very expensive by comparison. The clay tablet classified as No. 16.180 tells us that this
horse, probably a fine thoroughbred, cost 200 shekels, or half as
much as the whole consignment of slaves.

We also read how Ulmi, a woman of the highest rank, begged
her daughter, who was Queen of Ugarit, for help: "May the gods
of Ugarit and the gods of Amurru preserve you in the best of
health. Is it well with the King of Ugarit and yourself? Answer!"

The writer of the letter went on to say that her house had been burned down, that all her possessions had been destroyed and that she was in urgent need of assistance. It seems apparent that the Queen of Ugarit and her mother hailed from Amurru, hence the latter's reference to the gods of that place. She was able to mention them because of the tolerant and liberal atmosphere in Ugarit (which perhaps explains why the Canaanites' own gods disappeared in so far as they were not absorbed into later religions).

The deciphering of the clay tablets of Ras Shamra has meant that for the past thirty years our knowledge of Canaanite mythology has been steadily increasing. The French scholars Virolleaud, Dussaud and Nougayrol have shed light on the hidden secrets of this amazing people's religious faith. The main interest and importance of their findings lie in the fact that although the writings date from the fourteenth century B.C. their content is very much older. This information must either have been passed on verbally from generation to generation or transmitted through the medium of a very ancient and as yet nonalphabetical system of written characters. Since Canaanites and Israelites inhabited the same country, led a similar life, were familiar with the same legends and worshiped the same god, we are forced to assume that both peoples had a common origin. Thus the Ugarit tablets take us back into the earliest history of the Israelite people, and their discovery is one of the most important events to have occurred in the field of Biblical research.

The Canaanites' religion was anything but primitive. A tightly organized priesthood served regular spells of duty in the temples, which were numerous. The supreme deity was known as El, a word which means "god" in the Phoenician as well as in all other Semitic languages. The Canaanites' El is also the origin of Elohim, the Old Testament's term for the Almighty.

El stood high above the dealings and activities of mere mortals and was far removed from mundane affairs. He was the "father of the years" and his hand was "as great as the sea." He did, however, live on earth, somewhere on the coast "where the rivers flow into the sea." The Canaanites probably regarded their supreme being much as do many races surviving today, particularly those of the circumpolar regions. The deeper we probe into early history and prehistory the more clearly we recognize that the supreme being was little concerned with the petty affairs of mankind and, more especially, that he was not a distributor of punishment. An upright stone or stele found in Ugarit marked the place where El sat enthroned and where the kings of Ugarit made sacrifice to him.

El's female consort was Asherat, whom we rediscover many centuries later as the Ashera of the Bible. There her symbol is described as a sacred tree or pole—still an object of worship among certain primitive peoples today and one with a tradition going far back into the Stone Age.

The god who was most involved with the Canaanites' daily life was Baal, the hero of a great mythological epic preserved for us in the Ugarit tablets. We know that this Baal, against whom the prophets of the Old Testament preached so stubbornly, represented a great danger to the Israelites, who repeatedly threatened to defect and embrace the Canaanite religion. Baal exercised such a hold over the life of the Canaanites that he was still worshiped long after their cities had been captured by the Israelites. The two largest temples in Ugarit were dedicated to the god Baal and to his father, Dagon. Final testimony to the Jewish religion's bitter struggle against a slowly dying but tenacious adversary is their name for the devil, Beelzebub. *Baal* means "owner," "husband" or "devouring" and *zebub* is the Hebrew for "fly."

The age-old myths about this god were first disclosed by the Ras Shamra-Ugarit finds, so our knowledge of the background behind all Biblical references to Baal is only thirty years old.

The clay tablets tell us that the sister of the god Baal was called Anat and that, as was so often the case in the East and in Egypt, in particular, brother and sister were married. Virginity, fertility and savagery were strangely combined in this goddess. From time immemorial, therefore, a close association existed between innocence, sacred birth, perversion and devotion to orgiastic cults.

When men started to forget Baal and their religious zeal dwindled, Anat instituted a great bloodbath among the apostates. In the north of the country there was, we are told, a mountain of gold. Anat made her way to this mountain and there recounted her victories. She had slain an enormous snake called Litan or Lotan, the Leviathan of our Bible. Ugarit is the only place where we find a reference to the name Leviathan prior to its introduction into the Book of Job.

This shows the great antiquity of the myths of a gold-guarding dragon or treasure-guarding snake.

The famous cedars of Lebanon were also mentioned in the Ugarit tablets long before the Old Testament's Books of Kings came to be written. When Anat complained to the supreme god El that her brother and husband Baal possessed no temple like other gods, celestial architects were bidden to build a temple of brick and wood from the cedars of Lebanon. I Kings: vi, 9 records that Solomon, too, "covered the house with beams and boards of cedar." The wise king's collaborator in building this temple was no less a person than the Canaanite king Hiram of Tyre. Hiram reigned from 969 until 936 B.C. and Solomon from 972 to 932, but the clay tablets of Ugarit tell of the building of a temple to Baal five hundred years earlier, and the story is probably much older still.

The library of Ugarit also tells us of men's eternal wish to bring their nearest and dearest back from the world of the dead. While out hunting, Baal was lured into an ambush by his enemies and killed, together with his son Aleyn. Anat descended into the underworld and mourned her loved ones, sacrificing seventy oxen, seventy buffalo, seventy sheep, seventy rams, seventy ibex and seventy antelopes. This sacrifice was not only a funerary offering but was intended to provide her son and husband with food in the world hereafter. None of this, however, brought them back to life.

The person responsible for Baal's murder was Mot, or death itself. Anat alone knew of Mot's abode, and with the aid of the sun-goddess she slew him with a sickle. Only then did Baal and Aleyn return to the light of day. The same theme recurs in Greek myths of a later age, in which Heracles snatches Alcestis from death.

Long before the first clay tablets of Ugarit were written, its inhabitants—like the Christians long after them—had ceased to believe in the finality of death. Charles Virolleaud stresses that the Canaanites were never quite sure whether spring would really follow winter. Their uncertainty may have stemmed from an ancient remembrance of the last Ice Age, which ended about 8000 B.C. At all events, the Canaanites fell prey to a short spell of disquiet and anxiety each year, especially when the first rains were late in arriving, for each year might mean the end of the world. This was why they held Anat responsible for the reappearance of spring and the victory of life over death.

The souls of the dead, known in the Canaanite and Hebrew tongues as *rephaim*, were invited to a feast prepared by the goddess Anat. To quote the words of one clay tablet: "Today and tomorrow eat ye, O Rephaim, and drink . . . and do the same until the seventh day." The feast of the dead lasted for a week, after which the supreme god El called the souls and said: "Go now, ye Rephaim, into my house; enter ye the palace."

Who, then, was Anat, the goddess who rescued Baal, vanquished the dragon and feasted the souls of the dead? She was the same Astarte to whom Pharaoh Thutmosis III erected a temple at Thebes in the fifteenth century B.C. She was the same goddess Asterot whom the children of Israel worshiped from time to time when their faith in Yahweh faltered.

The clay tablets of Ugarit were not deciphered until thirty years ago, so we are much more familiar with the Greek version of the name, Astarte, whereas the original name, Anat, lay buried for more than three thousand years beneath the hill of Ras Shamra.

The Canaanite goddess Anat may well have affected the Greeks' ideas about Aphrodite, their goddess of love. It is certainly noteworthy that on the island of Cyprus, which was inhabited by Canaanite seafarers and boasted the Phoenician city of Alasia, there were two world-renowned temples dedicated to Aphrodite, those of Paphos and Amathus. And also that to Homer, Aphrodite was a Cyprian goddess. The Greeks' tradition undoubtedly shows symptoms of an eastern and Semitic origin, for to them Aphrodite was the goddess of fertility and love just as Anat was to the Canaanites.

We can see, therefore, that a considerable number of mythological and cultural ideas from the Canaanite-Phoenician world insinuated themselves into ancient Greece and into our own religious conceptions. It is one of the world's great mysteries that a mutual relationship exists not only between all cultures but between all gods.

TYRE AND SIDON

The conquest of the sea is man's most important feat. New horizons, new stars have always held an irresistible attraction for the imagination of man. The sea enabled unknown island races to conquer immense areas and establish lasting sovereignty on foreign soil. In a remote time when no one had yet founded any proper trading colonies or established a navy, a small people living on the eastern shores of the Mediterranean discovered the art of navigating by the Pole Star and, over a period of about a thousand years, built up a maritime empire, a thalassocracy, which was safe from the clutches of any land-based army. 1,200 years before the Christian era, when the power of Egypt was waning, the Phoenicians gradually debouched upon the Mediterranean scene, where for many centuries they dictated the course of other nations' economic activity in their capacity as veritable merchant princes and grands seigneurs. And all this happened while Italy was still waiting for the dawn.

—A. POIDEBARD AND J. LAUFFRAY, *Sidon,*
Beirut, 1951

PHARAOH Rameses II was a high-spirited king. No Egyptian ruler made a stronger impact on posterity than this unusual man whose insatiable lust for building devoured such huge sums of money. He erected dozens of temples and obelisks, completed his father's famous funerary temple at Thebes, and set aside the temple now known as the Ramaseum for the use of his own death cult. At Luxor he ordered the completion of the huge Hall of Pillars in the Temple of Karnak. No Pharaoh erected larger statues, some of them hewn from a single block of stone. His statue at Tanis was nearly 90 feet high and had to be sculpted from a monolith weighing 900 tons. (A large modern truck can haul between 50 and 60 tons.)

Rameses II may have desired to immortalize his fame in stone, but he also sought to enjoy his days on earth. Looking at his features portrayed in the colossal relief at the great Temple of Abu Simbel or in the granite statue in the Temple of Karnak, we can see a subtle, vivacious smile playing about his mouth. We can also sense that he was a pampered and pleasure-loving man. His numerous marriages brought him 79 sons and 59 daughters whom he proudly depicted in long reliefs on the walls of his temples. He ruled for

43

67 years, from 1290 until 1223 B.C., and died at the age of ninety. Even death has failed to conquer his body, for his mummy still survives today.

It is scarcely surprising that it was this Pharaoh who caused the Israelites to perform such feats of forced labor in Egypt, and still less surprising that Moses and Aaron one day presented themselves before Rameses II and asked him to allow their people to set off into the desert. Inquiring ironically what god it was whose voice he was supposed to obey, the Pharaoh dismissed them with the words: "I know not the Lord, neither will I let Israel go." Since his urge to build was all-consuming and he knew that large numbers of Israelites lived in Egypt, he refused to sacrifice such a valuable source of manpower. On the contrary, he ordered them to step up their production of bricks. With all the delights of the world at his fingertips, he was still anxious to preserve his memory in stone for all eternity, so he commanded them to redouble their efforts. "Let there be more work laid upon the men ... and let them not regard vain words." The Israelite overseers, who were in turn appointed by Egyptian taskmasters, were beaten and abused if they failed to produce their daily quota. They protested, but the Pharaoh's reply to all entreaties was: "Ye are idle, ye are idle!"

We learn these historical facts from the fifth chapter of Exodus. Not until his country had been ravaged by the ten plagues did the Pharaoh reconsider his decision and leave the children of Israel free to make their exodus from Egypt. This took place about 1300 B.C., or some 3,300 years ago. Later on in Exodus we read that Rameses II regretted his decision to let the children of Israel go and sent six hundred of his best chariots in pursuit of Moses and his people.

There is still extant a letter from a man called Hori, a senior officer in Pharaoh's cavalry, to a colleague of his, Aman-appag, one of the Egyptian army commanders. Its interest lies in the fact that it dates from a time when Rameses was still seeking to set the stamp of his mind and his race upon the world, a time when Moses was conducting one of the largest and most hazardous emigrations in history. The document, which now reposes in the British Museum under the name Papyrus Anastasi I, also mentions some of the thriving Canaanite cities which were later captured by the Israelites.

The Pharaonic master of horse addresses his correspondent as Mahir, a Canaanite word used to describe a skillful writer or generally erudite individual. Mahir has apparently traveled through Syria and seen the Canaanite-Phoenician cities. Hori pokes fun at him in his letter, and it is not uninteresting to read how friends corresponded 3,300 years ago. "When you halt in the evening your body is quite pulverized and your limbs in pieces. You have to harness your horses by yourself because no one comes to help you. Then people break into the camp and untie your horse, pilfering and stealing your clothes. Your groom appropriates what is left and goes off with the thieves. When you wake up you cannot find their tracks. They have carried off your possessions. You tug at your ear." What more graphic and striking description of a rueful gesture could the Egyptian have given?

The letter goes on to imply that Mahir has been sadly unobservant during his travels. "I wrote to you about a city, Byblos by name. What does it look like? Did you not visit it? Tell me about Berytos and Sidon and Sarepta. What does Uz look like? There is talk of another city which stands in the sea, Tyre by name. Water is brought to it by ship, and it is richer in fish than sand."

It is immensely informative to draw back the veil and look into past millennia. Paul Claudel has said that the past is even more unattainable than the future—but is not the past a part of the present and the present a part of the future? The life of the world's peoples, especially the unspoiled races who live much as their ancestors did, the discoveries made by archaeology and the information about advanced civilizations transmitted in their writing can all teach us much about the past. Hori's sarcasm brings us close to the Egyptian tourist in Syria. "Tremors seize you, and your hair stands on end. Your heart is in your mouth. The chasm lies on one side, the mountain on the other. You continue, you walk beside your carriage and are afraid. Your heart thumps. You walk on foot. The sky is open. You imagine that the enemy is behind you. You tremble. . . ." Seldom has a lonely traveler's fear been more graphically portrayed.

"When you come to Joppa you find a field of verdure. You enter an unwalled vineyard, where you find a lovely girl guarding the grapes. She takes you as her companion and grants you delightful tokens of her favor. You are caught, and confess. They upbraid you, and you hastily surrender your apron of fine Upper Egyptian linen. Once more you sleep and do nothing. They steal your bow, your

dagger, your quiver. Your horse crosses boggy ground. The road
is long. Your carriage falls to pieces. You lose your weapons in
the sand. 'Give me food and water,' you say, 'for I have arrived.'
But they pretend to be deaf and do not listen."

Has there ever been a letter which described a disastrous journey
by a government official more vividly, more observantly or with
more delicate sarcasm? Men have changed little since Rameses, Moses
and the golden age of Syrian culture.

When Mahir roamed through the Phoenician cities, the maritime
fortresses already had a history of thousands of years behind them.
They had felt the influence of Asia, Egypt and Crete. That the
Egyptians maintained good relations with a city like Byblos is
proved by the excavations carried out by Montet (1921–1924) and
Dunand (1925–1957). It was at Byblos in 1923 that Pierre Montet
made one of the most interesting finds of the century by discovering the sarcophagus of King Ahiram in a burial chamber there.
In its interior, among other funerary gifts, were two Rameses II
alabaster vases. King Ahiram was a contemporary of the great
builder and Byblos was at that time the most important city in
Phoenicia, although strongly under the influence of Egypt in
politics, trade and art. One side of the stone sarcophagus depicts a
bearded King Ahiram seated on a sphinx throne, his feet on a stool,
a lotus blossom in his left hand and a cup in his right. Seven men
stand before the king. The first is brushing flies from the sacrificial
table with a swat. Two others are carrying in dishes and cups,
while the other four are saluting the king with raised arms, palms
facing forward. The other side of the sarcophagus depicts eight
mourning figures: two women, two porters with pitchers on their
shoulders, a man leading a billy goat and, finally, three bearded
servants with their hands raised in greeting. The lid of the sarcophagus bears a life-size figure of the great king and—something
of inestimable importance—an engraved inscription running along
both its sides. It is the earliest Phoenician text in existence and
antedates the alphabetical mode of writing, proving that even in
1300 B.C. the Phoenicians were on the way to that most important
invention in human history: the alphabet. The find was important
because it solved a mystery which had been puzzling scholars. It
had long been assumed that the Greeks adopted their written
characters from a foreign people, probably as early as the tenth

century B.C. But unless it could be proved that the Phoenicians possessed written characters several centuries previously, the theory of the take-over was open to doubt. Dussaud attributed Ahiram's sarcophagus to the thirteenth century. If this is correct, the Phoenicians already possessed the rudiments of written characters at that time and the dead king has bequeathed us an immensely important piece of information.

Thieves had removed the most valuable objects from the burial chamber and the king's corpse was no longer there, but the sarcophagus itself now reposes in the National Museum at Beirut.

Because the coastal city of Byblos was renowned for processing Egyptian papyrus, *biblos* became the Greek term for book, and our Bible owes its name to the same source.

One of the most famous Phoenicians cities was Tyre, an island fortress possessed of two harbors, the Sidonian in the north and the Egyptian in the south. The Sidonian harbor is not only still in existence today but is still in use. The Egyptian, however, has disappeared. Since 1934 the French archaeologist Poidebard has been conducting explorations on the site of the former Egyptian harbor under the aegis of the Académie des Inscriptions et Belles-Lettres of Paris.

Research in the past twenty years has shown that many vanished cities, both on land and beneath the sea, are discernible only from a great altitude where their general outlines emerge more clearly. Poidebard exploited this knowledge by taking aerial photographs before sending his divers down. When they reached the sea bed the submerged walls of ancient Tyre unfolded before their astonished eyes. On the southern side of the city they discovered a mole half a mile long and some twenty-five feet wide with a well-fortified entrance at its center. The Egyptian harbor had not been created by nature but wrung from the sea by human endeavor, and was complete with quays, breakwaters, loading sheds and every other prerequisite of a thriving maritime metropolis.

The city stood on an island. According to information given by the historian Arrian, who lived in the second century A.D., it had walls more than 160 feet high and was built on rocky ground. Since the surface area was small, the inhabitants lived in multistoried houses. Opposite the city on the mainland stood Palaityros, a large metropolis which stretched for eight miles along the coast. Today,

Tyre (now called Sur) forms the tip of a tongue of land projecting into the sea, testimony to the fact that Alexander the Great not only conquered the world but altered geography itself. While preparing to capture Tyre in 332 B.C. he built a causeway out to the island city, which lay 650 yards from the mainland. Using rubble from the ruins of mainland Tyre, he pushed a wall of stone nearly two hundred feet wide out into the sea. We can only guess how many thousands of laborers must have worked to realize Alexander's grand design. In the course of more than 2,000 years silt has gradually increased the width of the dike until today one can only imagine what the mightiest maritime fortress in human history must have looked like when it was still an island. Only about 6,000 people now live in Sur, whereas the former island was once the fulcrum of a great sea power and accommodated 25,000 inhabitants within its walls.

The coastal strip opposite the island belonged to the kings of Tyre and supplied the seagirt city with grain, fruit and vegetables. Fantastic as it sounds, the Phoenicians installed an excellent system of water supply here over 3,000 years ago. On the mainland, nearly five miles south of Tyre, was—and still is—the spring of Ras el-ain. Leading its waters northward to a point almost opposite the island, the Phoenicians used them to irrigate the fields that supplied them with food. They also set up a regular ferry service to carry water from the canal to the island and so provide a source of drinking water for its 25,000 inhabitants. In time of siege, a water ration was distributed from the city's storage cisterns, and the system's efficiency is vouched for by the fact that Nebuchadnezzar besieged Tyre in vain for thirteen years, from 585 to 572 B.C.

In the coastal plain and the hilly country that rises to the north, all of which once belonged to Tyre, modern archaelogists have discovered widespread traces of habitation, among them graves, sarcophagi, remnants of houses, oil presses, cisterns and stone reliefs. The imagination boggles at the antiquity of Tyre. When Herodotus visited the place about 450 B.C. he was told that the Temple of Heracles Melkert was already 2,300 years old. But the city itself was far older. Who knows when the god Melkert ordered the first purple robe for his beloved, the nymph Tyro, from the purple refiners of Tyre? Weaving, glass manufacture, metalwork and, above all, purple dye—all these things contributed to the city's wealth.

Tyre is a place where the beginnings of Christianity go back to the time of Jesus' presence on earth. A Christian community existed there in the middle of the first century A.D., and it was through the narrow alleyways of Tyre that Paul passed on the way back from his third missionary journey. Even earlier, the prophet Ezekiel, who fought against the Phoenicians' gods, foresaw disaster: "How art thou destroyed, that wast inhabited of seafaring men, the renowned city, which wast strong in the sea. . . ." He even predicted that the southern harbor was destined to collapse into the sea, for he went on: ". . . I shall bring up the deep upon thee, and great waters shall cover thee." We can also read in Ezekiel's prophecies something of the pride and arrogance that must have inspired the Phoenicians at the height of their power. ". . . Thou [the prince of Tyre] hast said, I am a God, I sit in the seat of God, in the midst of the seas."

This mysterious race survived many vicissitudes in the course of its long history. At the beginning of the third millennium B.C. forty ships arrived in Egypt laden with cedarwood from Lebanon, exported from Byblos. The walls of Pharaoh Sahure's funerary temple at Abusir illustrate the items which his war fleet brought back from Phoenicia in 2700 B.C.: bears, numerous other beasts, prisoners and, last but not least, slaves without number. While Pharaoh Thutmosis III occupied the throne between 1504 and 1450 B.C. the Phoenicians' great maritime cities played, as so often in their history, the role of shrewd vassals. Tyre, Sidon, Berytos and Byblos sent the king of Egypt corn, oil and incense and placed ships at his disposal. Then the "sea peoples" invaded Syria, and between 1200 and 750 B.C. the maritime cities fell upon hard times, Sidon being almost destroyed. Later they were forced to pay huge tributes to the kings of Assyria. In Tyre we see King Hiram—not to be confused with Ahiram of Byblos—augmenting the surface of his island city by reclamation work, building new temples to Melkert and Astarte and erecting a golden pillar in the shrine of Baal. As we have already heard, this king was a friend of King Solomon and had probably met his father David in person.

The walls of Tyre witnessed dramatic scenes of hope, love and hatred—not to mention numberless royal assassinations. Abdastartos, who reigned from 918 to 910 B.C., was a victim of one such plot, and it is symptomatic that the murderers were the four sons of his own wet nurse.

The Phoenicians were descendants of the Canaanites and called their country Canaan. This much we know, but we do not know what instilled in them their unique yearning for travel. Perhaps they had inherited it from their predecessors, the seafarers of Crete. At all events, their questing, roving, restless love of the open sea drove them to Spain, to the city of Tarshish (Tartessus) in the estuary of the Guadalquivir; and the merchants of Tartessus. in their turn, plied their trade as far afield as England and the Baltic Sea. Tarshish was probably not a Phoenician city, but the Israelites had learned the name from Phoenician sailors and so they called any large galleys "ships of Tarshish." The ships which Solomon and Hiram I of Tyre jointly sent to Ophir, the land of gold, were so described, although they sailed nowhere near Tarshish. The Phoenicians planted colonies everywhere: on the islands of Thasos, Cythera, Melos, Rhodes, Malta and Sicily, and on the North African coast. Their last colony, founded in 814 B.C., was Carthage, where the Phoenician or "Punic" way of life survived long after the mother cities had been submerged in the Graeco-Roman world.

The Phoenicians bequeathed the ancient world the invention of purple. Small wide-meshed nets were baited with mussels to attract the purple-bearing mollusks which preyed on them. Then, when the snails had attached their long suckers firmly, the nets were raised and the valuable harvest reaped. The mollusks, the largest of which could weigh twelve pounds or more, were then smashed and their purple glands extracted. These were salted down and left to stand for three days, after which the mass was tipped into a leaden caldron and diluted in the proportion of 4½ gallons of water to 4 hundredweight of purple. The caldron was heated to an even temperature by steam, which was introduced—3,000 years ago, it must be remembered—through a long pipe leading from the furnace. When the caldron began to simmer, the fragments of flesh which rose to the surface were skimmed off. After about ten days the solution was clear and ready to be tested on wool which had previously been steeped in lye. If the initial test proved satisfactory the wool was immersed in purple for five hours.

Exposure to the rays of the sun enhanced the wool's glowing color but also gave off a revolting stench. The Papyrus Sallier 2, which was written in the time of Rameses II, gives us some idea of the purple dyer's unpleasant working conditions. "The hands of the dyer stink like rotten fish, and the man eventually comes to detest any cloth."

Sunlight turned the dye first dark green and then violet or sometimes mauve. Generally speaking, however, the purple of the ancient world was almost always violet in shade. The Jews, who may have learned the art of purple refining during their sojourn in Egypt, became skilled in the technique of purple manufacture. In later years the curtain which hung before their Holy of Holies was purple, and purple came to be used in religious ceremonies— hence the four liturgical colors: white, violet, crimson and scarlet. Sacrificial tables and other sacred objects were draped in purple, too. The Egyptians, who imported purple from nearby Phoenicia, not only swathed the mummies of distinguished men in purple bandages and robed their dead in purple shrouds but also used purple on papyrus as a form of ink. In order to make clothes wear better, the ancients mixed purple with honey. Among the Lydians, purple was worth its weight in silver. Clement of Alexandria, who was born in 150 B.C., tells us that a certain Egyptian courtesan paid 10,000 talents for a purple robe although she only charged 1,000 Attic drachmas for her services. This meant, in modern terms, that her dress cost her about $250 while her regular fee was only fifty cents.

However, nothing in life—not even purple—endures forever, and the genuine purple of antiquity finally disappeared for good. When the Mohammedans took Constantinople in 1453, purple refining was discontinued.

Is man intended to unearth the past? Reading the inscription on the sarcophagus of a Sidonian king, one is smitten by a strange feeling: "I adjure every king and every man not to open this resting place or search for jewels, for I have none with me. Let no one take my couch away nor carry me off elsewhere. I adjure kings and men not to uncover me nor lay me bare."

The sarcophagus, which anyone can inspect in the Louvre in Paris, is empty.

QUEEN OF THE SEAS

I shall describe the most notable of all wars, the war which the Carthaginians waged against the Roman people under Hannibal's command. Never did more powerful states and nations engage in armed conflict. The fortunes of war were so changeable and the struggle so arduous that those who won were in the greater danger. Indeed, they fought with almost more embitterment than strength: the Romans from displeasure that they, the victors, had been attacked by the vanquished; the Punians because they believed that Rome had often behaved toward them, the vanquished, like an arrogant and covetous overlord.

—TITUS LIVIUS, *History of Rome*, xxi, 1

FEW cities in antiquity were as wealthy as Carthage, and few of them met as tragic an end. Her inhabitants sat in their six-storied houses drinking the best Greek wine while their ships sailed to every quarter of the world.

Carthage was founded by the Phoenicians who from their base at Tyre set sail for the west, founding colonies and establishing trading posts and cities as far afield as Gibraltar and, beyond Gibraltar, Gadir, known to the Romans as Gades and to us as the Spanish town of Cádiz. In the Phoenician tongue Carthage was called Kart-Hadasht, which meant "new city." Presumably the Tyrians regarded Carthage as their most important daughter city and, consequently, as a new Tyre (see map p. 54).

Carthage is reputed to have been founded in 814 B.C., 38 years before the first Olympiad. The story of its founding is generally regarded as a legend, but such legends usually contain a grain of historical truth. Timaeus, who lived between 356 and 260 B.C. and wrote a history in 38 volumes, gives us some details of the city's founding. We glean further information from the foremost and most celebrated poet of the Augustan age, Publius Virgilius Maro (Virgil), who spent the eleven years before his death working on his great poem the *Aeneid*, a national epic which chronicled the wanderings of Aeneas.

Elissa was the daughter of the king of Tyre. Her husband Sychaeus was murdered by his brother Pygmalion, who made himself king of Tyre and forced Elissa to flee the country, accompanied by a number of native Tyrians. The emigrants, whose first port of call was Cyprus, included a high priest of the goddess Astarte, who had stipulated that his family should supply the priesthood in any future colony. Also among the fugitives were eighty virgins who were to be at the disposal of emigrants and foreigners in the temples of Astarte. Eventually, at the point where the North African coast juts closest to the island of Sicily, the Tyrian refugees founded Carthage, having secured the land peacefully by paying the indigenous population an agreed rent. The king of Libya tried to force Elissa into marriage, but she built a pyre as though intending to do sacrifice and then leaped into the flames. Elissa's Carthaginian name was Dido.

In Virgil's version of the story, Aeneas was wrecked on the Libyan coast and brought to Dido's palace. She fell in love with him and later, when he deserted her, committed suicide by leaping onto a pyre.

Elissa's story is really the story of Carthage, for it follows the same pattern and ends in the same manner.

The Carthaginians, known to the Romans as Poeni and to us as Punians, forfeited their Mediterranean supremacy as a result of the three Punic Wars which were fought between 264 and 146 B.C. Although their city was ultimately annihilated, their greatest leader, Hannibal, merits comparison with Alexander the Great, Julius Caesar and Napoleon as one of the most brilliant military commanders in history.

Carthage stood by the sea only about six miles from modern Tunis. Slightly inland is the hill of Byrsa, and at its summit stood a temple dedicated to the Punic god Eshmun. The Carthaginians had built a wall around the sacred hill, turning it into a citadel. Today the heights are occupied by the monastery of the White Fathers and the Cathedral of St. Louis. It is no accident that the richest place in the ancient world not only gave its name to some of the world's most famous stock exchanges, notably the Paris Bourse, but also to that humbler article of use, the purse.

Carthage had two harbors, one rectangular and the other round. These harbors were linked, leaving only one egress to the sea. The rectangular outer harbor was used for merchant ships and the circular inner harbor served as a naval base. In the center of the naval harbor lay an island on which was situated the headquarters

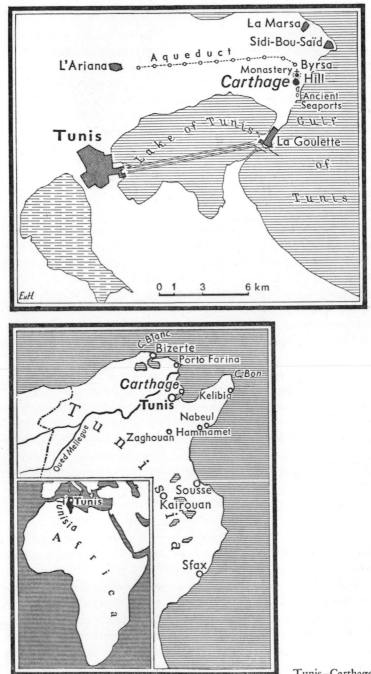

Tunis—Carthage

of the fleet. Facilities included berths for 220 warships, arsenals, wharfs, quays and warehouses. The only exit could, when necessary, be barred with iron chains and the whole city was protected by walls with a total length of over twenty miles.

From this secure base, Carthage dominated the North African coast from Egypt to Gibraltar and sent forth her five-tiered galleys to southern Spain, to the islands of Sardinia and Corsica, and to Sicily, always maintaining contact with her erstwhile mother city Tyre. Carthaginian ships sailed far into the Atlantic Ocean. It is likely that they reached Britain via Cádiz, and they may well have touched the Azores.

Carthage derived immense wealth from her worldwide trading connections, for the shrewd merchant princes of Byrsa saw to it that foreign countries traded only with them and never with their colonies. Ships belonging to those who disregarded this rule were ruthlessly captured or sunk.

The city did a thriving trade in foodstuffs from the rich African hinterland. Valuable metals such as tin, copper and silver were imported from Spain and England and reshipped. Astute Punic businessmen sold textiles, African hides and thousands of slaves to customers throughout the known world, thereby filling the coffers of their countinghouses and swelling the revenues of their miraculous city which, like some New York of the ancient world, was a place of tireless activity and ultramodern methods. Gold, pearls, Tyrian purple, ivory, incense from Arabia, Egyptian linen, fine vases from Greece—all these goods were displayed in the warehouses and market places of Carthage. The world's first joint stock companies originated there, and it was Carthage which floated the first government loans, built machines and invented the first artillery in military history. The strongest Negro slaves and the loveliest dusky slave girls in Rome, Athens, Spain and the Bosporus were all supplied by her. (Some Carthaginian aristocrats owned as many as 20,000 slaves.)

Carthage evolved a constitution which combined elements of monarchy, aristocracy and democracy, a system which certainly suited the contemporary world but may well have contributed to the city's ultimate downfall. At the head of the city-state were two men known in Latin as *suffetes,* from the Semitic *shopet.* (The word is translated as "judges" in the Bible.) These two annually elected officials ruled in conjunction with a parliament consisting of three hundred of the wealthiest citizens, all of whom held office for life. In addition to them there was the "council of the hundred judges." In reality there were 104 of these men, who controlled the courts and exercised considerable influence on general policy.

All military matters were entrusted to a supreme commander. The moneyed aristocracy of this extraordinary city had devised a solution to their military problems which looked effective but contained latent dangers: the supreme commander had to win every war. If things went awry he was called to account and, if necessary, crucified. The sons of wealthy aristocrats would not deign to become soldiers and Carthaginians in general prided themselves on never having had to go to war in person, so the only answer was to maintain a large and potentially dangerous army of mercenaries recruited from every land.

It is uncertain how many people lived in the Carthaginian metropolis during its prime. The Greek geographer Strabo puts the number at 700,000, which, allowing for foreign residents and slaves, does not appear to be an exaggerated estimate. Conditions in the city can be deduced from a thorough study of ancient sources. Magnificent marble temples, gold and silver pillars, statues and statuettes gleamed in the African sun. The goddess Tanit was worshiped here in peculiarly lavish style, for archaeologists have found thousands of urns containing the charred bones of children in the ruins of her temple. It was the practice in Carthage to sacrifice children, probably only those belonging to leading families. Diodorus tells us that one such sacrifice in the year 310 B.C. cost the lives of no less than five hundred children. The goddess Tanit was considered to be more powerful than the god Baal, although the great Carthaginian generals incorporated the latter's name in their own. Hasdrubal, for instance, means "Baal is my help," and Hannibal "favored of Baal."

Viewed in a contemporary light, the three Punic Wars, which covered a period of 119 years, were world wars. When Hannibal suffered his first defeat at Zama, when Carthage was forced to pay Rome the fantastic sum of 10,000 talents and her aristocrats in their tall houses swore never to make war again without Rome's permission, the downfall of one of the most amazing sea powers in history was already sealed. Rome waited another fifty years, and then the city was burned, destroyed and smashed, house by house, temple by temple and terrace by terrace. The walls were overthrown, the quays demolished, the lighthouses battered down and any Carthaginians who still survived sold into slavery by the Romans.

Were the Carthaginians cowardly? This Semitic race of Phoenician stock sailed the seas of the world more boldly than men had ever done before. The objects of their voyages and explorations were almost always unknown and unfamiliar lands, uncharted and unfriendly waters. Only stout hearts could have overcome such perils. The Carthaginians were not artists or poets. They were seduced neither by Greek nor Roman culture, nor did they live in the despotic style of the East. In the end, they defended their city and their way of life to the last man.

They possessed something worth defending, for they lived in their metropolis by the sea in a style unequaled by any other race in the contemporary world.

THE SILENT STONES OF MALTA

Although the artistic sense of the people is not always on a par with their moral and civic attainments, it is very probable that the neolithic population of the Maltese islands had, in addition to their artistic achievements, elaborated a religious system of a type which we usually attribute to much later generations.

—SIR THEMISTOCLES ZAMMIT, *Prehistoric Malta,*
p. 16, London, 1930

THE island of Malta is small, and there are few other places in the world where so many people live so closely packed together. Towns, suburbs and villages almost melt into one another, and all are seething with people. The peasants of Malta hate stones because they interfere with their plows—and there are plenty of stones on Malta, stones so big that they waste cultivable ground, stones that provide the island with its greatest mystery.

Seventeen miles long and nine miles wide, Malta is inhabited by the most persevering peasant farmers in the Mediterranean area, an island of innumerable tiny fields surrounded by low stone walls, an island breeding the finest and sturdiest goats and donkeys, an island which supplies the finest honey in Europe. The fossilized bones of long-extinct elephants and of rhinoceros and various types of deer that have been found there suggest that the Maltese group, which includes the islands of Malta, Gozo, Comino and Filfla, is all that is left of a land bridge which once linked Africa with Italy. Man was living in the area possibly as long ago as 100,000 years or even more. Six miles from Valletta, the capital, in Ghar Dalam, "the cavern of darkness," eight human teeth were discovered with fossils belonging to the extinct dwarf rhinoceros. The anthropologist Arthur Keith suggests that two of these teeth belong to the Neanderthal people who roamed the world between 130,000 and 30,000 years ago. To ascribe them to the Neanderthalians is, however, a bold piece of conjecture, for Neanderthal traces have not been definitely identified here.

Nevertheless, it is still possible that the inhabitants of the islands lived through many of the paleolithic periods even though the available evidence would not take us back 30,000 years, let alone 130,000.

It was on Malta's shores that Paul the Apostle was wrecked while on his way to Rome as a prisoner. "And when they were escaped, then they knew that the island was called Melita," we are told in Acts: xxviii. The anniversary of Paul's landing is still celebrated by the inhabitants to this day.

Nowhere else in Europe can we see such an amazing number of early buildings as on this small group of Mediterranean islands where, over thousands of years, men developed an architectural technique which bordered on the miraculous. In such a densely populated place every square foot of ground is valuable, and Maltese peasants have been clearing away the stones and stone buildings for thousands of years. However, enough still remains to provide an almost inexhaustible archaeological paradise. To catch a glimpse of this wonderland is to travel backward in time to a period which lies four or five thousand years in the past and to speculate about people who handled vast blocks of stone as though they were the legendary Titans of old.

A megalith is a large stone, and megalithic buildings are buildings composed of huge individual blocks of stone. We shall never know exactly what prompted men to construct such immense megalithic buildings here in prehistoric times. The builders are no longer with us and we do not even know their precise race, although we can at least try to gain an inkling of the mystery.

On July 20, 1915, Themistocles Zammit began to excavate some megalithic buildings near the village of Tarxien, about two miles south of Valletta. Two years later, the ruins of the golden age of these unknown builders had been unearthed. The superficial observer will not immediately discern any plan in the immense jumble of stones, yet each was laid with a deliberate intent. Semioval chambers were built in pairs with their axes of length parallel to one another and a central corridor connecting them. The ground plan can be likened to two Ds set close together but facing outward in this fashion: ⅭⅮ. The entrance leads into the corridor dividing the two oval chambers, whose side walls and floors consist of huge stone slabs, and the whole arrangement is surrounded by an enclosing wall.

For decades it was thought that these oval buildings had been

Malta

erected by the Phoenicians, but the megalithic buildings of Malta date back to far more ancient times.

Archaeologists have debated whether the megalithic buildings were dwelling places, palaces, enormous graves or temples. The layout of the buildings indicates that they were used for a religious purpose. The broad central corridor almost invariably leads to a large niche at the rear which appears to have been the most important place in the whole complex, rather like the apse of a cathedral. Other small niches, stone tables and storage places for animal bones also point to the religious significance of the oval buildings. Several monoliths may have been altars, and stone covers have been found which probably served as water catchments or fireplaces. Beneath a number of stone blocks diggers found fragments of receptacles, tools of stone or bone, shells and pebbles, all carefully placed there by human agency before the megaliths were superimposed on them. This indicates that the oval buildings were neither dwelling places nor palaces, but sanctuaries. Wherever in the world man has erected his largest and finest buildings and wherever he has excelled himself creatively and artistically, he has almost invariably been motivated by a religious impulse. These massive megalithic buildings were likewise erected for purposes of divine worship.

In one chamber at Hal Tarxien the lower portion of a female statue was excavated. The figure was seated on a block of stone decorated in relief and was almost life-size. Various statuettes in clay and stone were also discovered, mostly female figures which probably had religious significance. One thing we do know is that the prehistoric Stone-Age inhabitants of Malta worshiped a female deity. The director of the Valletta Museum, Professor Sir Themistocles Zammit, has also established by dint of exhaustive research that oracles were bestowed in the sanctuaries of Malta. Such deductions demand an extremely wide knowledge of other similar places in all parts of the Mediterranean area.

In the interior of many of the temples, rectangular stone blocks almost twelve feet square had been let into the ground. These were surrounded by walls on three sides and bordered by a stone step. Each block of stone had five holes in it, and in the right-hand corner of the stone step was a sixth. Zammit has tried to interpret these strange cavities. They may have been used for storing flour or loaves for temple use, but it is also conceivable that the oddly shaped blocks had something to do with the numerous small stone marbles which were also found. Over a hundred little balls of varying sizes were discovered some yards away. This would suggest that we are dealing with an oracle. Perhaps the stone balls were thrown at the stone from a distance and the purport of the oracle depended on the particular hole in which they landed.

Peculiar stone chambers with niches and apertures unearthed not only at Tarxien but at other sites such as Hagiar Kim, Mnaidra and Gigantia, all suggest that a system of sacrificial rites was practiced in the megalithic sanctuaries.

No human skeletons were found in the megalithic buildings, but there were many bones belonging to domesticated animals, particularly oxen and sheep. Professor Zammit considers these bones to be the remains of sacrificial beasts. Some of the stone blocks portray whole rows of goats which were undoubtedly destined for sacrifice.

The year 1902 saw the discovery of the Hypogeum at Hal Saflieni in the neighborhood of the Tarxien ruins, and in 1907 it was opened to the public. Derived from the Greek *hypogeion*, the word is used to describe a subterranean vault and consisted in this case of recesses, passages and small chambers hewn out of the solid rock, together with some external buildings. In order to clear the Hypogeum a shaft thirty feet deep had to be driven into the ground. Debris from the mysterious catacombs was carried out through this tunnel and electric lights were later installed so that the interior could be inspected with ease.

In ancient times the Hypogeum must have been a sanctuary. It seems safe to assume this because the roof of one of the vaults is decorated with spirals in red ochre, a well-known feature of prehistoric religious art. The Italian authority Luigi Ugolini considers this chamber to be the seat of an oracle. If one speaks into one of the artificial niches in a deep voice, the words re-echo from wall to wall and chamber to chamber throughout the whole vault—yet another feature of this astonishing place.

In Zammit's opinion, the Hypogeum at Hal Saflieni and the temples of Tarxien are older than any other known oracles: "Yet they filled the visitor with reverence and directed his mind to the mystery and power of unseen spirits. Perhaps the Hal Saflieni caves and the Tarxien temples attracted people of distant lands who believed in the power of the oracle which could be consulted there."

Toward the close of the Stone Age the Hypogeum served as a huge burial vault. Chambers on each of its two levels were filled with red earth and the skeletons of over seven thousand people placed inside. The absence of large bones indicates most of them had not been buried in this spot originally, but had presumably been brought there from other burial places and then interred in the Hypogeum. The practice of waiting for bodies to decompose and then burying them elsewhere in a common grave is one which has been identified in other places in the Mediterranean.

The Hypogeum contained potsherds and fragments of statuettes. Two female clay figures wore strangely pleated bell-shaped skirts. One of the women was lying on her belly on a couch and the other was sleeping on her side. This dormant and amply proportioned figure is one of the finest neolithic sculptures in existence. The sculptors of Malta, who lived roughly four or five thousand years ago, probably excelled all the other artists of the western Mediterranean, particularly where the human figure was concerned.

The whole complex, especially the hollowing out of the subterranean vault, was an astonishing achievement. People who accomplished such things had undoubtedly formed highly organized communities and were culturally very advanced, or they would never have been capable of such feats.

We know that animals were sacrificed to a god or gods; we also know that they were slaughtered before a sacred image and then burned. Complicated oracular rituals and the interpretation of god-sent dreams, too, have been inferred—and all from the silent ruins, the echoing chambers and broken statuettes of the Hypogeum at Hal Saflieni. What a high degree of intellectual attainment, what an intricate system of religious observance it summons up! The Maltese islands offer us what is probably the most interesting example of man's quest for spirituality in pre-metallic times. In the Mnaidra sanctuary, which consisted of two massive oval buildings, mountains of neolithic vessels were found. Seen from the air, this veritable miracle in stone looks like a half-finished game played by giants.

A similar impression is created by the Gigantia, which comprises the ruins of two enormous temples on the neighboring island of Gozo. Blocks and slabs of stone must have been brought there from miles away, for heavy building materials were not available in the immediate area. Many of the Gigantia's upright stones are over sixteen feet high, and one is more than twenty-six feet long and thirteen feet wide.

Equally astonishing is the size of several monolithic pillars and slabs in the ruins of Hagiar Kim, which, incidentally, means "standing stones." One of the pillars there is over sixteen feet high, and one of the slabs nearly two and a half feet thick, ten feet high and twenty-three feet long. It would be impossible to load such a weight onto a modern truck without using elaborate technical equipment. Analyzing the remarkable engineering feats of five thousand years ago, we can only assume that the immense stones were moved over a period of months or even years by a whole community employing levers, stone balls and wooden rollers.

The almost incredible amount of energy expended by the prehistoric inhabitants of Malta in their timeless struggle with the huge stones is manifested by deep tracks cut into the hard limestone.

These tracks, which occur throughout the islands and run in every direction, are testimony to the exertions of a large population, to the transportation of heavy materials, perhaps to the first stone wheels or to the centuries-long rumbling of the big stone balls which have come to light in all Malta's megalithic ruins and very probably acted as rollers for transporting immense loads.

Megalithic culture was still at its prime in Malta long after other places in the Mediterranean area had discovered metal. Eventually, an entirely alien population took over the island and the huge megalithic sanctuaries fell into decay. No writing, no verbal traditions, no portraits in stone or paint, were left behind by the people who piled these mighty blocks of stone one upon the other, nor is it possible to reconstruct their appearance or tell their race from the formation of their bones and skulls.

The mute evidence is there. Once upon a time, with endless perseverance and enormous effort, thousands upon thousands of men reared the great rocks skyward. The people of Malta must have devoted their whole energies to building these sanctuaries for eternity, but what their motives were, what language they spoke and what gods they served must forever remain a mystery.

Only the stones know the answer.

[15] A particularly fine Punic gravestone, now in the Bardo Museum at Tunis. Some historians assert that the Carthaginians did not believe in an afterlife, but it is difficult to believe that the creator of this stone was not convinced of the existence of a life after death.

[16] Carthaginian sculptures are extraordinarily rare. This gravestone depicts the face of a Carthaginian noblewoman. It is now in the Museum of the White Fathers at Carthage.

[17] [1] The Bardo Museum at Tunis displays a number of these strange ceramic works from the mysterious city that was one of the greatest commercial centers in the ancient world.

[18] [2-4] These small heads in brightly colored glass from the Museum of the White Fathers at Carthage are only a few centimeters high and may have served religious purposes.

[19] The Hypogeum, a two-floored, many-roomed subterranean building carved into the rock. The spirals painted on the ceiling in red ocher indicate that the place had religious associations.

[20] The "Sleeping Woman of Malta" was found in the Hypogeum, and is Malta's finest neolithic sculpture. Four or five thousand years ago, the island's sculptors were the finest artists to be found in the western Mediterranean.

[21] This terra-cotta head was also found in Malta but appears to belong to a later period.

[22] The huge complex of Hal Tarxien, excavated by Professor Themistocles Zammit between 1915 and 1917. These blocks and slabs of stone were cut by human hand and assembled into megalithic buildings, probably about 3,000 years before the birth of Christ. Prehistorian Karl J. Narr, however, states that in his opinion the site is not older than the Middle Minoan period, somewhere between 2100 and 1600 B.C.

[23] Overall plan of the temple at Hal Tarxien, showing the characteristic double-oval shape of its buildings. The dark outlines indicate walls built of large vertical slabs, and the darkest gray, shaded portions represent the horizontal blocks composing the perimeter walls. Filling materials in the intervening spaces are shown in lighter gray, while the lightest tint indicates the position of large floor slabs.

[24] Thousands of bizarre constructions like this can still be seen on the plains and hills of Portugal. They are the remains of megalithic graves.

[25] "Tholos da Fariosa," a megalithic grave discovered in the west of the Iberian Peninsula. The entrance (*background, center*) can be clearly distinguished.

[26] Stonehenge is the most celebrated and interesting megalithic complex to have survived from the period between the end of the Stone Age and the beginning of the Bronze Age. It is generally assumed to have had religious associations.

[27] This passage grave, known as Vjälkinge 9, was found in the Swedish province of Schonen. Folke Hansen discovered forty humeral bones there, together with the remains of hand and foot bones. It is estimated that twenty-five persons were buried in the grave during prehistoric times.

[28] The palace of Mari was decorated with splendid mural paintings. Here we see a killer of sacrificial beasts painted on the wall of "Courtyard 106" in ocher, red, black and white. This work of art is some 3,700 years old.

THEIR FAITH MOVED MOUNTAINS

Avebury and Stonehenge are among the most astonishing pre-historic monuments, not only in the British Isles but in the Old World. Each might be fairly compared to a cathedral.

—V. GORDON CHILDE, *Prehistoric Communities of the British Isles*, p. 101, London, 1949

WHEN you wander across a hill overgrown with grass, undergrowth or trees and get the feeling that there is something artificial about the rising ground, pause a moment. What lies beneath your feet may be a mass grave built by man in prehistoric times. *Megas* and *lithos* are the Greek words for "large" and "stone," so a megalith is a large stone. It was out of large stones like these that, between roughly 3000 and 1500 B.C., man erected monuments whose existence has always been known but whose purpose has in many respects remained a mystery for thousands of years. Sometimes they were only dolmens or cromlechs, a few massive stones topped by a large slab; sometimes they took the form of large burial chambers or rings or long avenues of stones; sometimes, again, the men of about four thousand years ago placed a single stone upright and so left us one of the famous menhirs. This term is derived from the Celtic words *maen* and *hir*, meaning "stone" and "long." All these things—the single stones, the rings and complexes, coupled with the creative impulse and the ideas that gave birth to them—together go to make up the great and almost worldwide phenomenon which we call megalithic culture. There is a fascination in endeavoring to divine what thoughts animated the men who sought eternity through the medium of the monolith, or "single stone."

Extending in a huge arc from Norway, Denmark and southern Sweden to northwest Germany, England and Ireland, and from Brittany, Spain and Portugal to the islands of the western Mediterranean, the relics of this mysterious culture include barrows, cairns, tumuli, groups of monoliths, stone rings, tracks bordered by vast blocks of sandstone and monuments constructed of unhewn rock and built to withstand the ages. Western Europe alone has between forty and fifty thousand megalithic graves.

People have wondered why all these monuments were built either in coastal regions or, if inland, not too far from the sea. This may have been because coastal areas have always held the lead in cultural development. It is as if the sea and ships have been mankind's greatest educators; as if sea travel enhanced man's capabilities, made him inventive and stimulated his mind through an exchange of ideas with foreign peoples. It should not be surprising, therefore, that some of man's earliest advanced civilizations came into being around the shores of the Mediterranean, that our alphabet was invented in the Near East and that the Mediterranean was one of the principal cradles of architecture and religion. Civilizations developed much more slowly on the great continental land masses than in the maritime regions of Central America, on the coasts of China, in Greece, Italy, Spain and the Mediterranean islands. It was in the Aegean that man first learned how to hew blocks of stone, fit them together in layers and construct domed graves. In the remaining areas, in the western Mediterranean and on the Atlantic coasts, blocks of crude stone lying in the fields were merely piled up to form compartments, and menhirs were still being erected there long after the people of Mesopotamia, Syria and Egypt had started to hew stone into squared blocks.

What surprises one about the earliest stone monuments erected by Europe's prehistoric inhabitants is the sheer size of the building materials used. Near the township of Carnac and the village of Locmariaquer, both in Brittany, lie the most interesting megalithic areas in France and probably the entire world, for they contain the finest stone monuments ever discovered.

The grouping of the megaliths, the three series (*alignements*) comprising 2,935 menhirs and extending over two and a half miles, the covered galleries (*galeries couvertes*)—all these bear witness, in their arrangement, planning and selection of stones, to a once-advanced culture. Prehistorian Z. Le Rouzic believes that the *alignements* were cult sites or open-air temples and that the cromlech of Ménec was the chief sanctuary. Cromlechs are megaliths arranged in a circle or rectangle. The *alignements* may have been processional routes used by a death cult. Certainly, the fact that the avenues of stones usually lead to an open space surrounded by a ring of stones and close to a megalithic grave suggests some connection with a cult of that nature.

Research conducted by Commandant Devoir has revealed that

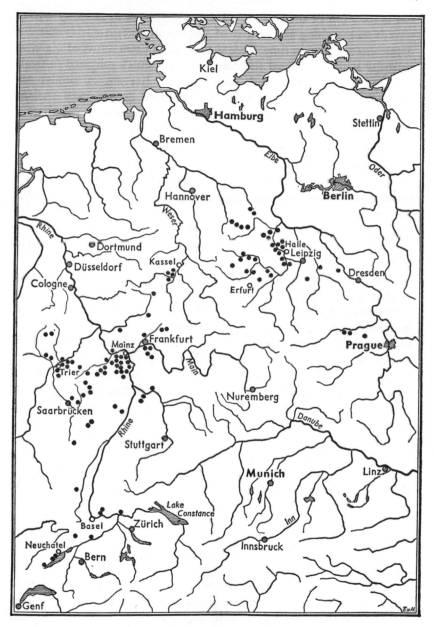

The black dots indicate German menhirs.

the orientation of the rows in all the *alignements* in Brittany corresponds to the rising and setting of the sun at certain astronomically determinate points in time. This would make them a sort of gigantic calendar which indicated the dates of a sun cult's religious festivals and had a connection with seedtime and harvest. A similar astronomical orientation has been attributed to certain very ancient roads in Brittany, but there is no scientific evidence for such a theory and it would seem to be no more than a product of wishful thinking.

The *alignements* of Ménec extend for a distance of some 1,300 yards, are about 100 yards wide and contain 1,099 menhirs. They form eleven parallel rows running in a west-southwesterly or north-northwesterly direction.

The *alignements* of Kermario extend for some 1,250 yards at a depth of just over 100 yards and consist of 1,029 menhirs ranged in ten rows.

The *alignements* of Kerlescan are just under 1,000 yards long and contain a total of 594 menhirs arranged in thirteen rows.

Whereas at Carnac it is the sheer mass of the megaliths that impresses one, at Locmariaquer it is the vastness and dimensions of the individual stones. The menhir which has been christened Mané er H'rolk, or "fairy stone," must have measured over sixty-five feet long when it was still intact. One day, we do not know when, it fell and broke into four pieces. This monolith is between ten and thirteen feet thick and its weight has been estimated at 350 tons. Five of our largest modern trucks would be needed to transport such a load. Not far away stands a magnificent dolmen called the Table des Marchands. This enormous stone slab was part of a subterranean chamber beneath a hill. A passage now leads into the chamber, enabling the visitor to marvel at the elemental majesty of this simple but breathtakingly impressive construction.

The mass and dimensions of the building materials used in many different places are a constant source of amazement. The largest stone at Stonehenge is almost thirty feet long. A stone in the Mount Browne dolmen in County Carlow, Ireland, weighs over a hundred tons. The megalithic grave at Bagneux in the neighborhood of Saumur, central France, boasts one stone which is just over sixty feet long and about sixteen feet wide and a roof stone weighing some ninety tons. It has never been fully explained how the men of 4,000

The extent of megalithic graves in the west of the Iberian Peninsula

years ago managed to shift such immense weights. In 1840 one of the largest megaliths at Saumur was used to bridge a river. Thirty-six yoked oxen and huge oaken rollers three feet in diameter had to be employed to move it. It is certainly conceivable, therefore, that even in early days a large number of men using primitive devices such as wooden rollers and towropes could have transported and erected such massive stones.

A few years ago, British archaeologists undertook a further thorough examination of Stonehenge, which stands on Salisbury Plain just over two miles from the Wiltshire village of Amesbury. Some of the fallen stones were re-erected, and the Institute of Atomic Research at Harwell ascertained the location of internal fissures by using the latest scientific aids.

Stonehenge is one of the most interesting megalithic complexes in the world. Stuart Piggott declared in 1954 that it was the unique and individual creation of an architect whose sense of overall planning and proportion far surpassed the general ability of his contemporaries in the barbaric northwest regions of Europe. He went on to say that anyone on the lookout for comparisons would have to turn to the world of the Aegean. The way in which the stones were fitted together, the ground plan and the technical mastery displayed were things which could not be deduced merely from the archaeological findings—but it was at least possible to elicit the sequence in which the separate phases occurred and determine their chronological boundaries.

In the center of the complex is a longish stone, the so-called altar stone, whose exact significance cannot be gauged. Around it in a horseshoe arc stand stones ranging from six and a half to eight feet in height. Five massive triliths formed an outer horseshoe, and around them stood a ring of thirty stones nearly fifteen feet high and linked by horizontal slabs. The whole arrangement was enclosed by a circular rampart measuring 130 yards in diameter and approached by a broad avenue which ran straight through the altar stone. Also on the path's axis but outside the whole circle and in front of the entrance stands the so-called "heel stone," the astronomical stone, surrounded by a small ditch. The slaughter or sacrificial stone may also have been situated here at one time. It has been estimated that the central axis is focused on the exact point on the horizon where, in the second millennium B.C., the sun would have risen on June 21st, though even if this were true it would be wrong to conclude simply that Stonehenge was a sun temple. Most of the world's holy places, from prehistoric graves to modern cathedrals, face eastward because birth, creation, God and the rising sun have always been symbolically associated.

Piggott tells us that this edifice was built at the beginning of the second millennium B.C. or, more precisely, that building was *begun* early in the second millennium B.C. The remains and objects discovered in the graves are, he says, typical of the so-called Secondary Neolithic Culture of Britain. Radiocarbon tests conducted on charred remains which were dug up here in 1950 dated them somewhere between 2123 and 1573 B.C.

Stonehenge is partly built of tertiary sandstone blocks which were once available on Salisbury Plain itself and are known in England as sarsens or Saracen stones. In addition, however, there are the so-called "bluestones" which form the inner circle and the smaller horseshoe. H. H. Thomas has ascertained that these bluestones came from the eastern end of Prescelly in South Wales, some 130 miles from Stonehenge as the crow flies. How were they transported to Salisbury Plain from so far away? By sea the route would have been roughly 400 miles long and overland they would have had to cover a distance of more than 170 miles. As the British archaeologist Glyn Daniel rightly says, the transportation of the bluestones was an amazing technical achievement and covered, so far as we can ascertain, the longest route ever used by the builders of any megalithic monument.

About two hundred stone rings have been discovered in the British Isles, but they are all inferior to Stonehenge and Avebury in grandeur of design and execution.

Avebury, an even larger megalithic complex than Stonehenge, lies only a few miles away. Originally, more than 650 blocks of stone were erected there in circles and rows, but many of the larger boulders were removed at a later date, some by local builders in search of materials and others by overzealous medieval Christians who bore them off and piously buried them.

Avebury's general outlines are hard to distinguish today because the village of that name nests immediately inside the ring of stones. The level ground in the center was once crowned by a ring of gigantic unhewn slabs. Each monolith measures about thirteen feet both in height and width and is about two feet six inches thick. The ring was encircled by a rampart and ditch, the latter running inside the former. Inside the large ring were two nonconcentric smaller rings whose edges almost touched. Of the stones which composed them, five and four have survived respectively. In the center of the southern inner ring stood a particularly tall stone, while the northern ring contained three monoliths.

What was the object of these ancient and gargantuan creations? Obscure as the history of the people of the time appears, two facts are apparent. Having been a hunter and a collector of wild fruit for a million or six hundred thousand years, man began, in the neolithic and megalithic period, to domesticate animals, inhabit a fixed abode and cultivate the soil. Concomitantly, there arose a desire to bury the dead in a more elaborate and secure fashion. Throughout the entire European and Mediterranean area there came into being enormous stone burial places, with Egypt leading the field by a considerable margin. The idea of building stone edifices for the dead was one that became disseminated throughout the regions mentioned above. Everywhere save in Egypt, provision was normally made for the interment of a considerable number of dead—probably members of one particular family or tribe. The forerunner of the chamber constructed of boulders was probably the cave, and archaeologists have, in fact, discovered worldwide evidence of cave burial going back hundreds of thousands of years.

The infinite pains which men took with the construction of megalithic graves indicate that they were concerned with preserving more for eternity than the mere physical remains of their dead. The size of the graves shows that they also served as cult sites and that there was a belief in something which survived after death. Contact and intercourse are practicable only with something that is alive, so it must be assumed that one of the driving forces of the amazing megalithic culture was a belief in the soul and its continued existence after death.

Many of the later megalithic graves were sealed with stones which had a round or oval hole cut into them. This "soul hole" was intended as a means of communication between the souls of the departed and the outside world, and may also have been used for supplying the dead with food and drink. Even today, one can still see "soul holes" in old French-Swiss houses on the upper reaches

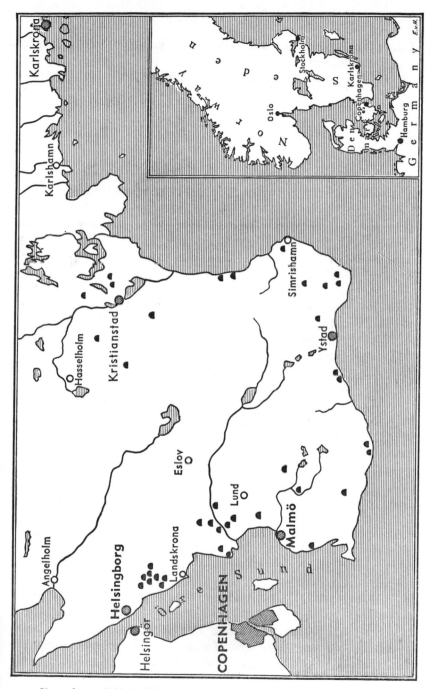

Sites of megalithic buildings found in Skåne Province, southern Sweden

of the Rhône, though the local inhabitants have no inkling of their age-old significance.

Stonehenge, Avebury, and other megalithic buildings cannot have been only graves. Had that been their sole function, their builders would have been guilty of needless overelaboration. It is far more likely that these immense constructions were holy places, sanctuaries which had originated in and were bound up with the death cult and other religious conceptions.

In the opinion of some authorities, the huge buildings on the Maltese islands set the pattern for all subsequent megalithic edifices, though whether they really represent such a point of departure seems highly questionable. Nevertheless, since the buildings there are clearly recognizable as temples they do lend support to the assumption that tribal sanctuaries were planned and built throughout western Europe.

How graves became cult sites and how cult sites—our own churches included—came to include graves is the material counterpart of a great spiritual mystery, for there is fundamental truth in the assertion that all death comes from life and all life from death.

The secret of the menhirs, too, can only be elucidated in religio-magical terms. Wherever these stones occur in Europe, people living in their vicinity have believed that miraculous powers emanate from or are associated with them. Professor Horst Kirchner of Berlin University has collected many of these ancient traditions. A Breton peasant woman declared that a year after touching the Saint Cado menhir she gave birth to a fine healthy son, and a number of other women who had visited the stone told the same story. In Germany the Long Stone at Tiengen in Kreis Waldshut was formerly called the Chindlistein ("little child stone") because wet nurses were supposed to remove newborn children from it at night. It is said of the Kindstein at Unterwiddersheim in Kreis Büdingen that anyone who lays his ear against it can hear children crying inside. The Langstein at Sulzmatt in Upper Alsace is supposed to have revolved on its axis one Good Friday as the midday bells were ringing, and the young girls who witnessed the phenomenon were all married within the year. The German menhirs known as Brautsteine ("betrothed" or "bride stones") are also said to ensure a happy marriage. Menhirs are often the object of pilgrimages by the sick. Some of these stones once marked medieval execution places, as, for instance, the Long Stone at Tiengen im Klettgau, the Long Stone near Ober-Saulheim in Rheinhessen and the "Flitch of Bacon" near Aschersleben. It is to be assumed that thousands of years ago people likewise believed that there was some vital force imprisoned in these stones.

One or two burial chambers of the megalithic period were found to contain a single upright stone. The late Sir Arthur Evans, who unearthed the Minoan culture of Crete, suggested that the Greek grave-pillar originally stood inside the burial chamber and was not erected over the grave in the form of a stele until later times. This indicates that it retained some magical significance from its "burial-chamber days" because it was supposed to house the spirits of the departed.

All this encourages one to assume that the menhirs, too, were not only monuments but possessed a magical or religious significance as well. When a dead man's soul left his body it went in search of another abode, and this other abode was provided by the menhir. It acted as a receptable for the soul of a person who was buried nearby or at some distance away, which may be why some menhirs were roughly hewn to represent the human form.

The stone giants of Sulzmatt and the Meisenthal Stone, incongruously adorned with its cross from a later age, the menhir of Alberschweiler and central Europe's largest upright megalith at Blieskastel, the menhirs of Carnac and Locmariaquer, standing erect like an army of silent dwellings for the human soul—all these are an irresistible reminder that the people of the megalithic cultures who set up these "soul stones" four or five thousand years ago possessed a faith which almost literally moved mountains.

THE MEGALITHS OF MORBIHAN

It is clear that, where the dolmen signs are concerned, we are groping in the dark. We can only rely on our gift of observation and draw certain conclusions from it. Our sole aim is our burning thirst for knowledge. Despite the imperfections of our methods, we have attempted to probe the spiritual and mystical domains of our oldest ancestors and grasp the thoughts that guided their hand.

—MARTHE and SAINT-JUST PÉQUART and ZACHARIE LE ROUZIC, *Corpus des Signes Gravés des Monuments Mégalithiques du Morbihan*, p. 92, Paris, 1927

THE greatest mystery surrounding megalithic monuments concerns the strange symbols engraved on them. The massive stone slabs and supporting stones of dolmens in the region of Morbihan on the southern coast of Brittany have long aroused particular interest among archaeologists the world over. Although there is no doubt that the marks on them are genuine and actually date from the megalithic period, they remained undiscovered for centuries simply because many of them are extremely hard to see.

Marthe and Saint-Just Péquart and Zacharie Le Rouzic have spent forty years working in Morbihan, examining stones and recording their observations, but not even they have managed to catalogue all the symbols. The following story may serve to show how easily they can escape the eye.

One year, the Péquarts and Le Rouzic discovered several signs on a stone in the dolmen known as Kerham. Returning next year to photograph their discovery they found to their great surprise that the signs seemed to have disappeared. Undeterred, one of the party spent many hours inspecting the monolith until, suddenly, the signs sprang to view, seeming to become more and more distinct as he watched. It seems that in the case of some stones special lighting conditions are necessary before the signs will emerge. The celebrated dolmen known as the Table des Marchands is adorned with a sun, but its existence has been denied and disputed in many learned treatises because it is clearly visible only between four and five o'clock in the afternoon, being indistinguishable at any other time of day.

Many marks have disappeared in the course of time as a result of wind and weather, changes in temperature and growths of moss

The Table des Marchands is a *dolmen à galerie* or passage grave at Locmariaquer which was first explored in 1814. The supporting stone (1) and the undersurface of the tablelike slab (2) in the chamber bear engraved symbols which were discovered by Le Rouzic. This sketch shows how such a passage grave was laid out.

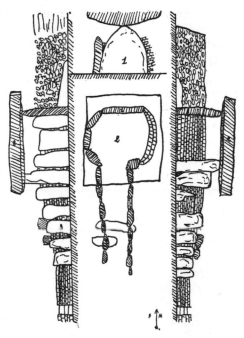

and lichen—and one day, no doubt, it will no longer be possible to discern what people carved on these stones some four thousand years ago.

These interesting signs appear on numerous menhirs as well as on dolmens, but because menhirs stand in an isolated position and are particularly exposed to the weather the signs carved on them have often been entirely obliterated by wind and weather. The menhir of Manio, for instance, displays a pattern of fine serpentine lines, but only where the earth has been dug away from around its base. The portion which protruded from the ground exhibits no marks that could have been made by human hand.

At Morbihan all the signs were *pounded*, not *carved* into the rock as they were in the Magdalenian, the paleolithic cultural phase of about 20,000 years ago. Hammer blows produced uneven furrows in the granite which normally provided the material for these stone monuments and the clarity of the lines suffered accordingly, but it has been ascertained that decoration was usually applied before the monoliths were placed in their allotted position.

The Franco-Cantabrian artists of the Magdalenian period in southern France and northwest Spain took great pains to make their mural paintings and sculptures naturalistic, so that they would achieve the greatest possible identity between them and the animals they portrayed. Only in this way, they reasoned, could they gain a hold over their potential prey. The engravings on megalithic monuments, by contrast, were left behind by people who had succeeded in reducing their ideas to the simplest possible terms. They had already abandoned art as a means of expressing their ideas and begun to evolve symbols and emblemlike designs. The pronounced schematization of these symbols in itself shrouds them in mystery, and the meaning of the ideograms has largely escaped our comprehension.

Nevertheless, the meaning of some signs is quite obvious. We can recognize axes, suns and sizable boats with raised prows and sterns. Snakes are often clearly identifiable in the granite, as are oxen, geometrical figures and even insects. Archaeologists naturally differ over the interpretation of a number of signs. Cephalopods or marine mollusks such as the calamary or inkfish are very often depicted. I believe that I myself have identified the mollusk *rondeletiola minor* or *spirula spirula* on one of the stones in the *"Allée couverte du Lufang."* It is interesting to note that mollusks occur only in covered galleries near the sea. But, if dolmens are also found not far from the coast, we are led to wonder why the people of the megalithic period never used them to depict cephalopods. This question has never been resolved. No genuine portrayal of a human form has ever been found except on the dolmen called Petit Mont, where two feet are shown. Perhaps they represent the feet of the man buried beneath the tumulus, for they are surrounded by lines not unlike a megalithic ground plan. The Roch Priol bears the outlines of six pairs of feet, but it is probably not a monument of the dolmen type. The Dolmen de Mané Lud seems to depict four standing figures, but it is not certain that the engravings actually represent human beings because they consist merely of crosses, some of them surmounted by round dots which may, or may not, be heads.

We do not know what the people of the megalithic cultures looked like, what race they belonged to or whether they were blond or dark, light- or dark-skinned. Glyn Daniel surmises that they belonged not to an Indo-European but to one or more Mediterranean linguistic groups, but it is just as likely that they resembled the present-day customers in the harbor cafés of Brest or the fishermen of Saint-Jean-de-Luz and San Sebastian. The men who drew boats and cephalopods must have been skilled seafarers or they would never have been able to spread their building methods and religious ideas from coast to coast throughout western Europe. They must, too, have had a firm belief in a life after death, or they would never have summoned up the energy to handle gigantic boulders as though they were playthings.

Is there any form of writing on megalithic monuments, do they express language in symbolic terms and do they bear alphabetical symbols?

In 1893 the French scholar Letourneau identified certain similarities between megalithic symbols and the earliest alphabets known, drawing for comparison on the neo-Punic, Phoenician, Etruscan and Coptic scripts. The Péquarts and Le Rouzic, however, decisively reject Letourneau's assumption of "Inscriptions on the Burial Monuments of Morbihan."

By and large it is quite clear what the megalithic sculptors, if so they can be termed, had in mind. Their drawings had a ritual and religious significance and may have been instructions or notes on religious observance. The details, however, remain obscure, and thousands of symbols will fade away completely in the next few thousand years without ever having been deciphered.

MARI, THE WONDER CITY

The story is told not only by clay tablets but by walls which have been devoured by fire and demolished by picks, by paving stones which have been trodden by countless thousands of feet. Never was ancient architecture so alive.

—ANDRÉ PARROT, *Le Palais*, p. 6, Paris, 1958

THE outstanding archaeological site found in the Near East during the past thirty years owed its discovery to a headless statuette picked up by wandering Bedouins. Tell Hariri had lain lonely and undisturbed in its grave by the banks of the Euphrates for thousands of years. No one guessed that a nondescript hill in eastern Syria, five miles north of Abu Kemal and close to the Iraq border, concealed one of the most famous cities of the third millennium B.C.

Excavations were organized at the instigation of the distinguished orientalist René Dussaud and financed by grants from the French National Museums and the Ministry of Education.

Work began on Tell Hariri on December 14, 1933. Only a few minutes after the surface had been broken by the first strokes of the pick, some statuettes came to light. On January 23, 1934, just forty days after digging had started, small sculptures were unearthed which portrayed three important personalities: Lamgi-Mari, the king; Ebih-il, the city's senior dignitary; and Idi-Nârum, the man who may have been responsible for supplying Mari with grain. The statuettes bore written symbols which provided the key to one of the great mysteries in the ancient history of the East. They not only made it clear that the diggers had found a temple dedicated to the goddess Ishtar, but revealed something of far greater import: that beneath Tell Hariri lay the lost and almost legendary city of Mari.

The discovery of the statuette of King Lamgi-Mari was particularly important because, in a sense, he carried the name of the city on his person. Engraved on the right-hand side of the back and the reverse of the right upper arm was the inscription: *Lamgi-Mari, King of Mari, the great Patesi of Enlil, has dedicated his statuette to Ishtar.*

From 1934 to 1937 a large section of the Temple of Ishtar was

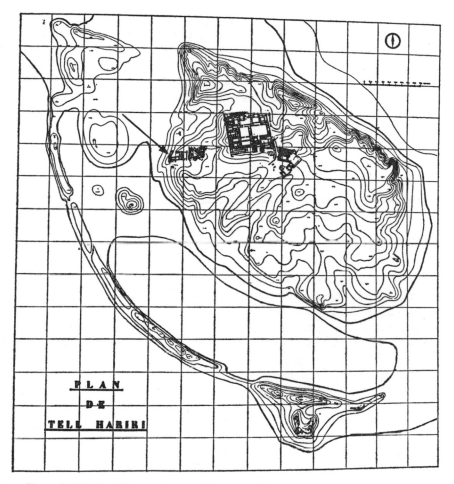

Plan of Tell Hariri. Beneath the hill on the left (*see arrow*) lay the Temple of Ishtar. Adjoining it can be seen residential quarters. The large rectangle represents the palace, and the building adjoining its lower right-hand corner was a temple for the god Dagan.

laid bare, an operation which entailed clearing an area of roughly 5,000 square yards to a depth of twenty feet. Excavation of ruins as ancient as these has to be carried out very carefully. The ground is painstakingly broken up, inch by inch, and much of the earth sieved and taken away in baskets. Considering how laborious this process of disinterment is, it seems amazing that within three years

more than 30,000 cubic yards of earth had been removed from
Tell Hariri. André Parrot, the brilliant French archaeologist, has
labeled the various layers of the miraculous city by different letters,
A, B, C, D and E, in descending order. It could be deduced from
layer E that the Temple of Ishtar had remained in existence for a
very long time. It was built of unbaked bricks and its floors were
laid with finely polished stucco. The temple's core consisted of a
"cella" in the form of a hearth house. On the short wall of the
chamber the altar was erected, while the exit was situated in one
of the long walls, as far as possible from the holy of holies. Adjoining
it were rooms for priests and temple administrators. The whole
sanctuary resembled the typical inward-facing Oriental house with
its central courtyard. In the temple courtyard itself Parrot found
a number of troughs, the so-called "longboats," two to the left of
the door and five to the right. These receptacles were used during
drink-offering rites.

The main chamber or cella must have occupied an exceedingly
important position in the temple and was obviously regarded with
great reverence. We know this to be so because Parrot found some
very peculiar objects there. Bronze wedges had been driven into
the ground, their apexes topped by handles set in bronze and
adorned with small rectangular plates of lapis lazuli, white stone or
silver. Just as we lay foundation stones today, so the architects of
Mari used to sink foundation wedges, anchoring them in the ground
for tutelary and religious reasons. Of the thirteen foundation wedges
found within the temple boundaries seven were in the cella, which
indicates the great sanctity of that room.

The citizens of Mari presented their deities with statuettes, small
figures of reddish stone, limestone or white alabaster which the
priests arranged on shelves. Most of them were only six or eight
inches high, but the largest measured about twenty inches.

Mari's inhabitants were evidently of a pious disposition, for they
commissioned these small statuettes as a means of worshiping their
particular god or goddess. The figurines stood in the sanctuary
where they would receive any blessings the deity might bestow,
their hands folded in prayer as befitted true believers.

Parrot has made some interesting observations on the nature of
these figures. The highborn and prosperous citizens of Mari were
not content to let themselves be personified by any old sculptures

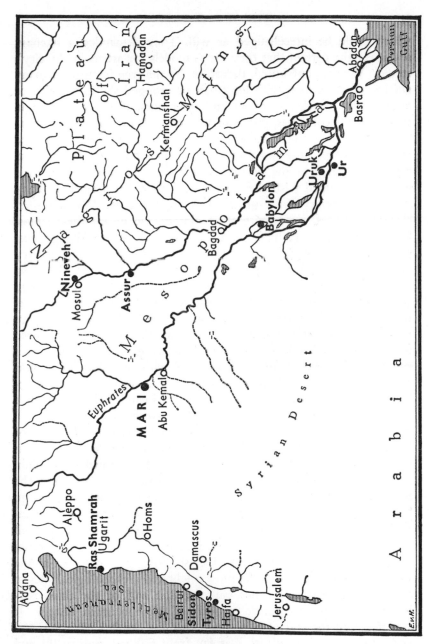

Mari

which could be interchanged at will. They demanded a likeness, and it is quite certain that they sat as models for artists in the city's studios. We are confronted, therefore, by the true features of many citizens of Mari, men with long hair or cropped skulls, bearded or clean-shaven cheeks, warriors and governors of the city-state in truly magnificent robes, girls and women with extraordinarily vivacious expressions—the standing or seated figures of people who lived at a time which now lies four or five thousand years in the past, captured forever in the posture which they assumed before their deity and stamped with the sincerity of their fervent belief. They stare into eternity with great, dark-pupiled eyes. We see their elegant coiffures, we admire their clothes, we notice their almost invariably confident smiles, and before us is one of the greatest treasures in the world: the crystallization of the life and artistry of a Semitic people who evolved an amazingly refined culture on the banks of the Euphrates in times beyond our ken. A man and a woman sit close together, his hand almost tenderly holding her forearm, just above the wrist. Although the heads are missing we can tell from the living quality of the stone that a great love united these two people—"lovers without face or name," André Parrot calls them. The people of Mari were not without a sense of humor, either. A clownlike pair of musicians laugh at us in the same timeless way in which the pious citizens of Mari carried their reverence and their faith in Astarte with them into eternity.

The fact that a Semitic people had so highly cultivated a way of life and such a highly developed religion as early as 3000 B.C. is remarkable in itself. During the first half of the third millennium B.C. the whole of Mesopotamia was Sumerian territory, and the Sumerians were not Semites. The beginnings of their culture go back to the fourth millennium B.C. and their sphere of cultural influence embraced the whole of southern Mesopotamia. It is well known what remarkable finds have been made in Sumerian cities such as Ur, Eridu, Larsa, Uruk, Lagash, Suruppak, Kish, Es-nunna and Upi—to name some of the most celebrated archaeological sites in the area. Modern authorities call the first half of the third millennium the "early dynastic period" of Mesopotamian history. It was not until the end of this epoch that the Semites emerged, and even then Sumerian culture was far from finished. Spiritually and culturally the Sumerians retained their dominance, but the Semites possessed greater powers of resistance and a stronger temperament. About 2600 B.C. the Semites seized power under the Akkadian dynasty. The newly founded city became the center of the known world, the Semites learned how to use cuneiform writing from the Sumerians, and the two races became fused. The Semites contributed their greater vitality, the Sumerians their artistry, their brilliant craftsmanship and good taste. The whole of Babylonian-Assyrian culture and the Semitic way of life were permeated by old Sumerian elements. The Semitic city-kingdom of Mari had also inherited much from Sumer but it evolved its own individual style as well. Three thousand years before the birth of Christ, it was already far advanced in its art and architecture, in its religion and general way of life.

Mari's most remarkable feature was its palace, which is the grandest example of Near Eastern architecture of its period, the beginning of the second millennium B.C. André Parrot, who excavated this amazing building, unearthed a vast complex covering two and a half acres and containing corridors, courtyards and three hundred rooms.

The palace, which probably took many years to build, grew out of various courtyard systems, for it seems obvious that the architects of Mari had no fixed plan in mind when they began their huge undertaking. The palace was at once a royal residence, a fortress, a granary, a seat of government, an administrative center and, above all, a symbol of regal authority. We even know that it was King Zimrilim who adorned the palace with its splendid murals. The excavations of the past forty years have shown that mural painting was a very ancient art in Mesopotamia, and that even in early times artists had acquired a high degree of technical proficiency in this field. Zimrilim's frescoes were based on this ancient Mesopotamian tradition. Parrot emphasizes that beneath the relics of the mural pictures in Zimrilim's palace there have survived fragments of another mural depicting a religious procession composed of people whose physiognomy and dress reveal alien, West Semitic characteristics.

Five temples have so far been excavated beneath Tell Hariri, together with a ziggurat or terraced tower of the Babylonian type. Also found were vases and ritual jugs ornamented with lions, massive earthenware vessels, a schoolroom with twenty-eight stone benches and the little plates of shell which served the pupils as slates. Small stone cylinders depict ships, a banquet, and scenes in which men fight with animals and King Gilgamesh subdues some rampant monsters. The courtyard of the palace yielded the figure of a goddess inhaling the scent of a flower with evident delight. One of the most beautiful statuettes is the water-pouring goddess of fertility dating from 1800 B.C. Almost five feet high and sculpted in white stone, this figure has eyes inlaid with precious stones, plaited reddish hair, and six rows of necklaces.

Even if what was discovered beneath Tell Hariri had been confined merely to the temple, the palace, the statuettes, the houses and the city walls, our knowledge of the ancient East would still have been immeasurably enriched. But Mari yielded up yet another huge treasure which affords us a profusion of information about the culture, daily life and history of these unique people and their relations with other city-kingdoms in the contemporary world. This hoard consists of the twenty thousand inscribed clay tablets which were found in King Zimrilim's palace. They represent the state archives of Mari and include the political and private correspondence of the city's last king. Many of the letters come from Shamsi-Adad of Assyria and contain instructions to his son Yasmah-Adad, who ruled Mari for some time on Assyria's behalf and was eventually succeeded by Zimrilim, the legal heir to the throne.

The tablets make it clear that rulers of the time were always worried about war, that they besieged fortified towns, forged defensive alliances and carried off people into slavery. If a city resisted too stubbornly, the conqueror would sometimes enslave the whole population. When the fortress of Sibat was taken the victors acquired so many prisoners that even private soldiers received an allotment of slaves to serve their personal requirements. On capturing Mari, King Shamsi-Adad decreed that the young daughters of Yahdunlim should be brought into his son's house. There he had them trained as musicians, advising his son to make them play wherever and whenever he had a mind to.

In another tablet Shamsi-Adad writes to his son Yasmah-Adad as follows: "I had resolved that you should keep the sons of Vilanum with you against the possibility of making a treaty with them later on. Now that I know it will never come to a treaty with Vilanum, have his sons arrested and execute them the same night. Let there be no ceremony and no mourning. Prepare their graves, kill them and bury them. Take away their head ornaments and their clothes, their money and their gold, and send me their wives. Keep the two musicians yourself, but have Sammetar's serving-women brought to me. This tablet I send you in the month of Tirum, on the evening of the fifteenth day."

God is often mentioned in the tablets. He was a single god, perhaps Mari's senior deity, and was called Dagan. Also referred to is a god called Itur-Mer and, in the neighboring city of Terqa, another called Ikrub-Il. So Mari, too, was familiar with the Semitic god Il or El who later dominated the Old Testament. It was, however, the goddess Ishtar who bestowed war and peace and governed the daily life of Mari's citizens. Since nothing could ever happen without divine sanction, attempts were made to discover the will of the gods by reading auguries in the entrails of sacrificial beasts. The augurs were consulted on private matters and important government decisions, and were also taken to war. As in all the world's most ancient civilizations, the snake played a role here. On one occasion the future could not be foretold until a particular species of snake known as the zarzar had been obtained. King Shamsi-Adad postponed a campaign because he wanted to sacrifice first and because the "bath ritual" had to be performed before war could begin. He also traveled to his home city of Terqa for the sake of a funerary sacrifice.

All this we learn from the twenty thousand cuneiform documents which have been found in the palace at Mari. We know that building operations were not confined to houses, temples and palaces but also embraced canals and river embankments. We read of sheep and cattle breeding and the danger of predatory animals. Lions were not to be killed because King Zimrilim had a special predilection for them. Once, when a lion got into a neighboring town and took up its abode on the roof of a house, the townsfolk had to feed the beast until the king decided what was to be done. Even when it had reduced the whole town to panic it was still not killed. Eventually the garrison commander caught it in a cage and shipped it off to Mari.

Zimrilim's game with the lions one day came to an abrupt end. Hammurabi, the great king and lawgiver from Babylon who ruled from 1728 to 1686 B.C. and whose empire ultimately included the whole of Babylonia, Assyria and Mesopotamia, launched a fearful assault by night. He defeated King Zimrilim and in the year 1695 B.C. devastated the city of Mari so completely that it never recovered from the blow. The great artists of Mari ceased to sculpt, paint and build. The Paris of the Euphrates forgot how to tailor elegant clothes, and life, which had once held such infinite charm, was finally extinguished, not to reappear until our own century. Mari is such an inexhaustible site of civilization that its remains are still being explored to this day.

ISLAND OF 8,000 TOWERS

Numerous similarities between the Sardinian and Aegean cultures indicate that the Aegean world left distinct traces on the island many centuries before the Phoenicians' arrival there.

—CHRISTIAN ZERVOS, La Civilisation de la Sardaigne,
Paris, 1954

SARDINIA is a hot and barren island whose hills, mountains and valleys are steeped in solitude. Parched aridity and silent grandeur are the main features of this austere countryside, where one can walk for miles without encountering a living soul.

At one time merged with Corsica in a single land mass, Sardinia is geologically very ancient. Older than the Alps and the whole of Italy, it protrudes from the sea as a reminder of a continent which has largely sunk from view. This took place several hundred million years ago, long before the Italian peninsula emerged. Indeed, geographers assume the existence of a land called Tyrrhenis which lay where the Tyrrhenian Sea is now but was eventually engulfed by water.

Sardinia, however, remained to form a fragment of land which has survived from times immemorial. It is by no means a sunny southern land, but a land pitilessly scorched in summer by the southern sun, which beats down as though with malevolent intent. The granite cliffs and basalt crags, the lonely magnificence of the mountains and the all-pervasive melancholy which seems to clothe the whole island grip the beholder and leave him with a sense of being far from Europe.

The winds of Africa prevail there, for no protective belt of land shields the island from the Sahara. The granite and gneiss cliffs in the east of the island tower steeply into the sky, often with vertiginous overhangs. Deep blue water pounds thunderously away at gigantic natural walls so inhospitable to man that they often stretch for miles without offering a foothold to the potential castaway. The sea has eroded them at the base, leaving deep caves in which the water booms and roars. Then, again, there are deserted beaches of snow-white sand, squat watchtowers dating from the time of the Arab occupation, cork woods, unfamiliar flowers, taciturn men with

89

smoldering tempers and an almost medieval code of chivalry, women
who combine a regal bearing with madonnalike humility, beautiful
pitchers apparently floating through the countryside on the queenly
heads of girls who still wear long skirts and white blouses and, on
Sundays, bright peasant costumes.

Many races have ruled here, but the only permanent feature of
the place is its prehistory, its stones and its age-old towers, the
nuraghi which are the island's greatest mystery.

Sardinia is shaped like a foot or a sandal, which is why the
Greeks called it Ichnousa ("footprint") or Sandaliotis ("sandal").
The island was certainly uninhabited during the last Ice Age, which
lasted until about 8000 B.C., and no paleolithic sites yielding human
relics have ever been found there. Man did not arrive until the
neolithic period, which lasted here from 4000 until 2000 B.C. We
do not know where these early immigrants came from or what they
looked like, but we must assume that they were not Indo-Europeans.
The islands of the Mediterranean had been gradually populated
from the fifth millennium B.C. onward by seafarers from the East
who had rowed or paddled their way westward. On Sardinia they
lived in caves, cavities in the rock or straw huts, mainly on level
ground and at first always in the vicinity of the sea or by lakes
and rivers. The island's many imposing caves have yielded relics
of these bold mariners and their tools.

A second influx, probably from Asia, peopled the island with
one of the most interesting races in the world and one which, after
their strange towers, we shall call Nuraghians. In complete contrast
to the neolithic inhabitants, these people possessed a considerable
knowledge of architecture and an advanced culture from the very
start. The Nuraghians landed on the east coast during the third
millennium B.C. and began to build the circular towers with sloping
walls of natural stone which are their principal legacy to us.

Finally, about 1400 B.C., a third race arrived, bringing an urban
culture with them. These Sardi or Shardena probably hailed from
Asia also and intermarried with the earlier arrivals.

Of the 8,000 nuraghi which once stood on the island about 6,500
still exist in a ruined and dilapidated state. Only a very small
proportion of these strange towers has survived in good condition.

We do not know what language the Nuraghians spoke. They
left behind no recorded history because they unfortunately had

no form of writing. But megalithic towers of this design and in this quantity are to be found only on Sardinia. The Sardinians themselves call them *nurakes, nuraxis, nuragies* and other variants of the same name, according to the dialect spoken in the particular part of the island. Professor Giovanni Lilliu, the leading authority on ancient Sardinian architecture, thinks that the term derives from a pre-Indo-European tongue. In the interior of the island *nura* or *nurra* means "mound" or "hollow," and *nur-aghe* means roughly "high pillar" or "hollow tower."

The nuraghe consists of rough unhewn stones piled layer on layer to form a tower with inward-sloping walls. Many of the nuraghi are only a few feet high, but some soar more than sixty feet into the blue Mediterranean sky. Their walls are between six and sixteen feet thick. The low towers contain only one chamber, but the tallest are divided into three stories.

What was the purpose of these towers, and from what part of the world was their prototype imported? Did the idea for them come from Spain, Africa or the East? We do not know.

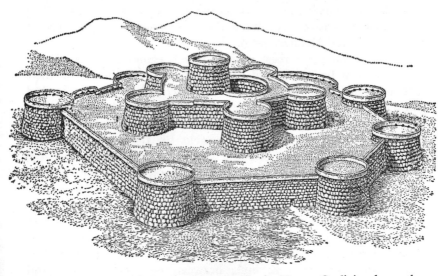

This reconstruction of the Orrubiu nuraghe in Nuoro, Sardinia, shows the ultimate development of this type of defensive tower. It is the fruit of research carried out by Professor Lilliu into this remarkable building, which is more than 2,000 years old.

They were neither sanctuaries nor burial places, but seem rather to have been defensive positions used by people who were exposed to continual attack. Sardinia was never politically united in its entirety, and its regional groups or tribes were ruled by chieftains who used these towers as houses and strongholds. In the course of time, the towers were extended to form larger fortified systems where several hundred people could take refuge in an emergency. The island was repeatedly attacked by Ligurians, Phoenicians, Carthaginians and, eventually, Romans, so the Sardinians were obliged to fight and fight again, even though it was always a losing battle.

Even if an enemy succeeded in penetrating a tower, he was still in mortal danger. The buildings were provided with doors opening on pitch-black cul-de-sacs and all manner of pitfalls and blind alleys from which the lurking Nuraghians could pounce with spear and sword to cut down the unwary intruder.

A flat roof installed at the summit of the tower for purposes of observation and defense and surrounded by a parapet, probably of wood, together with projecting attachments for the launching of stones and missiles, made any assault a perilous undertaking. The Sardinians' defensive bays were the first military installations of their type in the Mediterranean.

Towers from the earliest period, which came into being about 1500 B.C., can be recognized by the pronounced incline of their exterior walls. Later nuraghi were steeper, and between 1000 and 500 B.C., in the early Iron Age, nuraghe construction reached its prime. In the end the Sardinians erected fortified citadels of massive proportions to ward off coastal attacks by the Semitic Punians. Professor Lilliu remarks that the shepherds and warriors of the island must have shed a great deal of blood in defense of their political autonomy. A race of simple, hardy people, like their modern counterparts, they were in daily peril of losing their freedom, and defensive war must have become a sort of religion to them. Being accustomed to an austere life, they learned to be tough, unpretentious and mutually helpful in time of need. The last of the nuraghi were built between 600 and 250 B.C. and eventually served as hiding places, for by 231 the Romans had succeeded in conquering the island. The Sardinian guerrillas crept into the most remote towers in their wild countryside, but the

Romans ruthlessly hunted them down with trained bloodhounds. In the province of Cagliari, so named after the island's capital, a hill has stood for more than 2,000 years which is known to the Sardinians as Su Nuraxi. In 1940 a few test diggings were made there, and in 1951 Professor Lilliu started on the planned excavation of one of the most interesting prehistoric sites in Europe.

I have stood in the plain of Barumini and seen this lonely, deserted place for myself. All is silent, all lies open to the sky, a powerful system of fortifications with an original central tower, four corner towers built subsequently, massive external walls and, in front of them, a whole village with ruined stone roundhouses.

I have also visited Professor Lilliu, who occupies the chair of archaeology at the small but active university which stands on a hill overlooking the rest of the capital. Lilliu told me that he had spent five years, from 1951 to 1956, excavating the place. He had sent a fragment of wood from one of the supporting beams in the lower chamber of the central tower to the laboratory of the National Museum at Copenhagen. Using the radiocarbon method, Danish scientists established the age of the wood at about 1270 B.C. (A margin of error of two hundred years either way should always be allowed in such cases.) During the second phase of construction the four outer towers were built, and during the third all the towers and the walls were reinforced. This was probably done in order to withstand the battering rams used by the Carthaginians. Lilliu and his associates have also found defensive bays, fireplaces, sacrificial pits, large stone receptacles for kneading dough, stone balls which could be launched at besiegers, millstones, troughlike receptacles for ground corn, stone seats, bakery equipment and traces of various handicrafts from the later stages in the stronghold's history.

When I suggested that the excavation of the citadel and settlement, which were covered by stones, debris and thousands of cubic yards of earth, must have made enormous physical demands on men working in such high temperatures, Lilliu merely looked down modestly at the papers in front of him and did not reply. However, anyone who has seen Barumini lying there in the plain, ringed by the desolate hills which are the sole surviving witnesses of the life that once flourished there, and anyone who knows the iron-hard ground, the parching sirocco, the arid, stubborn and unyielding nature of this melancholy land will not underestimate the archaeologist's achievement.

In the sixth century B.C., after a long siege by the armies of Carthage, Barumini was overwhelmed, the nuraghe fortifications dismantled and the population driven from the burning village. However, the tough and resilient Sardinians returned in later centuries to settle once more amid the ruins and live on in the same way and with the same customs as in the golden age of their culture and renown.

Because the Nuraghians had no script, scholars have attempted to deduce the nature of their earliest language from such expressions as have remained unaltered for hundreds if not thousands of years. These are largely place names and names of animals, plants, mountains and rivers. It has been suggested that the Nuraghians came from Asia, since the island has certain expressions which could have originated in the Altai Range, Mesopotamia, Azerbaidzhan, the Caucasus, Nuristan (Kafiristan), Kazakhstan or even in Tibet and Sinkiang.

Nevertheless, the towers' interiors bear a certain resemblance to Aegean buildings and, more particularly, to those of Tiryns, Mycenae and the Creto-Mycenaean civilization. And the spiritual life and many aspects of the Sardinians' material culture also correspond to the Aegean culture as exemplified in Crete, Cyprus and Greece.

In addition to their towers, the Sardinians bequeathed us yet another legacy. This unique and unrivaled cultural heritage is the magnificent bronze art of gifted people who were not only warriors but outstanding exponents of the sculptor's art.

The bronze statuettes of Sardinia still have the power to grip and enthrall us today. They regard us with expressions of vitality and taut attention, unique and incomparable figurines whose lonely beauty is 2,800 years old, yet immediate in its appeal and, in a mysterious and inexplicable way, almost uncannily modern.

A PRE-CHRISTIAN MADONNA

*At the head of the nuraghi pantheon stood the Great Goddess.
All figurative representations of her hark back to fertility and to
water. She is portrayed sometimes with a basket of fruit on her
head, sometimes embracing a child; sometimes, again, holding a
jug on her head, and sometimes nursing the lifeless figure of a
young god, slain by some hostile power, on her lap. The goddess
reigns eternally over the birth and growth of all creatures, over
the fertility of the soil, the sanctity of water and the eternal
renewal of a lavish but inexhaustible Nature.*

—CHRISTIAN ZERVOS, *La Civilisation de la Sardaigne,*
Paris, 1954

THE mountain, the spring and the tree were the first natural features
to be associated with the holy places of the earth. Religion must
have played a very large part in the lives of the Sardinians as early
as 2000 B.C. or even earlier, for archaeologists have found the remains of cult sites all over the island. These holy places, the great
majority of which were probably open to the sky, were situated
on cliffs or high ground, beside springs and in woods. The altars
stood on mountaintops, on hills or in caves, always close to a source
of running water, the symbol of fertility. The holy mountain, the
nearness to God, the "high places"—these are ideas which human
beings have brought with them from the earliest paleolithic times,
via hundreds of thousands of years of prehistory, into our own
historical epoch.

The "cosmic mountain" is an age-old Mesopotamian idea. The
Altaic peoples believed for many thousands of years that certain
trees and poles led upward to the supreme being, that they represented the center of the earth and that the Pole Star stood above
them. The Greeks rediscovered the cosmic mountain in Olympus,
the men of the Old Testament in their Mount Sinai. Tall mountains
whose summits pierced the clouds were held to be the abode of
the gods in ancient China, Japan, Finland, Crete, Phoenicia and the
entire Mediterranean area. The Tower of Babel and the ziggurats
of Mesopotamia were nothing other than symbols of the cosmic
mountain. The early inhabitants of Sardinia or paleo-Sardinians also
dwelled in a world of ideas which was dominated by the sanctity of

prominent natural features, and, believing in the religio-magical power which emanated from high places, they sited their sanctuaries on remote hills or mountains. The sanctuary of Mazzani stands nearly 2,300 feet up in the Villacidro mountains, Santa Vittoria de Serri at almost 2,000 feet, Santa Lulla d'Orune at 1,600. All these sites have a fountain or spring close at hand, just as did the Acropolis at Athens, whose spring has only recently been found. Christian Zervos, the distinguished French authority on Sardinian culture, does not think that the spring, fountain or pool played so important a role on the island merely because of the scarcity and consequent importance of fresh water. Resurrection via water, emergence from water and water as a fructifying force are all ideas in which humanity has believed from time immemorial, ideas which have found their culmination in the baptism of the Christian religion. Some springs on the island of Sardinia are said to cure eye diseases, and in the region of Mongolia known as Barga, far away in east Asia, I have personally visited a spring which, so the nomads believe, can give sight to the blind and make cripples walk. Thousands of pilgrims had stuck their crutches in the ground or hung their spectacles on branches in token of their recovery.

It is certainly apparent that there were open-air temples in Sardinia at a very early period. By the very beginning of the nuraghi era, in the eleventh and tenth centuries B.C., the Sardinians were already laying out sanctuaries whose central or focal point was a healing spring or source of water. Examples of such places are Sardara, Mazzani, Rebeccu, Lorana and Milis. The sacred water was enclosed by stone walls or rings, and paths paved with blocks of stone led to the inner sanctum. Standing on the heights of Santa Vittoria de Serri and looking down from that mountain fortress on the landscape beneath, one can sense the air of tranquillity and of sanctity that pervades the place. Serri, which was excavated by the archaeologist Taramelli between 1909 and 1929, gives us some idea of the exalted significance which must have invested such a spot in 600 B.C. At the center of the sanctuary one can see the circular spring shaft and descend the ancient stone steps into its cool depths. Above, one can still make out the stone blocks of the enclosing walls. Everything is in ruins, but it is suddenly borne in on one what great religious significance the water from such a spring must once have possessed.

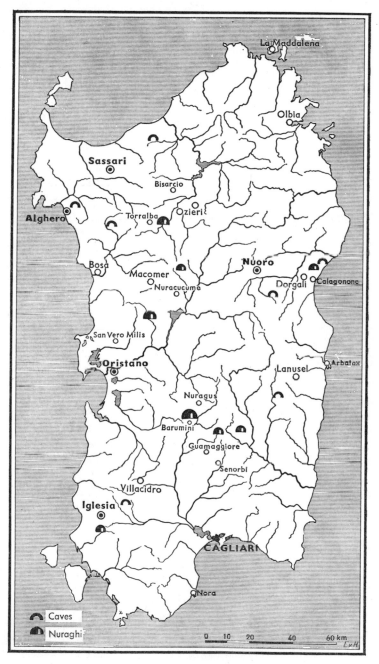

Caves

Nuraghi

Sardinia

Is there any chance of learning more about the religion of the Old Sardinians? Their mythology will always remain a closed book to us, but the nuraghe bronze statuettes, those enigmatic manifestations of an extinct way of life, may yet reveal something. They are, at all events, unusual testimony to a vanished religion. The large, heavy-lidded eyes and delicate construction of these little figures tell us of a people whose art is unique in the West. Sardinian art is an unwritten book which discloses to us the whole of the island's ancient religious hierarchy. This included senior priests, male acolytes of the cult and even musicians. Senior priests wore a close-fitting garment that fell to the thigh and a cloak thrown over one shoulder. They carried a staff or emblem of office in the left hand. Zervos conjectures that tribal chieftains of the nuraghe period also acted as the highest earthly representatives of the nuraghe religion.

Priestesses occupied a very important position. In this respect, the island of Sardinia appears to be one link in a chain that goes back thirty or forty thousand years. The earliest figurative portrayals in the world, the Venus statuettes of the paleolithic age which have been found throughout Europe, are presumed to be goddesses of fertility, and the portrayals of the goddesses and priestesses of ancient Sardinia are their latter-day descendants. In so far as we can understand the Nuraghians' religion and look back into the mists of prehistory, the first idea we meet is always that of the Magna Mater, or great mother, and her fertility cult. The tall basalt statuettes of Macomer are mother-goddesses of this nature. Marble idols which portray female symbols have been found at Porto Ferro and in the environs of Senorbi. Rarely has the religious conception of a female deity survived in a simpler, more consistent or magnificent form than it has here. From the first wave of Asiatic immigration to the centuries preceding the Christian era and the period of Roman domination, this Stone-Age "Madonna idea" retained its essential vitality. The Sardinians may have learned the Romans' language (the inhabitants of central Sardinia are, incidentally, the only people in the world to have preserved it to this day) but they rejected their religion and their gods.

The islanders began to portray their deities at a very early date, the earliest such portrayals being long stones three or four feet high and half buried in the ground. As time passed, these stones were given human form, and the ancient Sardinians were already portraying divine figures before the introduction of bronze casting. Three of the Perdas Marmuradas of Tamuli, some vertical stones standing near Macomer, betray female characteristics, but the remainder do not. From this it can be deduced that the stones represent male and female deities. That the Bronze-Age art which later drew on these early religious ideas reached the remarkable heights it did, is attributable to the fact that its exponents were constantly searching for the mainsprings of life and faith. Unique examples of creative artistry, Sardinia's bronze statuettes first appeared about 1000 B.C. and reached a peak of perfection in the eighth century B.C., which means that the men who made them were contemporaries of Homer, the world's greatest epic poet. Bronzes are still found from the fifth and fourth centuries B.C., but Phoenician conquest and Punic colonization ultimately brought their manufacture to an end.

The statuettes portraying priestesses clearly show what their role must have been. Shrouded in cloaks, they hold a bowl—probably containing drink offerings or consecrated water—in their left hand. The great significance of springwater in the Sardinians' religious cult is reflected in the senior status of these priestesses. Solemn, serious, distant and contemplative, the little figures stand in their showcases in Cagliari Museum and gaze into eternity.

The bronze statuettes also tell us that sacrifice was performed by male priests. One figure, now in the Bibliothèque Nationale at Paris, represents a man carrying sacrificial animals in a satchel. Cagliari Museum displays figures of other sacrificial priests, some carrying goats or jugs on their backs or holding consecrated rope in their hands. One priestly figure, only just over five inches high, has its right hand raised to shoulder height in supplication. Indeed, it seems to have been a general practice among the Nuraghians to pray with the right hand raised and palm facing forward.

As in the Minoan culture of Crete and in other parts of the eastern Mediterranean, religious festivals were accompanied by games and dances performed to music. The musicians of ancient Sardinia are portrayed with haunting realism, beating tambourines and blowing horns in a state of orgiastic ecstasy. Religious festivals, it should be remembered, were also fertility rites.

Like the inhabitants of Mari on the central Euphrates, the believers of 2,500 or 3,000 years ago used to set up statuettes of their deities in the temples and pray to them, believing that these tangible embodiments of the divine would receive their prayers with benevolence. Had the incomparable Bronze-Age culture of the Nuraghians not been sustained by these religious ideas it would never have attained such an artistic zenith. The fruit of this translation of faith into bronze represents an expenditure of spiritual and creative energy which would not otherwise have been possible.

Some statuettes were mounted on blocks of stone and others on bronze spits or pins, the lower ends of which were stuck into metal blocks or pierced stones. The supposition that these strange attachments had a religious purpose is reinforced by their length, their remarkable thinness and their fragility. Apart from that, many pins were found on stone benches in the vicinity of altars, sometimes mounted in groups of three and possibly symbolizing a trinity composed of the earth-mother and two male beings associated with her.

The Nuraghians' bronzes attained a peak of perfection in their portrayals of the goddess and her son. One such statuette reposes in the National Archaeological Museum at Cagliari. The divine mother's features express deep sorrow, and her son, whom she is cradling in her left arm, is unmistakably dead. This bronze, which was dug up in the neighborhood of Urzulei, is only four inches tall. Another statuette of the mother-goddess and the young god was found at Santa Vittoria de Serri and also stands four inches high. The woman has her right hand raised as though in blessing. Her lips are twisted with grief and her eyes swollen from weeping. A third bronze, this time four and a half inches high, gives the mother an expression of such sympathy and the son a face so deathly calm that no one who sees the piece can escape its dramatic impact. The same museum possesses a highly stylized mother-goddess in marble dating from long before the Bronze Age. Over sixteen inches tall, this figurine was dug up at Senorbi and takes the shape of a simple cross, the cross of an age which lies well over three thousand years in the past. It could well serve as an example to many of our modern sculptors.

Evidence of many centuries of faith and suffering, conflict and daily toil has been found on the island, captured forever in bronze. Archaeologists have unearthed casting molds and discovered complete treasuries. Some of these depots contained whole or fragmentary copper ingots, others double- or single-edged axes and still others blocks of metal and various objects in bronze. Seven hundred and fifty pieces were dug up at the Abini depot and no less than 1,976 pieces at that of Portotorres. Repositories of votive offerings and religious objects were normally found near springs and pools which were probably cult sites. Other smelters' and bronze workers' stores contained no jewelry or bronze figures; only tools, weapons, casting molds and fragments of objects which were obviously destined for recasting.

Of particular interest are the copper ingots which were used for bartering purposes. These copper plates were made in the shape of cowhides and stamped with ancient Cretan characters of the Linear B type. Since *pecus* means "cattle" in Latin, and *pecunia* was the Romans' word for "money," the Sardinians' hide-shaped copper plates are far closer to the Latin expression than is the thought that hide was once used as a medium of exchange in ancient Rome. The Sardinians were a peaceful, hard-working, domestic-minded people, as we can see from relics of their livestock, their agriculture and the countless appurtenances of their many-sided daily life.

A total of between four and five hundred bronze statuettes has been found so far, and fresh treasures are being brought to light every day. The value of a single nuraghe statuette is impossible to assess because its irreplaceability renders it literally priceless. Such pieces are the material expression of a race whose considerable pride, high morality and deep religious faith are still mirrored today in the faces of Sardinian women as they emerge from Sunday service in their superb peasant costumes.

LINEAR B

Among all the records known to us there is mention of only a single royal family strong and rich enough to play the role required to fit into the palace that frames the scene at Englianos. That is of course the family of the Neleids. Neleus, an invader from Thessaly, was the founder of the dynasty....Nestor, sole survivor of Neleus' twelve sons, inherited the throne and through "three generations of men" he ruled over a realm of nine cities. It is most likely that he, too, was a builder, adding perhaps the second of the large units of the palace, if not more. As the intimate associate, adviser and trusted friend of Agamemnon he won fame and universal respect in the expedition against Troy. Nestor returned from the war and continued to reign at Pylos where ten years later he received the visit of Telemachus.

—CARL W. BLEGEN, *"The Palace of Nestor,"*
American Journal of Archaeology,
April, 1960, p. 159

THE ruins of the most famous citadel in ancient Greece lie only 900 feet above sea level, but the history of the place has provided an inexhaustible source of material for the poets, dramatists and artists of Western civilization as a whole. No family ever afforded the tragedians and playwrights of Europe more themes than the lords of the citadel of Mycenae. It was Agamemnon, king of this city-state, who mustered the tribes of Greece and sailed against Paris, the Trojan prince who had abducted Helen, the wife of his brother Menelaus.

Mycenae stands on the Peloponnesian peninsula, which the earliest Greeks looked upon as an island. The place was named after one of Agamemnon's ancestors and means literally "Pelops-island." The *Iliad* paints Agamemnon as the principal antagonist of Achilles, whose fury forms the basic theme of the poem. Homer sang this epic in the eighth century B.C., but the golden age of Mycenae lasted from 1400 to 1150, and the battles that raged around Troy occurred in the ten years between 1194 and 1184. It was these centuries which saw the building of the great ramparts and Lion Gate of Mycenae, the palace, the huge tomb and the Treasury of Atreus, who was probably the king responsible for planning these architectural marvels.

As we all know, Heinrich Schliemann accepted the historical
authenticity of Homer's accounts and proceeded to find tangible
evidence of them by unearthing Troy not far from the entrance
to the Dardanelles in modern Turkey, as well as Tiryns and Mycenae
in the Peloponnesus. Beside the remains of seventeen bodies, Schliemann found a hoard of golden objects which weighed nearly thirty
pounds and are now displayed in the National Museum at Athens.
His discovery unleashed a spate of archaeological research into
periods of Greek history which antedated Homer by many centuries.

Agamemnon's citadel has given its name to the whole Greek way
of life in the second millennium B.C. The most important sites of
this pre-Homeric "Mycenaean" culture so far discovered are the
fortresses of Mycenae and Tiryns, the ruins of Pylos and the palaces
on the island of Crete.

Arthur John Evans, later Sir Arthur Evans, was born at Nash
Mills in England in the year 1851. He studied at Oxford and
Göttingen, traveled extensively in Finland, Lapland and the Balkans,
and was arrested by the Austrians in 1882 on suspicion of having
taken part in an uprising in Dalmatia. In 1893 Evans began to dig
on the island of Crete, and, by unearthing the palace of Knossos,
bequeathed us our knowledge of the splendid Minoan culture, which
represents the earliest advanced civilization on European soil. Evans
was knighted in 1911 and died, an internationally respected figure,
at the age of ninety, in 1941, just in time to miss the news that
the Germans had landed on his beloved island and that the German
General Staff had chosen to take up its quarters in, of all places,
his Villa Ariadne near Knossos.

The palaces of Crete were built at two separate periods, and
each period ended in their almost total destruction. The first or
"great" palaces came into being in Knossos, Phaistos and Malia
about 2000 B.C. These famous buildings were destroyed after several
centuries, and it seems likely that the first golden age of Cretan
architecture ended in 1700 B.C. In about 1600 B.C. new palaces began
to go up, though the period is principally famous for the "mansions"
or personal residences of senior officials who probably performed
governmental and religious duties. Then, between 1525 and 1520 B.C.,
a catastrophe occurred whose cause remains an enigma to this day.
The mansions and the newly built palaces were, to all appearances,
violently and suddenly destroyed. No one knows whether this

devastation was caused by foreign invaders or by some natural agency. Archaeologists, historians and scientists have put forward many theories to explain the mystery, but none of them has settled the question beyond dispute.

Just over sixty miles north of Crete lies a small horseshoe-shaped island known in the ancient world as Thera and in the Middle Ages as Santorin, after its patron saint Santa Irini. About the middle of the second millennium B.C. a major volcanic eruption destroyed all organic life there. Basing his conclusions on the ceramics of Knossos and the fresco styles and mirror imprints in the palace there, the Greek archaeologist Marinatos dates this upheaval at somewhere between 1550 and 1500 B.C. The eruption coated the slopes of the Elias Range on Thera with a layer of lava two hundred feet thick in places. Under a similar layer on the south coast of the small neighboring island of Therasia were found the remains of a Minoan settlement dating from between 1800 and 1500 B.C. The eruption was so immense that the whole of the volcanic cone caved in and seawater gushed into the crater.

Marinatos postulates that the eruption also produced enormous tidal waves which caused widespread devastation along the coasts of Crete. He believes that the outbreak on Thera was four times as great as the one which killed 36,000 people on Krakatoa in the Dutch East Indies in 1887, and calculates that there were "83 square kilometers of devastated and sunken land on Thera as opposed to 23 square kilometers on Krakatoa."

The same period also saw the destruction of palaces built in the Cretan interior during the second architectural phase. Marinatos admits that places like Knossos, Phaistos, Hagia Triada, Tylissos and Sklavocampos could not have been directly affected by the tidal wave, but suggests that major earthquakes may have followed the Thera eruption, causing fire and destruction among the buildings of Crete itself. Crete is, incidentally, severely shaken by three or four earthquakes each century.

The third possibility is that the fire and devastation were caused by some human agency, namely an invasion by mainland Greeks.

So much survived the holocaust that the island continued to throb with life for another hundred years, until, about 1400 B.C., the civilization began to wane and eventually all but disappeared.

The three types of writing that have been found in Crete include

a very ancient picture script as well as the two linear scripts which
Evans christened Linear A and Linear B. The earliest or hieroglyphic
script was used between 2000 and 1750 B.C. and consisted of picto-
grams such as heads, hands, stars and arrows. Between 1750 and
1450 these pictorial symbols were simplified into the linear script
which Evans called Linear A. This script has been found at many
places in the island of Crete, and one palace a few miles from
Phaistos yielded no less than 150 clay tablets inscribed with it. The
site, whose ancient name is unknown, is now called Hagia Triada
after a chapel in the vicinity. It was early recognized, long before
anyone had deciphered Linear A, that these clay tablets were inscribed with lists of agricultural products.

Outside Crete, Linear A has been found on the island of Melos
and, in fragmentary texts, in Mycenae and Cyprus.

At some point in time—probably about 1400 B.C.—Linear A was
superseded by a new form of writing which Evans designated as
Linear B. It is noteworthy that in Crete itself Linear B was found on

A clay tablet inscribed
with Linear A characters
from the palace of Pylos.
Original tablets have been
photographed and traced
so as to produce accurate
line drawings like this
one. The fragment illus-
trated here is only one-
third smaller than the
original. Most tablets
were only inscribed on
one side, and fine lines
were drawn between the
separate rows of char-
acters. The writing runs
from left to right.

only three or four thousand tablets in the palace at Knossos. The explanation may be that clay tablets survive for thousands of years only if they are baked hard. But the Minoans dried their tablets in the sun, and sun- or air-dried tablets are not hard enough to withstand the effects of the passage of three thousand years or more. Since the palace of Knossos suffered several great conflagrations the clay tablets there were baked to the consistency of stone. None of this, however, explains why Evans found such a quantity of Linear B tablets only at Knossos. Other palaces also went up in flames and any Linear B tablets which happened to be on the premises would likewise have been hardened and preserved, so the burning of Knossos does not alone account for the fact that the large majority of Linear B tablets were found at this one spot.

Perhaps we shall come nearer the truth if, like the men who eventually solved the problem, we ask ourselves whether there could have been a special reason why the strange script was used exclusively in the palace at Knossos. In order to answer that question, it is essential to know what language Linear B was devised to express. What was written on the clay tablets, and was there any means of deciphering them?

Many scholars strove to solve the enigma, putting forward the most audacious theories. Some attempted to find a solution in the ancient scripts of Egypt, the Hittites or the Indus Valley, while others compared the unintelligible symbols with Phoenician or Etruscan texts. But still the tablets refused to yield their secret.

Then Professor Carl Blegen of Cincinnati University set out to find and excavate the palace of Nestor, the ancient Greek warrior-king whose advice is repeatedly sought by his fellow countrymen in Homer's *Iliad*. Like Schliemann, Blegen proceeded on the assumption that the Homeric figures must have been historical. Homer tells us that Nestor lived in the citadel of Pylos, but no trace of the palace could be found on the site of the present port of that name. In 1939 Blegen began, in conjunction with the Greek archaeologist Kourouniotis, to dig at a place called Epano Englianos in Messenia on the southwest side of the Peloponnesus, nearly ten miles north of modern Pylos. During his first year's work there he discovered six hundred clay tablets bearing the same Linear B script which had been found far away in the palace of Knossos on Crete. The Pylos tablets date from a period later than 1300 B.C. Tablets with Linear B

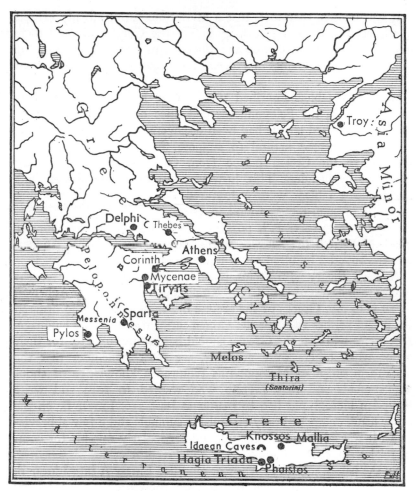

The Aegean area

inscriptions were also found in the citadels of Mycenae and Tiryns. Of these the so-called "spice tablets" found by Wace in 1954 in the House of the Wine Merchant at Mycenae are of especial interest. These listed varying quantities of spices such as might have been sold to individual customers, including red and white safflower, caraway, sesame, coriander, mint, fennel and a medicinal plant called polei.

It was known, therefore, that a mysterious script already existed in Greece about 1300 B.C., long before the Greeks adopted their more familiar alphabet from the Phoenicians at about the time of the first Olympic Games in 776 B.C. and began to record their own history.

Since clay tablets inscribed with Linear B had been found at three places in the Peloponnesus and since on Crete examples of similarly inscribed tablets had been discovered only in the palace at Knossos, it seemed natural to suppose that the script had been brought to the Cretan palace from Greece, either by visiting sailors or by invaders. This, however, was most improbable since the Knossos tablets were a hundred years older than the first examples of such tablets found in Greece.

Or are we so sure? Is it possible that Evans and his collaborator Mackenzie dated the Knossos strata inaccurately and that Knossos was destroyed a hundred years or more *after* 1400?

A third theory also seems possible. This holds that after the widespread devastation of Crete, Knossos was occupied by Achaeans —that is to say, Greeks of the second millennium B.C.—who ordered the palace scribes to adapt the Cretan script to the Greek language. If it seems odd that the Greeks should have gone to Crete for their script when others were available, we must remember that the cuneiform script of Mesopotamia required a knowledge of about 300 symbols and that anyone who wanted to read and write Egyptian hieroglyphs had to master at least 350. Linear B, on the other hand, comprised only 80 syllabic symbols and a few abbreviations. It was a kind of shorthand, and particularly suitable for commercial transactions, bookkeeping and inventories.

So the palace scribes of Knossos modified Linear A into Linear B, and it was then introduced into Greece, though only for the lords and masters of great palaces and fortresses such as those at Pylos, Mycenae, Tiryns and Thebes. Evans himself had noticed that several cups in the Palace of Cadmus at Thebes bore similar pre-Hellenic symbols and assumed that during the pre-Hellenic period the same language was spoken there as in Crete—though precisely what language no one yet knew.

Blegen's excavations at Pylos had yielded great scientific dividends. So many clay tablets in Linear B were now available that there were far more opportunities for comparative study than before.

However, the characters had been scratched on the clay by many different hands and exhibited countless slight variations. The deciphering of a modern secret code would have presented less difficulty because the expert at least knows what language it disguises, whereas with Linear B neither script nor language was known.

In 1952 Michael Ventris, an Englishman, succeeded in identifying a number of the mysterious symbols and realized that the language behind Linear B was Greek. Ventris was an architect, not a philologist, but he carefully established contact with all the scholars who had studied the problem hitherto. He was one of the first to gain access to the clay tablets of Pylos, he had complete command of the Greek language, and he possessed imagination and ingenuity. Above all, he found an experienced adviser in John Chadwick, the Cambridge philologist who collaborated so effectively in the young architect's publications and—a most important point—provided the requisite scientific pull.

For years beforehand, Ventris had mistakenly assumed that the language disguised by the mysterious symbols was that of the Etruscans, and this had put him off the track. It was now known, however, that what lay behind the clay tablets not only of Pylos, Tiryns and Mycenae but also of Knossos was an ancient form of Greek, and in the course of the intervening years all the characters have been identified. It is a truly remarkable scientific achievement and one, moreover, in which many scholars have collaborated, notably the Americans Alice Kober and Emmett L. Bennett (the leading authority on Linear B), A. Furumark of Sweden, Chantraine and Lejeune of France, Ernst Sittig and Hans Stoltenberg of Germany, Fritz Schachermeyr of Austria, B. R. Palmer, E. G. Turner and A. P. Treweek of Great Britain, P. Meriggi, V. Pisani and C. Cappovilla of Italy and K. Ktistopoulos of Greece.

Professor Fritz Schachermeyr, the Austrian authority on ancient history, has recently explained in an extremely interesting paper why Linear B texts are not easy to understand even now that the script in which they are written has been deciphered. The tablets of Knossos and Pylos contain virtually nothing but inventories and book entries designed to help administrators keep their accounts. Just as many a modern businessman's jottings can only be understood by people with specialized commercial training, so the meaning of the clay tablets must remain partially obscure because they were only an *aide-mémoire* containing commercial terms which would have seemed quite unexceptional to literate businessmen of the time. Schachermeyr describes the Greek language of the Linear B texts as a "language of bookkeepers and specialists." He assumes not that Linear B was commissioned by the Greeks but that, as a variant of Linear A, it was already used for an ancient Cretan language and was subsequently adapted for Greek. As we have already seen, the finds at Knossos do not permit us to date the origins of Linear B with any accuracy.

The tablets contain particulars of herds of rams and ewes, he-goats and she-goats, wild boar, bulls and cows. Bronzesmiths are mentioned by name, together with the weight of the metal they worked in. We find inventories of tableware, furniture, utensils of all kinds, wine and many types of foodstuffs, memoranda on war chariots, entries dealing with sales and purchases of male and female slaves. The Pylos tablets even record the quantities of oil and scent used by two groups of royal servingmen and serving-women.

History invariably begins with writing. The knowledge that the Greek language could be recorded in writing as early as 1400 B.C. has pushed back the frontiers of Greek history by six hundred years; from Homer, as it were, to Nestor and the men who constructed the fabulous fortresses and palaces at Mycenae, Tiryns and Pylos.

And so there unfolds before us a remarkably colorful and lively picture of people whose existence we could only guess at, until recently, from the mute ruins of their buildings and the relics of their art.

LIFE IN THE MYCENAEAN AGE

*I should like to say that I believe Agamemnon to have been a
historical character who flourished at Mycenae about 1200 B.C.*

—ALAN J. B. WACE, *Mycenae*,
p. 1, Princeton, N.J., 1949

IT IS always fascinating to explore a people's origins, even though
we can rarely see very far into the depths of prehistory.

The Greeks are an Indo-European race. Before their arrival,
Greece was inhabited by quite a different people, a pre-Indo-European population classified by ethnologists as Aegean. The Aegeans
were resident not only in Greece but in the islands of the eastern
Mediterranean, in Crete and southwest Asia Minor. The later Greeks
called the original population Leleges, Carians and Pelasgi.

We know that an Indo-European race migrated to the territories
and islands of the Aegean because there is evidence that the whole of
southern Europe was swept by an influx of Indo-Europeans. The
Greek language is the end product of a development in age-old
Indo-European tongues and originated in the great plains that
stretch between Poland and Turkestan. Greek also contains many
relics of *pre*-Greek language. For example, place names ending in
nthos and *ssos* are un-Indo-European and cannot be reconciled with
Greek linguistic conventions. Many names for plants, rivers, mountains and islands were obviously adopted by the Greeks from the
aboriginal population.

Crete was a repository of "Aegeandom." The Minoan language
hails from the Aegean world and the texts written in the ancient
Cretan script known as Linear A seem to have been composed in that
tongue, although it is also possible a Semitic language was employed.
We also know from Homer's *Odyssey* that Crete was inhabited by
"true Cretans, Sidonians, Dorians and Pelasgians." It is almost certain that the Pelasgians spoke a "barbaric" or non-Greek language,
as we are told by Herodotus.

Towns and the concept of urban life were introduced into Greece
between 3200 and 2500 B.C., imported from the East by the Aegean
pioneering spirit, and because the idea of the city took root in the
Aegean domain, Crete became the first advanced civilization in

Europe. Fritz Schachermeyr has demonstrated that the Hellenic *polis* or city-state, that foremost cultural and political achievement of the ancient world, was based on the early penetration of Greece by the Aegeans' city idea. The Greek talent for sculpture, the genre portrayal which reached perfection on Greek vases, and many other fundamental ideas—notably that of the heroine in Greek myth—all these things sprang from sources that originated in the dawn of the Aegean age.

Those who visit Greece should, therefore, remember that at the back of Greek culture and the Greek people stands the ancient spirit of Aegeandom.

The first Greek migration took place between 2000 and 1900 B.C. and came from the north. It is interesting to examine the surviving skulls of people who lived in the early dawn of Greek history. Twenty-seven skulls found at Asine and dating from between 1900 and 1580 B.C. prove that the population there was a mixture of Aegean and Indo-European. Twenty-one skulls were dug up at Kalkani in a burial place almost 4,000 years old. The men belonged to the Indo-European race, the women to the Aegean, so anthropology, too, confirms that a mingling of two racial groups was taking place. Presumably the Greek immigrants took native-born wives, a common practice in eras of conquest.

We do not know if Agamemnon, Odysseus, Telemachus or Nestor could read and write, but the clay tablets written in Linear B and dating from between 1300 and 1100 B.C. found by Professor Blegen at Pylos and Professor Wace at Mycenae make it probable that Nestor did, in fact, sit in his palace at Pylos and read his stewards' reports. The same may go for Agamemnon, king of Mycenae. At all events, the Homeric heroes were Greek in language, religion and way of life, and it is becoming ever clearer that they were historical figures who lived in a sort of Viking epoch distinguished for its long voyages and seaborne raids, its love of adventure and thirst for booty. By the time the great age of the Mycenaean heroes began and the massive domed grave—the Treasury of Atreus—and the Lion Gate were built at Mycenae, about 1350 B.C., the burgeoning strength of that seat of power had already made itself felt throughout the eastern Mediterranean.

Shortly before this, about 1400 B.C., the palaces of Knossos collapsed in ruins for the last time. This third and final destruction of

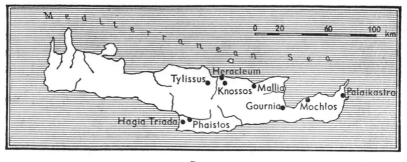

Crete

Minoan culture was, in the opinion of many scholars, the work of Greeks. No nation senses the waning of its strength, of its intellectual interests or of its art while it still survives, but in retrospect we know that about 1400 B.C. Crete began to lose its vitality and creative energy, whereas the Peloponnesus was witnessing the birth of magnificent and richly appointed palaces destined for the rulers of Pylos, Mycenae, Tiryns and Orchomenos. The relationship between the Greeks' Mycenaean culture and the Cretans' Minoan culture is by no means as obvious as is generally supposed. The whole of the pre-Homeric way of life has taken its name from the citadel of Mycenae because Schliemann discovered six shaft graves there in 1876, royal graves unopened since the sixteenth century B.C. and containing the now celebrated hoard of gold vessels and funerary gifts. It is assumed that the nine men, eight women and two children buried there were members of a great ruling dynasty, for five of the men wore golden masks. Wace, who followed Schliemann's example by unearthing large areas of Mycenae, inquires on page 114 of his book *Mycenae,* published in 1949, as to the real source of this fortified city's wealth. Why was it so powerful, large and prosperous that Homer himself extolled its wealth? The countryside around Mycenae is not overabundantly endowed with agricultural products. On the other hand, not far north of Mycenae, in the vicinity of Nemea, an old copper mine has been discovered. Wace thinks that the Argive Hills behind Mycenae have not yet been explored sufficiently and that it is possible that they conceal other ancient copper mines which were exploited by the lords of Mycenae. Copper, one need hardly add, was an excellent basis for power and wealth during the Bronze Age. The gold that was found at Mycenae undoubtedly came from far away, for Argolis itself possessed none.

Did the Greeks carry their Mycenaean culture to Crete or did they, as it were, import elements of culture from that island? There is even a vague possibility that the Cretans themselves brought their art and way of life to Greece.

Most authorities now assume that the Greeks adopted Minoan culture as a result of raids, wars and commercial dealings with the island. It is known that a refined way of life always held a considerable attraction for Indo-Europeans and that, in general, a high standard of living has always been the magic door at which races with harder beds and ruder customs one day come knocking.

In the opinion of the late Sir Arthur Evans, the distinguished British archaeologist who excavated Knossos, it was the Minoans themselves who carried their cultural assets northward to Greece. If, however, the Minoans had really crossed from Crete to the mainland, colonized the Peloponnesus and introduced Minoan culture into the peninsula, the palaces of the early Greeks would probably have been more labyrinthine in character, like that of Knossos, and would not have exhibited the clean-cut outlines of Pylos and Tiryns.

Many things are common to both the Minoan and Mycenaean cultures: brightly painted murals and vases, the secondary role of sculpture, ivory carvings, long sea voyages, and a pleasure-loving and wealthy aristocracy.

It is probably nearer the truth to assume that, while Greece was permeated by the culture of ancient Crete, the Greeks themselves brought a great many things with them when they migrated from the north. All these things differentiate their culture from that of Crete. For example, they brought their mode of dress with them. Warriors and hunters wore the short-sleeved chiton or brief shirt, and women depicted driving a wagon in a wall painting at Tiryns are similarly dressed. Cretan costumes, on the other hand, were much more elaborate and much more finely and artistically made. The fibula or safety pin did not exist in Crete, whereas the Greeks used it widely, as witness the fact that fourteen examples of this type of pin were found at Mycenae, four at Thebes, one at Tiryns and several at various other pre-Homeric sites. Amber, too, was very probably brought from the north by the Greeks: in Crete it was a rarity. The horse was known in Greece far earlier than in Crete.

Mycenaean graves yielded numerous female statuettes, Minoan graves very few. Wars were conducted on the mainland, hence the fortresses and citadels there, strongholds so stoutly built that only starvation could reduce them; life in Crete was far more peaceable. It was from the north that the Greeks brought the idea of the megaron, the main hall found in large houses of the second millennium B.C., a throne room heated by a fire burning in a central hearth. (The term *megaron* is derived from the Greek word *megas*, meaning "large.")

Almost all the early Indo-European religions have the same supreme deity, a being known to Indians, Greeks, Illyrians and Romans alike as Dyaus, Zeus, Jovis and similar variants. The Romans' Jupiter was derived from the additional title "father" which both the Indians and Greeks appended in very early times to the original name, making *Dyaus pitar*. This ancient tradition also gave rise to the idea of the tribal father or patriarch, a feature of the social order among all Indo-European peoples. Also associated with this was the cult of the hearth, the sanctity of which was a conception hailing from pre-Greek times. Anyone who inspects the fireplace in one of the Mycenaean palaces will grasp the profound relationship between paterfamilias, God and hearth, symbolized in these ruins by the proximity of the throne to the large circular fireplace.

During their golden age—between, say, the building of the old palaces about 2000 B.C. and the decline of their civilization about 1400 B.C.—the Cretans lived a life of almost unimaginable luxury. The palaces of Knossos, Phaistos, Hagia Triada and Mallia, the family seats and villas, the amazing frescoes, the cups, bowls, jugs and vessels with their splendid, inimitable colors, all bear witness to what were probably the most cultivated tastes of the age.

It is also worthy of note that in ancient Cretan society the woman's status equaled that of man and that her appearance was enhanced by clothing, jewelry and various beauty treatments to a degree unrivaled until the present day. It is no coincidence that a fragment from a circa 1500 B.C. fresco in the six-pillared chamber of state in the west wing of the palace at Knossos has been christened "the Parisienne." It depicts the head of a woman with large dark eyes, long braided hair falling to her shoulders, a red-tinted mouth and very elegant clothes. Cretan women's dresses create such a modern impression that they might well have originated in our own day.

Skirts varied according to the prevailing fashion. Sometimes bell-shaped skirts were in vogue, sometimes crinolines, sometimes the Cretan version of the "princess line." Waists were invariably slim and tightly laced. Clothes were always sewn, never pinned, draped or held by clasps as were those of Greek women. The Cretans of 3,500 years ago lived in an age of *haute couture* and must have kept a veritable army of professional dressmakers fully occupied. They also lived in an age which boasted fine cosmetics, perfumes and hair preparations. On Mochlos archaeologists even found tweezers for plucking out superfluous hair!

The subterranean treasure chambers in the central sanctum of the palace at Knossos have yielded a female statuette in faience. This small figure, which dates from between 1600 and 1580 B.C. and is only eleven and a half inches tall, portrays a girl holding a snake in either hand. A talented modern fashion designer might find it a rich source of inspiration. Minoan tiaras, earrings, necklaces, bracelets, pendants and rings all display the most intricate workmanship. One is continually struck by the white skin and lustrous dark eyes and hair of the Cretan women. It is noteworthy that they left their breasts uncovered, and that one of the frescoes at Tiryns also shows a lady-in-waiting with her breasts exposed by a short jacket.

We can tell from murals, statuettes and the famous Poros sarcophagus, which was found in a burial chamber near the palace at Hagia Triada, that Cretan women were extremely graceful in their movements. The same conclusion can be drawn from our knowledge of the acrobatic "bullfights"—probably a form of sacred cult—in which young girls were obliged to participate. In these, female acrobats used to seize a charging bull by the horns, vault onto its back and then leap off. Slave girls were probably schooled from a very early age in this technique, which presents so much danger and difficulty that it has not since been imitated in any other country or period.

Women set the tone in Minoan society. They attended religious festivals and games unescorted. They were dancers, priestesses and spectators. They played a predominant role at all religious functions, and it seems likely that the fervent, indeed passionate, character of Cretan religion stemmed from feminine influence.

We are ignorant of the true nature of the Cretan faith. We only know that there were no temples in Crete and that holy places consisted of caves, sacred groves and mountains. Important religious rites were conducted in the royal palace, as evidenced by the altars, sacrificial tables, shelves, rhytons and sacrificial jugs which have been found there. The king himself was also a priest. Sacred emblems included the tree, the pillar and the snake, but the symbol of the double-edged ax and the horns has never yet been explained satisfactorily. Crete also had a Mistress of Animals, a goddess whose origins lie deep in European prehistory.

Since the Linear B tablets of Knossos, Pylos, Mycenae and Tiryns were deciphered, we have been able to catch glimpses of everyday life in 1400 B.C. and after, reading between the lines of the Homeric epics and glimpsing something of the remarkable administrative organization of the time. The businesslike tone of the text of the clay tablets almost savors of the East.

With the scientific publication of about three hundred of these tablets, Dr. John Chadwick of Cambridge University and the late Michael Ventris, who lost his life in an untimely automobile accident, opened up an almost unknown world. We know that princes ruled at Knossos in Crete just as they did at Pylos in the southeastern Peloponnesus. A tablet from Pylos may even have supplied us with the name of one of these princes or kings: Ekhelawon. There were princes and retainers, feudal lords, mayors and slaves. There were also officials who governed towns on behalf of Pylos and Knossos, and were called *pa-si-re-u*, a title which we rediscover in the Homeric *basileus* and the Christian basilica.

Work was strictly apportioned among specialist craftsmen. Many types of craftsmen are mentioned in the tablets, including wood carvers, masons, carpenters, bronzesmiths, bowyers, cabinetmakers and potters. Shepherds, goatherds and hunters are also listed, and there seem to have been professional incense burners, too. Women ground corn, made cloth, did the spinning, weaving and wool carding, performed sundry duties in the palace and acted as bath attendants. Cloth fulling was a male occupation, and clothes were probably made by men as well as women. There is also an allusion to a doctor.

Slavery undoubtedly existed. The children of unemancipated parents became slaves by birth, a rule which applied even if only one parent was a slave. The huge labor force needed to build palaces was provided by prisoners taken in raids, and their womenfolk and children were taught a trade. The majority of the Pylos slaves were called slaves or slave women of the god or goddess, as the case might be, but it is not known what their precise duties were.

It is interesting to note that by Mycenaean times, or about 1300 B.C., almost all the Greek gods figure in the clay tablets: Zeus, Hera, Poseidon, Ares, Hermes, Athene, Artemis, Dionysus and Hephaestus. Ventris and Blegen meticulously give the scientific designation of each tablet in which the name of a particular deity appears. Sacrifices were probably confined to wheat, barley, flour, oil, wine, figs and honey, and did not include human beings or animals. Tablet G 866 indicates that even wool was presented to the gods. The priest-king was assisted by a large number of auxiliary priests.

The tablets have no direct historical or literary value and the texts are brief and meager, it is true, but a great deal of information can be derived from them if one is prepared to read between the lines. One tablet, for instance, bears the note: *38 girl-children, 33 girls, 16 boys.* Another remarks: *8 women, 2 girls, 3 boys,* and goes on to list the foodstuffs that were evidently allotted to them: *300 quarts of grain and 300 quarts of figs.* Yet another tablet runs: *In Pylos, 37 female bath attendants, 13 girls, 15 boys; 1,170 quarts of grain, 1,170 quarts of figs.* Tablet Ad 686 reports: *In Ke-re-za, Pylos, 15 prisoners' sons; Alkawon did not appear* or *did not report.* On tablet Eo 02 we find a woman called E-ra-ta-ra and the description *slave woman of the priestess.* Tablet Ae 04 tells us that *Ke-ro-wo, the herdsman in A-si-ja-ti-ja, tends the ox of Thalamatas.* Tablet An 18 mentions: *16 fire makers, 10 me-ri-du-ma-te* (?), *3 mi-ka-ta* (?), *4 tackle makers, 5 weaponsmiths, 3 bakers.* We do not know the meaning of me-ri-du-ma-te and mi-ka-ta, but they were obviously trades—perhaps of a kind which no longer exists today. Several tablets list coast-guard commanders and their subordinates by name. There are tablets containing notes on landed property and seed planting, tablets listing tributes and sacrifices, tablets referring to textiles, vessels and furniture. Tn 996 mentions: *3 tubs for bath water with outlet, 3 water containers, 3 cooking vessels, 2 amphorae, 1 hydria and 7 bronze jugs.* Tablet 713 refers to stone tables and ivory inlays, ivory tables with feather patterns and small ebony tables, likewise richly decorated.

The Dorian migration—or the return of Heracles' descendants to the land of Argolis—set the seal on the flourishing Mycenaean culture and destroyed the old citadels and palaces. What remained was the Cretans' great artistic contribution to Mycenaean culture and their lasting influence on every aspect of the plastic and graphic arts throughout the Greek world. What remained, too, was their almost unrivaled proficiency in handicrafts, the idea of the fortified city (a conception which survived until the Middle Ages), their sense of style, their creative impetus, the many facets of their mythology and religion, and their general quest for spirituality.

The effects of the Mycenaean way of life are still felt in our own age, for it was not only the first but one of the strongest cultural impulses that Europe ever received.

THE CULT OF APOLLO

From its earliest beginnings, Delphi was always the world's fore-
most seat of divination. The god and adviser of mankind who came
to Delphi had of necessity to bestow oracles there or have them
bestowed in his name. He came there less in order to demand
and receive worship than to keep a personal watch over the
oracle. His spirit pervaded the oracle far more than the sanctuary.
...As lord of the place, Apollo chose to reveal his thoughts
neither through the ambiguous rustling of leaves nor the hum of
swarming bees. He rejected the confused pictures which run
through dreams or mirror themselves in the surface of springs.
When speaking to mankind he used the speech of man.

—Pierre de La Coste-Messelière, *Delphes,*
pp. 17 and 20, Paris, 1957

Many different things are related of Delphi itself and of the
oracle of Apollo. In earliest times, for instance, the seat of divina-
tion is said to have belonged to Ge.

—Pausanias (circa A.D. 150)
Description of Greece, Book x

THE ultimate realization of the Hellenic world might be said to be
embodied in two words which express the summit of knowledge
attained by mankind in its struggle for wisdom. Preserved for us
in an inscription on the Temple of Apollo at Delphi, they read:
KNOW THYSELF.

There is an infinity of meaning in these two words. They mean
that God can be found only in the innermost recesses of the human
mind. They mean that man comes closest to the truth when he
harkens to his inner voice. They cry out for the thing most urgently
needed by a civilization sated with the marvels of science: modera-
tion. They warn man to know his limitations and acknowledge his
mortality, but they also demand that he give freely of what lies
within him and so fulfill his destiny.

"Know thyself" was one of the maxims attributed to the Seven
Sages, as the seven most prominent figures in the first half of the
sixth century B.C. were called. These were: the aristocrat Solon,
who gave his native city of Athens its first constitution; the tyrant

Periander of Corinth, who founded cities, sponsored Delphi and Olympia, ushered in a golden age in art, handicrafts and trade and prohibited idleness and luxury; Bias of Priene in Ionia, who, when forced to flee his native city empty-handed, remarked, "I am taking with me all that is mine"; the statesman Pittacus of Mytilene, who enacted a law by which any crime committed in a state of intoxication incurred a double penalty; Thales of Miletus, who accurately predicted the solar eclipse of May 28, 585 B.C.; Chilon, a Spartan hero; and the poet Cleobulus of Lindus, who also composed riddles. The distilled experience of these seven great minds was embodied in aphorisms engraved on the Temple of Delphi.

Before anyone was permitted to approach the Delphic god or question him, therefore, the god demanded the utmost that any human being can undertake: a completely frank examination of his own conscience. The admonition "Know thyself" serves to show what sort of spirit ruled the place and to convey the unfathomable wisdom, infinite truth and human understanding of the Greek god.

Delphi stands on the lower southern slopes of Parnassus, almost two thousand feet above the Gulf of Corinth. Here in the lonely splendor of the mountain scenery, the mind is impelled irresistibly toward God, eternity and the supernatural.

The site is one of the great enigmas in human history. It is as though the god who ruled there withdrew before the downfall of ancient Greece and the victory of alien religions were complete, to ensure that no one should degrade him, approach him or measure him by petty, human standards for all eternity to come. Poets and scholars, ancient historians, students of religion and archaeologists have tried for two thousand years to discover the secret of the Delphic god, but Delphi has never raised the veil of its exalted sanctity. Despite all human endeavor, it has remained sealed and silent in the face of research and excavation. It speaks no more, nor will it ever give voice again.

The name Delphi conjures up before our eyes a nebulous and impalpable vision of the Pythia. Actually Pythia was not a proper name but a title or designation signifying roughly "priestess of the Pythian cult." We tend to think of the oracle alone, but who was the *god* that dwelt and spoke there? Delphi was a holy place, not merely a source of opportune and practical advice. It was the largest and most important sanctuary in the Greek world, and the god who owned it was Apollo. Even though we are the spiritual descendants of the Hellenes and so of their god, even though we still are influenced by the culture of Greece in all we do and think, we know less about this god than about great religious figures of the East such as Buddha, Zarathustra and Mohammed. Of all the gods of mankind Apollo is the hardest to comprehend, yet from time immemorial his oracle provided an abundant source of religious energy.

Delphi was world-famous as early as 1600 B.C., although people of that time knew it not as Delphi but Pytho, a name probably derived from Python, a being that guarded the sacred place. Python was a large male snake and was the son of Gaea or Ge, a goddess who symbolized the earth, the abyss or subterranean realm. She and her kinswoman Themis were the first and earliest prophetesses to utter oracles on the slopes of Parnassus.

This is yet another version of the ancient myth of the snake that represents God's eternal adversary. The snake symbolizes not only the earth, demonic powers and dark forces but also healing, which is why it has become the emblem of medicine. It is the monster that, like the Midgard Serpent, embraces the earth and causes earthquakes. It is all-knowing as well, and thus responsible for introducing sin into the world. Many races have regarded it as an oracular creature. Just as the snake in Genesis:iii brought about the Fall, so Apollo became guilty of sin when he killed the Python. He then went to Crete, where he underwent a form of purification or atonement for the murder. Religious ceremonies of peculiar sanctity were performed in ancient Crete while the embers of the once-great Minoan religion still glowed.

Snakes were not only feared and respected for their omniscience: the people of the ancient world kept them as domestic animals and used them, like weasels, to keep down mice. Children played with them and women used them to cool their necks and bosoms when the weather was particularly hot.

At Delphi, however, Python the snake and Ge the earth formed the origin of the world's most famous oracular site. It was there that the spirit of the earth gave voice long ago, speaking to those in need of help and divine guidance.

The French archaeologist de La Coste found traces of pre-Greek sacrifices in Delphi. It is probable that the earliest form of divination involved casting lots, and that the future was interpreted from small stones lying in a basin supported on a tripod. Archaeologists found the spout of a Minoan fountain in the shape of a lioness's head among the ruins of the Temple of Apollo, a piece dating from a period fourteen, fifteen or sixteen hundred years before Christ's birth. At the spot where the altar once stood, the soil was found to contain traces of many organic substances and ash from burnt bones interspersed with fragments of Mycenaean pottery, ample proof that sacrifice was made there in Mycenaean times, or in approximately 1500 B.C. A still more important find was a small Minoan terracotta figure of a nude woman sitting in a three-legged chair. Since the Pythia does not go back as far as that, one is led to wonder if it portrays Themis or the earth-goddess Ge.

With the decipherment of Linear B, the relationship between ancient Greece and Crete has become much clearer. It is probable that the priesthood of the Delphic oracle was yet another importation from the world of Minoan culture—that is to say, from Crete. The Homeric *Hymn to Apollo* dating from the seventh century B.C. tells us that as the god was looking about him for priests he saw in the distance a shipload of Cretans outward bound from Knossos. Assuming the shape of a dolphin, Apollo lured the ship to Crissa, where the sailors built an altar to Apollo Delphinios. And this, so legend has it, was the origin of the name Delphi.

We cannot tell when Apollo became the god of Delphi, but the oracle was undoubtedly in existence long before Apollo took up his abode there. Apollo was the most "Greek" of all gods, worshiped at many places in Greece and Asia Minor, but particularly in Sparta and other Doric cities. He was the most radiant and splendid figure in the Greek heavens and in the dwelling place of the gods that lay above Olympus, at 9,570 feet the highest peak in the Greek peninsula and the massif whose isolated bulk separates Macedonia from Thessaly. Apollo was the supreme ideal of young masculine beauty.

We do not know what Apollo was originally, although most probably he was the sun-god. But we know what the Greeks made of him. He was the guardian of herds and god of herdsmen, reminding us that throughout Greece and the Near East and from Bethlehem to Persia, herdsmen have always been close to God. Apollo was the healer of the sick, the preserver of crops and the patron of music, spiritual life and philosophy. He was the coordinator of measurement and time, the friend of planned activity, the custodian of high morality and, above all, the god of the oracle.

Apollo possessed oracles at many places in Greece and Asia Minor, and the methods of obtaining an oracle were very varied. In Argos, the priestess sought inspiration by drinking the blood of slaughtered lambs. At Hysiae, Apollo's decision was ascertained by drinking from a sacred spring. At Thebes, soothsayers read the future by inspecting the entrails of sacrificial beasts. At Colophon, in the oracle of the Apollo of Claros, soothsaying was performed not by a woman, as in Delphi, but by a priest who was told only the name of the oracle seeker. He would then descend into a cave and, having drunk water from a sacred spring, give advice in verse form on the unspoken problems of the applicant. This we learn in Tacitus's *Annals*, II, liv.

At Patara in Lycia the priestess was locked up in the temple at night "whenever Apollo came," so Herodotus tells us in his *Histories*, II, clxxxii. Patara was, so to speak, Apollo's winter quarters. He visited Delphi only in summertime.

It is hard to say where the name Apollo came from. It could have come from the Doric word *apella*, meaning "herd," which would suggest that he was originally a herdsmen's god. Wilamowitz asserts that it came from the Lycian tongue, which would make him not Greek but foreign. On the other hand, Ernst Sittig, the leading authority on the Lycian language, has demonstrated that the god's Lycian name was borrowed from the Greeks, and that Apollo must therefore have been a Greek god in earlier times. But in Homer's *Iliad* Apollo is always on the Trojan side, never on the Greeks'. Since Troy stood not far from the Dardanelles in what is now Turkey, we can deduce that Apollo at one time belonged not to Greece but to Asia Minor.

There are two more very interesting indications that Apollo was Asiatic in origin. The Greeks got their lunisolar calendar from Delphi, that is to say, from the Delphic Temple of Apollo, in the second half of the seventh century B.C. The oldest and most renowned center of astronomical study was Babylon, where a lunisolar calendar had been astronomically determined long before that. The Swedish historian and authority on Greek religion Martin P. Nilsson points out that festivals of Apollo fell on the seventh day of the month. The especial significance attributed to the seventh day or *sibutu* is purely Babylonian. (Our own Sunday has a similar origin.) The

Greeks, however, divided their month into three spans of ten days, each decade corresponding to our week. Thus the seventh day is a totally alien element in such a decimal system, and the fact that seven was Apollo's sacred number is yet another indication that he originated in Asia Minor. His mother's name, too, is of similar origin, for Leto was worshiped as a goddess in her own right principally on the southwest coast of Asia Minor. Nilsson thinks that Apollo came from the interior of Asia Minor, from the Kingdom of the Hittites, which owed a great deal to Babylonian culture.

If this is so, we can only wonder at what the Greeks made of their once foreign god. They based a great process of spiritual evolution on him, developed his morality to encompass the limits of human understanding and forgiveness, and made of him a god who substituted purification by atonement for the traditional blood feud, a god who demanded repentance and granted divine forgiveness even to the tormented murderer—once he had submitted to purification and reconciliation. If Apollo came from the East, he must once have been a god of vengeance. The Greeks turned him into what Pindar described as "the most friendly of the gods," a European god and a true healer of the soul.

But, whatever his origins, Apollo was endowed from the very first with the power to interpret all manner of signs and occurrences. Homer himself calls him "the seer." He was a god who not only accepted prayer but answered it, although ecstatic prophecy became one of his attributes only at a later stage. We do not know when this form of soothsaying, which was performed in a state known as "mantic ecstasy," was first ascribed to him, but it, too, probably hailed from Asia Minor, an area famous for its oracles.

THE DELPHIC ORACLE

After Théophile Homolle and Émile Bourguet, neither of whom is with us any longer, it was Pierre de La Coste-Messelière, artist and scholar, who devoted the better part of a lifetime's research to the sanctuary. He was fortunate in his digging and lived for a long time on very close terms with the ancient stone ruins.

CHARLES PICARD, *Delphes*, Paris, 1957

DELPHI, sanctuary of the god Apollo, was the religious fulcrum and most important seat of divination in Greece. It was regarded as the center of the earth or "navel of the world." The Greek word for navel was *omphalos*, and in the holy of holies, the *adyton* or cella of the temple of Apollo, near the golden statue of the god, there was a stone which actually symbolized the navel of the world. Apollo was more closely associated with the cult of stones than any other god, and a kindly fate has preserved this particular stone for us. Shaped like a small mound, the ancient design of heroic graves, it is only 11 inches high and 15 inches in diameter. This ancient and sacred object was found against the southern wall of the cella by the French archaeologist F. Courby, who identified it as the famous Omphalos. The stone not only represented the center of the world but marked the grave of the murdered Python. Three letters from an archaic alphabet have been deciphered on the Omphalos: the letters GA, signifying the name of the earth-mother who gave birth to the Python, and the mystic E of Delphi, whose meaning not even Plutarch knew.

The Omphalos may once have stood over a crevice in the rock which emitted steam, fumes or sweet-smelling vapors. These vapors, which were assumed to emanate from the sacred snake or other subterranean gods, were said to send the Pythia into prophetic ecstasies. She used to wash herself at the Castalian Spring, burn a little laurel and barley meal, and then ascend into the main chamber or adyton of the temple. There, seating herself on a tripod in front of the Omphalos, she drank water from the spring of Massotis, and plunged into a divinely inspired state of "mantic ecstasy."

And here we come to Delphi's greatest enigma. The cleft in the rock and the steam that issued from it are mentioned in many ancient

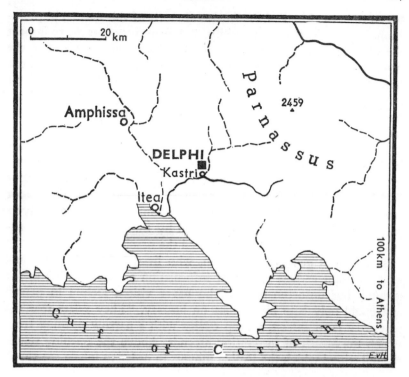

Delphi

texts, none of which, however, is really old. Do they prove that such
a thing existed—a subterraneous breath or *pneuma* which sent the
Pythia into ecstasies and rendered prophecy possible? It is extremely
interesting to study the tradition in the original texts rather than
hear them at second hand.

Writing between 60 and 30 B.C., Diodorus reported that the
Delphic oracle was discovered in ancient times by some goats. (The
herdsman who found Edessa, the ancient capital of Macedonia, was
likewise led to the spot by goats.) In the most sacred part of the
Delphic oracle, Diodorus continued, there once yawned a cleft in
the ground. Whenever one of the goats approached this cleft it
would leap miraculously and utter strange cries. Seeing this, the
goatherd went up to the cleft and, as he approached it, underwent
the same experience. He lost his senses, became "enraptured" and

began to have visions of the future. Reports of this natural phenomenon and its effects spread rapidly, and many people came to inspect
the place and experience the strange delirium. However, after the
ground had swallowed up a large number of those who ventured too
near the crevice, the inhabitants of the region decided to appoint a
virgin to be sole prophetess and distribute oracles on behalf of all,
building her a three-legged contrivance or tripod which she could
mount in order to prophesy in safety.

Justin tells us in Book xxiv of his *Philippic Histories* that roughly
in the middle of the heights of Parnassus there was a patch of level
ground with a deep hole running down into the earth. A cold vapor
rose from it as though borne upward by a strong wind. This vapor
from the interior of the earth roused the souls of female soothsayers
to frenzy and impelled them, inspired by the deity, to bestow answers upon people who had consulted the oracle.

The famous geographer Strabo, who lived between 63 B.C. and
A.D. 19, is our earliest source of information on the opening in the
ground, but unfortunately Strabo never visited Delphi in person
and could only base his reports on hearsay. "They relate that the
sanctuary is an *antron*, a deep cavity with a narrow opening from
which the breath of inspiration ascends. Above the opening stands
the tall tripod which the Pythia mounts in order to inhale the vapor
and give the oracle in verse or prose."

One of our best witnesses is Plutarch (A.D. 46–120), who knew
the oracle well because he was himself a priest at Delphi for some
time. He wrote: "The Oikos or room in which those who consult
the god are seated becomes filled with a sweet-smelling vapor. This
happens neither often nor regularly, but at varying intervals. The
adyton allows this vapor to stream forth like a spring, comparable
with the sweetest and most costly of perfumes." Plutarch speaks of
a vapor, therefore, but does not mention any opening in the ground.

Lucan, a Roman author who lived between A.D. 39 and 65 and
whose only surviving work is an epic poem about the civil war
between Pompey and Caesar, gives in it (v, 169–174) a dramatic
description of a Pythia who becomes crazed with excitement and
eventually falls prey to her divinely inspired frenzy.

Interesting though they are, all these accounts date from the post-
classical period. Justin's *Philippic Histories* did not appear until the
third century A.D., and even the earlier sources fall within a hundred

[29] A fertility goddess from the palace of Mari, found in several pieces and later reconstructed. In her hands she holds a vessel from which flowed the "water of life." The water was conveyed to the jug through a pipe ingeniously situated inside the statue itself. Height: 34".

[30] Statue with folded hands portraying the city administrator of Mari, Ebih-Il, and placed in the temple at his behest. On his back are engraved the words: *Ebih-Il, the administrator, dedicated to the goddess Ishtar.*

[31] Clay bathtubs still survive in the palace bathroom at Mari. On the left, the somewhat primitive W.C. Waste water drained off into a cesspool located over 50 feet below ground.

32] Looking up through the interior of a nuraghe. These austere buildings provided Sardinian chieftains with living quarters and their warriors with an almost impregnable stronghold.

[33] A typical nuraghe, a massive circular tower with inward-sloping walls, born of a people's love for liberty about 3,500 years ago.

[34] These ruins were once inhabited by simple but staunchly courageous people. Each ring of stones represents one of the numerous houses that were built close together by the shelter of the Barumini fortress about 1270 B.C.

→

[35] Weeping goddess with her right hand raised in prayer and her young son on her lap—a pre-Christian "Madonna" of 800–500 B.C.

[36] A bronze statuette of an archer, standing with hand upraised as though in prayer, dug up at Abini, Sardinia. He wears a coat of mail, greaves and a horned helmet and carries a quiver.

[37] The priestesses of the nuraghe culture, circa 800 B.C., played an important role in the religion of the ancient Sardinians. This priestess is holding a drink offering in her left hand. The bronze statuette, which is only 4 inches tall, was found at S. Vittoria de Serri and is now in Cagliari Museum.

[38] We shall never know what this strange bronze sculpture portrays, but it probably represents a symbolic religious struggle. Six inches long and 4 inches high, it is one of the showpieces of the Archaeological Museum at Cagliari.

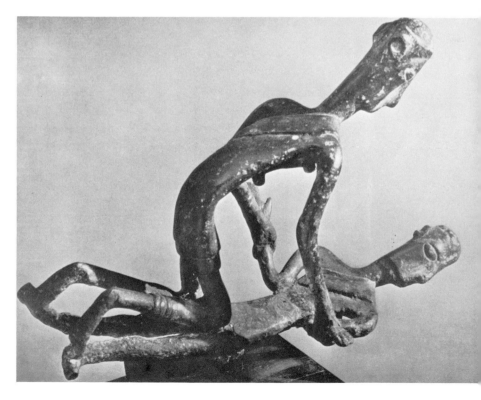

[39] Gold death mask of a Mycenaean prince, found by Schliemann in Grave V in the citadel of Mycenae and designated as "Agamemnon." The remains of the man whose face the mask had covered were also found.

years either side of the beginning of our era. The Pythia, on the other hand, had been soothsaying since about 700 B.C. and Delphi was radiating its greatest spiritual influence in the sixth century, a period when the treasuries of Corinth, Sicyon and Siphnos were built and the kings of Lydia sent costly votive offerings.

Classical authors such as Herodotus (c. 468 B.C.), Euripides (c. 450 B.C.), Plato (c. 400 B.C.) and others tell us much about the oracle, the Pythia, the priests and the questions and answers, it is true, but they never mention the cleft in the rock. Was there a crevice in the rock or the ground, and was there any prophetic vapor, any mysterious *pneuma*, air or breath from the earth's interior?

Let us hear what modern science has to say. The French archaeologist Émil Bourguet, who participated in the excavation of Delphi, tells us that he had expected the unearthed ruins to disclose the oracle's inner construction, i.e. its mode of operation, but adds resignedly that "what used to go on in the most important part of the prophetic sanctuary remains a mystery to us, too." The archaeologists were constantly pursued by one thought as they worked: "It seemed as though we were confronted by the products of systematic destruction." What was responsible for it—heathendom on the retreat, or a youthful Christianity anxious to wipe out the heathen god once and for all? The last Pythia took the secret to her grave.

If there ever were a fissure in the rock, signs of it should still be apparent today. Delphi was not built on the limestone of the mountain itself but stood on a sort of terrace composed of shale. This shale could not, in the opinion of A. P. Oppé, have been eroded by water, but he concedes that a cavity might have been formed at the place where the shale reposed on the limestone and that this could have been the source of rising vapors. Oppé himself believes that the fabled cleft in the rock was really the Castalian Spring, which can still be seen between two walls of rock quite close to the sacred precincts of Delphi, and dismisses the vapor and the hole in the ground beneath the Temple of Apollo as fabrications by the priests and historians of antiquity.

In 1913 another French archaeologist, F. Courby, conducted a careful examination of the floor of the cella, where the *stomion* or cleft was assumed to have been. He reached the conclusion that the ground beneath was undisturbed and declared that there had never been a fissure, natural or artificial, in the stone. He found no trace of an opening and could not see signs of any former geological subsidences.

Robert Flacelière, on the other hand, thinks that the tradition is so unambiguous that there are no grounds for doubting the existence of the vapors and the cleft, and holds that landslides or earthquakes could have effectively changed everything. It may be added that Delphi is no stranger to earth tremors.

Massive fragments fell from the Phaidriades or Shining Rocks and badly damaged the northern part of the temple terrace as long ago as the sixth century. Flacelière suggests that the opening in the ground may already have ceased to play its role in the oracle by Plutarch's time, or about A.D. 100, and that this would account for his silence on the subject. I would certainly agree that a biographer's or historian's silence is not always evidence for the non-existence of a phenomenon. Herodotus visited the Pyramids at Gizeh but did not mention the Sphinx—yet it was there. In fact, when Herodotus was in the area the enormous lion couchant had already been there for two thousand years! Plutarch may possibly have had religious scruples about disclosing the mysteries of the *pneuma*, since he was at one period a Delphic priest himself and, as such, had to keep certain secrets.

Finally, E. Bourguet states flatly that there must have been a cleft in the rock which emitted stimulating vapors, and that we should not dismiss the phenomenon even if proof of it is no longer forthcoming.

Two facts, neither of which has received sufficient attention hitherto, seem to be of the utmost importance. In the year 373 B.C. the entire Temple of Apollo at Delphi collapsed. The cause may have been either an enormous conflagration or—as Homolle thinks—an earthquake. The fact that apart from small quantities of ash no traces of fire have been found supports the earthquake theory, especially as the whole Parnassus massif lies in a traditional earthquake area. The effects of a violent earthquake might well have closed a narrow fissure in such a way that no trace of the opening would be visible after more than two thousand years.

One more thing: in the whole of the literature on Delphi I have found not a single reference to research carried out by a trained modern geologist who had a thorough acquaintanceship with the

limestone and shale formation of Parnassus. To my knowledge, the
only geologist to ever work there was Professor Philippson. Admit-
tedly, he thought that the famous cleft was nonexistent and that
the whole tradition was a "priestly fraud," but his findings are too
old to carry weight today. Writing as long ago as 1938, Flacelière
says that it would be interesting to consult a modern geologist. The
fact that no one has done so is one more mystery surrounding Delphi
—just as the history of mankind in general is more a story of omis-
sion than discovery.

Another interesting theory was put forward and argued with great
acumen by the American authority Leicester B. Holland in 1933.
The Omphalos or mound-shaped stone over which the Pythia's
tripod stood displayed one unusual feature: it had been pierced from
top to bottom, and thus had a small channel running through its
center. Since the stone pedestal on which it reposed was similarly
pierced, Holland thinks that this channel or pipelike aperture was
used to convey the vapor to the foot of the Pythia's tripod, and
that the sweet-smelling smoke was artificially produced somewhere
beneath the stone floor and the Omphalos.

The idea of a pipe is an enlightening one. Holland does not, however, explain why the vapor must have been an artificial device
rather than a natural phenomenon, but relies solely on statements
by other authorities that there was no natural opening in the rock.

But, even if he is right, Delphi was certainly not a place devoted
to trickery and witchcraft. However her ecstasy was induced, the
Pythia herself was no fraud. Plato calls her condition "mania," an
apt expression because it described a state of divine inspiration which
had no psychopathic element.

The Pythia's words were inspired by Apollo but recorded and
announced in verse form by priests, who molded and interpreted
them as it seemed politic to do. The Delphic god had many temple
slaves, some of them prisoners taken in holy wars and others gifts
from various cities and private citizens. It received a constant flow
of foreigners from every part of the known world, laden with
veritable fortunes in votive offerings, since the more they gave the
sooner they got a chance to consult the oracle.

The Panhellenic Pythian Games (founded circa 590 B.C.) transformed Delphi into a seat of artistic activity and competitions
devoted to the Muses. The crowds of visitors from distant lands

also made it a scene of bustling commercial activity from which the Hellenic language and way of thought spread throughout the world. The priests plied their sacrificial knives diligently, and Plutarch tells us that their victims had to tremble from head to tail during sacrifice or no oracle could be pronounced. Sacrificial feasts were not uncommon.

During the oracle's prime, three virgins took turns in performing the duties of Pythia. Chosen from among girls of Delphi itself, they had to live a life of absolute chastity and were held under strict surveillance in a "house of the Pythia" inside the sanctuary of Apollo, cut off from all human contact. Xenophon says that a Pythia had to be completely inexperienced and must have seen and heard nothing, so that she could confront her god with a truly virginal soul. The office was not without its dangers, since the vapors induced such an abnormal state of excitement and the Pythia had to expose herself constantly to such abnormal forces that several priestesses lost their lives in the course of their duties.

THE PYTHIA REPLIES

Just as in ancient times there were people who complained of the oracle's obscurity and equivocation, so now there are some who criticize it for excessive clarity—an attitude which is extremely unjust and stupid. People of this kind are like children who take far more delight in rainbows, comets and mock suns than in the sun and moon themselves.

—PLUTARCH, *De Pythiae oraculis*

OF ALL the seats of religion in Greece, the Delphic oracle had the greatest spiritual influence. There was no important occurrence, no momentous undertaking, no war nor state of peace in which Delphi did not play a part. Forms of prayer, sacrifice, atonement, dedication and divine service were all prescribed by Delphi. Each individual Pythia was not only endowed with religious and civil power but was the supreme authority on ethics and morality in general. Delphi's influence radiated far into Asia. Even the Lydians consulted the Delphic oracles as to whom they should choose as their king, Gyges or a member of the former dynasty. The Pythia advised on Gyges, who lived circa 670 B.C. and was the first ruler to be given the name "tyrant"—probably a Lydian word. Naturally enough, the rulers who succeeded this king were among the most devoted adherents of Pythian Apollo.

The priest who recorded and passed on the Pythia's words was known as the *prophetes*. This individual did not foretell the future but was simply the god's mouthpiece or medium of communication. The relationship between the prophetes and the Pythia is obscure. If his sole function was to formulate the Pythia's answers in intelligible terms, her wide knowledge of human, political and even geographical questions bordered on the miraculous. Nilsson's view is that the prophetes either elaborated the Pythia's utterances and put them into plain speech or actually gave her guidance on her answers. There is no full solution to the problem, but we know that the oracular priests were anything but charlatans and frauds. They were excellent judges of human nature and men of wide knowledge. They were brilliant astronomers, as the Delphic calendar proves. They knew the history of the various city-states, were well informed

on geography, had a working knowledge of commercial practice
and were acquainted with the burial places of all the heroes.

The priests found it easy to solve run-of-the-mill problems, but
if a question was vague or too skillfully framed the questioner
received a vague answer. Exceptionally difficult or ambiguous answers could be laid before the *exegetes*, who examined them and
offered their considered and often valuable advice. The exegetes
remained in office for life, which was a measure of the importance
attached to their duties.

The original temple, a small and unpretentious building, was
destroyed by fire in 548 B.C. In 1939 archaeologists found several
works of art which had been saved from the fire and concealed
beneath a stone in the sacred path. The second temple was completed in the year 510, having been financed by voluntary contributions of which one of the biggest came from the Alcmaeonid family,
who had been banished from Athens and lived at Delphi in exile.
Croesus and the Egyptian king Amasis also lent their support.

During the reign of King Amasis there lived in Thrace a girl
called Rhodopis, who was a slave belonging to a certain Iadmon.
(Strangely enough, the celebrated fabulist Aesop was a fellow slave
of hers in Iadmon's establishment.) Apparently, Rhodopis was pur-
chased from Iadmon by a wealthy slave trader from Samos known
as Xantos. Being a shrewd salesman, he took the girl to the place
where she would fetch most, in this case the famous trading settlement of Naucratis in Egypt. Before long a man from Mytilene called
Charaxos fell in love with the delectable piece of human merchandise
and bought her at a very high price. Having done so, Charaxos gave
her her freedom, thereby incurring the mockery of the famous
poetess Sappho, who happened to be his sister.

Rhodopis used her new-found freedom to become the talk of the
town not only in Naucratis, which lay between Alexandria and
present-day Cairo, but throughout the Hellenic world. Her grace
and charm became a byword on every coast and she earned a large
fortune for a girl of her sort—though nothing like enough to build
the Pyramid of Mycerinus at Gizeh, as the Hellenes loved to boast.
Herodotus tells us that although Rhodopis's fortune would not run
to a pyramid she was extremely ambitious and wanted to leave the
Greeks some souvenir which would always remind them of her.
She accordingly made the Delphic sanctuary a strange bequest com-

prising a large number of spits, each so big that it could accommodate a whole ox. The value of the gift represented a tenth of her entire capital. Herodotus says that these spits could still be seen in his own day (c. 450 B.C.), lying behind the altar dedicated to Apollo by the inhabitants of Chios.

The significance of this bequest was not understood until the German scholar Waldstein found a bundle of iron spits of equal length, tightly bound by iron bands at either end, in the Heraeum at Argos. This peculiar object found its way into the National Museum in Athens and remained there unnoticed for years, until the Greek archaeologist Svoronos made a detailed examination of the dusty relic. Thirty-two spits, each nearly four feet long, had survived intact, but the original bundle had contained 180. It was a heavy bundle of iron like this, weighing several hundredweight, which the industrious Rhodopis had once sent from Naucratis to Delphi. Like the 1,000 talents' worth of alum sent by King Amasis and the 20 minas sent by the Greeks of Egypt, this was a contribution toward the building of the temple. Thus, the answer to the enigma is that these spits were a very ancient form of money which the Delphians found they could not use and so stacked away behind the altar.

In the year 373, as we have already heard, an earthquake caused the temple to collapse, only to be replaced by yet another Temple of Apollo, also financed by voluntary contributions. This temple survived the coming of the Romans and was repaired by Emperor Domitian, the bulk of the Delphic treasury having previously been seized by Sulla. Emperor Hadrian tried to restore the sanctuary's ancient status and Emperor Julian attempted to instill new life into the place after his abandonment of Christianity. However, the oracle's sole prediction to Julian was that its own end was nigh, and in the year 390 Theodosius closed it down in the name of Christianity. The Pythia spoke no more, and rubble and earth marked the former site of a place whose fame had spread throughout Greece and the contemporary world, a place to which kings, statesmen and sages from every quarter of the earth had once made pilgrimage. On the ruins of Delphi there arose a small and wretched village called Kastri. The Greek government bought it up and demolished the houses, and the French built the inhabitants new houses in a different spot. Then, after years of work by the French School of Archaeology at Athens under the direction of Professor Homolle,

Delphi re-emerged and its temples, treasure chambers, sculptures and over five thousand inscriptions saw the light of day once more.

Why did the Greeks' most sacred place meet its downfall? The waning of the ancient faith, the loss of former convictions, the relaxation of traditional morality, the growth of enlightenment and the Peloponnesian War between Athens and Sparta—all these things helped to undermine the oracle's reputation. During the latter conflict Delphi took the Peloponnesians' side and assisted Sparta with grants of money, thereby winning the Athenians' distrust for the first time—an attitude which Pericles did everything to foster. As time passed, the oracle fell prey to the general disunity of the period, the mockery of the comic dramatists who have always been quick to seize their chance in any age—in short, skepticism. Here, as in Egypt so long before, disbelief and doubt proved to be harbingers of doom; for a civilization survives only for as long as its members are still prepared to build pyramids, temples or cathedrals to the god of that civilization.

The veneration accorded to the Delphic Apollo during the oracle's prime can be assessed by the treasures assembled there by all the tribes and cities of Greece—indeed, of the whole world. These included vast numbers of the three-legged bronze caldrons which were sacred to Apollo, and a multitude of sculptures erected in Delphi by the various competing clans and states. Although the Roman emperor Nero confiscated five hundred of them he left more than three thousand behind.

Most of the questions addressed to the deity at Delphi were really requests for advice. Very few of them concerned the future. The Delphic oracle was consulted, for instance, as to when a new city should be founded or a devastated city rebuilt. The Pythia was questioned about the outcome of wars, about illnesses, physical infirmities and dire disasters such as crop failures, famines, epidemics and wartime defeats.

Above all, the Delphic Apollo was, through his mouthpiece the Pythia, the divine authority and supreme arbiter in all religious matters. People went to the god of Delphi and consulted the virgin seated on her tripod at the center of the world to learn the will of the gods on subjects such as the founding of temples, the offering of sacrifice, dedicatory gifts to the dead, graves, cults, demons and heroes.

Thus there existed a single regulating and arbitrating authority equipped to deal with all the crucial problems, disputes and emergencies in the contemporary world: a god who did not remain dumb in the face of every request and every entreaty but had a mouthpiece through which he spoke directly to mankind.

The citizens of the wealthy gold- and silver-mining island of Syphnos in the Cyclades once asked the oracle how long their good fortune would last. The Pythia answered that they should "secure themselves against the wooden horde and the red herald when their council house and market glimmered white." The Syphnians had decorated their market and council house with Persian marble, but they did not understand the oracle until the day when the ships of Samos (the wooden horde), painted with red lead, lay moored off their coasts. When the Syphnians refused the Samian envoy (the red herald) a loan, the Samians devastated the island.

In common with all the Greek oracles, Delphi predicted a victory for Croesus, the fabulously rich and fortunate Lydian king who reigned from 560 to 546 B.C. In the autumn of 546 both King Croesus and his capital, Sardis, fell into the hands of Cyrus of Persia. The downfall of this noble and philhellene ruler and his kingdom exercised a decisive influence on the attitude adopted by every subsequent generation of Greeks toward the fickleness of fortune, the impartiality of fate and the envy of the gods. Having erred in the case of Croesus, the Delphic oracle tried a hundred years later to reinterpret history and so eradicate the poor impression made by its inaccurate prediction. By then convinced that the Persians were invincible, Delphi counseled the Greeks, through the Pythia, not to offer them armed resistance. The oracle was guilty neither of timidity nor pusillanimity nor Persian bias. As Nilsson so aptly puts it, this was one case where the god knew a little too much about the future!

Having been defeated by the Tegeans, the Spartans sent religious emissaries to Delphi to ask what they had to do in order to conquer them. The Pythia advised them to find the remains of Orestes. Not knowing where Orestes' burial place was located, the Spartans asked the god where Orestes lay buried. The Pythia answered: "At Tegea in Arcadia there is a large fallow field where two winds rage. There is blow and counterblow. That is where the earth harbors Agamemnon's son Orestes." The Lacedaemonians failed to solve this riddle, but Lichas eventually found the grave in a blacksmith's yard complete with two bellows (the raging winds) and hammer and anvil (blow and counterblow).

Perhaps the Pythia's most bewildering pronouncement was made in response to a question from Chaerephon, a devoted pupil and follower of Socrates who went to Delphi and asked the oracle if any man were wiser than Socrates. The Pythia's unqualified reply was: "No one is wiser." The man most amazed by this answer was Socrates himself. Being fully aware how little he knew, he inferred from the oracle that other men who seemed to be extremely clever or erudite must know even less than he did. Accordingly, he examined the foremost of his contemporaries in the gymnasium, in the academy, in the Lyceum, in the market place and craftsmen's workshops, and refuted their belief in their own infallibility. "God alone is wise," said Socrates. "If the oracle declares that I, who know nothing, am the wisest, it means that human knowledge is a cipher. But the most fearful thing of all is to believe that one is learned in things of which one understands nothing."

What sort of answer would Chaerephon receive today? No modern institution could name the wisest man alive—not because there are no wise men left, but because it is virtually impossible for the present to assess or truly apprehend the present and simultaneously take the future into consideration.

The god who expressed himself so clearly on the subject of Socrates sat enthroned high above all earthly standards and criteria. He recognized Socrates for what he was, whereas men in their pettiness forced Athens' greatest son to drink the poisoned cup.

OLYMPIAS, ZEUS AND ALEXANDER

It is said that during his youthful years, when Philip was initiated into the Mysteries in Samothrace in company with Olympias, he fell in love with that princess, who was likewise still very young and an orphan, and took her, with her uncle Arymbas' consent, as his wife. The night before, when she was locked up in the bridal chamber, the bride dreamed that a shaft of lightning pierced her body during a storm, and that from the stroke there arose a raging fire which burst into bright flames on every side and then was suddenly quenched.

—PLUTARCH, *Lives*, Alexander, ii

THERE was once a woman who decisively affected the course of human history not by taking a personal part in international affairs but by exerting her influence in the secret and mysterious way that is woman's alone.

This unique figure on the sidelines of world history was Olympias, daughter of King Neoptolemus, wife of Philip of Macedon and mother of that brilliant and cometlike apparition, Alexander the Great. Although Alexander's grand design, a political amalgamation of Europe and Asia, was frustrated by his untimely death at the age of thirty-three, Hellenism, the spirit of Greece, followed in the train of his armies and found its way to the Far East. To this day every image of Buddha betrays the influence of the Greek artists of Gandhara.

In her girlhood, Olympias was known as Myrtale. She was born in the Kingdom of Epirus, probably at Passaron, the ancient city where the kings of the Molossians used to be crowned. It is set in an imposing region of rugged mountain chains interspersed with deep and narrow but partially fertile valleys. The Gulfs of Avlona, Butrinto and Arta bite deep into the land there, and the mountains are not far from the Albanian border. The wind that blows there is quite different from the winds of Athens or the Peloponnesus.

I have seen the village of Gardiki, the district where Olympias was born. There is an ineffable stillness about the place. Nothing can be seen of the former royal city of the Epirotes save a circular grass-grown hill which marks the spot where the citadel or acropolis of Passaron once dominated the surrounding countryside. Its ruins still await the archaeologist's attentions.

The importance of Olympias is that her ardent soul and strong belief in the supersensual world convinced her that her son Alexander was the offspring of her association with Zeus, and therefore a son of God. Olympias' belief in Alexander's divinity took root and lived on in him after her death.

So we are confronted, 350 years before Christ's birth, by another man who claimed to be the son of God. His father Philip avoided Olympias because of her association with the supreme being, and this sense of immediate nearness to God filled and obsessed Alexander throughout his life. If it is not generally known that Alexander was obsessed by the belief that he was the son of God, it is because history is written by historians and not psychologists!

There is no other possible explanation of the fact that a young man who lived only thirty-three years should have transmitted the spirit of Greece to the entire Orient, should first have subjugated whole nations and empires and then made them thrive under the impact of his genius for organization, should have blazed a trail to the Indus and deep into the wastes of Africa, should have given mankind a totally different conception of the world and, finally, should have been indirectly responsible for the subsequent clothing of Christ's teachings in the Greek language, on whose wings they conquered the world.

To anyone who stands on the lonely hill above Passaron and reflects that Alexander's mother Olympias grew up there, such thoughts seem inconceivable. There is nothing to be seen but the open sky, an expanse of grass and marshland, and an apparently meaningless jumble of time-worn stones.

Have we any means of discovering how Olympias came to believe in her son's divinity?

As a child Princess Myrtale was taken to the island of Samothrace, which lies in the northeast corner of the Aegean Sea, there to undergo religious instruction. Samothrace was well known for its Mystery Cult, and the island was the site of a mysterious sanctuary dedicated to the Cabiri, who were probably gods of Asiatic-Phrygian origin. Mystic and orphic rites were performed there and sacrifice was done in their honor.

Little is known about these secret cults because initiates were forbidden to speak of the sacred mysteries during their lifetime. Men also took part in the religious ceremonies, which is how the young Macedonian prince came to meet his princess. He immediately fell head over heels in love with her. Myrtale was still very young, but her eyes and lips seemed to have partaken of the wild beauty and solitude of the countryside of Epirus, and she devoted herself to the Mysteries and the gods of Samothrace with passionate intensity.

There was much that was unusual about young Myrtale. She was a hypersensitive girl who had the gift of finding her way to the unseen gods and communing with them spiritually, as though in a dream. It was a faculty which must have exercised a great fascination over Philip, a gifted boy who had just come into contact with the supernatural for the first time in his impressionable young life.

Myrtale's father Neoptolemus had died in 360 B.C., leaving her in the care of her uncle Arrybas, who had meanwhile succeeded to the throne of Epirus. Arrybas agreed without demur when Philip asked for his niece's hand in marriage. He was pleased, for he saw in Philip the future king of his large but chaotic neighbor, Macedon, and probably recognized his statesmanlike qualities even at that early stage.

On the night before her marriage, Myrtale was shut up in the bridal chamber in accordance with Greek custom, and there she had a dream which was to change her whole life. She saw a storm and in it a shaft of lightning that struck her body and caused bright flames to burst forth. Then, so Plutarch tells us, the fire was suddenly extinguished. What did the portent mean? To the Greeks there could be only one answer: a storm, a flash of lightning and peals of thunder signified the presence of no less a god than Zeus himself.

Just under twenty miles south of Passaron lies the lovely valley of Dramissos, site of the oracle of Dodona, a famous sanctuary dedicated to the Greeks' supreme god and, so we are told in Homer, Herodotus and Plato's *Phaedrus*, the oldest oracle in Greece. It was the abode of heathen Europe's most important deity, Zeus, whom the Romans called Jupiter. *Ju* is Zeus, and *piter* or *pater* means father. Zeus is the Greek equivalent of the Indo-European Dieus. The Latin word for God, *deus*, and the French *dieu* are derived from Dios, the genitival form of Zeus. Zeus was also the origin of

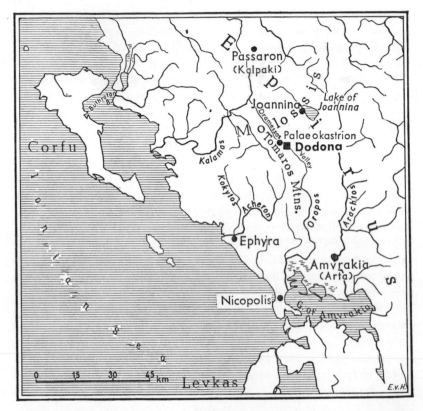

Dodona

the Latin word for day, *dies*. The Germanic god Ziu, the Lithuanian Diewas, the Lettish Dews, the Gothic Tius and the English Tuesday are all derived from the name of the Indo-Europeans' supreme god.

The question of Zeus's origins has never been settled beyond dispute, but there is considerable evidence to suggest that the idea of this god arrived from the north and became disseminated throughout central Greece before finding its way to Dodona. It seems likely that the god also touched the Mycenaean world during his travels, for the Mycenaean double ax became one of his emblems.

Zeus never created any human or divine beings, but he was the paterfamilias and patriarchal chieftain of all Olympus. His daughter Athena and his son Apollo, the god of the Delphic oracle, were intimately associated with him, and most of the other gods were children of his.

The oracle of Dodona was spreading the spirit of Zeus abroad even in early heroic times, and was visited by some of the most illustrious people in the ancient world despite the long and fatiguing journey involved. The wealthy King Croesus consulted this oracle as well as that of Delphi. Pindar composed a paean to Dodonaean Zeus. Aeschylus and Sophocles spoke of the sanctuary with the greatest veneration, and even the Spartans turned to Dodona in cases of especial importance.

Those who travel from Passaron to Dodona and stand in the valley of the oracle looking up at the summit of the Tomarus can visualize what Olympias must have seen there as a child: the throngs of pilgrims arriving from all over the world to consult the oracle, the echoing caldrons on their tripods, the priests going about their duties. As for Princess Myrtale, she must have watched all this with wondering eyes and sensed the omnipresence of Zeus. The god was no stranger to her. On the contrary, he was by her side day and night. And her dream held an extraordinary significance not only for the subsequent careers of Philip and Alexander but for the history of mankind as a whole. Without it, Alexander might never have become "the Great" nor his kingdom a far-flung empire.

Epirus is truly a land of kings and gods, a land where the mountains still converse secretly with the sky. It was the proper site for a place which, like Dodona, mediated between earth and heaven.

Has everything really vanished, and is nothing left of Dodona? Two such distinguished scholars as Ernst Kirsten and Wilhelm Kraiker included the following note in a report on Dodona published as recently as 1957: "No trace of temple or sacred oak grove." Yet the oracle is a reality and can still be seen, even though Zeus speaks no more and his cult is extinct, even though the god who once dominated Europe has retreated forever into the past.

The correct location of Dodona was long ago predicted by the Frenchman Gaultier de Claubry, and Christopher Wordsworth mentioned in 1868 that the ruins of Palaeokastrion were connected with the former sanctuary of Dodonaean Zeus. Palaeokastrion, which means "old citadel," was the name given in more recent times to

the walled city complete with acropolis which stood at the summit
of the hill overlooking the sanctuary of Zeus.

In 1876 the Greek archaeologist Constantin Carapanos began to
dig in the area of the Dodona sanctuary and unearthed various
objects, notably inscribed plaquettes of lead and bronze, which
indicated that he had probably found the actual site of the oracle.
When deciphered, the inscriptions on the small lead tablets proved to
be written questions addressed to the oracle by pilgrims. They
covered a wide range of subjects. One, put by a certain Lysanias,
inquired whether the child which his wife was expecting was really
his. Another man wanted to know whether the purchase of some
land was likely to be advantageous. Although the priests' answers
were mostly given orally, they were sometimes written on the
reverse of the tablets. Such tablets are of great value because they
give us an inkling of the actual nature of an oracular pronouncement.
Answers were given in a form of officialese. One tablet, for instance,
bore the words: *Reference plot of land: the matter is profitable.*
Someone who was obviously worried about his health received the
reply: *Reference health: sacrifice to Zeus.* Other sample questions
concerned missing articles and whether it was expedient to let
the upper floor of a house.

Although Carapanos had found the actual sanctuary, he did not
identify it correctly. The small finds made round about were important enough in themselves, but Carapanos had partially unearthed the ruins of a Christian basilica and, since he found votive
offerings dating from pre-Christian times in an annex belonging to
the church, concluded that he had found the Temple of Dodona
itself.

It was not until between 1929 and 1935 that the mystery of
Dodona moved closer to solution. Professor Evangelides unearthed
three small temples, two Roman buildings, a grave and numerous
votive pedestals. He also found copper statuettes, handmade pottery,
fragmentary copper vessels and other votive offerings, all of which
offered evidence that the origins of Dodona went back to the
second millennium B.C.

Digging was discontinued in 1935 and was not recommenced
until a short time ago. The man in charge was Sotiris Dakaris,
a young and talented archaeologist who was born in the district

and has known every stone, every hill and valley of his native district since childhood.

In order to gauge the significance of these ancient buildings we must examine the relationship between Zeus and his sacred tree, the oak. The cult of the oak hails from a very early period during which the tree was sacred to many Indo-European peoples.

The Swedish authority on Greek religion, Martin Nilsson, interprets the significance of the oak in religious history by suggesting that its fruit provided mankind's first food. Edible acorns were described by Hesiod circa 700 B.C. and by Ovid at the time of Christ's birth as the food of the "Golden Age." They were no doubt thinking of the sweet acorns that supplied the whole of the northern hemisphere with its principal source of vegetable nourishment before the age of grain cultivation. The oak was reputed to be the world's first tree. Pliny, who lived from A.D. 23 to A.D. 79, referred in his work on natural history to oaks that were as old as the earth and mentioned the ancient tradition that human beings sprang from oaks.

There are, however, far more intelligible grounds for this belief in the sanctity of the oak tree. Oaks can attain a very advanced age. One oak tree at Schwanheim, near Frankfurt, displayed 630 well-defined annual circles. With a diameter over 9 feet, the oak of Bischofswald, ten miles east of Helmstedt, is estimated to be 1,190 years old. When the colonists arrived in America they found ancient oaks which had long been held in veneration by the Indians as landmarks and meeting places. Two such oaks played a role in American history—the famous Charter Oak at Hartford, Connecticut, and the Wadsworth Oak near Genesee, New York, a venerable tree 27 feet in circumference, under whose lofty branches Robert Morris and the Seneca Indians signed a peace treaty.

Another thing: perhaps because of their greater height, oaks are struck by lightning more frequently than other trees, and the linking of sky and oak tree through that medium was recognized very early. In one wood near Lippe-Detmold composed of 70 percent birch, 13 percent spruce, 11 percent oak, and 6 percent pine, it is recorded that the numbers of trees struck by lightning over a period of sixteen years were as follows: 310 oaks, 108 pines, 34 spruces and 33 birches. Subsequent inspection brought to light a further 34 oaks struck by lightning as compared with 12 other deciduous trees, 9 coniferous trees and a single beech tree. The oak's abnormal susceptibility to damage by lightning did not, however, detract from its reputation in prehistoric times, for trees struck by lightning were regarded as sacred.

The most renowned of all sacred oaks stood in the grove at Dodona in Epirus. Since we know that the cult of the oak was an ancient Indo-European conception, we must assume that the first Greeks to migrate to Epirus brought this cult with them from their original home. Writing about 450 B.C., Herodotus mentioned that Dodona was regarded as the oldest oracle of the Hellenes.

Religions are composed of many overlapping cultural strata and often represent an amalgam of the very old and the more recent, just as Christianity contains relics of many ancient heathen practices. The oak tree is intimately associated with the earth. Since Gaea or Ge, the earliest earth-goddess, was worshiped at Dodona, the priests in the sanctuary there slept on the bare earth in order to maintain the closest possible contact with her. Another strange custom of theirs was never to remove dust or earth from their feet, on the grounds that it would be desecration.

Thus, oak and earth formed the nucleus of the earliest cult at Dodona, which lasted until about the thirteenth century B.C. Zeus did not arrive there until after the oak, but he was the newer god and stronger, greater and more powerful than the earth-goddess Gaea and her sacred tree. His female consort Dione, who accompanied him, became the new earth-goddess in place of Gaea. (Dione is the feminine version of the name Dios.)

At Dodona the new god received the additional name Naios, possibly an abbreviation for "he who lives in the oak tree." For the idea that Zeus and his consort Dione dwelt in the tree was constantly stressed, and it was held that the god manifested his will through the tossing of its massive branches. Dodona must already have been very ancient when Homer composed his epics about 750 B.C., for he mentions in Book XIV of the *Odyssey* that Odysseus asked the sacred foliage of the great oak of Zeus Dodonaeus for advice as to how he was to journey home to Ithaca.

But how did the holy place come into being in the first place?

Herodotus of Halicarnassus, ever an inquisitive student of early Western history, visited Dodona in person and questioned the sooth-

According to Herodotus, these were the routes taken by the black doves that flew from Egyptian Thebes to Dodona and Siwa.

saying priestesses about the origins of the oracle. They told him that once upon a time two black doves had flown from Egyptian Thebes, one to Libya and the other to Dodona. The latter, it was said, had perched on an oak in Dodona and demanded in human tones that an oracle sacred to Zeus be established there. The oracle was duly founded and the branches of the oak became a favorite haunt of the sacred doves of Zeus. The other bird, which had flown to Libya, commanded the Libyans to found an oracle sacred to Ammon, and the Libyans likewise complied. The oracle of Ammon at the oasis of Siwa in northwest Egypt was also dedicated to Zeus, as we read in Herodotus's *Histories* (II, lv). It was no mere coincidence that Alexander the Great had it in mind to bestow upon the sanctuary of Dodona the enormous sum of 1,500 talents (the equivalent of 9 million Attic drachmas or between fifteen and sixteen million dollars), and that he undertook the perilous march to the oasis of Siwa in order to visit his "father" Zeus-Ammon. Alexander also planned to build a huge Temple of Zeus at Dodona, but his premature death put an end to the project.

At Dodona, as in the Parthenon on the Athenian Acropolis, one forgets only too easily that this is a holy place and that one is standing on holy ground. The ancient abode of the earth-goddess

Gaia and the oak became the abode of Zeus and Dione. Zeus held sway there for twenty centuries until, about A.D. 350, he forfeited his sovereignty. Yet even today an aura of sanctity permeates the silent ruins in the bright and open valley, and even now they tell the story of their strange and fascinating past.

LATEST NEWS OF DODONA

At first, so I was told at Dodona, the Pelasgians used to offer all sacrifice and prayer to the gods without giving any one of them a name because they had not yet heard of one.... After a long time had elapsed they learned the names of the gods from Egypt. ...Then, after a further period, they sought a divine decision about the names at Dodona, for that oracle is held to be the oldest oracle of the Hellenes and was at that time the only one. When, therefore, the Pelasgians sought a decision at Dodona as to whether they should use the names which they had got from the barbarians, the oracle gave voice: "Use ye them!" So from thenceforth they used the names of the gods when sacrificing, and the Hellenes in turn received them from the Pelasgians.

—HERODOTUS, *Histories,* I, lii

SOTIRIS DAKARIS, who has devoted his life to a study of the Greeks' most mysterious sanctuary, conducted me through the whole district of Dodona. It is a place where life has long since ebbed. It is one of mankind's earliest and most important sites of religious activity, yet few people visit it.

Dodona boasts one of the finest and most imposing amphitheatres in the world. Next to it is a building whose significance has not yet been determined. Its perimeter walls have already been laid bare, but only test diggings have been carried out so far. It may have been an *adyton* or cult chamber corresponding to the holy of holies, or it may, alternatively, have been the *enkomitirion* used by pilgrims for the "temple sleep" in which they were visited by oracular dreams. There is a pilgrimage site of this type at Epidaurus. Only a few yards away from the building can be seen the foundation walls of the sanctuary itself, the oracle of the Greeks' oldest god, around which are scattered the ruins of several smaller temples together with the remains of a much more recent Christian basilica.

It is a scene that effectively conveys the impermanence of human handiwork and the remoteness of God from all human considerations. At some stage, probably between A.D. 360 and 370, the Christians dethroned Zeus, destroyed his temple and silenced the sacred oak forever. Then they built the basilica to their own god, only to see life in the valley extinguished for a second time

149

by the constant depradations of warlike tribes. About 550 the church was destroyed, although its walls continued to point at the sky, lonely and neglected, until at long last even they collapsed. Torrents gnawed at the stones, earth clothed the ruins, and ultimately everything was blotted out.

The sacred oak, of course, was not enclosed in a temple. The earliest rites of Zeus were performed in the open air around the tree, which was surrounded by bronze tripods supporting caldrons. When the caldrons brushed together or were struck by hand the vibrations were taken up by each in turn, filling the air with sound.

The Greek expression *dodonaion chalkeion,* meaning "Dodonaean bronze," was used to describe loquacity because these caldrons continued to reverberate for a long time after being struck. The metal drums did not always make the same sound, however. Their tone varied with the way they were struck, with the wind, and with the temperature and humidity of the air, and it was from the nature of the reverberations that priests and priestesses interpreted the oracle and translated it into words.

This, at least, is how we think the oracle of Dodona functioned, although we cannot be certain because Aristotle, writing between 335 and 323 B.C., declared that there were not as many tripods in the sanctuary as one might suppose. Aristotle described a votive offering from Corfu which consisted of two pillars. On one of them stood a caldron and on the other a bronze statue of a boy with a whip in his hand. The chains suspended from the whip hung free, so that with every breath of wind they touched the caldron, producing a sound which was interpreted as an oracle. *Korkyraion mastix* or "whip of the Corcyrans" was yet another idiomatic expression for loquacity.

Numerous fragments of bronze tripods were found during excavations at Dodona. These pieces of bronze date from the eighth century B.C., and Dakaris infers from them that the sanctuary was surrounded by bronze vessels at that period. This would correspond with a report by the Athenian historian Demon (circa 330 B.C.), who related that the sanctuary of Zeus originally had no walls but was fenced in with tripods.

Homer's references to Dodona are based on conditions prevailing in the thirteenth century B.C., the time of Mycenae. Once again, archaeology confirms the truth of what used to be regarded as the

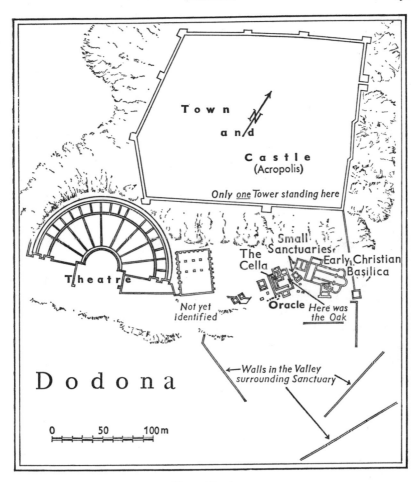

Plan of Dodona

product of poetic imagination, for many of the objects dug up at
Dodona date from that period. They are principally votive offerings
such as pots, stone mattocks and Mycenaean weapons. But Dodona
goes back even further into the mists of prehistory. Excavation has
brought to light even older finds, and it is now recognized that the
sacred precincts were already the home of a religious cult as early
as 1900 or 2100 B.C.

All these finds are cult objects of varying sizes. Where archi-

tectural remains are concerned, on the other hand, nothing earlier
than the fourth century B.C. has been found. Nevertheless, what has
been discovered—and above all the holy of holies, the temple itself—
is breathtaking enough.

The oldest temple, built in the fourth century B.C., measured
only 21 feet by 19½. It consisted of a cella and a small projecting
structure without pillars. Between 350 and 325 B.C. a low wall of
uniform stones was built, forming a largish courtyard enclosing the
sacred precincts once occupied by the tripods. On its southeast
side a sensational discovery was made—perhaps the most sensational
of all the revelations of Dodona. Sotiris Dakaris came upon a deep
pit in the natural rock containing hewn stones which had evidently
belonged to an altar, and a few votive offerings. It was the cavity
that had once housed the mighty roots of the sacred oak! The oak
must, therefore, have existed, and the Christians were so anxious to
eradicate it that they removed the roots that represented the vital
link between the abode of Zeus and the earth itself. So Dakaris
has positively identified the exact location of the oak which was
until recently often dismissed as a fable, and we now possess, through
the medium of his published findings in the great Pyrsos Encyclo-
pedia, an idea of this mysterious cult site dedicated to the supreme
god of ancient Greece.

Pyrrhus of Epirus, the famous Molossian king who ruled from
297 to 272 B.C. and was the last Greek leader to resist the Romans
successfully, replaced the enclosure around the oak with a much
larger wall forming a rectangular courtyard measuring 68 feet by
62. This courtyard, whose eastern side was left free for the sacred
tree, incorporated a hall with Ionic pillars in its interior.

A small Doric temple with four pillars was erected at about the
same time, probably for the cult of Heracles, together with another,
Ionic temple with vestibule dedicated to the cult of Dione, wife of
Zeus Dodonaeus.

On a hill to the north of the sanctuary stood the old city, today
known as Palaeokastrion, crowned by an acropolis built of uniform
stones. This fortress was fortified by ten wall turrets and two corner
towers. The wall of the acropolis that faced the temples had only
one rectangular tower built into it to enhance its appearance when
seen from the sacred buildings in the valley 100 feet below.

Like the acropolis, the theatre also came into being during the reign of King Pyrrhus. It is a true architectural masterpiece, larger than that of Epidaurus and the best-preserved edifice of its kind in Greece.

The builders carved the enormous semicircle out of the solid rock, displaying an almost frightening disregard of practical difficulties. The theatre is divided by two precipitous gangways into three levels containing 21, 16 and 21 tiers of stone seats respectively —58 in all. The lowest semicircle in the theatre, known as the *proedria*, was reserved for privileged spectators. Between the lowest semicircle and the *orchestra*, or stage, was a narrow gangway 3½ feet wide with a groove running along it. This was a channel for the rainwater that accumulated there from all over the theatre, including the orchestra, and unobtrusively drained away. Beneath the gutter in the drainage cavity were found stalactites up to 8 inches long, evidence of 2,200 years' growth.

Ten steps led from the orchestra to the spectators' seats. The theatre held 18,000 spectators, and if all its seats were placed side by side they would stretch for nearly 4½ miles. The audience could gaze down at the orchestra or past it into the blue vistas of one of the most beautiful valleys in the world. The stage itself was backed by a wide hall supported by thirteen octagonal pillars. A stone proscenium or antestage was added later, supported by eighteen Ionic half pillars. In the center of the orchestra stood the foundation stone of the altar or *tymele*, which still survives today. It should be remembered that the twin origins of the theatre were drama and religion, and that dances and songs used to be performed around the altar. *Choros* was, in fact, the Greek word for "dance."

During the reign of Augustus the Romans modified the theatre's shape and turned it, typically enough, into a circus. They did not, however, succeed in destroying the building's chiseled beauty and strength. To increase the size of the orchestra they removed the first five tiers of seats and built a nine-foot-high wall between the orchestra and the crescent-shaped auditorium to protect the spectators. This made it possible to stage duels, gladiatorial contests and fights with wild animals. At the extremities of the arena one can still make out the stone cells where trained or savage beasts were kept in preparation for the slaughter to follow. Large quantities of bones have been found there. In addition, the layer of chalk beneath the orchestra was threaded with natural cavities, though it is impossible to say for what they were used.

The huge semicircle of the theatre is bounded at either end by massive buttresses and further strengthened by three monumental towers. A flight of steps leads up through the first tower to the middle and upper sections of the crescent, the latter being on the same level as the acropolis. Acropolis, theatre and sanctuary thus formed a unified and magnificent complex of buildings protected by an immense exterior courtyard. It was a fortified area of vast proportions and one that must have evoked the admiration and envy of the entire world in the third century B.C.

I have looked down on the theatre from above and felt my head swim with vertigo. I have also sat in the extreme corner of one of the highest tiers. Wherever the eye turns, there is a harmony and elegance about the theatre's lines and perspectives. Looking up from the stage, one can see the seats towering up and away into the brightness of the sky. It is a breathtakingly beautiful spectacle.

For some reason—probably a violent earthquake—the massive stone blocks composing the spectators' benches had been thrown into disorder. Dakaris has restored them to their original position, a very laborious task even with the help of modern engineering equipment.

Dodona's amphitheatre fills the puny mortals who stand before its massive bulk with a sense of wonder and admiration. It helps us to understand why the dramatists of the West are still feeding on the unquenchable source of inspiration provided by a small nation which, two and a half thousand years ago, evolved all the basic themes that are still in use today. Far from increasing in beauty since then, stages and theatres have become no more than wretched little huts in comparison with their grandiose predecessors.

When Pausanias, the Greek traveler and geographer, visited Dodona about A.D. 150, the great oak was still standing, the oracle was still giving voice and the Roman emperors had rebuilt all that their own legions had destroyed during the conquest of Epirus. Two hundred years later, the world's earliest place of pilgrimage stood desolate and forlorn, and the people who lived on the hill above the sanctuary had fled to Ioannina.

Ioannina stands dreaming by the lake a few miles northeast of Dodona, a small and remote Balkan township with white walls and gray roofs. Expert craftsmen, carpet knotters, weavers, embroiderers and probably the best silversmiths in Greece live in this rugged, industrious, garrulous and congenial place. Anyone who ascends the hill overlooking the town and visits the Aslan Aga mosque, now a museum, can discover in the relics displayed there the wonder that was once Dodona.

If we could only look down on our little world in a godlike and timeless fashion we should see that life crawls across it at an almost imperceptible pace. Abandoning Dodona, it moved on to Ioannina and soared to a splendid prime there. Ioannina became the capital of Epirus and the seat of venerable archbishops. It was annexed to Serbia, was conquered by sultans and witnessed desperate Christian uprisings. Under Ali of Tepeleni it became a world-famous center of learning whose schools taught Greek literature, Latin, French and other branches of knowledge. Pressing onward, history left the town in its wake. Ioannina struggled for mastery over the whole of Greece. Emissaries from France, England and Russia met there and shared Lord Byron's admiration for the place.

Growing apprehensive that one pasha should command so much power, the Turkish government besieged Ali in the fortress above the town. Finally he surrendered, and on February 22, 1822, was treacherously assassinated on an island in the lake, ordering with his last breath that his wife should be killed to prevent her falling into the hands of his enemies. His severed head was publicly displayed in Ioannina, and the inhabitants filed silently past their former master. Ninety-one years later, on the anniversary of his murder, Ioannina was recaptured by the Greeks.

Ioannina weaves the tapestry of its life from timeless threads, but twelve miles away in the lonely valley of Dramissos the bare brown mountains face the sky in mute inquiry. Who tore the ancient oak from the bosom of its mother earth? Why was the plaintive voice of the bronze caldrons stilled? Where did the priests go, and how did the priestesses meet their end? And why did Zeus, the god in whose language our New Testament was composed, leave heaven and earth forever without hope of resurrection?

ATLANTIS, FACT OR FICTION?

*Thus the muddy shallows and the estuary show that Plato
visualized his island of Atlantis on the coast of the Western Ocean,
and he is kind enough to satisfy our curiosity as to whether it
was the Libyan or the Iberian or the Celtic coast. He says that
Poseidon's second son Eumelos was also called Gadeiros and that
Gadeiros's allotted (eastern) end of the island of Atlantis lay near
the Pillars of Heracles and extended into the region of Gades.
That is his sole fairly precise topographical allusion to Atlantis, but
it is of inestimable value.*

—ADOLF SCHULTEN, *Tartessos*,
p. 98, Hamburg, 1950

OF ALL the vanished civilizations of man, Atlantis is possibly the
most intriguing. The question of whether Atlantis is only a legend
or whether the story of the remote island is based on fact was a
bone of contention even in antiquity. Aristotle, for example, regarded all the accounts of Atlantis as pure fiction, whereas Posidonius
took it for granted that Atlantis actually existed at one time.

The fascination which Atlantis has always exercised over men's
minds originated in their yearning for a climatically mild, fertile
land of the unknown, in their escapist longing for a better world
untroubled by mundane cares. The Greek poet Hesiod, who lived
about 700 B.C., was the first to write of the Islands of the Blest.
Sickened by years of civil strife, the famous Roman poet Horace
counseled his fellow men to go in search of the *arva beata* or
"blessed fields." Sertorius, who served as a praetor in Spain in
83 B.C., heard master mariners from Gades, the present-day Cádiz,
tell of "fortunate isles" in the Atlantic Ocean—probably Madeira
and the Canary group. The Sicilian writer Diodorus went so far as
to give a glowing description of Madeira, probably based on reports
by the explorer Pytheas of Massilia (Marseilles), who toured
northern Europe about 325 B.C. and reached the Shetland and Orkney
islands. As the author of a book entitled *The Ocean* (unfortunately
not extant) Pytheas probably gave an account of Madeira's wonderfully mild and temperate climate and its extremely fertile soil. From
Homer to Daniel Defoe and Thor Heyerdahl, poets, explorers and
sailors have always dreamed—in company with their readers—of
faraway islands, perilous or paradisiac.

Was Atlantis an island, a distant continent, or a mainland region that seemed like an island?

The world has had to wait until our own day before seeing a ray of light shed on the mystery surrounding the country and its inhabitants. Ever since Columbus discovered a new continent in the Atlantic Ocean in 1492, there has been a tendency to equate America with Atlantis. Despite the hundreds of volumes devoted to solving the riddle of Atlantis, recent scientific research into the subject justifies yet another attempt to define the Atlantides and their culture geographically, for there is abundant evidence that Atlantis existed. Troy, too, would have been an "Atlantis" had no one dug it up!

The most celebrated reference to the city and island of Atlantis is to be found in the writings of Plato, who was born in May of the year 427 B.C. The son of an aristocratic Athenian family, he received a first-rate and comprehensive education. He might well have become a great statesman, but a study of political events in Greece convinced him of a truth which was destined never to lose its validity: that the social and political conditions of a country will never improve until politicians become philosophers or the destinies of a nation are controlled by philosophers with statesman-like qualities. The word "philosopher" is not, of course, used here in the strictly technical sense. We are dealing with the well-proved fact that politics and statesmanship are not merely special branches of knowledge but rooted in human wisdom.

Plato wrote poems, epigrams, dithyrambs and tragedies, but his true immortality arose out of his friendship with Socrates, the unique genius whose teachings he enriched with the fruits of a deeper and more widely based education. After Socrates' execution in the year 399 B.C., Plato traveled to Megara, southern Italy and Syracuse, where, at the court of the tyrant Dionysius I, he formed an intimate friendship with that ruler which endured until the latter's death.

Plato was the originator of higher education in western Europe, for with his Academy, a school of philosophy outside the gates of Athens named after the hero Academos, he laid the foundations of all future universities. He taught there without fee until his death in the year 347 B.C., displaying true charity and self-sacrifice in his constant quest for the truth. Plato was, to put it crudely, the inventor of the "idea." He realized that human life and endeavor are focused far more on the ideal than the material, and recognized the existence of "ideals" as such. This was Plato's extremely simple but grandiose discovery. He had faith in the immortality of the soul and strove to find evidence for that faith. His assertion that virtue was something real and imperishable was not a universally accepted truism four hundred years before Christ's birth, but he realized that material things perish while only what is intangible and ideal survives. He also knew that eternal moral values are not determined simply by the arbitrary whim of the individual but denote the existence of a more perfect world divorced from the specious reality of material objects. Thus Socrates and Plato must be numbered with men like Confucius, Buddha, Mohammed and Paul among the truly great geniuses of history, overshadowed only by the incomparable figure of Christ.

In addition to his passionate defense of Socrates, his *Protagoras*, a book on the communicability of virtue, his works on piety, love and immortality, Plato wrote two treatises which convey an idea of the lost island, vanished city or country of Atlantis. They are entitled *Timaeus* and *Critias*.

The work was really intended to be a trilogy, but for reasons unknown to us the philosopher never came to write the third or concluding volume, and even the second, *Critias*, remained uncompleted. Plato wrote these essays while Athens was going through a critical period, probably intending to console his fellow mortals with the picture of a remote and better world. It was a bold undertaking. He recounted the story of mankind's earliest beginnings and described the nature of man and his physical and moral constitution—a colossal and all-embracing design. *Timaeus* and *Critias* cannot be compared to his most brilliant works, as, for example, the *Symposium*. They are not purely literary in conception and their often dry and didactic flavor robs them of any element of drama. All in all, there are few more difficult books to assess in the whole of ancient literature, even though the knowledge and human insight contained in them is beyond praise.

Generations of scholars have puzzled over the contents of this unfinished work. Albert Rivaud, professor at the Sorbonne, declared in 1956 that it embodied not only ancient traditions but also the results of the latest contemporary research carried out during Plato's lifetime. That a distinguished French scholar who had spent decades studying the Platonic texts should reach this conclusion is most significant because it invests the geographical and ethnological allusions in the two books with greater weight.

It is possible that as an old man Plato wanted what was probably the last literary work in his prolific life to transport him in advance, as it were, to the Islands of the Blest.

Was Plato's Atlantis no more than poetic fiction? Was his account of a happy island that ruled the world merely a sympathetic refurbishing of legends handed down from the dawn of prehistory? Or did he have factual knowledge of a vanished city and empire, of a vanished Atlantic civilization? The pupils who immediately succeeded the great philosopher accepted the entire account of Atlantis as fact rather than fiction. Crantor, who lived between 335 and 275 B.C. and taught philosophy at the Academy, was the first to write a commentary on Plato's *Timaeus*. The philosopher, scientist and historian Posidonius (circa 100 B.C.) also tells us that Plato probably based his accounts on real knowledge and actual events.

In later times, scholars and adventurers of every nationality made repeated attempts to ascertain the location of Atlantis. It has been sought in every part of the world, from America to Australia, from Spitsbergen to England, from Helgoland to the southern coasts of Africa, from India to the Far East.

In 1611 Thomas Campanella, an Italian Dominican, described a "sun city" composed of seven circles divided by walls and ditches— an arrangement strongly reminiscent of the capital of Plato's Atlantic realm. Campanella later atoned for his "heretical theories" by spending thirty years in the dungeons. Francis Bacon asserted that Plato's Atlantis was none other than America, but died in 1628 before he could complete a book entitled *Nova Insula Atlantis*. The Swedish scholar Olf Rudbek wrote in 1675 that Plato's allusions fitted no other place on earth so accurately as Sweden and, in particular, Uppsala and its environs. (Rudbek was Rector of Uppsala University.) Georg Caspar Kirchmaier suggested at Wittenberg in 1685 that Atlantis lay in South Africa, while Jean Sylvain Bailly declared in London in 1779 that the Atlantis of antiquity was really the Nordic island of Spitsbergen. Undeterred by the fact that Plato's island sank beneath the waves, Bailly explained that Spitsbergen had only been "frozen up," not engulfed by the sea. In the same year Jean Baptiste Claude Delisle de Sales transposed Atlantis to the island of Sardinia. In 1762 F. C. Bär found it in Palestine, Bartoli in Attica. In 1838 Gottfried Stallbaum, author of several commentaries on Plato's works, declared that the Egyptians and their Asian neighbors had an obscure tradition concerning a Western continent, namely America, and that the latter was Atlantis. The French scholar Cadet surmised that there were traces of the sunken island in the Canary Islands or the Azores.

One of the wildest and most fantastic theories was put forward by the American Augustus Le Plongeon, who declared that the Maya race had recorded the downfall of Atlantis as early as 2500 B.C., and that it had taken place 11,500 years earlier. The famous student of Africa, Leo Frobenius, concluded from the results of his scientific work and numerous travels that the vanished city must have stood somewhere in the neighborhood of Benin in Nigeria. Professor Dr. H. H. Borchardt believed that Atlantis once existed in Tunis. Professor Albert Herrmann conducted excavations in Shott el Djerid in southern Tunisia and found remains of settlements "which are peculiarly reminiscent of Plato's city of Atlantis."

Finally, mention must be made of two Germans, Professor Hermann Wirth of Marburg, who identifies Atlantis with a Stone-Age realm of Nordic civilization located near Iceland, and Pastor Jürgen Spanuth, who is convinced that Atlantis lies in the North Sea near Helgoland. Spanuth believes that while diving in the shallows northeast of the island he has seen ruined fortifications belonging to the ancient citadel thirty or forty feet below the surface. Twelve of the blocks of flint which Spanuth brought up, under the impression that they revealed signs of human handiwork, were examined by the Institute of Geology at Kiel University. The Department of Marine Geology found, however, that the plate-shaped stones had been split naturally and not by human agency.

Anyone attempting to solve the mystery would be well advised to stick closely to Plato's text. While traveling in Egypt, he reported, Solon learned to his astonishment how far back the Egyptians' knowledge of history went. Apparently an Egyptian priest had confided certain secrets to him. We read in *Timaeus* (25 and 26):

In those days one could sail through this sea. In front of the straits, the Pillars of Heracles [Gibraltar], there was an island. This island was larger than Libya and Asia combined. The travelers of those times could voyage from this island to the other islands, and from the other

[40] No one will ever know the identity of the man buried in Shaft Grave IV at Mycenae, but he wore this gold mask over his face. Excavated by Heinrich Schliemann, it is now on display in the National Museum at Athens.

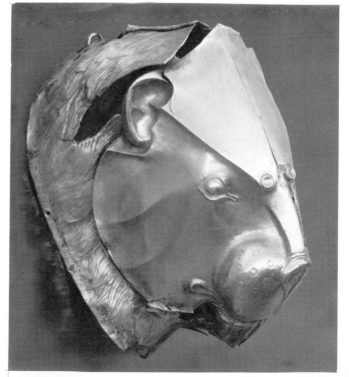

[41] Solid gold rhyton in the shape of a lion's head. This ritual vessel was beaten out of a single sheet of metal and is a remarkably fine work of art. It was also discovered in Shaft Grave IV in the citadel of Mycenae and dates from the 16th century B.C.

[42] Head of a bull vaulter in ivory, found in the palace of Knossos (circa 1550 B.C.). This fragment is part of a complete bull-vaulting group, but the remainder of the sculpture is lost.

[43] Spouted jug and cup decorated with the double ax, a sacred emblem in ancient Crete. These fine pieces were found in the New Palace at Phaistos. (Circa 1500 B.C.)

[44] This bronze statuette of a man praying from Tylissos, Crete, was made around 1550 B.C. and shows the stance customarily adopted during prayer. The figurine is only 6 inches tall.

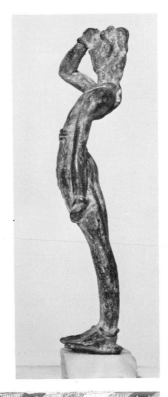

[45] Bull vaulting held a religious significance for the people of ancient Crete, who trained girls and boys in the technique from an early age. Since men were always painted in red and women in white, we can tell that two girls (left and right) and one boy (center) were taking part in the dangerous maneuver illustrated here. (Fresco in a small courtyard in the east wing of the palace of Knossos, circa 1500 B.C.)

[46] The so-called temple grave at Knossos, beneath which lies a pillared vault.
Visible in the background are the forecourt and entrance hall.
[47] Throne room in the palace of Knossos. The throne and benches are of alabaster
and the frescoes painted in vivid colors. The chamber has been restored with
complete accuracy.

[48] The stadium at Delphi, site of the Pythian Games. This view shows the track and spectators' benches.

[49] On the right, the massive Temple of Apollo at Delphi; on the left, the amphitheatre. Built in the 2nd century B.C., it had thirty-five tiers of seats and could hold 5,000 spectators—not many compared with the 16,000 seats in the Theatre of Dionysus at Athens.

[50] Caryatid composed of three young girls holding up their short robes as they dance. They are wearing the *polos*, a hair style common to priestesses.

[51] Figure of an Amazon on the Athenian Treasury at Delphi, sculpted about 500 B.C.

[52] Portrayed on the frieze on the north face of the Siphnian Treasury are the god Apollo, the goddess Artemis and a fleeing giant. The treasury was dedicated to the Delphic sanctuary by the people of the island of Siphnos.

[53] Fivefold enlargement of a remarkably fine seal dating from 420 B.C. (The original is only 1½ inches in diameter.) It was found south of Ioannina in the neighborhood of the Dodona oracle. The relief shows Orestes and his mother Clytemnestra, who has been stabbed in the heart with a dagger and is seeking refuge on the altar. Orestes is trying to drag her from it in order to complete the revenge of his father Agamemnon's murder.

[54] These stone mattocks are over 3,500 years old. They were found in the oracle of Dodona and offer evidence that the sanctuary came into existence before 2000 B.C.

[55] An example of the most durable pottery ever made in Greece, this Minyan bowl of gray clay dates from the period 1900–1700 B.C. The Minyans were the people who built the domed graves at Orchomenos, and whose culture immediately pre-dated the Mycenaean period. This vessel was found in the Dodona district and is now in the Archaeological Museum at Ioannina.

[56] This Phoenician sculpture from circa 500 B.C. was discovered in San Fernando, not far from Cádiz. The features are distinctly Phoenician with a Nubian admixture, and the subject may have been brought to Spain by the Carthaginians.

islands they could reach the whole continent on the far shores of the
sea which really merits its name [Atlantic]. On the one side, in the
interior of the straits of which we speak, there appears to be only a
harbor with a narrow entrance. On the other side, without, there lies
this real sea. The land which it encloses must be described as a continent
in the true sense of the term. On this island of Atlantis kings had founded
a large and wonderful empire which ruled the whole island and many
other islands and parts of the continent. It possessed in addition, on our
side, Libya [Africa west of Egypt] and Europe down to the Tyrrhenian
[western Italy]. In later times there were frightful earthquakes and
inundations in Atlantis, and during a single day and a single terrible
night the island of Atlantis sank beneath the sea and vanished. Because
of obstruction by deep silt, the submerged remnants of the vanished
island, the ocean there is difficult to navigate to this day and can hardly
be explored.

In *Critias* (114) Plato goes on to say that the island's earliest king
was called Atlas and that it was he who gave the island and the whole
ocean their names. His twin brother was given the extreme tip of
the island near the Pillars of Heracles and opposite the Gadeiran
region—hence Gadeiros, his name in the language of the country.

So Atlantis can only be located somewhere *in front of* the
Pillars of Heracles, i.e. to the west of Gibraltar, not in the Mediterranean but on the Atlantic coast in the area of Gades, the present-
day town of Cádiz, and the "Gadeiran region" must therefore be
assumed to be somewhere north of it.

The writers of antiquity rarely gave entirely imaginary geographical details or ones which were completely at odds with the
facts because they had a highly developed sense of topography.
From the time Schliemann excavated Troy and Evans unearthed
Knossos, modern archaeology has repeatedly supplied proof that
the directions of ancient writers can be followed, and that even
poetically embellished topographical allusions were not entirely
fabricated. It is dangerous therefore to dismiss Plato's accounts as
pure fantasy, especially in an age when sensational archaeological discoveries have been made on the basis of ancient sources. Apart
from that, well-known geographical details are rarely tacked onto
a purely imaginary location. The "Gadeiran region," the Pillars of
Heracles and the words "without, there lies this real sea" are relatively precise directions, which is why German scholars as meticu-

lous as Richard Henning and Adolf Schulten have insisted that Plato's description of Atlantis is based on concrete facts.

The late Professor Schulten devoted fifty years of his life to an historical and archaeological study of Spain. In 1940, on his seventieth birthday, the University of Barcelona bestowed an honorary doctorate on him. He also received the highest Spanish decoration for cultural services, the Grand Cross of the Order of Alfonso X.

While reading Appian's *Iberica* one night in Göttingen during the winter of 1901-02, Schulten was struck by the detailed description of the siege of Numantia by Publius Cornelius Scipio in the year 133 B.C. As soon as an opportunity presented itself, Schulten set off for the Douro, where he carefully scrutinized a hill near its banks. At 2 P.M. on August 12, 1905, he and his six laborers began to dig, and four hours later he had discovered Nurmantia, the lost Iberian city which people had been vainly seeking for centuries. By autumn 1908 Schulten had also excavated Scipio's seven camps. He published his archaeological findings in five volumes, wrote a geographical, ethnographical and historical survey of the Iberian Peninsula and a study of Iberian customs, edited twelve volumes of classical references to the peninsula complete with Spanish commentary, and wrote a book about the Etruscan city of Tarragona. He also identified Atlantis with the city of Tartessus.

In order to prove that Tartessus and Atlantis were identical, we must first examine what is known of Tartessus and establish the possible location of the city or country of that name.

All sources indicate that Tartessus should be sought in the south or southwest of Spain; that is to say, in modern Andalusia. Andalusia has always been and still is to this day the richest part of the Iberian Peninsula. Indeed, classical authors regarded it as the richest country in the world. Baetica, as Andalusia used to be called, was praised for its fertility by Pliny about A.D. 100. Posidonius has left us a description of Tartessus preserved in the first and second chapters of Strabo's third book.

Posidonius tells us that the banks of the Baetis (the Guadalquivir's original name) were densely populated, and that the river was navigable for 1,200 stadia (135 miles), from the sea to Córdoba and a little beyond. The land near the river was intensively cultivated. Posidonius mentions olive groves and large plantations, and tells us that "Turdetania" was extremely rich in exportable goods such as wax, honey, pitch and ruddle. Ships were built of indigenous wood, and there was an abundance of oysters, mussels and fish. Turdetania and the adjoining regions were particularly rich in metals; in very few places in the ancient world were gold, silver, copper and iron available in such quantity or quality. Posidonius goes on to describe the extraction of gold, silver, copper and tin. Even though we read his reports at second hand in Strabo, the latter's pages are illuminated by the lively style of the original. The wealth of Tartessus lay principally in the mountains of Andalusia, the Sierra Morena, whose mineral resources are still not exhausted at the present day. Strabo gives some almost incredible details of the Iberian El Dorado, a place where Phoenician sailors exchanged their leaden anchors for anchors of silver, and whose precious metals found their way into the treasuries at Olympia and Delphi. Southern Spain is the home of one of the oldest mining industries in the Western world. It was probably in the valley of the Baetis, near the copper mines of Río Tinto, that copper was first alloyed with tin to make bronze. And Tartessus was a metropolis which stood by the sea somewhere in the estuary of the Guadalquivir. It was the predecessor of Seville and an international seaport like Lisbon, Bordeaux, Antwerp, Hamburg or London.

The city was founded about 1150 B.C. by seafarers from the ancient Lydian city of Tursa, which, incidentally, is not to be confused with Tyre, the famous Phoenician port on the Mediterranean coast of what is now Syria. Gades, present-day Cádiz, was established by the Phoenicians as a trading station on the southwest coast of Spain.

Tursa, on the other hand, has vanished from the face of the earth. This is a great misfortune, because if we could find and excavate Tursa we might have a clearer idea of where the Etruscans came from, for the Tyrseni or Tyrrheni, Strabo tells us, were the race whom we know by the later, Roman, name Etruscans. Strabo adds that the Tyrrhenians were of Lydian stock and came from Asia Minor. Lydia occupied the center of modern Turkey's southern coast and bordered the Aegean. Being a Tyrrhenian colony, Tartessus thus belonged to the Etruscan world. One of the kings of Tartessus was called Arganthonius, a name which in the late Professor Schulten's opinion is connected with the Etruscan name *arcnti*.

Moreover, Andalusia has a number of Etruscan place names which come from the Lydian home of the Tyrrhenians. We read in the Old Testament of the kings of Tarshish and the ships of Tarshish, noblest of harbors. "The ships of Tarshish did sing of thee in thy market: and thou wast replenished, and made very glorious in the midst of the seas," writes Ezekiel: xxvii, 25.

The year A.D. 400 saw the appearance of an important work by Rufus Festus Avienus, a Roman aristocrat and author who described, for the benefit of a friend, the shores of the Mediterranean from Spain to the Black Sea. Avienus was a student of ancient geography, so his picture of these coasts, countries and islands was not a contemporary one but based as far as possible on ancient sources. Thus for his description of the Spanish coast he used a report by a Greek sailor from Massilia (Marseilles) who undertook a voyage from Tartessus to Massilia in 530 B.C. His account is of inestimable value, for he gives a description of the west coast of Europe, then regarded as the edge of the world, from Gibraltar to the far north. In it we find the first recorded mention of Albion (England) and references to Oestrymnis (Brittany), the island of Ierne (Ireland) and the countries of the North Sea, renowned for their amber.

The Greek seaman from Massilia also described the legendary city of Tartessus, which apparently stood on the west coast of Spain somewhere near the place where the Guadalquivir joins the sea. There is a description of the Tartessus River, i.e. the Guadalquivir, from its mouth to the "Mountain of Silver." Tartessus ruled large tracts of the west coast of Spain and its influence extended deep inland to the metal-rich Sierra Morena. The inhabitants of Tartessus evolved what was probably the most advanced civilization in the contemporary Western world.

Wandering through the Andalusian countryside today, one realizes how magnificent a past the cities of southern Spain once enjoyed, how rich the country still is, and with what uncanny clarity the culture of Tartessus still emerges from the numerous objects on show in museums there.

Did this ancient and still undiscovered city really stand at the mouth of the Guadalquivir, or is Tartessus identical with modern Seville? Was it, in any case, the fabulously wealthy metropolis which Plato called Atlantis?

In the next chapter we shall endeavor to find out.

CITY BENEATH THE SANDS

And so, by assembling all manner of riches in their country, the inhabitants of Atlantis built temples, palaces for kings, harbors and dry docks, and in addition developed the whole of the rest of the country. They built bridges across the curved inlets that enclosed their native city and so opened up a road to the royal residence and to the outside. Each king inherited the palace from his predecessor and enhanced what his predecessor had already invested with such splendor.

—PLATO, *Critias*, 115c

IN EARLIER times—and until about 500 B.C.—there lay not far from the estuary of the Guadalquivir a lake known in the ancient world as the Lacus Ligustinus. In those days the river flowed from the lake in three channels, forming several islands or one large island in the estuary. We learn from Strabo and from Pausanias' works on travel that later on, between 500 and 100 B.C., the river's outlets were reduced to two in number because the central channel had become silted up.

Today the old Lacus Ligustinus is a marsh and the northern outlet of the Guadalquivir is also silted up and unrecognizable save as a chain of lagoons. If the island formed by the channels in the estuary of the Guadalquivir was the Atlantis described by Plato in *Critias* and *Timaeus*, a number of things become clear: the floods mentioned by Plato; the fact that Atlantis or part of Atlantis "vanished into the sea"; the "deep mud" and the "submerged remnants of the Island." We can also understand why people have been searching vainly for the island for two thousand years. The Guadalquivir leaves the marsh by only one channel now, so the island no longer exists.

Professor Adolf Schulten hit upon the brilliant notion that the lost city of Tartessus and ancient Atlantis were identical. He suggested that the city lay on the island formerly delineated by the channels of the Guadalquivir—not on the sea side but a mile or two inland in the hunting grounds now known as the Coto de Dona Ana.

Schulten pointed to the existence of a number of parallels between the city of Tartessus and the city described by Plato.

Tartessus

Plato's Atlantis extended as far as Gades, so Tartessus must have been somewhere in the immediate vicinity of Cádiz.

According to *Critias*, the Atlantides' capital stood on an island enclosed by a triple ring of water: Tartessus stood on an island between the three mouths of the Baetis, the modern Guadalquivir.

Atlantis was not actually on the coast but stood on a connecting channel or estuary nearly six miles inland: Tartessus stood on an island just over six miles north of Sanlúcar, a town in the estuary of the Guadalquivir which serves as an export center for the famous wine of Manzanilla. The former island may have extended either farther into the Atlantic or farther inland, but the vanished city itself may be assumed to have stood about six miles from the coast in an area which has been greatly altered by the formation of marshes.

We read in *Critias* that there was a "moat" one stadium wide (roughly 200 yards) which split into two arms enclosing a plain longer than it was broad: the Guadalquivir, whose average width at this point is 220 yards, flowed through a long plain, divided at Tartessus, and then flowed into the sea.

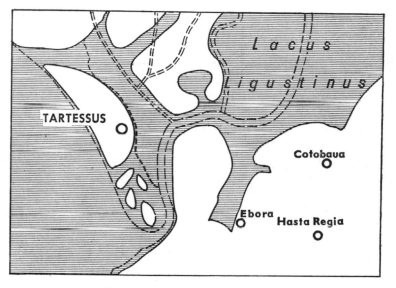

Tartessus used to stand on an island.

We also read in *Critias* that the plain was threaded with canals, and Strabo describes a similar system of oblique canals in the valley of the Guadalquivir. Plato's account is extremely precise and for that reason unlikely to be mere invention. The ancient river-mouth cities of the Mediterranean seldom installed canal networks of this kind, but many such canals have been found on the Atlantic coast.

The wealth of Atlantis was reputedly so great that it has never been rivaled before or since: Tartessus was not only the wealthiest city in the West but one of the richest cities in the whole of the contemporary world, and its store of precious metals must have been fabulous. *Critias* mentions that silver, gold, iron and copper were the chief sources of the Atlantides' wealth, a description which would have applied equally well to the city on the Spanish coast.

The sacred bulls mentioned by Plato are an equally consistent feature, for the bull was a sacred animal in ancient Iberia. The cult of the bull probably came to Spain from Crete and the Cretan art of bull vaulting later became transformed into the bullfight.

Atlantis was a great maritime empire whose influence extended to Egypt and Tyrrhenia, or western Italy: Tartessus must have been the most powerful maritime power of its day, for the ships of Tarshish penetrated deep into the Mediterranean and sailed as far north as Scotland and perhaps even farther.

According to *Critias* the Atlantides used the river that linked them with the sea as a harbor: the inhabitants of Tartessus lived on the landward side of their island and used the Baetis as their access to the sea, just as the city of Seville, some thirty-eight miles up the Guadalquivir, does today.

The people of Atlantis were in contact with the "islands of the ocean" and, via these islands, with the "mainland opposite" (*Timaeus*). We do not know if Plato was referring to the islands of Brittany or to England or even to the American continent, but sea voyages to continents and islands must have been made by the ships of Tarshish mentioned in the Old Testament.

The Atlantides' chief sanctuary was a temple by the sea dedicated to Poseidon. In this temple stood a pillar of *oreichalkos* or brass on which were engraved the laws of Poseidon and other official records. The geographer Strabo tells us that Tartessus had prose records, poems and laws which were six thousand years old. Both Schulten and Niebuhr before him recognized the advanced nature of Tartessus' civilization. Its inhabitants seem to have been among the most intellectually active people in Europe between 1100 and 500 B.C.

Atlantis was a kingdom, a great metropolis whose industries, trade, bustling activity, docks, large-scale bronze industry, warehouses and temple of Poseidon made it a jewel in the crown of the ancient world. The vanished city of Tartessus must also have been ruled by kings, for we know two of their names: Geron and Arganthonius. According to Avienus, Tartessus once possessed a royal citadel known as the Arx Gerontis, and Plato tells us of a similar fortress.

Finally, we know from *Timaeus* and *Critias* that the island of Atlantis, having enjoyed a long prime, was suddenly engulfed by the sea during an earthquake. There are two interpretations of Plato's story. He may have been referring either to the destruction of the mysterious city of Tartessus by the Carthaginians in 500 B.C., or to the fact that the whole area became waterlogged and two of the three channels of the Guadalquivir dried up.

Adolf Schulten was convinced Atlantis should be equated with Tartessus. When I visited the elderly scholar at Erlangen in 1956 he advised me to dig, or encourage someone else to dig, on the former island in the Coto de Dona Ana. There was sadness in his voice, for his own excavations there had been unsuccessful and although he yearned for his beloved Spain, he felt too old at eighty-six to travel and try again.

Between 1922 and 1926 Schulten explored the extensive Coto de Dona Ana hunting preserves in company with General Lammerer. At the close of their investigations, Lammerer wrote: "There is no doubt that in early antiquity a sandy island some 18 kilometers long lay obliquely in front of the estuary of the Guadalquivir, which was then wider and more lakelike. The banks of the two arms through which the waters of the Guadalquivir used to flow into the sea could be distinguished from the surrounding countryside with considerable accuracy."

Schulten, who was the first to explore this area for relics of Tartessus, had already spent some time in 1910 combing the shore. In 1922 he discovered a Roman settlement at Cerro de Trigo, nearly four miles north of Marismilla, where he unearthed walls and a number of Roman amphorae. More extensive excavations carried out between 1923 and 1926 revealed that the Roman settlement covered an area measuring about 200 by 750 yards. On October 4, 1923, Schulten found beneath a Roman house a stone on which lay a copper ring with a Greek inscription on its inner and outer circumference. The inscription read, roughly: *Owner, be fortunate!* or *Guard the ring well!* Schulten concurred with Professor Rehm in assuming that the inscription was extremely ancient and dated from the sixth or even the seventh century B.C.—the days of Greek voyages to Tartessus.

The Roman settlement dated from A.D. 200–400 and had been inhabited by fishermen. The finds made there included about twenty graves, late Roman pottery and amphorae for wine and oil. Indeed, everything was of Roman origin except the ring. Since groundwater starts at five feet in this area, no deeper excavations could be carried out. A few boreholes sunk to a depth of twenty feet yielded no trace of any older ruins, but Schulten's view was that the stones of the Roman fishing village were originally brought partly from the district of Huelva and partly from Cádiz. Considering that the town of Sanlúcar was already in existence when the Romans erected their village, one is tempted to wonder why the fisherfolk did not get their stones from there, and this leads one to infer that building materials were available nearer at hand, namely in the ruins of Tartessus. The people of Tartessus may have brought them by ship from the area of Huelva and Cádiz, ultimately to be reused by Roman fishermen 700 years after their city had collapsed in ruins!

Schulten believed that the fishing village was located on the very site of ancient Tartessus, that it was built of materials taken from the ruins of Tartessus, and that the latter have been at least partly absorbed by the village. It is well known that many ancient cities were built of rubble taken from even more ancient settlements. At any rate, what Plato says about the location of his Atlantic city is remarkably consistent with the site which Schulten excavated without success.

Tartessus flourished for 600 years, from 1100 B.C. until its destruction in 500 B.C., yet people have been searching for it for two thousand years. Schulten told me that he thought borings made fifteen feet or more beneath the Roman settlement could well prove informative. Further excavations would have to be pursued with the latest technical aids, although to clear an area of any size would be a costly business and powerful pumps would be needed to drain off the groundwater. Schulten insisted that Tartessus lay buried somewhere beneath the dunes of the Marismilla. If these dunes were already covering—and therefore protecting—the ruined city in ancient times there was a distinct hope that sizable remnants of Tartessus might some day be unearthed.

There is an eerie stillness about the place today. It is a wilderness of pines, dunes and marshy tracts inhabited by deer, boar and rabbits, a paradise for the successive owners of the hunting rights. Somewhere in the solitude of the Marismas, Tartessus has slept for 2,500 years. The broad ribbon of the Guadalquivir flows slowly down to the Atlantic through an infinity of reddish dunes to mingle its yellow waters with those of the vast ocean beyond....

But Tartessus is not the only famous estuary city to have vanished. Somewhere on the coast of Lucania, for example, Sybaris lies buried beneath the alluvial deposits of the ancient river Crathis. Digging is equally difficult there because groundwater begins at a depth of six feet. Yet the city was so wealthy and its inhabitants so pampered and fastidious that the "sybaritic life" has become proverbial.

It was tragic that Schulten should have failed in his attempt to wrest Tartessus from its millennial sleep. He was a true scholar, not a visionary, as is shown by his discovery and excavation of Numantia, Scipio's camps and numerous other Spanish sites.

But Tartessus was not just a city; it was also the capital of a country whose culture is the greatest single archaeological discovery of the past twenty years. The kingdom of Tartessus embraced the whole of southern Spain, notably Andalusia, Granada and Murcia. Professor Schulten was aware of this before he died, and described the kingdom and its culture as "a marvelous historical phenomenon."

Tartessus was the earliest city-state in the pre-Roman West, and ruled over towns inhabited by an Iberian, that is to say, pre-Phoenician and pre-Roman, population. The aristocrats of Tartessus referred to their Iberian subjects as Turdetanians.

The men of Tartessus must have been lordly beings not unlike the Spanish noblemen who live in the region today. They loved hunting, wine and sailing, and owned serfs like their Italian cousins the Etruscans. We learn from Justin that King Gargoris of Tartessus was held to be the originator of beekeeping.

Traveling through the south of Spain, through Jerez, Cádiz, Seville, Córdoba, Granada and Cartagena, one can still sense something of the spirit of this proud and ancient seafaring race. Iberians, Etruscans, Phoenicians, Celts, Greeks and Romans all contributed to the creation of a unique culture in Tartessus. Its works of art invariably betray the artistic influence of one or another of these races to a greater or lesser degree, yet the characteristically "Tartessian" quality nearly always predominates. The cultural heritage of Tartessus still makes itself felt today. Life in the south has a brisk, vital flavor born of nearness to the sea. Heir to Tartessus, Seville boasts the hottest summers in Europe and the loveliest springs, warm autumns and mild winters, subtropical palms and magnificent gardens that still blaze with color in October, enchanting patios with little fountains and drowsy nooks. Seville is dominated by one of the largest and most elaborate Gothic cathedrals in existence. In Seville one can see how a minaret in the principal Moorish mosque has become transformed into a Christian campanile, the 305-foot-high Giralda, and in Seville Cathedral one can stand before the tomb of Europe's greatest explorer, the discoverer of the New World, whose remains are said to lie in the sarcophagus which was brought back to Seville from Cuba after the island's secession in 1898.

The narrow old streets of southern Spain are lined with shops and craftsmen's establishments very like those of ancient Rome and Carthage. The bodegas and halls of Jerez still serve dry wines like those that were drunk there 3,000 years ago, and southern Spain offers the finest lobsters, cuttlefish, mussels and other more exotic varieties of seafood prepared much as the people of Tartessus must have prepared them more than 2,500 years before.

The air is filled with the roar of the breakers as they pound at the jutting rocks around Cádiz, erstwhile center of the tin and copper trade, whose walls tower as much as fifty feet into the sky. And if one listens, in the thunder of the waves, one can almost hear the ocean singing the ancient song of vanished Atlantis.

THE CIVILIZATION OF TARTESSUS

Written sources define the greatest incentive for the long voyages made by foreign traders to the Iberian Peninsula as the riches of the city of Tartessus, gateway to the whole of Southern Iberia from the Portuguese Algarve to the territories of the Mastians, where the Punians later established the colony of Nova Carthago. Tartessus was the center of an area rich in mines, cattle and agriculture. The power of attraction which Tartessus must once have exerted can be inferred from the location of the Phoenician colonies on the Andalusian coast and from the Greeks' attempt to establish themselves at Mainake, near present-day Malaga. The discoveries of the past few years—the Valdegamas jug, the Carriazo bronze and others—present us with an enthralling problem whose solution could well confirm the picture of Tartessus given by the authors of antiquity. In the people of Tartessus and the Turdetanians, their successors, they saw a people with an old and major civilization which had expressed itself in their literature, urban life and social order.

—ANTONIO BLANCO FREIJEIRO, Madrid

WRITING in the year 1761, a Swedish scholar called Johan Podolyn related a strange experience. While staying in Madrid he had met a certain Father Florez, a distinguished numismatist with a thorough knowledge of his subject. The priest showed Podolyn some rare coins which had been found in the Azores and went so far as to present him with a few. What Podolyn learned subsequently was to shed an interesting light on sea travel in 400 B.C.

One day in November, 1749, a violent Atlantic storm was battering the coasts of the Azores. On the beaches of Corvo, a small island only seven square miles in extent, the waves undermined a stone building and demolished it, revealing a black clay vessel. It was smashed to pieces, but among the fragments a quantity of coins was found. Taken to Lisbon, they were later forwarded to Madrid, where Father Florez had already made his name as a numismatist.

In those days, when archaeology was not as well-founded and reputable a science as it is now, the majority of such finds were lost. And, in fact, only nine pieces reached Madrid: two Carthaginian gold coins and seven copper coins of which five were Carthaginian and two Cyrenaican.

The Azores are generally supposed to have been discovered by the Portuguese between 1430 and 1460, but the island group must have been known earlier, since we find it sketched in on a few early medieval maps. Certainly, sailors had landed in the Azores before the reign of Alfonso the Magnanimous (1416–1458). In fact, amazing as it seems, Punic ships from Carthage must have reached the islands at the end of the fourth century B.C. It is well known that the Phoenicians were the greatest navigators of the pre-Christian era. Nevertheless, the Azores lie more than 1,100 miles out in the Atlantic Ocean, west of Gibraltar, and the fact that the primitive ships of the time could have made such a voyage casts an entirely new light on the range of Phoenician sea travel.

Some authorities, notably Alexander von Humboldt, have suggested that the coins were brought to Corvo in the Middle Ages by Vikings or Arabs, but there is no evidence that Vikings or Arabs ever put in at the Azores. Then, too, it is far more likely that the coins were brought to the islands when they were still accepted currency, or they would not have been so carefully hidden. Professor Richard Hennig, who wrote an interesting work on the subject in 1927, concluded that there was absolutely no doubt that the Azores were visited by Carthaginians. One strange feature is that the Punic-Phoenician mariners should have put in at the most remote, most northwesterly, smallest and least fertile island in the whole group. It is possible that they were cast up on the beach by a storm or were heading for countries even farther west—North or South America, perhaps. We do not know, but we can assume that they either meant to return and collect their buried hoard or never left the island at all, otherwise they would probably have taken the coins with them. Since the prevailing current flows in the direction of the Strait of Gibraltar, it is unlikely that a derelict would have been cast up from the eastern quarter. The ship which carried the coins must, therefore, have been manned. Having sailed from Madeira, Porto Santo, some port on the coast of southern Spain, or even from Carthage itself, it had traversed an immense distance, perhaps 1,250 miles. Such, at least, was the remarkable story told by the nine mute and abandoned coins.

Mysterious inscriptions in an unknown tongue were said to have been found with the coins, or so J. Mees reported at Ghent in 1901,

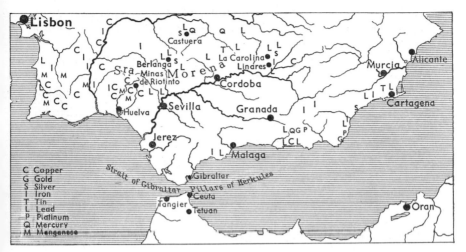

Southern Spain

but the engraved tablets have disappeared, whereas Podolyn's original account at least contained illustrations of the coins.

In the year 1628 a work dealing with Portuguese discoveries in the Azores was published at Madrid. The author, Manoel de Faria e Sousa, reported that the Portuguese had discovered an equestrian statue on a promontory on one of the islands. The mounted figure, which was pointing westward, was thought to be an effigy of a heathen deity, and the Portuguese promptly destroyed it in an excess of religious zeal. Perhaps the Carthaginians had undertaken a daring voyage farther westward and the statue, whose pedestal bore an inscription, was intended to commemorate it.

We know that the Phoenician Tyrians founded the city of Gadir (modern Cádiz) about 1100 B.C., but no archaeological finds older than circa 700 B.C. have been made in the area. We also know that somewhat to the north of Cádiz was the metal-trading center of Tartessus, a place which in those days enjoyed almost legendary renown and was inhabited by people of great artistic ability. Here again, our only relics of these people go back no farther than 700 or 800 B.C. What makes the location of these two mysterious cities so interesting is that Cádiz was a Phoenician commercial center, whereas the vanished city of Tartessus was an Etruscan-Tyrrhenian metropolis. Thus, two centers of international trade belonging to two very different cultures were situated quite close together. Only sixty miles of coastline separates Cádiz from the estuary of the Guadalquivir, where Tartessus is assumed to have stood.

Until the vanished city, market or harbor of Tartessus is actually located we shall never know for certain whether Tartessus was only a market place or harbor at the mouth of the Guadalquivir, whether the real capital stood farther inland, or whether the name Tartessus was applied to the whole kingdom. Nevertheless, the fact that our only evidence of the antiquity of the great Tartessus civilization consists of written traditions and that archaeological finds belonging to that civilization are of more recent date does not disprove the existence of the kingdom of Tartessus.

The Spanish authority Antonio García y Bellido has emphasized that written accounts given in ancient sources may deserve credence even if no archaeological evidence is forthcoming, and that the absence of such evidence is not sufficient reason to discount written traditions. For instance, Odysseus' palace has never been discovered, but this does not mean that Homer's assertion that it was in Ithaca is incorrect. We have found no tangible evidence of the Spaniards' march across the Andes, through Patagonia and the Amazon jungle in the sixteenth century, yet we know that it took place. The daring Spanish explorers Loaisa, Queirós, Mendaña and Torres left nothing behind on the islands of the Pacific, but we know that they visited them. The Vikings who landed on the Atlantic coast of America in the eleventh century left few archaeologically identifiable traces, but we know that their voyages to the west are an historical fact. Any settlement has to survive a number of storms, has to thrive and eat its way into the ground if it is not eventually to be blotted out by the passage of time. A myriad traces of human existence have been swallowed up by the past, and where natural catastrophes, floods, tidal waves and earthquakes have taken their toll the sites of whole cities can easily become lost beyond all hope of rediscovery.

So it is a reasonable assumption that the Phoenicians were already in the far west, in Spain and perhaps even in the Azores before the eighth or ninth century B.C., and that the Tyrrhenians were living in the city and kingdom of Tartessus at an even earlier date.

In this connection, mention should be made of some people who were in contact with Tartessus and whose domain extended far into the north, to Ireland and the fjords of Norway. These were the

Ostimians, principal trading partners (after the Phoenicians) of the people of Tartessus and spiritual ancestors of the Frisians, Saxons, Vikings, Dutch and English. Avienus tells us that the Ostimians were a seafaring race renowned for their hardiness, daring and commercial enterprise.

It is interesting to note that the Ostimians used large leather-covered boats. This kind of vessel, which is possibly the earliest type of boat in the world, appears to have been known along the entire Atlantic coast from Portugal to the North Sea. The Celtologist Julius Pokorny informed me that leather boats were also used by the pre-Celtic inhabitants of Ireland and that the aboriginal Irish were known to the Celts as *Fir-bolg*, or "people of the hide-boats." Dio Cassius, an historian of the imperial age of Rome, stated that the coastal peoples of the Western Ocean were using leather boats in his day (xlvii, 18). We do not know if the people of Tartessus used leather boats of this kind because both wood and leather would have disintegrated in the course of more than 2,500 years. Much older boats have survived in Egypt, of course, but only because they were funerary ships carefully preserved as cult objects in massive stone chambers. The "ships of Tarshish," by contrast, formed a commercial link between places hundreds if not thousands of miles apart and have vanished into the void, either sunk at sea or burned or destroyed in unidentified ports and harbors throughout the ancient world. We are told that vessels like these could cover 1,200 stadia (about 135 miles) in twenty-four hours. This not only indicates that the people of Tartessus possessed sailing ships but is consistent with Avienus' reference to the fact that a ship entering Tagus Bay needed first a westerly and then a southerly wind.

Such relics of the Tartessus culture as have been found in the past few decades are interesting principally because they are a late reflection of a rich and glorious past. Anyone who sees them will realize that they date from the evening of a splendid civilization.

On September 30, 1958, workmen on a building site on the hill of El Carambolo near Seville came upon a priceless hoard consisting of necklaces, armbands, pendants, breast ornaments and plates which had once formed a crown or belt. These objects, all made of gold and twenty-one in number, were evidently the product of a highly developed goldsmith's technique. Professor Antonio Blanco has suggested that some of the decorative motifs on these articles of adornment correspond with those found on Mycenaean vases, ivory gaming boards from Megiddo and mural paintings in the Assyrian and Syrian palaces of Khorsabad, Arslan Tash and Tell Barsib. Yet nowhere else in the world have pieces of jewelry quite like these come to light!

Kukahn and Blanco believe that the gold plates are more likely to have been components of a crown than a belt. Similar pieces have been found in an ancient grave in Cyprus, so it is thought that the idea of this type of ornamentation may have come from there. The necklace bears a series of punched impressions reminiscent of the Phoenician-Punian culture. Despite all these influences, however, the El Carambolo cache is evidence of an independent and creative goldsmith's art in the southern part of the Iberian Peninsula, evidence of a Tartessus culture which, in the words of the eminent Spanish scholar mentioned above, "is daily becoming more tangible." The articles of adornment found at El Carambolo are attributed to the sixth century B.C. and were deliberately hidden by someone who scooped out a cavity in the side of the hill and buried them in a vessel of some kind. Another who concurs with this view is the Spanish professor J. Maluquer, who thinks that in pre-Christian times a small house or hut stood on the site of the discovery and that it was later destroyed by fire.

1953 saw the discovery near Don Benito of a bronze wine jug which, once again in the words of Antonio Blanco, surpassed in beauty all vessels of this type found in the Iberian Peninsula so far. A farm laborer had turned up the jug while plowing a field on the Valdegamas estate, which adjoins Don Benito. Having no conception of the value of his find, the peasant threw the jug onto a pile of firewood. However, after further plowing had revealed the remains of a house with four rooms of varying sizes less than eighteen inches beneath the soil, and after fragments of pottery had come to light among the ruined walls, it was realized that the site had once been a settlement. The Donoso Cortés family, who owns the Valdegamas estate, took the bronze jug into safekeeping. Professor Blanco has identified its style as part Greek, part Phoenician, and attributes it with a fair degree of certainty to the sixth century B.C. But where did it come from? Was it manufactured by the Phoenicians of Gadir or imported from some center of bronze industry outside Spain, or may the birthplace of such wine jugs have been Etruria in Italy?

By the Guadalquivir near Sanlúcar de Barrameda lie the fields of Évora. Some Spanish scholars believe this region to be the site of the vanished city of Tartessus, and we have already heard that Professor Schulten of Erlangen placed it only six miles or so to the north on the Coto de Dona Ana. Be that as it may, the fields of Évora probably conceal the Roman town of Ebora, which, like so many thousands of buried settlements, remains unexcavated to this day. An eight-year-old boy, Francisco Bejarano, found a number of gold ornaments in freshly plowed soil there and took them to his father. The articles were soon sold, but the owner of the field alerted the police and the police confiscated the little hoard in the interests of archaeology. Unfortunately, six of the priceless pieces had already been melted down and beaten into wedding rings, while the remainder had been acquired by a silver dealer for 2,565 pesetas. The Spanish archaeologist Concepción Blanco de Torrecillas reports that the cache now consists of forty-seven pieces, richly ornamented and all of pure gold. A few of them have been bent by the pressure of the earth and most have lost their inset stones. All of them—armbands, earrings, rings, diadem components, necklace and pendants—appear to date from the fifth century B.C. Once again there is evidence of part-Greek, part-Oriental-Phoenician influence, and once again it is uncertain whether these fine pieces were imported or manufactured by an indigenous goldsmith. They may even, so de Torrecillas believes, have originated at the court of King Arganthonius of Tartessus.

In the words of de Torrecillas: "If one knew for certain that Tartessus lay unrecognized in the heart of the Évora Estate one would be able to make some extremely interesting excavations there. But, even though the city still preserves its anonymity, the hoard recently found there has brought fresh confirmation of earlier suppositions about the splendor and advanced culture of this legendary metropolis, whose walls cannot be far to seek."

On February 29, 1920, laborers found a cache of jewelry in a jar buried only three feet beneath the ground at La Aliseida on the northern slopes of the San Pedro Range. They had evidently uncovered the burial place of an Iberian noblewoman, for the presence of 194 small dress ornaments implied that the dress itself was once buried there. Among the fine examples of goldsmith's work in the cache were a gold headband used for keeping a veil in place, a gold diadem, gold earrings, armbands, a 53-piece necklace and a 62-piece belt of very skilled workmanship—articles which would grace the window of a modern jeweler.

De Torrecillas, who is a director of the Museum of Archaeology at Cádiz, showed me a sarcophagus which has raised a number of archaeological problems. It is a marble coffin shaped to fit the human body, and contained the remains of a distinguished nobleman. Coffins of this type are known as anthropoid sarcophagi and this particular archaeological relic is known in Spain as the Sidonian Sarcophagus. P. Bosch-Gimpera states that it is of genuine Phoenician workmanship but betrays the stylistic influences of Egypt and ancient Greece. The bearded and majestic features of the prince show him to have been a man of truly royal mien with certain Semitic traits. The interior of the marble coffin still contained his body. Was he brought posthumously from Phoenicia in one of the famous ships of Tarshish? Was he a king of Gadir who wished to be interred in his native soil? We may never know, but we can at least see in this magnificent piece of fifth- or fourth-century B.C. Phoenician workmanship the links that once bound the seagirt fortress of Cádiz to the ancient Orient.

The most interesting archaeological discovery made in southern Spain and probably the most valuable work of art found in the whole Iberian Peninsula is still the so-called Lady of Elche. Elche (the Ilici of ancient Iberia) is near Alicante and has an even warmer climate than the latter town. The summers are unusually hot there, even though the place is only ten miles from the Mediterranean coast. It is also the site of Europe's largest palm grove. One hundred and seventy thousand of these trees, many of them well over 100 feet high, stand "foot in water, head in the fire of the sky," as an Arabic proverb has it, artificially irrigated by water brought from over three miles away.

The Lady of Elche was unearthed in 1897. It is a remarkably beautiful bust sculpted in chalky limestone, and is twenty inches high. Traces of color indicate that the figure was once painted all over. The pupils of the eyes were probably filled with molten glass. Since the figure was found in a burial ground, it was at first assumed that the Lady of Elche (also known in Spain as the Reina Mora) was an effigy of a dead woman decked out in her ceremonial finery. However, Professor Blanco says that "her expression reflects an

encounter between the human and the divine" and believes that the
unique figure may have been a goddess.

I have inspected the sculpture closely in the little room on the
lower floor of the Prado where it has reappeared after being bought
by the French and then returned to the Spaniards. The longer one
looks at this pre-Christian Madonna the more the beauty and
serenity of her features work their uncanny spell. The head ornaments and the heavy chains on her breast are, so it is believed,
intended to represent metals such as bronze, silver or gold. I went
to the Instituto Valencia de Don Juan, a little-frequented museum
elsewhere in Madrid, in order to compare gold ear pendants and
jewelry in a showcase there with the sculpted ornaments on the
Lady of Elche. The similarity was so striking that I was left convinced that the originals of the jewelry on the finest ancient sculpture
in Spain were gold.

Even though both Greek and Punic stylistic traits can be discerned
in the figure, it still remains a genuinely Spanish "Mona Lisa."
Sculpted some 2,500 years ago, it fits Strabo's descriptions of what
the women of ancient Spain wore in the way of jewelry. The circular ornaments on either side of the head are, in Blanco's opinion,
decorative disks of silver similar to fragments of other ornaments
from Estremadura which he found in the Museum of Archaeology
at Madrid. Since they were of a type worn in an artificially enhanced coiffure they may have been partially formed by the hair
itself. When the girls of Valencia turn out in their old native costumes today they wear a similarly elaborate hair style with so-called
"snails" on either side of the head. Twenty-five thousand years are
a mere drop in the ocean of human history and prehistory. Perhaps
the girls danced as passionately in the kingdom of Tartessus more
than two and a half millennia ago as they do in the south of Spain
today.

THE GUANCHES

Since I wished to know more about the Satyrs I talked of them with many people. Euphenos of Caria told me that on the journey to Italy he was blown off course by a storm and driven into the outer sea, where no one ever ventures as a rule. There, he said, are many desert islands and other islands inhabited by savage people. They had not wanted to land because they had been there and encountered the inhabitants on an earlier occasion, but once again they were forced to put ashore. These islands were called the "Satyrides" by the sailors. The inhabitants are fiery red and have tails on their hind quarters as big as those of horses. They came to the ship when they saw it, uttering not a sound but laying hands on the ship's womenfolk. In their fear, the sailors eventually marooned a barbarian woman, on whom the Satyrs took their pleasure.

—PAUSANIAS, I, xxiii, 5 and 6

IN THE Atlantic, only fifty miles off the coast of the Spanish Sahara, lie the Canaries, a group of islands formed by volcanic eruption, blessed with pure air and healthy northwest sea winds, crowned by mountains as high as 11,000 feet, richly endowed with an abundance of geraniums, lilies, dahlias and roses, figs, olives, sugar cane and bananas, bathed in radiant sunshine throughout most of the year and well provided with pure springwater. The thirteen small islands lie scattered across the ocean for a distance of more than 300 miles, with Madeira another 300 miles farther away to the north.

The Canary group was known in ancient times as the Islands of the Blest, and the islands and their fortunate inhabitants provided a favorite theme for historians, geographers and poets. Plutarch may have described them as the Atlantides but we do not know if he was really referring to the Canary Islands. Gaius Plinius Secundus (Pliny the Elder), who was born in A.D. 23 and lost his life during an eruption of Vesuvius in A.D. 79, mentioned the islands in his work on natural history, which he entitled *Naturalis Historia*. Pliny had gleaned his information about these distant islands from a certain Statius Sebosus and the works of Juba, the Numidian king of Mauretania, who lived between 50 B.C. and A.D. 23. Juba was brought to Rome as a boy in Caesar's triumphal procession after the latter's campaigns in Africa, and received his education there. He wrote a large number of books in the Greek language dealing with Libya, Arabia, Syria, philology, botanics and probably archaeology as well.

Pomponius Mela from Tingentera near Gibraltar, who wrote a geography of the inhabited world in three volumes about A.D. 40, likewise mentioned the Gorgonian Islands under the name Hesperides. Homer may have visualized them as the site of the Elysian Fields to which souls retire after the death of the body to receive suitable recompense for their behavior during their lifetime. The great poet saw the Elysian meadows as the end of the world, a place where the hero Rhadamanthus dwelled, where people lived in tranquillity and bliss, where there was no snow and where mild breezes were forever wafted from the ocean to cool the inhabitants with their gentle breath.

Why should the souls of the dead have traveled westward?

The Islands of the Blest were formerly the Islands of the Dead, and all the world's oldest races visualized them at the western extremity of the inhabited world because the dead were thought to follow the course of the sun as it sank to its evening abode in the west. The people of the ancient world imagined the fields of paradise to be on geographically determinate islands: in the time of Hesiod and Homer, somewhere to the north of Spanish West Africa, i.e. the Río de Oro; and toward the end of the Roman Republic and at the beginning of the Imperial era, on Madeira and the Canary group.

Place names often have very ancient historical and ethnological associations, and the word Canaria is no exception. Some authorities trace the name back to Canaan. Pliny speaks in Book V, xv, of the Canarii people in northern Río de Oro, while the African writer Arnobius, who died circa A.D. 330, extended the scope of the name to embrace the whole group, calling them *Canariae Insulae*.

It is interesting to note that the commonest assumption is that the Canary Islands derived their name from the Latin word *canis*, "dog," because the inhabitants used to fatten hairless dogs for eating just as people did in certain of the advanced civilizations of Central America.

Canna meant tube or reed, but it is quite certain that the name has nothing to do with sugar cane, which was unknown in the ancient world. Sugar cane was introduced into southern Spain by the Arabs and did not find its way to the Canaries until later. But when the islands were conquered, sugar cane became their most important

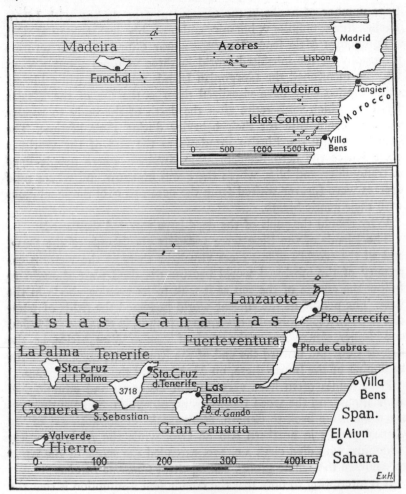

The Canary Islands

source of revenue. The conquistadors made vast fortunes from their
cane plantations and mills, and it was not until enterprising planters
introduced sugar cane into the West Indies from the Canaries that
Canary sugar was ousted from the world market by the competition
from that new source of supply.

There is probably no justification for the theory that anyone
reached America from Europe before the Vikings, but a passage in

Pausanias does hint at the possibility that someone may have been driven ashore there by a storm. Pausanias, a Greek born in Asia Minor, wrote a ten-volume *Periegesis of Greece* circa A.D. 175, which was really a cultural history containing much valuable information about the life, religion, geography and art of the ancient world. Where did Euphenos, the Carian mentioned by Pausanias (I, xxiii, 5 and 6), actually land? A storm had driven him through the Strait of Gibraltar and out into the Atlantic Ocean, to the Satyrides, islands inhabited by fire-red savages. This sounds at first as though they may have been American Indians, but it is more likely that Euphenos had encountered the inhabitants of the Canary Islands. The islanders apparently behaved in a very hostile fashion and forced their attentions on the women in the stranded ship so that the sailors got away unscathed only by leaving behind a barbarian (i.e. non-Greek) woman, whom the natives shamefully maltreated.

Probably the first men to visit the islands in more recent times were the Arabs. Putting ashore at Gando Bay, Grand Canary, in the year 999, Admiral Ben Farroukh found the local inhabitants willing to barter and trade. They told him that strangers had landed there earlier, but we shall never know who they were, nor do we know how the Arab sea captain managed to communicate with the natives, although the Arab historian Ebu Fathymah reports that he visited several of the other islands. The Arab geographer Edrisi, who lived between 1099 and 1164, tells us that observers on the African coast saw plumes of smoke issuing from two mountain peaks, and Alexander von Humboldt confirms the likelihood of this report.

The islands were also visited by other long-forgotten navigators and explorers, among them the Genoese, whose fleet landed there in 1291 but never returned. Learning that a French sailing ship had reached the islands in the year 1330, Alfonso IV of Portugal sent ships there four years later, but their crews were driven back into the sea by the natives of the island of Gomera.

The Portuguese visited the Canary Islands yet again in 1341 and brought back a great deal of information. In 1344 Pope Clement VI, who resided at Avignon, commissioned a French prince of Spanish origin, Louis de la Cerda, to sail to the mysterious islands and convert the natives there to Christianity as best he could. In 1360, missionaries landed on Grand Canary, converted a few natives and taught them one or two handicrafts, but most of the worthy men of God died a martyr's death. In the year 1393 the Spaniards dispatched an expeditionary force which contented itself with plundering the island of Lanzarote and achieved little else of consequence.

The recent history of the Canaries really begins with a Norman nobleman called Jean de Béthencourt, who sailed off into the Atlantic in 1402 with the express intention of conquering the islands. Having erected a fortress in the north of Fuerteventura, he found that his crew was not numerically strong enough to subdue the whole island, and so, leaving a small garrison behind, he sailed home to ask Henry III of Castile for more money and sailors. That was how the King of Castile succeeded in bringing Fuerteventura, Lanzarote, Gomera and Hierro under his flag.

As so often in the history of foreign conquest, the natives welcomed the strangers with great hospitality and the best of intentions. Only when they realized that the white man was chiefly interested in plunder did they turn into "savages." Béthencourt was received on the island of Gomera with the utmost friendliness, and when he sailed away the Canary Islanders swam beside his ship for miles, begging him not to leave them.

An old legend was still current on the island of Hierro according to which, when the remains of King Yore fell to dust, white houses would come from across the sea to save the people. When Béthencourt's caravels approached the island for the first time, their sails gleaming white in the distance, the archpriest hurried to the burial place of King Yore. Seeing that his bones had crumbled to dust, he at once declared that the redeemers from the sea had arrived. However, the friendly attitude of the Hierro natives soon turned to hostility. In the neighborhood of the present capital, Valverde, there stood a tree (later called El Garoe) from whose foliage water dripped in sufficient quantity to supply the whole island with drinking water. The tree may have stood by a spring. At all events, the natives camouflaged the tree and probably the spring, too, with twigs and dry grass to give the strangers the impression that there was no fresh water on the island. Inevitably, one of the island girls fell in love with a Spanish caballero and betrayed the secret. Fighting broke out, many natives were carried off as slaves, and the girl was condemned to death by her own people.

The islanders of La Palma had an old tradition that the rock known as Idafe would collapse if ever the island were conquered, and one of their prayers was: "Idafe spare us." When the Spaniards were trying to storm the interior of the island, the islanders prayed that Idafe would fall. The crag duly broke off and plunged to the ground, crushing the last heroic defenders of the island and entombing them forever. The native prince Tanausu was captured alive and taken to Spain, but died of self-imposed starvation.

After many bloody engagements, during which the inhabitants of various islands helped the invaders to subdue their neighbors, the entire Canary group was conquered by the Spaniards. The natives were remarkably courageous fighters and put up some very stiff resistance, but after sundry fluctuations in the tide of battle the Spanish conquistadors, notably Diego de Herrera, Diego de Silva and Don Alfonso Fernandez de Lugo, secured the Canary Islands for the Spanish crown.

When a large English fleet commanded by Sir Francis Drake and Sir John Hawkins attacked the new masters of the islands in 1595 they were repulsed off Las Palmas. Later Admiral Nelson himself lost one arm to a cannon ball when his fleet tried to capture Santa Cruz on Tenerife in 1797.

The natives of the Canary Islands represent one of the most fascinating and puzzling problems in the field of anthropology and early history, a problem which remains largely unsolved to this day.

It seems likely that the average Guanche was tall and well built. The inhabitants of the more westerly islands had lighter hair than the natives of the islands nearer Africa, who were dark-haired and thick-lipped. However, stories that their womenfolk were distinguished for their beauty should probably be attributed to the wild imaginings of sailors who would have found any girls attractive after weeks at sea! The allegedly abnormal strength of the Guanches, too, is probably one of the exaggerations so often indulged in by the explorers of olden times.

Not all the Guanches were massacred. Most of them died a natural death, but not until the women had fraternized with the invaders and some of the Guanches had married Spanish or Portuguese wives. As a result, although the islanders' racial characteristics became submerged in those of their conquerors, the features of the modern Spanish population often betray faint traces of aboriginal blood.

The islanders' old way of life, with its primitive tools of wood, bone and stone, survived until the sixteenth century, but evidence of an advanced neolithic culture has also been found in the large subterranean buildings on Grand Canary, which are reminiscent of ancient Mediterranean cultures, in the ground plans of temples, in ruined houses, former roads and elaborate burial practices.

Many Guanches lived in artificial caves carved into the mountainside and others lived in natural caves, but where cave life was not practicable they built small circular houses and fortifications.

Their clothing was made of goatskin or vegetable fibers, materials of which many traces have been discovered on Grand Canary. Necklaces and other articles of adornment made of wood, bone and mother-of-pearl were worn by men as well as women. The Guanches painted their bodies in bright colors, using stamplike implements made of baked clay. Clay vessels, either undecorated or with primitive finger-impressed ornamentation, have been dug up together with wooden spears, clubs, lances and shields. The Guanches were unfamiliar with iron, the potter's wheel or the bow and arrow. Their spear points were either fire-hardened or tipped with horn spikes.

One puzzling feature is that the Guanches never learned to sail. They could often see across from their own island to the next, but the Spaniards reported that they had no form of communication with each other. It is probable, however, that the islanders were in touch at lengthy intervals and that a raft or primitive boat occasionally managed to make the crossing.

The Italian traveler Leonardo Torriani, a native of Cremona, visited the Canary group in 1585 and in 1590 wrote a most interesting book on the islands and their aboriginal population. His view was that the Guanches possessed dugout boats with sails of matting and palm leaves. He believed that these boats were an indigenous cultural asset and that the islanders already knew how to sail before the Spaniards arrived. If Torriani's suppositions are correct, it is hard to understand why no remnants of such vessels have been found. All in all, the problem remains unsolved.

It is a fact that the Guanches overcame the difficulties of verbal communication over great distances by means of a type of birdcall, passing messages from hill to hill in a "whistle language." Curiously enough, a few modern islanders still command the art of transmitting various signals and even names by whistling.

The Guanches' wealth was based on their herds of sheep, goats, dogs and rabbits, all of which animals were used as food. Plump young dogs were considered an especial delicacy. All food was boiled, the staple diet being fish caught in the shallow water around the coasts. Like many primitive peoples, the Canary Islanders made fire by drilling one stick with another or rubbing them together.

When a Guanche grew very old or had contracted an incurable disease and was no longer fit for work, he could ask for death. Relatives were not permitted to refuse such a request, but laid the dying man to rest in a remote cave with a little food and left him to die in solitude.

The islanders tried to preserve the remains of their dead for all eternity, believing that the disintegration of the body would automatically destroy the immortality of the soul. Numerous embalmed mummies have been found, though mainly in a dilapidated condition. It is an astonishing fact that none of them weighs more than six or seven pounds.

The first stage in the embalming process was to gut the body of the deceased, a despised occupation performed by social outcasts. The actual embalmers, on the other hand, were normally priests or priestesses who ranked high in public esteem. The dead were embalmed by members of their own sex, who preserved the bodies with the dark red resin of the dragon's-blood tree. Dragon's-blood trees have always grown in these islands and can reach an age of 3,000 years. The few surviving examples are under official protection. Their gum does, in fact, make an excellent preservative, but we shall never know who originally discovered its properties.

Mummies were swathed in straw mats and as many as six goatskins or sheepskins, which were sewn together. Then, if the dead man was a king, his corpse was hidden in an inaccessible cave shaft or hurriedly buried beneath a hill. No member of the public was admitted to such a burial and the priests carefully guarded the position of the grave.

Guanche kings went to eternity in a standing position, whereas their wives were laid to rest lying on their side. A king often remained unburied for years and was interred only on the death of his successor. In this way there were always two kings, one living and one dead, the latter acting as adviser to the former!

Ordinary mortals were embalmed and their mummies simply placed one on top of the other in layers, men with their arms at their sides, women with arms folded. The departed were buried with bowls and jugs of butter and milk, dried figs and other fruits.

It seems reasonable to suppose that the custom of embalming hailed from Egypt, and some authorities have gone so far as to deduce that the earliest inhabitants of the islands were Egyptians who later intermarried with Nubians. However, the Egyptian process of conservation was quite different from that of the Canary Islands. Moreover, when the Spaniards landed in the archipelago the islanders had no form of writing. If they had come from Egypt they would presumably have brought a system of writing with them, yet no linguistic similarities have been found either. On the other hand, marriage between brother and sister was not only permissible on the island of Hierro but customary, just as it was among the royal families of ancient Egypt.

The natives must have been established on their islands for a very long time, perhaps since 2000 B.C. or even earlier. Their name, Guanches or Vanches, may be derived from Chinet, the hill on Tenerife, and *guam* or "man." Guam-Chinet would thus have meant "people of Chinet," a name subsequently distorted by the Spaniards into Guanche.

The islands were certainly known to the Semitic sailors of the southern and southeastern Mediterranean—that is to say, the Phoenicians and their Carthaginian cousins—long before the Romans extended their sovereignty to Spain. The Carthaginian navigator Hanno, who was dispatched to West Africa about 480 B.C., found the archipelago seemingly uninhabited but discovered the ruins of some large buildings. One cannot infer from the apparent absence of human beings that the aboriginal population had become extinct and that new immigrants had not yet found their way there. Hanno may have landed on an island that happened to be uninhabited, or perhaps he did not look farther than the beach. In any case, like the Spaniards and Portuguese in the time of the conquistadors, the Carthaginians kept the location of many islands and trading posts to themselves in order to eliminate unwelcome competition. Thus the world heard virtually nothing more of the Canaries for centuries, and there was no further news of the natives until their island home was rediscovered by the Arabs.

Anthropologically, the Canary Islanders belonged to the Cro-Magnon type and were similar to the begetters of the Aurignacian culture in continental Europe and Asia, who made the celebrated Venus statuettes of thirty or fifty thousand years ago. In much later times they probably became interbred with Berbers from North Africa.

The Spanish invaders reported that the Guanches were a people of more than average height, that some of the men and women had blue eyes and blond hair, and that they were endowed with colossal physical strength. These romantic descriptions of "noble, handsome, courageous but culturally primitive cave dwellers" were energetically impugned by Dominik Josef Wölfel in 1939, and it is hard to disagree with him. Many explorers, even those of the nineteenth century, had a penchant for sending back highly colored reports about unknown countries.

The islanders believed in the immortality of the soul and in a supreme and invisible being known on Grand Canary as Acoran, on Tenerife as Achaman, on Hierro as Eraoranham, and on La Palma as Abora. Archaeologists have unearthed the remains of extensive temples protected by strong exterior walls. Tradition had it that there were also a male and a female deity who lived in the mountains and came down to hear the prayers of the people. Belief in an evil spirit was equally widespread. This demon, who was known on Tenerife as Guayota, lived at the summit of the Teide, a 10,750-foot peak. In times of extreme drought the Guanches used to drive their herds to holy places where they separated the lambs from the ewes in the hope that their melancholy bleating would melt the heart of the supreme being. All personal feuds and wars had to be postponed during religious festivals.

The islands evidently had a sort of caste system founded upon a complicated mythology. There were many social strata, ranging from serfs to priests and royalty. On some islands the king was an absolute ruler, while on others the chieftains and nobility formed a council which controlled the decisions of the head of state. Again, one or two islands were inhabited by numerous small tribes who owed allegiance to no single master. The title of king or prince was handed down from father to son. The emblem of authority was the armbone of a deceased king or, according to other sources, a dead king's skull. Oaths were sworn on such relics at coronations, and they were also used as scepters during councils of state.

Despite the existence of various dialects, the inhabitants of all the seven islands formed a linguistic unity. Some expressions and names corresponded to Berber words and some were common to all the islands. *Aemon* meant "water" on Lanzarote, Hierro and probably some of the other islands. *Aho* meant "milk" on Lanzarote, Grand Canary and Tenerife.

On many of the islands the danger of overpopulation was so great that men were punished with death if they so much as approached a strange woman or spoke to her in the road. It is interesting to note that, small though the islands were, twin paths were laid out in the mountains of Tenerife and Grand Canary for just this reason, one for men and one for women. From time to time, when the population reached a certain density, the people received a general decree to kill all newborn babies, the only exceptions to this inhuman measure being firstborn children. All this proves that at the time of the Spanish conquest a considerable number of Guanches lived on the islands and that in earlier times the islands may well have been even more densely populated.

On Lanzarote there was a pit into which those who had been condemned to death were lowered and given the choice of either food or water. However, the death pit was abolished after one prisoner chose milk and stayed alive so long that the penalty lost its meaning.

The strange symbols which have been found on the rocks of La Palma and Hierro remain an unsolved scientific mystery. Scholars have been unable to recognize any form of writing in these inscriptions, and, apart from that, they seem to have been made not by the Guanches but by an older race which had long been extinct when the islands were taken by the Spaniards.

Only some 500 years have elapsed since we discovered the natives of these lovely, lonely islands in the Atlantic, since we tried to turn them into "civilized beings" and so exterminated them. How much "foreign aid" primitive peoples can absorb without becoming extinct is a vital but unanswered question. It is a symptom of primitive thinking when advanced nations imagine their own way of life to be the only one worth imitating, and insist on exporting their machine-made comforts at all costs. On the Canary Islands, so Leonardo Torriani reported, people had been living "healthily for a long time without serious illness or need of a doctor."

A whole people has vanished from the earth without our devoting

[57] The origin of this little figure is still in doubt. It may have been sculpted by a Greek artist and brought to a port on the Atlantic coast of southern Spain or it may, on the other hand, be a product of native Tartessus art.

[58] Roman amphorae exhibiting Phoenician influence, salvaged from the sea off Cádiz. The bronze had been deeply eroded as a result of 2,000 years' immersion in seawater.

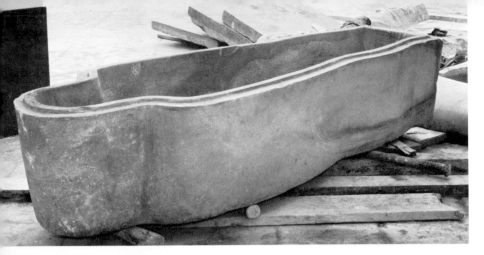

[59 and 60] One of the most interesting finds of the Tartessus era. The stone-faced vaults and burial pits discovered at Punta de la Vaca, Cádiz, yielded this 5th century B.C. sarcophagus complete with original occupant and closely fitting lid (*left*). It is assumed that the sarcophagus was brought to Cádiz from the Phoenician city of Sidon, but we shall never know why the prince for whom this handsome stone coffin was made should have found his last resting place at Cádiz.

[61] This fine Greek bowl was transported to Tartessus in one of the famous "ships of Tarshish" which King Solomon knew so well, and is probably between 2,500 and 2,600 years old.

[62] Unusual burial stele in the Museo Arqueológico at Seville. The palm tree and doe with calf are reminiscent of Tartessus art but probably hail from the later, Roman period.

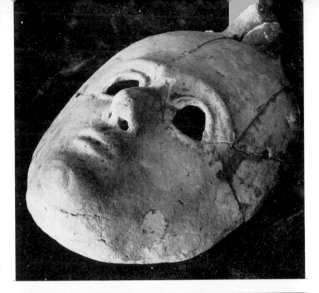

[63] A female mask, probably of Greek origin but found in a grave at Cádiz. This funeral offering was placed in the grave to drive away evil spirits, and dates from the period 500–300 B.C.

[64] This handsome children's drinking vessel in the shape of a cockerel belongs to the Tartessus culture and probably dates from the 7th or 6th century B.C. It is now in the Museum of Archaeology, Cádiz.

[65] Well designed jewelry of this sort was made by the descendants of the Tartessus people in the 4th century B.C. These pieces were photographed in the Museum of Archaeology at Cádiz. It is possible, though not probable, that they were imported from Phoenicia.

→

[66] "The Lady of Elche," found at Elche on the east coast of Spain. This Mona-Lisa-like portrayal is a unique example of the artistic skill of the 5th century B.C. The head ornaments, coiffure, ear pendants and chains are testimony to the splendor of the vanished culture of Tartessus.

→

[67] The celebrated treasure of El Carambolo, which was unearthed on September 30, 1958, comprised twenty-one articles of solid gold. In Professor Blanco's opinion, the plates are not components of a belt but of a crown. This valuable find bears witness to the remarkable technique of Tartessus goldsmiths.

[68] The Guanches are extinct as a people, but this wooden bust of a Guanche girl gives us some idea of their racial type, which may have been related to that of the Berbers of North Africa. The Spaniards described them as tall and strong-boned.

[69] This model of a stone building erected by the Guanches shows how far advanced their culture was. The place was enclosed by a massive wall and probably served religious purposes.

[70] Stone pestle and mortar used by the Guanches for grinding corn. Hand mills of this type have been found on several of the Canary Islands. (House of Columbus, Las Palmas.)

[71] A tripod of this type is known as a *ting*. T'ao-t'ieh masks can be seen on each of its three sides. The probable age of this sacrificial vessel is 2,500 years.

[72] This Shang Dynasty (1766–1123 B.C.) bowl is 23½ inches high and has a fine olive-green patina. The center of its girth is occupied by a T'ao-t'ieh mask in which the crescent moons have become modified into horns. Top center, the complete head of a horned beast.

sufficient study to them. Gone are the Guanches' buildings in the rock and beneath the ground, gone the work of their carpenters, ropemakers and tanners, gone their secret recipe for brewing an elixir of life from tree sap, gone the leather lines and goats' bones, the nets made of grasses and palm leaves with which they once fished so skillfully. Never again will the world's best stone-throwers engage in mortal combat with the balls of clay which they used for sport as well as war, dangerous missiles which only the agile could avoid; never again will spears quiver in the clear air, hurled by the hand of expert Guanche spearmen.

The people of these islands loved life and solitude and they believed in a supreme god. They made music and their songs drifted out across the waters of the Atlantic.

Today only the thunder of the surf tells the story of their vanished way of life.

THE MASK OF T'AO-T'IEH

The study of ancient bronzes has been industriously pursued in China by generations of scholars, who have the greatest veneration for the written script and find it better preserved on bronze than on stone, while the more perishable materials used in early times, such as tablets of wood and rolls of silk, have long since disappeared.

—STEPHEN W. BUSHELL, *Chinese Art*,
p. 65, London, 1914

ALL civilizations are related. In the six hundred thousand or more years that have elapsed since mankind came into being, the creature Homo has transmitted the intellectual and material fruits of civilization from continent to continent and from one river valley to the next. This was so even before man learned how to sail the seas, but once he had invented boats and ships the exchange of cultural blessings and evils became still more widespread.

One nation, however, has always felt itself to be the center of the world and has thus remained more withdrawn and self-contained than any other advanced civilization, namely the Chinese—though the men who live in Sinkiang, the Gobi desert and Manchuria or by the Hwang Ho, Yangtze and Canton rivers differ so widely in their racial characteristics that they are less a people than a family of peoples.

With its huge population of nearly seven hundred millions, China has long ago passed the danger mark. A nation's strength and capabilities cannot be equated simply with its numerical strength but are dependent on the foodstuffs available per head of population and —above all—on what each such head contains. In our century a country's technical progress can be likened to a ship, which goes no better with a crew of four thousand men than with a complement just large enough to supervise the efficient functioning of all its equipment. Availability of food should never be a dominant factor in the life of any nation. The equating of manpower with military strength ceased to be valid after the end of the Second World War.

The astonishing feature of the Chinese population is not its present size but the rapidity of its recent growth. In 1661, the Chinese numbered only 105 millions; in 1766, 182 millions; in 1872, some 330 millions; and today, almost 700 millions.

This huge nation is endowed with certain attributes which Westerners either consistently forget or simply refuse to take into account. For thousands of years, ideas and trade goods entered China via endless caravan routes or by sea. The stratification of various cultures throughout the world, and especially in China, is so fantastically intricate that we shall have to dig and explore for centuries to come before we succeed in identifying even a few of the relationships in mankind's cultural history. Yet, despite this many-layered complexity, it seems as though China has been permanently enclosed by visible or invisible walls for the past four thousand years. The reason may lie in China's abnormal creative vigor in craftsmanship and the arts, a vitality that has inspired her people since very early times and particularly during the Han and T'ang periods, when their numbers stood far below the fifty-million mark. The extraordinary national pride of the Chinese rests on their very ancient and, despite outside influence, entirely individual cultural strength, on the inward-facing attitude which prompted them to concentrate more on their ancestors than on what lay beyond their frontiers, and on an extremely refined culinary expertise which required no alien importations.

The Chinese have always cherished the conviction that all the races with whom they have to deal are inferior to themselves. Every Chinese is fundamentally convinced, for instance, that Tibetans, Turkestanis, the inhabitants of Outer Mongolia and the primitive peoples of Siberia belong to his own nation. China has never acknowledged another people or country as the center of the world. In fact, she has scarcely been surpassed in culture by any country in the world for five thousand years. China was the "Kingdom of the Center," and the Chinese have always regarded other nations as barbarians, an attitude which still persists today. Racially and culturally, China has always swallowed her neighbors, conquerors and defeated enemies, assimilated and absorbed them. The Chinese thought of their country as the largest and most powerful in the world and looked down on their Western conquerors with contempt. They despised the English, the French, the Germans and, above all, the Russians, who were always trying to infiltrate across the Amur into Manchuria and to threaten Outer Mongolia and

Turkestan. They despised the Japanese, and they despised the adjoining peoples of the south.

Since the Chinese were not a great seafaring race and their relations with other advanced cultures were, in a sense, unconscious, it was never in their nature to belong to a family of nations. This fact, together with their ignorance of other peoples' cultural achievements, their thousands of years of practice in their own individual way of life and their innate sense of superiority, has always made them seem arrogant in foreign eyes. If it is arrogance, however, it is an ancient arrogance unengendered by any sort of inferiority complex.

It has always been difficult to conclude treaties with the Chinese and quite useless to expect them to adhere to an agreement. Like most river-valley peoples, the inhabitants of the Hwang Ho and Yangtze plains have been astute businessmen for thousands of years. They produced great poets, talented writers, incomparable painters and some of the world's foremost sculptors. They were excellent smiths, fine weavers and silk manufacturers, brilliant architects, magnificent cooks—and appallingly bad cattlemen.

During the first five dynasties, or from 2205 B.C. until A.D. 220, this unusual people evolved a Bronze-Age culture which ventured to plumb the profoundest secrets of light and darkness, sun and moon, beast, man and god. Under the Shang and Chou dynasties (1766–256 B.C.) bronze was in general use and represented China's most important metal.

Articles of bronze being as durable as they are, the Chinese have contributed a vast literature to the study of this art. The *Illustrated Description of Antiques* in the Hsüan-Ho Palace, compiled by Wang Fu at the beginning of the twelfth century, comprised thirty volumes. A study of antiques edited by Lü Ta-lin in 1092 contained ten volumes. A magnificently illustrated catalogue of the imperial bronze collections in the palace at Peking, published in 1751 by Emperor Ch'ien Lung, occupied no less than forty-two volumes and the supplementary catalogue was housed in a further fourteen. Thus there is a veritable library of works by Chinese art historians and archaeologists devoted to the rich and extensive subject of bronze art, and modern students of this extraordinarily difficult field are forced to refer repeatedly to Chinese descriptions and catalogues for advice.

The earlier Chinese dynasties

Hsia	2205 B.C.–1767 B.C.
Shang	1766 B.C.–1123 B.C.
Chou	1122 B.C.– 256 B.C.
Ch'in	255 B.C.– 207 B.C.
Han	206 B.C.–A.D. 220
The "Six Dynasties"	A.D. 220–A.D. 589
Sui	A.D. 589–A.D. 618
T'ang	A.D. 618–A.D. 906
Five Dynasties	A.D. 907–A.D. 960
Sung	A.D. 960–A.D. 1279

During the Chou dynasty (1122–256 B.C.) Chinese writers compiled a work on contemporary art, the celebrated *K'ao kung chi*. This book lists the ratios to be used when alloying copper and tin to make various bronze articles. Bells, gongs, large bowls and other sacred vessels and objects consisted of five parts copper to one part tin. Axes and mattocks required four parts copper to one of tin. Double-edged swords and agricultural implements were cast from two parts copper to one part tin. Yet another alloy was prescribed for making arrowheads and small knives, and the famous Chinese mirrors were made of the above two metals alloyed in equal proportions.

Chinese bronzes do not, however, consist only of copper and tin, but contain zinc, lead, nickel, antimony, silver and a little gold, a combination of metals which produces a beautiful patina when an object has lain in the ground and been subjected to chemical changes over a period of hundreds or thousands of years. Being familiar with the chemical properties of his country's soil, the Chinese antiquarian knows how the lovely greens, turquoises and reds are conjured up on bronze and can distinguish fake from genuine by patina alone. Patina is often faked, but a spurious coating can usually be removed with a knife blade or boiling water, whereas genuine patina penetrates deep into the metal.

Very large articles have been manufactured from copper. Each of the five massive bells of Peking, which were cast on the orders of Emperor Yung Lo between 1403 and 1424, weighs just short of 60 tons, is about 16 feet high, has a maximum circumference of 36 feet and is about 1 foot thick. The inner and outer surfaces of these bells bear Chinese versions of Buddhist texts and prayers in Sanskrit. Cast on the spot where they were destined to remain, they were suspended on tree trunks mounted on massive wooden frames. Then, when the earth had been dug away from beneath them, a swinging wooden beam was hung inside to summon them to sonorous life.

The earliest bronzes, which served religious ends, were associated with ancestor worship and certain rites performed at the imperial court. Special vessels were used for offerings of meat, grain, fruit and wine. Archaic inscriptions discovered in many vessels and subsequently deciphered reveal the development of Chinese script from the earliest dynasties onward.

The discovery of an old bronze vessel was regarded as a great stroke of good fortune by the Chinese because they thought that the article's sanctity in some way transferred itself to the finder. Thus it was a sacred duty to keep bronzes carefully and pass them on from one generation to the next. In the fifth month of the year 116 B.C. a three-legged caldron of the sort known to the Chinese as *ting* was unearthed on the southern bank of the river Fen in Shansi Province. This happy event was regarded in such an important light that the reign of the emperor of the day, Wu Ti, was thereafter known as Yuan Ting. In the year A.D. 722, during the T'ang dynasty, a bronze caldron was discovered on the left bank of the Yellow River in the city of Yung Ho. The name of the place was forthwith changed to Pao Ting Hsien, or "City of the Costly Tripod." Not until about A.D. 960, when the Sung dynasty came to power, did bronzes lose their reputation for sanctity. From then on they were systematically dug up and placed in imperial palaces and museums, where they were catalogued and their inscriptions deciphered.

The first items to be mentioned in lists of old Chinese bronzes were *chung* (bells) and *ting* (bowls). Bells were often hung at the entrances of banqueting halls and later in ancestral temples, where their clangorous voices could summon the shades to funeral banquets.

One very famous example of the *ting* type of three-legged vessel dates from the Chou dynasty (1122–256 B.C.) and now stands in the Chiao-Shan Temple on the Yangtze. Its interior bears an engraved inscription running from lip to base, of which the following is an extract: "I, Wu Chuan, ventured to utter my grateful recognition of the great favor and honorable gifts of the Son of Heaven. I have made vessels for wine and this bowl for the presentation of sacrificial meat to my late deserving father. May I be rewarded with a long life of many days, and may my sons and grandsons continue to use this vessel and hold it in honor for ten thousand years."

From the style of the text and a reference to the position of the moon, Chinese scholars concluded that the vessel dated from 812 B.C. and that it and its inscription were the work of a privy councillor of Emperor Hsüan Wang.

The inscriptions of the Shang dynasty (1766–1123 B.C.) are composed in an archaic pictographic script and usually mention the name of the dead man to whom the piece was dedicated. No engraved examples are known to have originated in the still earlier Hsia dynasty (2205–1767 B.C.). By contrast, the interior of one sacrificial bowl of the Chou dynasty (1122–256 B.C.) bears more than five hundred engraved and gilded characters.

Bronze vessels used in the ritual worship of ancestors varied in shape according to whether they were employed as winejars, sacrificial cups or meat dishes. There were trumpet-shaped wine vases of considerable beauty, wine vessels with lids, wine vessels in animal form, and large flat bowls. All these forms originated in very early times. The vessels are usually distinguished for their simplicity and expressive power, and possess—if such a metaphor is permissible—an abundance of personality. They appear cumbersome at times, for they changed little in thousands of years, yet in some strange and mysterious manner they convey their great age and hallowed significance.

The decorative motifs are partly geometrical patterns and partly stylized portrayals of natural phenomena. The latter themes shed light on the earliest Chinese interpretation of nature. Human beings are rarely depicted, but the surfaces of the vessels bear allusive representations of hills, clouds, tigers, deer and other animals. They also depict a staggering profusion of mythical creatures, dragons, unicorns, phoenixes, toads, tortoises and fabulous beasts. The latter presuppose an almost inconceivable degree of imagination and surpass anything of their kind in the West. Fantastic monsters like those conjured up by the Chinese mind were never imagined, let alone portrayed, by any other people on earth.

Foremost among these mythical beasts is T'ao-t'ieh. The two Chinese characters composing the name stress only one attribute of this mysterious creature, their literal translation being "the Voracious One." T'ao-t'ieh was either a deity or the embodiment of various characteristics belonging to what was probably the supreme deity, for the so-called mask of T'ao-t'ieh appears on so many vessels that it must have been associated with an important god of some kind. The design and juxtaposition of various masks of this type and of other animals or beings were an age-old Chinese tradition. Sacred representations of such antiquity that we shall never plumb their origins, they may at one time have been carved in a perishable medium such as wood long before the appearance of the first bronze vessels.

The Greek word for effigy is *eikon*, the "icon" which we apply to a sacred image. What we find on Chinese bronzes is an entire iconography, the description of one of mankind's earliest worlds of sacred ideas.

With its double-looped horns, the T'ao-t'ieh resembles a ram, but a large fang often protrudes from the upper jaw of its gaping mouth, so it must be some form of predatory beast, perhaps a wolf or tiger. On the other hand, many T'ao-t'ieh masks suggest a buffalo's head.

Careful scrutiny is essential to the discernment and interpretation of the animals and mythical beings on the exterior surfaces of vessels and bells. Probably the most eminent authority on early Chinese bronzes and cult portrayals is Professor Carl Hentze, a distinguished member of Ghent University, who has studied this enthralling field of art closely, paying extraordinary attention to detail. All T'ao-t'ieh masks have crescent-shaped horns, and the earliest examples incorporate half-moons. The upper pair of crescents grew into horns, while the lower pair became the lower jaw of the mask. During the early bronze period, however, most of the masks displayed four distinct crescents. Hentze and Japanese scholars before him have interpreted these crescents as a cult symbol of the moon. Night and the moon go together, and owls are creatures of the night, hence the stylized coalescence of owl and t'ao-t'ieh.

The central portion of the mask is particularly important, although its significance remained obscure until 1937, when Hentze proved that it, too, corresponded to an iconographic formula. He interpreted it as a grasshopper, and defined the role of this ornament between the horns of the T'ao-t'ieh as a symbol of renewal or rebirth. Fantastic as it may seem, this may point to an association with the Indus culture of Mohenjo Daro. It, too, had a deity with crescent horns, and these horns, too, were separated by an emblem. On the T'ao-t'ieh mask it is an insect, in Mohenjo Daro a plant. In both cases Hentze interprets the symbol as a renewal motif.

Hailing from the obscure past, the portrayals of the T'ao-t'ieh masks are assumed to represent the manifestations, characteristics and functions of an age-old supreme deity. Night and darkness are symbolized by the crescent moons and the owl, light and rebirth by sun symbols and grasshoppers. Out of darkness, so we are informed by the remarkable bronzes of early China, come light and life. T'ao-t'ieh, so familiar to the Chinese four thousand years ago and so mysterious now, was a demon of darkness and a creature of the moon. It was, as Professor Hentze has so brilliantly demonstrated, a central deity during the Shang period of 1766–1123 B.C.

Where did the Shang people learn the art of bronze manufacture? This question remains unanswered, despite the fact that for many centuries magnificent works of art in bronze have been unearthed in the An-yang district of central Honan, where the capital of the Shang dynasty used to be.

There is some evidence that the bronze culture of the West spread to China at an early date. The ancient motif of rams and the tree of life, a feature of Sumerian culture, has been rediscovered in China. Nevertheless, even if a bronze culture existed in the countries of the eastern Mediterranean earlier than in China it does not necessarily mean that China inherited its bronze art from that quarter. Indeed, the unique characteristics of Chinese bronzes and the extreme individuality of Shang religious culture are inconsistent with the adoption of Western elements, and the predominance of entirely uninfluenced Chinese pieces indicates that the Far East underwent an artistic evolution of its very own.

There are apparent similarities between ancient Chinese and Northwest American Indian art just as there are similarities between Shang iconography and some Maya and Aztec symbols. But what explanation can there be for the gap of two or three thousand years separating the extremely ancient bronze art of China and the Maya and Aztec civilizations of the fourth and fourteenth centuries A.D. respectively?

It will never be possible to grasp the origin and content of the Shang people's mysterious symbolism in its entirety. The most remarkable feature of Chinese bronze culture is that, like Pallas Athene, it appears to have sprung abruptly into being four thousand years ago and to have attained a peak of perfection without passing through any preliminary stages. W. C. White, a Canadian authority on Shang culture who has lived in Honan for many years, states that there is absolutely no indication of the origin or even the background of this art. The bronzes are superbly cast, carefully planned with regard to strength and form, refined in their ornamentation and unsurpassed by any other bronzes in the world.

We know that the Shang priests frequently made human sacrifice, we guess at their cult animals and have a vague idea of their demons, we study their fertility symbols and can handle the receptacles that contained their food and drink offerings more than three thousand years ago—but what did they *know*? What did they know of the whence and whither of mankind? What did they know of God, and why did their thoughts revolve eternally around the mysteries of nature?

If the mute bronzes refuse to yield up all their secrets, we must remember that it is characteristic of the moon's pale crescent to leave much in semidarkness.

A MAN NAMED SIDDHARTHA

*If Buddha is only an apocryphal figure and the product of sym-
bolic speculation, if he never preached, if he never had disciples
who, united in a common belief, regarded one another as brothers,
there is no explanation for the sudden appearance of the community which modeled itself on him mentally and based itself on
his doctrines, which possessed a literature in which it preserved a
recollection of all his daily doings, a recollection of his earthly
pronouncements and of the people who surrounded him in his
lifetime.*

—(Jean Filliozat) L. Renou and J. Filliozat,
L'Inde Classique, Vol. III, p. 465, Paris, 1953

*The venerable Sariputta spoke there to the monks: "This nirvana
is bliss, ye monks. This nirvana is bliss, ye friends." And when the
venerable Sariputta had thus spoken, the venerable Udayi spoke
to him as follows: "But how, my dear Sariputta, can there be bliss
in that condition if there is no sensation therein?" "The bliss of that
condition, my friend, is precisely that there is no sensation therein."*

—Maximilian Kern, *Das Licht des Ostens*,
p. 110, Leipzig, 1922

About 500 B.C. a man was born whose teachings conquered the
whole of the Far East and who thus gave Asia's most widely disseminated religion its name. Far fewer wars have been fought on
behalf of Buddhism than of Islam and Christendom, yet those who
embrace Buddha's ideas include Burmese, Siamese, Cambodians,
Laotians, Tibetans, Chinese and many millions of people in Mongolia, Manchuria and Japan.

Buddha never wished to be a monarch, never wished to found
or rule kingdoms, yet this genius who had no taste for earthly
power created a realm of the spirit in which hundreds of millions
of Asiatics still live today. Buddha begged his daily food in the
bazaars of central India. Today, the effigy of the erstwhile beggar
stands in gilded and exalted tranquillity in hundreds of thousands
of temples. Clouds of incense wreathe his countenance, and for
twenty centuries men have prayed and performed their meditations
in his presence.

Asia is the great cradle of the world's religions. Within a period of approximately two hundred years, it witnessed the appearance of Zarathustra (circa 600 B.C.), Confucius (551–479 B.C.) and Buddha. All the great sages, holy men and religious founders of the world have one thing in common: the historical facts of their existence are to some degree veiled in obscurity. This baffling half-knowledge, this distrust of reality and quest for precise details about people who were close to their god are natural and inevitable, for their existence has been overwhelmed and obscured by their teachings. Nothing is left of the great saints and sages except their spirit. Details of their private life must remain lost to history because it is a cipher, merely an earthly accessory of immortal thoughts. Sanctification, deification and apotheosis need no biographical details.

Thus we have very little precise information about Buddha's life. His followers saw in him such an intelligence and supernatural moral force that he became in their eyes the divine embodiment of everything spiritual and a symbol of liberation from a world of suffering and confusion. They witnessed miracles and clothed his life in legends, recognizing him as one of the saviors of mankind.

Only two hundred years after Buddha's death, reports of the man and his wisdom had penetrated to every corner of India. The nucleus of his doctrines—his words—was faithfully passed on with a zeal born of religious sincerity. His truths conquered the whole of the East, but ideas of him were so glamorized by bold flights of fancy, by poetic imagination, glorification and prayer, that all details of the real man were soon obscured by a dazzling aureole of legend. We are told that he converted the envious and hostile, ascended into heaven and returned to earth, was revered by beasts, worshiped by human beings and urged by the gods to share his wisdom with them. The gods themselves became his most ardent adherents and kings humbled themselves before him and offered him their treasures. And all this was accomplished by the spiritual and moral force of a beggar, a starving ascetic! Huge libraries could be filled with the erudite works that have been written about Buddha, but no form of science or research can get to the heart of the matter. The figure of Buddha remains in some degree incomprehensible and shrouded in mystery.

Actually Buddha is not a proper name but an honorific title meaning "the Enlightened One." He was the son of Suddhodana, a prince of the Sakya clan, and his wife Mahamaya, who died seven days after giving him birth. Mahamaya reputedly did not actually die in childbirth, but because she had achieved her highest destiny and fulfilled her supreme purpose. Like so much in Buddha's life, the death of his mother was at once an historical fact and a religious necessity.

The Sakya lived at the foot of the Himalayas. In fact we even know that Buddha's place of birth was Kapilavastu in modern Nepal, 125 miles from Katmandu and 220 miles from Mount Everest. The site is marked by a pillar bearing an inscription by King Asoka.

Buddha was India's greatest philosopher, but "philosopher" is a very European term, and it is perhaps better to call him India's greatest sage. Buddha embodied the spirit of Asia, the multiplicity of its philosophy and the profundity of its religious introspection. He is at once the most human figure and the most remarkable phenomenon which India has produced. No other Indian ever surpassed him in wisdom, depth of thought or spiritual radiance, yet we have no precise idea of the actual content of the historical Buddha's original doctrines. It certainly differed from the Buddhism of today, and there are some authorities—C. A. F. Rhys Davies, for example—who believe that Buddha's actual teachings differed but little from the ethic of the old Indian Upanishads.

Buddha's adherents paint a very highly colored picture of his life. Even if Buddha had never existed and Asia possessed no more than this creatively fashioned life story, she would still be immensely rich in the religious and spiritual sphere. Figures such as Zarathustra, Confucius, Buddha, Socrates and Christ are not, however, susceptible of invention.

We are told that Buddha's mother, Princess Mahamaya, was transported in miraculous fashion to a lake in the Himalayas, where she was bathed by heavenly attendants and dreamed that she saw a large white elephant holding a lotus blossom in its trunk. (The lotus blossom is one of Asia's most venerated symbols and is associated with birth.) The next day, sages interpreted her dream as signifying that she was destined to bear a son who would be a ruler of the universe and a servant of God. The child was duly born, not actually in Kapilavastu, the Sakya capital, but in its immediate vicinity, just as Mahamaya was on her way to her parents' house.

At the great baptismal ceremony customarily held by families of high rank, the newborn child received the name Siddhartha. His "Gotra" name was Gautama. Soothsayers apparently predicted that the child would be a teacher of mankind. His father, King Suddhodana, was determined to isolate him from all the sorrows and afflictions of the world, and we learn that he grew up and received his education in a magnificent palace far removed from such things as death, disease, sorrow and suffering. He married a cousin of his and might well have lived happily if he had not had an inner yearning for something more. Then he saw the four signs which had figured in the soothsayers' predictions: a very old man in a pitiable condition, a sick man covered in ulcers and shivering with fever, a dead man being carried to his funeral pyre and, finally, a pious beggar in a yellow robe. Only the fourth apparition gave any appearance of serenity or contentment, and at the age of twenty-nine Siddhartha decided to follow his example. Leaving home, family, wife and child, he set off on horseback. In his rejection of the world he abandoned his princely clothes and exchanged them for the habit of a mendicant monk.

The future Buddha visited the schools of various celebrated ascetics in his search for a solution to the questions which were troubling him, but in vain. Then he withdrew into solitude.

Gautama Buddha arrived at his philosophy through meditation. When he was forty-five years old he sat down beneath a pipal tree and swore not to move from the spot until he had solved the riddle of human suffering, even if his body decayed first.

For forty-nine days and nights he sat beneath the tree in motionless contemplation. By the end of that period, during which he withstood numerous temptations, he had seen the truth and understood the secret of pain and suffering. He realized why the world was unhappy and how its unhappiness could be overcome. Having become a Buddha, an "Enlightened One," he remained beneath the Tree of Wisdom or Bodhitaru for another seven weeks.

It was not Siddhartha's immediate intention to communicate his experience and knowledge to the world at large, but the god Brahma came down from heaven and bade him propagate the dharma or doctrine. His disciples numbered first five and then sixty, and his name and teachings became renowned throughout the plain of the Ganges. Returning to Kapilavastu, he converted his father, his wife, his son, large numbers of courtiers and even his wicked cousin Devadatta.

Many miracles are attributed to Buddha, but the earliest accounts of his life contain virtually no reference to any miraculous deeds. For two-thirds of the year he roamed through the countryside with his disciples, teaching as he went. The remaining months he spent in one of the many groves which were bequeathed to the Buddhists by wealthy patrons. Buddha wandered through the Ganges valley for forty-five years, a beggar among beggars and the poorest of the poor, but never unhappy.

Unlike Christ, Paul and Socrates, Buddha was never persecuted on account of his teachings. When he was eighty he prepared his followers for his death. Only his doctrine, the *dharma*, was to survive. No new master was to step into his shoes. He probably died, like Diogenes, from a type of paratyphus contracted after eating pork. Dragging himself as far as the suburb of Kusinagara, he lay down under a tree at nightfall and died. Buddha's death occurred by Singhalese reckoning in the year 543 and according to European research in 477 B.C. His body was burned on a pyre according to Indian custom.

Buddha's doctrines and Christianity came into being quite independently, even though the Christian religion and Buddhist philosophy both have their origin in a belief in a supreme god. All attempts to correlate the Buddhist sutras with the Christian Gospels are doomed to failure. There are superficial similarities and very considerable divergences, but even the apparent similarities vanish under careful comparative analysis. Christianity and Buddhism are worlds apart in dogma and quite close in their morality, as Professor A. Foucher of Paris University has so clearly demonstrated. "Christian and Buddhist moral values are undoubtedly homogeneous, but their doctrinal basis and mental and spiritual atmosphere are entirely dissimilar."

The contrast between Buddhism and Christianity is immediately apparent from their attitude toward the soul. According to Christian theology the soul originates with the child and thereafter retains its immortality. It has a beginning, therefore, but no end. To Indian philosophers such a notion is absurd, for in their view anything which comes into being at one point in time is susceptible to destruction at another point in time. They hold that the soul is immortal and travels from body to body during the process of rebirth. Since it exists eternally it has no beginning and can have an end only in exceptional cases when meritorious behavior and good deeds have rendered it ripe for the supreme condition, nirvana, from which there is no return to earth.

With only one life, the Christian can receive eternal bliss or eternal damnation only once. "The Buddhist has traveled far, and has all eternity before him. His life is only a transient moment in the course of an eternal existence. He reaps the fruits of his previous existences and sows the seeds of his future forms of existence. For him, the death knell never heralds the advent of everlasting bliss nor signals the hour of irreparable doom. He believes that his approach to perfection is an infinitely slow process spanning thousands upon thousands of successive lifetimes, for only thus can he attain the supreme reward of eternal bliss. It is a salvation which we, in our Occidental impatience, expect to receive after a single lifetime.

"The peoples of the East have different conceptions of this salvation from our own. The Westerner wants only to live. Should he fail to reach heaven, his thirst for immortality is such that he is prepared to accept the everlasting torments of purgatory and hell. The man of the Far East already has an eternity behind him. After so many existences he is infinitely weary, infinitely fatigued by the endless succession of deaths which he has undergone. In short, the ambition of the West is never to die again: the ambition of the East is never to be reborn."

Like Christ and Socrates, the Enlightened One of India never committed a word of his doctrine to writing. He was not really a religious founder as such, nor did he have any intention of founding a religion. His sole concern was to serve people with his teachings and help them to escape from suffering. He was not interested in solving theological questions such as the essential nature of the gods, the soul and immortality. All these problems were disposed of by his belief that it was better never to have been born at all than to live and so to suffer.

Buddhism did not, however, remain merely a philosophy; it became a world religion. Even though their originator's only real concern had been to encourage wisdom and rectitude in human behavior, the teachings of Buddha were being variously interpreted

by no less than eighteen different sects only two hundred years
after his death. The two main forms of Buddhism, Mahayana and
Hinayana, have divided the Buddhist world into two separate camps.
Those who live in the spirit of Mahayana, "the great vehicle," in-
clude the Chinese, the Japanese and the Lamaists of Tibet, Bhutan,
Sikkim, Nepal and Mongolia. Ceylon and Indo-China follow the
Hinayana or "little vehicle."

Mahayana entails a perpetual striving, during life and through
life, to be reborn after death as a future Buddha or Bodhisattva. The
adherents of Mahayana accept rebirth out of sympathy for the
world and when it is for the salvation or happiness of the majority.
The adherents of the Hinayana seek only their personal salvation.

The most remarkable feature of Buddhism is that while its teachings still survive in vast tracts of Asia they have all but disappeared
in the land of Buddha's birth. In India, Buddhism has been swamped
by the much more ancient Hindu religion, and the Indian people
have remained true to their traditional polytheism, their penchant
for miracles, their splendid myths and peculiar world of magic.

Nevertheless, Buddhism has adopted numerous legends and countless rituals and deities from Hinduism. The unadulterated doctrines
of Siddhartha and his world of ideas have not remained entirely
intact. Buddhism did not meet its end suddenly in India, it should be
added, but survived there for about a thousand years until its
eventual extinction circa A.D. 750. In every other country in the
Far East its doctrines still live on, unaffected by new masters, new
cure-all philosophies and new methods.

A third of mankind obeys the tenets of Buddhism. It may not obey
them as sincerely as Buddha's disciples once obeyed the words of
their master, but Buddhists are still Buddhists.

Buddhism has also bequeathed the world a great legacy, something impermanent, perhaps, but something engendered by faith and
therefore magnificent. This is the Buddhist art which has given
birth to statues, portraits and reliefs of Buddha throughout Asia.

GANDHARA AND THE BUDDHA IMAGE

*The purpose of these sculptures was to glorify the Buddha. This
they did by recounting episodes from the story of his life and of
his previous births, or sometimes, but only rarely, from the subsequent history of the Buddhist Church. In the earliest monuments
the stories of his previous births, or Jatakas, as they were called,
greatly predominated. Later on, interest shifted to the events of his
last earthly life, and still later to his image, which was destined to
eclipse all else in Buddhist art.*

—SIR JOHN MARSHALL, *The Buddhist Art of Gandhara*,
p. 7, Cambridge, 1960

THE ancient land of Gandhara was situated on the northwest
frontier of India, roughly between the Indus and its large northern
tributary, the Kabul. It occupied the northernmost tip of modern
Pakistan and the region of Afghanistan adjoining it in the Kabul
bend. Of great cultural interest and scenic beauty, this area was
conquered by Alexander the Great in the years 327 and 326 B.C.
Alexander led an army of 35,000 men into Gandhara from Sogdiana
and Bactria, which more or less corresponded with the area of
Uzbekistan (now in Soviet Russia) southeast of the Aral Sea. He
was searching for the eastern and southern boundaries of the inhabited world. His army had long ago ceased to be solely Macedonian. A whole empire was on the march, an empire composed of
many nations and races, Macedonians with their wives and children,
scholars, exponents of all the sciences, doctors, geographers, engineers, bridge builders, ballistics experts, historians, ethnologists, and
in addition a huge column of commissariat officials, ancillary troops,
seamen and even contingents lent by Indian princes—a total of about
120,000 souls.

Alexander pushed onward into the Kabul valley, fighting off bitter
attacks by tough mountain tribes. He stormed their strongholds and
battered their towns with his heavy catapult artillery until he
eventually reached the banks of the Indus. The Macedonian king
took strong exception to the Indian philosophers who berated, re-
viled and insulted the native princes who defected to him, and hanged
some of them. The Gandharan king of Takshashila (the modern
town of Taxila stands about 23 miles east of the Indus) paid homage

to the foreign invader, accompanied by other tribal chieftains. Alexander's army was progressively reinforced by renegade Indian troops, and in the spring of 326 B.C. he crossed the Indus. We are told that Prince Poros lay in wait for him on the eastern bank of the Hydaspes, now the Jhelum, but that after his men had put up a desperate struggle Poros was wounded, his army annihilated and his two sons captured. When Alexander asked him how he thought he should be treated, the royal captive replied: "Like a king!" Typically, Alexander complied. Poros became Alexander's ally and his possessions were considerably augmented.

It was not until the King of Magadha advanced on Alexander at the head of 600,000 infantry, war elephants and cavalry that the Macedonian army's courage wavered. For Alexander, the banks of the Hyphasis represented the end of the world and the end of his unique career of conquest. Considering the enormous distances and the alien surroundings, there was nothing surprising about the mutiny. Like Achilles, Alexander withdrew to his tent for three days and waited for the army to regain its senses, but his men were deathly tired of bold excursions to the end of the world. Alexander turned to the gods. Erecting twelve altars, he ordered a general retreat. Only a few years after Alexander's withdrawal the Indian king Chandragupta made sacrifice on one of these altars, a significant fact because it illustrates the spiritual contact between Graeco-Hellenistic culture and the culture of India.

After the departure of the invading army and the great Macedonian's death, disorder broke out among the Greeks who were left behind. Poros was treacherously assassinated by Eudemos, and Alexander's successors, the Diadochi, quarreled among themselves over the division of his empire. An Indian adventurer of inferior caste who had won an evil reputation for his intrigues on the lower Ganges now felt that the hour had struck for the fulfillment of his ambitious hopes. Placing himself at the head of the Indian liberation movement, Chandragupta took the field against the foreigners and in 316 B.C. won supremacy over the Punjab. Before long he controlled an area stretching from the estuary of the Indus to the Ganges delta. Seleucus Nicator, master of Babylonia and of a vast empire, gave him his daughter's hand in marriage and abandoned his designs on India. Envoys were sent by the Indians to the court of Babylon and by the Greeks to Pataliputra, now Patna. It is to one

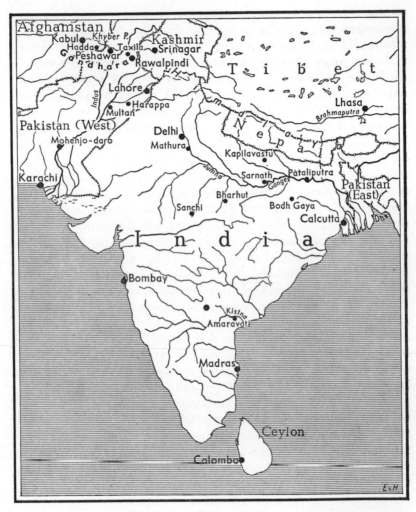

India

of these Greek diplomats, Megasthenes, that the West owes its first detailed and eyewitness accounts of the country and people of India. Megasthenes, who was an Ionian, wrote about Indian geography, religion and customs. His accounts are not extant, but such details of them as have survived in Arrian's *Indica* reflect the contemporary way of life in India, then known as the Kingdom of Maghada.

Megasthenes found the people sturdy, honest, sincere, temperate and peaceable at heart but ready to fight when provoked.

Chandragupta's royal line was known as the Maurya dynasty, after his mother, Mura. His grandson Asoka, who was the most powerful ruler ancient India ever knew, controlled the greater part of the subcontinent. He aroused emotions of such love, respect and veneration that his name is still held in awe from the shores of the Black Sea to the islands of Japan and from the borders of the Polar region to the equator. Asoka was the Constantine of India, a king who embraced the teachings of Gautama just as some 580 years later, on May 22, A.D. 337, Caesar Flavius Valerius Constantinus became the first Roman emperor to receive Christian baptism.

Once Asoka became an adherent of Buddhism, the people of Gandhara also embraced the teachings of Buddha. Asoka's religious zeal knew no bounds. In the thirteenth year of his reign he had inscriptions of a religious nature engraved on rocks, cave walls and pillars. They are the earliest surviving Indian texts of any historical value. Asoka's ambition was to conquer the world with the Buddhist religion, not by force of arms. A truly apostolic king, he brought Indian Buddhism to its zenith and gained his worldwide reputation not by means of conquest or political power but because of the spiritual insight which prompted him to follow Buddha. Under the Maurya dynasty ushered in by Chandragupta, Gandhara enjoyed its only spell of autonomy. Before that time it had been ruled by Achaemenides and Greeks, and it was subsequently to be dominated by Bactrians, Saka and the notorious Kushan. The latter infiltrated into Gandhara from East Asia, from the Chinese province of Kansu, and were a race of Scythian horsemen identical with the Yueh Chi of Chinese history. The most celebrated of the Kushan rulers was a man called Kanishka, who controlled a huge empire which extended from Margiana to Khotan and from the Aral Sea to Afghanistan, and incorporated almost the whole of India.

Like the great Asoka, Kanishka was also a Buddhist. He founded numerous monasteries, convened an assembly in Kashmir to reformulate the Buddhist doctrines and built some superb stupas. These buildings existed in India at a very early date and were originally burial mounds venerated by the local population. The stupa cult was revitalized and expanded by Buddhism. Stupas were like truncated cathedral domes containing a central chamber. The inner shell was built of unbaked bricks and the exterior of baked bricks coated with a thick layer of lime. The whole edifice was capped by an umbrellalike construction of wood or stone and enclosed by a wooden fence with massive gates, which was later superseded in some cases by a stone wall. Of all the stupas erected by King Asoka, the only one to have survived in its original form is in Nepal. The three most interesting stupas are those of Bharhut in Madhya Bharat, Sanchi in the state of Bhopal, and Amaravati at the lower end of the Kistna Valley. The largest stupas, which are to be found in Ceylon, sometimes exceed three hundred feet in diameter. Ever since Asoka's time, the inner chamber of a stupa has been used as a repository for relics of Buddha or Buddhist saints.

Chronological information has been handed down to us from this period and we can date many events with considerable accuracy. The Shaka chronology of India begins with the anointing of King Kanishka, which is traditionally supposed to have taken place on March 15, A.D. 78. This estimate is doubtful, however, and is disputed by many scholars. Estimates given by various authorities range between 57 B.C. and A.D. 278. Vincent A. Smith settled on A.D. 120 as the year of Kanishka's accession. Harald Ingholt, who bases his calculations on the Ghirshman chronology, puts it at A.D. 144. As we shall see, the question of dates is of vital importance to any examination of Gandhara art.

Kanishka ruled the Kushan Empire for twenty-seven years. The last of his line, Vasudeva, was defeated by the Sassanian dynasty of Persia, and in A.D. 241 Ardashir's son, Shapur I, captured Gandhara. The Sassanides left the Kushan ruling class to govern the country for most of the time, occasionally calling their deputies to order when they grew too independent for safety.

The inhabitants of central Asia are by nature wanderers. Its wide tracts of grassland and steppe and its vast, undulating hills and highlands have always been the cradle of races of herdsmen and horsemen. When the nomad left his own world and met lowland civilizations entirely alien to him, his usual reaction was to reach for his sword.

In the year A.D. 460 a great disaster occurred. The whole of northwest India, including Gandhara, was overrun by the contemporary world's most dangerous adversaries, a branch of the

Hun race known as "White Huns" or Hephthalites. The origins and racial identity of these horsemen from central Asia have never been established, but it was not until A.D. 562 that the Turks and Persians finally annihilated the mounted hordes. The White Huns wrought frightful havoc among the adherents of Buddhism and executed those who espoused its doctrines in the most inhuman fashion.

We know when the art of Gandhara ended, but when did it begin and when did men first venture to portray Buddha in stone?

The answer to this question owes its importance to the fact that Gandhara is the birthplace of the Buddha effigy and the birthplace of all such sculptures in Asia.

Buddhism first penetrated to Gandhara in the middle of the third century B.C., from the time of Asoka onward, and the beginnings of Buddhist religious sculpture date from the period 247–232 B.C. It was evolved by Greek and Graeco-Persian sculptors working in undoubted conjunction with Indian artists. However, the earliest sculptures of Buddha himself did not come into being until much later on, under the Kushan dynasty. Some scholars believe that the first statues of Buddha were made in the time of Kanishka, the most prominent of the Kushan rulers. Extant coins dating from the Scythian king's reign show Kanishka standing before an altar on one side and Buddha on the other. These coins are thought to be the earliest portrayals of Buddha, but the likeness on the coins must have been modeled on a statue of still earlier date. At all events, we have at least an approximate idea of the date of when Buddha was first portrayed. If we are correct in thinking that King Kanishka ruled from A.D. 144 to 173, the earliest statues of Buddha must have come into being a little earlier, perhaps between A.D. 50 and 100.

Gandhara submitted to a long series of alien rulers: Achaemenides, Greeks, Bactrians, Saka and Kushan. One by one they came, generally bringing misery and distress in their wake, only to be eventually obliged to withdraw. The people of Gandhara, however, remained rooted in their ancient culture, in their language and their faith in the Buddhist doctrine, which welded them to one another and to other peoples of India.

Gandhara had to endure foreign domination for almost a thousand years, but as a cultural area it derived unique benefits from its contact with foreign overlords. From the West, as a consequence of Alexander's conquest and of Greek and Graeco-Roman influence, the country received an artistic impetus which ultimately gave the world the Buddha effigy. One of the most momentous events in the artistic history of the world, it was something which sprang from the religious faith of the Gandharans (and probably, too, from that of the Indians in Mathura, nearly 100 miles south of Delhi), from the honest workmanship and stimulus of Western artists and, last but not least, from the considerable creative energy and artistic genius of the Indians themselves.

About six hundred years—roughly from the lifetime of Buddha until a century after the birth of Christ—had to elapse before the first portraits of Asia's greatest sage and saint came into being. No likenesses of Buddha, not even the most halfhearted attempt to portray the philosopher from Kapilavastu, existed in India in pre-Christian times. Asoka was, as we have heard, an adherent of Buddha, but his stone monuments dating from about the middle of the third century B.C. never venture to depict the object of his veneration.

During the first period of Buddhist art, or about 250 years after Buddha's death, only symbolic references were made to the great teacher. One such symbol was the "wheel of the doctrine" which the Buddhist scriptures envisaged as being turned by Buddha. In fact, to regard the wheel as a symbol of moral teaching was not a conception peculiar to Buddhism but dated from India's very earliest cultural period and originated in the Vedic hymns of fifteen hundred years before. During the Vedic era the wheel was the religious symbol of the sun, whose rising and setting was associated with the eternal mutability of all existence. Thus the earliest examples of Buddhist art depict the sun but not Buddha himself.

Another symbol which occurs frequently is the lion. Buddha, who came from the princely Sakya family, was sometimes known as Sakyasimha or "Sakya Lion," and Buddhist scriptures often refer to the *simhanada* or "lion's call" of Buddha.

At Sanchi in the State of Bhopal stands a large and celebrated stupa erected during the second and first centuries B.C. One of the most beautiful ancient monuments in India, it was intended to represent the universe. The four gates in the wall enclosing the shrine are engraved with scenes from Buddha's life, yet none of these reliefs portrays Buddha's features or even his figure. The gates date from the close of the first century B.C. On the central architrave

can be seen the *bodhi* tree beneath which Gautama received enlightenment. At the foot of the tree, flanked on either side by
reverent figures, stands a throne. It is the throne of the Master
himself, but it is empty! The fact that Buddhism's sacred figure
was regarded with boundless awe and humility but not portrayed
makes an immediate impact on the beholder. Everywhere, in every
monastery, every shrine and every stupa dating from before the
beginning of our era, the figure and face of the founder of Buddhism
is reverently omitted.

What is the explanation? Why did India's most exalted religion
or, more properly, philosophy wait until the end of the first century
A.D. before producing an effigy of Buddha? Why was it left to
foreign artists to bequeath the Buddhist world an idealized picture
of its founder?

The answer is as old as the idea of God itself. No representation
of God existed in the paleolithic or neolithic era of mankind. In
fact man himself was never depicted in the Aurignacian culture of
the Cro-Magnids. The earliest human likenesses of that period are
the Venus statuettes dating from thirty, forty or fifty thousand
years ago, but these are probably only symbols of the beginning
and continuance of life and emblems of immortality. Divine effigies
are a relatively late—one might say heathen—invention which first
originated when the idea of the supreme being was adulterated
with polytheistic elements. Brahmanism, the Indians' oldest religion,
did not tolerate idols as cult objects, either, and likewise confined
itself to symbols. This is the principal reason why no effigies of
Buddha were made until about six hundred years after his death.

There is yet another important factor. Buddha was moved by
suffering, by the transience of the flesh and the unreality of existence.
Seeing the grief which everything transitory brings in its wake, he
realized the quantity of tears mankind has shed on its eternal
journey from birth to death. He saw the thirst for life, the lust for
existence and the human passions which have no right of way on
the paths of suffering. And so he sought to abolish suffering by
the annihilation and dulling of the lust for existence, and thus to
demonstrate a way to abolish all suffering. He had tried complete
mortification of the flesh on his own person in order to find release
from the evils of all that is worldly, but he felt that this over-
stringent method concealed latent dangers. As the son of a prince,

he knew the ways of the world only too well, so he advised a middle way. The stages of the Noble Eightfold Path which he recommended are: right views, right intention, right speech, right action, right livelihood, right effort, right mindfulness and right concentration. It was a philosophy, a moral doctrine and form of guidance which Buddha did not intend as a religion because it did not demand a belief either in a supreme being or in himself.

As long as the doctrine retained its original character it was not a religion but a philosophical edifice. The Way and the Doctrine were all that mattered to Buddha, which was why symbols were best suited to represent his spiritual legacy. Symbols of the Master himself were also appropriate in this context, but he would never have wished his followers to make likenesses of him calculated to foster a religious cult of personality, for he rejected anything which did not pertain to the doctrine itself. It seems clear that Buddha's adherents honored his memory by respecting this wish for a few hundred years, until, in the first century A.D., the artists of Gandhara evolved an idealized picture of him. With the appearance of a figure which could be seen and worshiped, Buddha's philosophy became transformed into a religion.

The religious art of Gandhara served the Buddhist faith. For example, the plinth of a stupa from Sikri, now in Lahore Museum, is encircled by thirteen reliefs, each illustrating an event in the life of Buddha. They introduce us into the contemporary world of ideas concerning Buddha's life and reproduce in stone what legend relates of him.

These stone memorials were not, however, confined to his life alone. Artists began to portray him sitting and standing, in relief and in the round. Still other sculptors saw him as a Bodhisattva or being who declined nirvana in order to act as a mediator on mankind's behalf.

The English archaeologist Sir John Marshall, who excavated the ruins of three towns dating from between the seventh century B.C. and the fifth century A.D. in West Pakistan, also contributed greatly to research into the Buddhist art of Gandhara. He recognized an early school of Gandhara art in the first and second centuries A.D. and a later school which flourished between about A.D. 350 and 500. Not only was the art of these two schools different in character, but the media used by the sculptors of the two periods also differed.

Stone was employed in the first Gandhara period, stucco in the second. The artists of the early school worked in the Peshawar valley and the countryside west of the Indus. The later art covered a much wider area stretching from Taxila, east of the Indus, to ancient Bactria and the Oxus, i.e. Pakistan, India and Afghanistan. The early school displays a certain crudeness and rigidity, whereas in the finest pieces of the later school, matter has entirely given way to mind.

Most pictures show Buddha meditating with his hands cupped one inside the other. There are also some celebrated portrayals of him teaching, hands held before his breast in meditation. The *mudra* or hand positions of the so-called preaching Buddha later evolved into a series of subtle and varied gestures symbolizing—among many other things—concentration, instruction, encouragement, invocation and fearlessness.

The Master's robe, which reaches almost to the ground, is gathered at the waist and often leaves his right shoulder bare. It is actually a Greek robe or, still better, a Hellenistic or even Roman garment. One of the earliest known sculptures of Buddha, a standing figure in Peshawar Museum, portrays him wearing a toga like that of the Roman emperor Augustus.

Mahayana Buddhism evolved during the early centuries of our era, a period when the life of Alexander the Great was being romantically embroidered in the Roman Empire and when the idea of the Hellenistic god-kingdom had gained popularity throughout the Mediterranean area and far beyond. The deification of Oriental rulers who were so absolute, so wealthy and powerful that they were regarded as superior beings, the Egyptian Pharaohs, who were already gods and sons of Ammon during their sojourn on earth— all these strongly influenced the ideas of the Hellenistic and Roman world. Lysander, who delivered Greece from the twenty-seven years of misery brought about by the Peloponnesian War, was officially promoted to the status of divine hero during his lifetime. Alexander the Great was recognized in Egypt as Pharaoh and greeted with the title Son of Ammon by the priests of Siva. (To the Greeks, Ammon was the equivalent of Zeus.) The Diadochi, too, disseminated the idea of apotheosis throughout Asia Minor.

In the year 42 B.C., the Romans pronounced Caesar a god and invested him with the title Divus Julius, or "divine Julius." Augustus

was worshiped as a god in the East and by the end of his life enjoyed
a status far superior to that of other mortals in the Roman Empire.
Under his successors there grew up an emperor cult which encouraged Caligula and Domitian to feel and act like gods. In the
third century Aurelian officially decreed that he should be addressed
as *dominus et deus,* "lord and god." Virgil prophesied the birth
of a divine child in his *Eclogues,* written between 42 and 37 B.C.
Suetonius' glorification of Augustus and other Roman extravagances
of this nature all spoke in similar terms: a divine child, a divine
father, a particular astrological constellation present at the time of
the heavenly birth, mystic signs, miracles, a redeemer, an age of
peace and reconciliation. The British authority H. Buchthal com-
pares many of these phenomena with Mahayana Buddhism. The
life of Buddha, too, was tricked out with such a wealth of legendary
and miraculous occurrences that his divine origin and divine power
seemed to become ever more apparent. The resemblance to the
Hellenistic-Roman cult of royalty is most striking.

During the later phase of Gandhara sculptures the similarities
with those of early Christianity become so marked that the Christian
and Buddhist works must either have been derived from a common
source or, more probably, were directly linked. Certainly, Buchthal
has discovered some astonishing resemblances between devotional
sculptures of Buddha in Lahore Museum and early Christian sarcophagi in the Louvre in Paris and the Lateran Museum in Rome.
Some portrayals of Buddha are undeniably modeled on Christian
art and there are parallels between Gospel stories and some events
described in the Mahayana scriptures; for example, the feeding of
the five thousand and Peter walking on the water. As the American
scholar Alexander C. Soper wrote in "The Roman Style in Gandhara," an article published by the *American Journal of Archaeology*
in 1951, only one area in the Western world produced an art
comparable with the ideas and methods of Gandhara sculpture
during the century of its Kushan prime: the western Mediterranean
and its focal point, Rome. Links between West and East are discernible even more clearly in the sculptures of Hadda. Situated in
Afghanistan, five miles south of Jelalabad, Hadda was a famed place
of pilgrimage in Buddhist times. Digging there between 1923 and
1928, the French archaeologists Foucher, Godard and Barthoux
unearthed examples of Buddhist art dating from the third to eighth

centuries A.D. which can still be seen in the monasteries of Hadda, the Musée Guimet in Paris, and in Peshawar Museum. They include some very fine—one might almost say European—heads of Buddha, the head of Silenus, and horned monsters, demons and monks which are all closely related to French and Italian art of the eighth century. The famous demon of Hadda, a bent figure in cloak and hood with features apparently contorted with pain, is a portrayal of the Great Temptation and is reminiscent less of Gandhara than of the finest products of our own medieval religious art.

The Gandhara sculptures include not only Buddhist gods and Hindu gods such as Indra and Brahma, but also members of the Greek pantheon, a Harpocrates, a Silenus, centaurs and satyrs. Apart from these, Gandhara produced countless portrayals of patrons and benefactors, monks and ascetics, wrestlers and warriors, elephants and lions, fire altars and architectonic accessories.

Who were the foreign artists that gave the Indians their idealized vision of Buddha? What masters taught in Gandhara and probably Mathura as well? Who succeeded in giving visual expression to a figure who had become the supreme ideal of millions? What men were influential enough to set the pattern upon which gifted Indian artists based the growing splendor of their statues, reliefs and paintings—sacred works of art before which all the peoples of Asia were one day destined to bow down in devotion?

Although we shall never know their names, the genius of Alexander the Great, the spirit of Hellenism, the art of Greece and, last but not least, the artistry of Rome all made themselves felt here for centuries. That was how the picture of Gautama was first preserved in stone and how all Asia came to revere his features as a living reminder of the doctrine of compassion and of the road that leads to nirvana.

THE CAVE TEMPLES OF TUN-HUANG

One's impression on entering a chapel for the first time is indescribable, as though one had seen a vision. For a devout Buddhist, attaining this experience after a long and trying journey, it must be an experience of intense exaltation. Outside, one's very eyeballs have been scorched by the glare; the colors, though ranging through many subtle gradations, are few; the golden desert, green trees, the azure of the sky, an immense inverted bowl of porcelain over all. Within the shadow-filled chapel it was cool. The eye was first caught by a large statue of Buddha opposite the entry, which appeared to brood silently over little clay dishes of incense left by recent worshipers. In the quiet of this semi-darkness, which seemed steadily to dissolve, the great figure with its maroon robes might have meditated here through uncounted ages, more than a mere statue of plaster with broken arms. As we became accustomed to the subdued light, the scenes on the walls came into focus.

—IRENE VONGEHR VINCENT, *The Sacred Oasis,*
p. 67, London, 1953

SHIH HUANG TI was one of the most powerful monarchs that ever lived. He standardized weights and measures, systems of writing, calendar and laws. He decreed the proper width of vehicles and built long roads leading to his capital, Hsien Yang, near modern Sian. He divided his empire into thirty-six provinces and put each in charge of a military administrator. He divided court officials into twenty grades of seniority. He conducted major wars, extended his dominions southward as far as Canton and secured his northern frontiers against the Hsiung-nu or Huns by building the most massive fortified system of all time, linking his northern forts by means of earthen ramparts which later became the Great Wall of China. Such was the drive and energy of this absolute ruler that he diverted rivers, carried out vast irrigation projects, redirected the Min River through the side of a mountain, constructed a network of canals and built himself an enormous mausoleum patterned on the universe, with rivers, oceans and moving planets. The emperor decreed that peasants throughout the country could have land of their own, but since the vast government building projects could be implemented only by recourse to forced labor the peasants were obliged to abandon their small holdings and become little more than slave laborers, a process which has occurred again and again in the history of China.

When this mighty autocrat had given his orders and knew that his flights of fancy had been realized by the blood, sweat and tears of his subjects, he entered his litter and had himself carried through the countryside. Tax collection, government administration and military matters all came under his personal supervision. Shih Huang Ti wanted to obliterate the past and create the impression that nothing had existed before him. In his anxiety to be supreme emperor of the world and founder of the Ch'in dynasty he commanded that all annals, records and books by sages of former times should be destroyed. Wood, bamboo and parchment went up in flames. All criticism of the Chinese peasants' benefactor was prohibited, and swordsmen were kept busy severing dissenters' heads from their bodies.

But Shih Huang Ti reigned for only twelve years, from 221 until 209 B.C., and the Ch'in dynasty soon met its end under Shih Huang Ti's successors because the peasants rebelled under the frightful hardships of the forced labor system and because, needless to say, the emperor's own followers quarreled among themselves. The Ch'in dynasty was succeeded by the famous Han dynasty, which lasted from 206 B.C. until A.D. 220. It was a rich, great and flourishing period during which the two most powerful empires in the world were those of Rome and China. The Han spirit left such an indelible mark on China that the Chinese still proudly call themselves Han Yen, or Men of Han.

Perhaps the most important feature of the Han dynasty was the introduction of the Buddhist doctrine. The new world of ideas— the divine world of the Buddhas, Bodhisattvas and ascetic monks, the religious world of the Hinayana and Mahayana—all arrived in China from India at this time. The first Indian missionaries may have reached China as early as 217 B.C., but our information is unreliable on this point and the tradition that Ming Ti, second emperor of the eastern Han, sent envoys to India in A.D. 61 to fetch Buddhist books and priests is likewise open to doubt. Nevertheless, the foreign religion was certainly known in China and Buddhist monks were already living in the Kingdom of the Center during Ming Ti's reign. Before long, Buddhist pictures were imported into China along the

highroads of eastern Turkestan, Buddhist monastic settlements
sprang up beside the age-old caravan routes that linked western Asia
with the Far East, and here and there temples arose built of wood,
bricks and clay.

Tun-huang was China's gateway to the West. A rectangular
walled town in an oasis in the extreme west of Kansu, it received its
water from the Altyn Tagh mountains and was rich in fertile pasture
and herds of cattle. Kansu is a country of mountains, arid steppes
and fertile highland oases, oases spanned by the famous Silk Road
which linked the Far East with the Far West. The people who
lived, bartered and did business on this route became fabulously
wealthy. They saw caravans come and go, sold them provisions and
bought what they needed for themselves.

Ten miles north of the town of Tun-huang in the extreme west
of Kansu are the Caves of the Thousand Buddhas, a true wonder
of the world and one which was made possible because it lay on
the caravan route from India, because prosperous travelers of the
Han dynasty halted there and because missionaries decided to
immortalize their vision of Buddha there in pictures and sculptures
of dreamlike beauty. With the advent of Buddhism in the extreme
west of China there arrived, too, the Indian idea of hewing temples
into the living rock so that travelers between the two worlds who
halted at this oasis could linger before Buddhist works of art in
devotion and meditation.

The first artificial grottoes probably appeared between A.D. 357
and 384. There are several such cave precincts in central Asia, among
them the caves of Yün Kang, the caves of Lung Men near Loyang,
the caves of Lou Lan and the caves of Qyzyl, to name but a few.

At Tun-huang, access to the individual caves was usually gained
through a corridor leading into an entrance hall, behind which lay
one or more main halls. Caves on the same level were connected by
a form of balcony so that the visitor could pass from one shrine
to the next, and the walls of the caves were covered with beautiful
paintings.

The surface of the walls had to be painted with a layer of clay
followed by a layer of kaolin mixed with lime before color could
be applied. None of the cave murals of central Asia was properly
speaking *a fresco*, that is to say, painted directly on top of damp
and freshly applied plaster without supplementary binding agents.

73] A Chou Dynasty wine jug or *hu*, just over 18 inches high. The ornamentation consists of intertwined dragons. An inscription inside reads: *To be preserved forever and with care by sons and grandsons.*

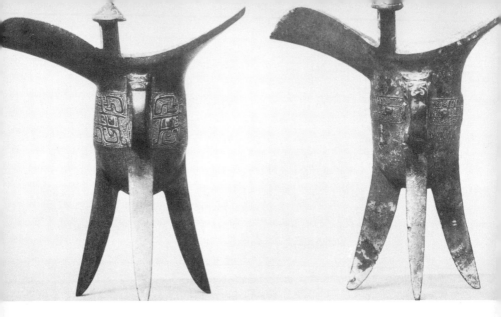

[74] Two three-legged sacrificial wine cups of the Chou Dynasty, of the type known as *chio*. These works of art also bear T'ao-t'ieh masks.

[75] A bronze stove from the Chou Dynasty (1122–256 B.C.), only 5.7 inches high, 9.4 inches wide and 18.1 inches long. A shallow vessel stands on each of the two circular apertures in its top. On the left is a vent to carry away smoke. Numerous ancient clay ovens have been found, but this is perhaps the earliest known bronze stove.

[76] This fragment of a dog-headed demon was found at Hadda in Afghanistan. It is a particularly valuable example of Late Gandhara sculpture and forms part of the collection in the Musée Guimet, Paris

[77] Hadda, on the northwest Indian border near the Khyber Pass, was a famous center for late Gandhara sculpture. The sculptors there perfected the Graeco-Roman-Indian style in the 5th century A.D. Here a demon in a fur coat is depicted. One of the most interesting pieces from the Hadda excavations, it is now in Musée Guimet, Paris.

[78] The head of Buddha, as conceived by Graeco-Roman artists in Gandhara during the 1st century A.D., was later "Indianized" by native sculptors, but the Gandhara style is evident in portrayals of Buddha throughout Asia and even in the far south. This splended stone head comes from Borobudur in Java and now reposes in the Musée Guimet, Paris. The ruins of the Buddhist temple at Borobudur date from the 7th and 8th centuries and are the world's finest example of Buddhist architecture.

[79] This bust with flowers clearly reveals the links between Roman sculpture and the Buddhist art of Hadda.

[80] Mural painting of Paradise from Tun-huang, showing Amitabha enthroned on lotus blossom between Avalokitesvara and Mahasthame. To left and right are smaller Bodhisattvas, and in the background a row of pupils. Extreme bottom left, woman kneeling on a mat in reverential devotion. The painting dates from circa A.D. 80[

[81] Scene from the life of Buddha. Prince Gautama, on horseback, encounters the three evils of earthly life: old age, disease and death. He is riding away from his father's palace, having renounced royal life. Beneath sits the Sakyamuni addressing three monks who kneel in an attitude of respectful attention.

[82] A very small section (the lower left-hand corner) of one of the finest paintings from Tun-huang. Not painted on silk like the other pictures, it is a piece of embroidery of the T'ang period, the golden age of Chinese culture. Sir Aurel Stein estimated that this remarkably fine piece of needlework dated from about A.D. 800. Stitched in red, brown and dull green, it depicts a group of pious women kneeling on mats. A child can be seen sitting beside the woman in the background, and the standing figure on the extreme left is a female attendant.

[83] Deep in the heart of central Asia, in the Chinese province of Sinkiang, Si
Aurel Stein's expedition came upon the ruined site of Miran. The ruins lie southwes
of the Lop Nor, between thirty and sixty miles from the Ansi-Khotan road, in a fla
region of a desert that stretches away in all directions as far as the eye can see. Thi
beautifully modeled head, which was found in an excavated temple there, is prob
ably a Bodhisattva. Parts of the face still bear traces of the original paint. Note th
remarkably detailed treatment of eyes and hair.

[84] The ancient burial places of Astana were dug up at Kara-Khoja, nearly twenty miles from the oasis of Turfan. This clay figure was a funeral offering. The horse is painted light and dark brown and the saddle is red, yellow and green.
[85] Cave 58 of the Tun-huang sanctuaries contained this remarkably fine altar depicting youths in prayer and good and evil spirits watching a sleeping Buddha.

[86] A Bodhisattva projects eerily from a cave wall in the light of torches, and hundreds of other sacred figures gaze from the adjoining wall. The sculptures in the Tun-huang caves owe their existence to artists and craftsmen whose influence traveled throughout Asia along the Silk Road.

[87] Scenic setting of the Tun-huang caves, artificial grottoes hewn into the rock. The Buddhist wall paintings and sculptures found in their interior are among the finest art treasures in the world. The men principally responsible for research into these sacred places on the Silk Road were Albert Grünwedel of Germany, Sir Aurel Stein of England and Paul Pelliot of France.

(The Italian expression *a fresco* here means "onto the fresh.") In this case the colors were blended with an adhesive binding medium and applied on a dry ground.

The extreme durability of the work done by Central Asian artists is vouched for by the fact that many paintings have survived for more than fifteen hundred years. However, the lasting qualities of so many of these splendid murals is also attributable to other factors. The oasis dwellers and their priests were anxious to ensure that the stream of pious pilgrims never ran dry, so they carefully protected their religious art and restored any pictures which faded with the passage of time or fell into decay. Renovations of this nature were carried out at Tun-huang under the Mongolian Yüan dynasty (1278–1368). By no means all the walls were painted over, however. The Mongols forbade the Chinese to learn the Mongol tongue or marry Mongol women, persecuted Chinese who owned weapons and horses, strangled China's trade and economy, abolished law and order and issued so much paper money that galloping inflation ensued, but they did not lay hands on the miraculous pictures of Tun-huang. Instead, they left them in the care of priests and even took steps to preserve their irreplaceable artistic value.

Nature itself can act as a preservative. Thousands upon thousands of almost equally splendid paintings housed in the large and densely populated cities of China vanished forever, but geographical location, remoteness and, above all, climate have combined to preserve the murals of Tun-huang until our own day. It is abnormally dry there, and the narrowness of the apertures leading into the interior of the caves helped to shield the pictures from the direct sunlight. Many entrances had collapsed, cutting the pictures off from the effects of weather, and still others had been blocked with sand by the perpetual storms of central Asia. They have only been cleared in the last forty years. Basil Gray, who visited Tun-huang in May 1957 and submitted the caves to further exhaustive scrutiny, relates that thousands of pilgrims from all over the world had scratched their names on the walls in many languages, among them Chinese, Uigurian, Japanese and even Russian. The cave murals originated in the dynasty of the later Wei (385–550) and painting ceased in the time of the northern Sung (560–1127). Five hundred years of superlative artistry, the chief legacy of Chinese painting as a whole, gaze down at us from the walls of Tun-huang.

The caves were first explored by Sir Aurel Stein, the celebrated British archaeologist and traveler. Stein was born in Budapest in 1862 and died at Kabul in the year 1943. While visiting the Tarim Basin in Sinkiang Province in 1900–01, he explored the city of Khotan on the Silk Road and unearthed the remains of a civilization that had once thrived there at 4,600 feet above sea level. Having examined a number of other important sites on the edge of the great desert, he reached China's western frontier and eventually came to Tun-huang in the Chinese province of Kansu. Stein's expedition left Kashmir in April 1906. He did not reach Tun-huang until March 1907.

It was known that there were hundreds of sacred grottoes in the vicinity of the oasis, and Stein was greatly intrigued by stories of the Caves of the Thousand Buddhas. On arriving in Tun-huang, he learned from a Mohammedan merchant that the many hundreds of shafts which honeycombed the cliffs north of the oasis contained yet another hidden treasure. In one of the larger caves the Taoist monk on duty there had discovered great quantities of manuscripts.

The monk had been trying to restore the shrine to its former splendor, a laborious task since sand had drifted in and the entrance had been blocked by fallen fragments of rock from the ceiling. When the sand and rubble was removed a fissure became visible in the painted inner wall leading from the antechamber to the temple. Soon an opening was found which gave onto a side chamber hollowed out of the rock behind the stucco wall, and this chamber was filled from floor to roof with rolls of manuscript.

Stein found that access to the hoard had been cut off by a wooden door, and by the time he returned a month later the monks had gone to the lengths of erecting a stone wall in front of it. Patiently, Stein persuaded the priest first to show him a few of the manuscripts and then to hand over the remainder.

Having cautiously unrolled one of the bundles of manuscript, the British archaeologist found that it contained paintings on silk, most of them in a fragmentary condition. It seemed, he said later, as though they had been hurriedly concealed during a sudden alarm— perhaps a raid by plundering Tatars or Tibetans. The manuscripts and pictures had certainly been deposited there shortly after the close of the tenth century A.D.

A year later the French scholar Paul Pelliot arrived in Tun-huang,

inspected the caves and took the rest of the pictures and a considerable number of manuscripts away with him. Thus part of this cache,
whose value is incalculable, is now in the Bibliothèque Nationale
and the Louvre at Paris, and part in the British Museum in London.

In London each bundle was carefully opened. The brittle, dusty
silk had sometimes crumbled into hundreds of pieces, each of which
had to be cleaned and reconstructed, an incredibly laborious and
time-consuming job. The colors had lost some of their depth and
luster, the silk had taken on a greenish tinge and many figures were
discernible only in outline or had completely disappeared, yet no
restoration work of any kind was undertaken.

Votum was the Latin term for a sacred vow or votive offering,
and a votive picture is a gift presented in token of gratitude and
respect. After reconstruction, some of the votive paintings of Tun-
huang turned out to be six or seven feet high. The portraits of their
donors which can often be seen at the foot of these works enable
one to date them with some accuracy because their style of dress
provides valuable information as to period.

One picture even bears a date which, when translated into our
own chronology, becomes A.D. 864. This takes us back to China's
golden age of art, a period when Chinese culture attained a zenith,
the time of the poets Li Po and Tu Fu, the golden age of Chinese
sculpture and a period of painting that was destined to remain
unrivaled.

At first sight the pictures seem to be similar and almost monotonous
in their subject matter and execution, but closer study reveals their
great diversity and latent symbolism.

Before the art of Tun-huang was discovered, little was known
about Buddhist painting in Europe, which was familiar only with
the famous Indian wall paintings of Ajanta and the Buddhist pictures
by great Japanese masters in the Horyuji Temple at Nara. The
Tun-huang pictures included some in Indian and Nepalese style,
others which betrayed Tibetan influence, others painted in typically
Chinese style and still others in which Indian, Chinese and Tibetan
elements were all represented simultaneously.

It was common knowledge that Buddhism had come to China
from India, but until these astonishing discoveries were made nothing had been known of the intermediate stages by way of which
Buddhist art journeyed eastward through Turkestan and Asia.

During his first expedition of 1900–01, Stein had found in the desert town of Khotan the remains of a settlement which had been abandoned in the third century A.D. and engulfed by the drifting sands of the Takla Makan. He discovered a quantity of letters and documents engraved in archaic Indian script on sealed and corded wooden tablets. The seals were of Greek design and carried representations of Athena, Heracles and other deities.

On his second expedition, Stein discovered Buddhist sanctuaries with mural paintings in late Graeco-Roman style dating from the fourth century A.D. at Miran, a ruined site near Lop Nor. These evidences of Western influence in the middle of the Asian desert constituted a major find. Hellenistic influence had not been the sole formative element, however. The culture of the flourishing oases that extended through the desert to the west of China found an inexhaustible source of inspiration in Buddhism and Indian art. Persian influence is also manifest, and some of the manuscripts at Tun-huang were written in the Iranian dialect of Sogdiana.

The art of Turkestan is interesting because it represents a point of contact between the great religions of East and West. There was an amazing wealth of religious ideas both in Europe and Asia in the first century of our era. Never before or since has mankind wrestled so earnestly with the problems of salvation and immortality. While Christianity and Mithraism were competing for supremacy in the Roman Empire, Buddhism was making its way eastward.

The new doctrine from India had now assumed the shape of Mahayana Buddhism, which sought salvation not merely for the individual but for the whole world. That is why pride of place among the paintings of Tun-huang went to the Bodhisattvas, who had earned the right to become Buddhas but waived it for suffering humanity's sake. Mahayana Buddhism was thus a late development of the original creed. Foremost among the Bodhisattvas was Avalokitesvara, known to the Chinese as Kuan-yin and to the Japanese as Kwannon. Curiously enough, Mahayana Buddhism's principal recipients of devotion were portrayed in male as well as female guise.

Apart from Bodhisattvas, the paintings of Tun-huang depict *jatakas* or scenes from the life of Buddha and visions of the "Western Paradise." The latter, which are distinguished for their amazingly intricate style and almost unrivaled sense of composition, include multitudes of figures, pavilions, terraces, oceans of lotus blossoms and other flowers, and heavenly beings singing and dancing.

Manichaeism was a gnostic religion founded in eastern Turkestan in the third century A.D. by a Persian named Mani. Born in the year 215 at Ctesiphon in Babylonia, then a Persian province, Mani preached in Persia and undertook long missionary journeys to Turkestan and India. He was ultimately persecuted as a heretic by the Zoroastrian priesthood, arrested, crucified, cut into two pieces, stuffed with straw and publicly exposed in the capital of the Jundisabur. Mani was a genuine Persian, but his religion was a blend of Christian, Buddhist and Persian ideas compounded with ancient Babylonian concepts and elements of gnosticism. Manichaeans could profess membership of any religious sect they wished, according to whether they lived under Christian or Buddhist rule. The basis of Mani's doctrine was a contest between good and evil, light and darkness. His inference was that light generally loses the battle and that darkness—interspersed with a few patches of light in keeping with the way of the world and its inhabitants—emerges victorious.

At the oasis of Turfan in East Turkestan, Manichaeans, Buddhists and Christians lived together in amity. Mankind owes Sir Aurel Stein a debt of gratitude for saving the silk paintings of Tun-huang, for the examples that he and Pelliot brought back to Europe are all that remain of an art that has been lost on the lonely roads of central Asia, stolen by marauders or scattered to the winds.

THE SILK ROAD

The silk roads via which China's goods were exchanged for those of India, Persia and the Roman East ran through the country-side to north and south, and the cities were everywhere inhabited by busy merchants from all the lands of the East. This explains why our second Turfan-Kara Khoja expedition brought back to Berlin a total of seventeen different languages in twenty-four different kinds of script.

—ALBERT VON LE COQ, *Auf Hellas Spuren in Ostturkistan*, p. 29, Leipzig, 1926

IT WAS the longest road in the world, an artery of communication between two vast empires, between people of many tongues, between the Mediterranean and the Pacific Ocean. It was a dream, a fairy tale, mankind's boldest venture. It went back to extremely ancient times but was destined to mold the future of the Asian continent. It carried tidings of alien worlds and some of the most sumptuous merchandise on earth, truly royal treasures endowed with the everlasting allure of the unattainable.

The Silk Road, which ran from Sian, capital of the province of Shensi in northwest China, to Palmyra and Antioch, measures about 4,700 miles as the crow flies. But the road is not a straight line. It surmounts the highest mountains in the world and weaves its endless way between East and West for more than 6,000 miles—a quarter of the earth's circumference.

As a trade route, it was perhaps the most important channel of communication in history, for it made possible some of the major economic, cultural and religious contacts and upheavals of mankind. The men who lived at one end of the world route had no idea where the goods in which they traded had come from. In Sian and Loyang, Kalgan and Peking, merchants all competed for the rare merchandise which the Phoenicians, Greeks and Romans had to offer, and at the many staging posts on the route middlemen computed the proceeds of international trade in the coins of many nations: Tocharians, Bactrians, Parthians, Medes and Syrians.

Silk was the lifeblood of these interminable trade routes. Several kinds of silk and an advanced weaving technique existed in China as early as the Shang period. Finds made in graves dating from between 1766 and 1123 B.C.—the period of the Shang dynasty—show that the Chinese used to write on ivory and bronze, that they obtained oracles from the fissures created in bone and tortoiseshell by the application of heat, that they were beginning to express themselves on shavings of bamboo and, above all, that they bred silkworms on mulberry trees.

Horses, glass vessels, precious stones, diamonds, ivory, tortoise-shell, asbestos and fine garments of wool and linen all reached the Kingdom of the Center by way of the most arduous thoroughfare in the world. Silk traveled westward along the same interminably winding road, across grassland, sandy wastes and desolate mountains, until it reached the Roman Empire.

In the year A.D. 120 some Roman conjurers arrived in the city of Loyang, accompanied on the last stage of their journey by a delegation from the countries on China's southern border. The magicians announced that they came from Ta Ch'ien, the region of the Western Sea. In the year A.D. 166, more dust-stained travelers from Ta Ch'ien arrived in Loyang, declaring that they were envoys of their king. The king was no less a person than Marcus Aurelius, the Roman Emperor. There are some indications that the Chinese in their turn had reached the Roman Empire as early as the lifetime of Christ.

Threads of silk are almost inextricably interwoven with the history of China. Its use was prohibited to many classes, and at certain periods even merchants were forbidden to deal in it. Certain patterns and colors, too, were regulated by law because they were an indication of official rank. Width, length and quality were all laid down by imperial decree. Silk was often used in the course of Chinese history as a medium of payment, and one of the country's main forms of taxation was collected in bales of that material. The collapse of Chinese silk manufacture and the invention of artificial silk are partially to blame for the economic exigencies of modern China. The quantity of silk paid in indemnities by China in the course of her history is almost incredible. When the "Golden Tatars" were expanding their Chin Kingdom to the south and had reached Kaifeng, capital of the Sung emperors, they demanded not only five million ounces of gold, five hundred million ounces of silver and countless head of cattle and horses, but also a consignment of five million bales of silk. China accepted these conditions. On Jan-

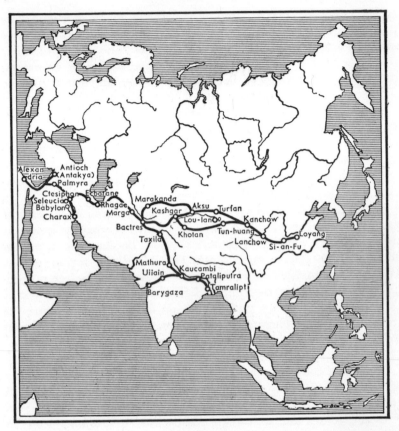

The Silk Road

uary 9, 1127, however, the Chin Tatars occupied Kaifeng and
carried Emperor Hui Tsung, the greatest painter who ever occupied
a throne, off with them into the inhospitable North. He was accompanied by senior officials and princes and princesses with pale oval
faces and delicate hands, all of whom were forced to undertake the
endless march into the remote wastes of Manchuria in bitter winter
weather.

For many centuries the technique of silk manufacture remained
a well-guarded secret. There were silk spies, fashion pirates and
experimental laboratories throughout the Mediterranean area even
in pre-Christian times. Silk, the queen of materials, was for centuries

the object of almost alchemistic attempts at imitation. Korea, Japan, India, Indo-China and West Indonesia all learned the imperial secret of silkworm breeding in due course.

The Silk Road survived every kind of human endeavor, greed and vanity. Bales of raw and woven silk swayed westward on camelback to be processed in Syria. In later times the Arabs became expert tailors in silk, to be succeeded during their great Renaissance by the Italians.

In Rome, silk became fashionable at court from the reign of Emperor Augustus onward. Roman patricians and their elegant wives and daughters selected the finest silks for their robes and preened themselves in the mirrors which were another Chinese invention. Silk (*sericum*) and silk cloth (*serica*) were in some mysterious way woven and exported by a distant people living somewhere far to the east, but the ladies of Rome had no idea of that remote and highly civilized people's identity.

The Macedonian merchant Maës Titanus must have had a commercial agent in the Far East. At any rate, he received an extremely accurate report of the eastern area of the Indian Ocean and the seas bordering the Pacific from a certain Marinos of Tyre. In the year A.D. 125, the geographer Claudius Ptolemaeus incorporated this report in his map of the world. It mentions a mysterious harbor called Cattigara, but we shall never know where it lay or whether it corresponded to Nanking, Canton, Singapore or—as Albert Herrmann suggested—Ha Tinh in north Vietnam.

The price of silk was extraordinarily high. In the time of the Roman emperor Aurelian (215–275), a pound of silk was worth a pound of gold. This in itself accounted for silk's extremely fine weave. The island of Cos in the Sporades group exported not only excellent wine in splendid amphorae and the fine salves known as *amaracinum* and *melinum* but also silken robes celebrated for their lightness and transparency, the *Coae vestes* of Pliny. These garments clearly revealed the contours of the body beneath and were consequently much favored by rich and famous courtesans. The Louvre in Paris displays a statue of Aphrodite dressed in a Coan robe, probably a classical copy of the celebrated "Aphrodite in the Garden" by the Greek sculptor Alcamenes, a pupil of Phidias.

The clothing, coverlets, cushions and curtains of the wealthy were all made of silk—an indescribable luxury. Emperors' wives wore

Asia

silken robes, but the fact that, despite a standing prohibition, vain and effeminate men also swathed themselves in silk was frowned upon. Emperor Elagabalus made a practice of bedding all the guests at his orgiastic summer fetes on silken cushions.

Caravan after caravan, long files of tortured beasts and toiling men, filled with a strange yearning for the unknown, journeyed along the Silk Road in each direction of the compass—yet another epoch-making Chinese device. Amber from the Baltic, Tyrian purple, incense, spices and gold were carried to the Far East. Caravans of this sort took four or five months to fight their way through the Tarim Basin. Death by thirst lurked in the sandy wastes and brackish marshes. In the high passes of the Pamirs the air was so thin that men fought for breath as they pressed onward. However, silk was a universal loadstone. To possess it was the pride and joy of all Europe. Silk rustled and gleamed from Persia to Constantinople, from Athens to Rome and Cádiz on the Atlantic coast of Spain, though thousands of priceless bales tumbled into the drifting sands to form the funerary offering of caravans annihilated by thirst.

East Turkestan, a huge depression filled with drifting dunes, consists partly of comfortless desert, large tracts of which are impassable for lack of water. All central Asia knows the buran or death-dealing sandstorm, an eruption of nature which is not only impressive to see but extremely hazardous. Abruptly, with almost inconceivable speed, the sky grows dark. The sun shines blood-red through a curtain of dust. Then the dust becomes so thick that even the sun is extinguished. The buran howls across the plain, unleashed with a fury that forces every caravan to halt and seek shelter on the ground. Huge masses of sand and pebbles are sucked up by the storm to form whirling funnels. The darkness grows ever deeper, the piercing roar of the storm ever louder. The strange clatter mentioned in so many travelers' tales is caused by stones rattling together in the storm-rent sky—a demoniacal sound, even if one does not equate it with the scream of the ghostly eagle which figures in Chinese legends.

No one has yet told the epic story of the men who lost their lives in such storms. Religious pilgrims, missionaries, merchants, scholars, even refugees from the Japanese and Communist reigns of terror during and since the last World War, all met their end in the buran. Needless to say, everyone knows the rules. Men, horses and camels have to lie down and allow the storm to rage over them for hours on end, but the buran is merciless. It whips them and lashes them with pebbles, causing man and beast to lose their reason and plunge wildly into the desert to die on trackless dunes. Many have been found as mummified cadavers, but, as Le Coq always said, a sandstorm generally likes to bury its victims.

East Turks, Dolans, West Mongols, Kalmucks and Kirghizes are hospitable, likable, greathearted people, the sort of people that only nomadic life and the country's untrammeled vastness could have bred. Perhaps the only exceptions are the Chinese-speaking Mohammedans known as Tungans. Nature is harsher and life cheaper than in many other parts of the world, and numerous explorers have perished there, most of them at the hands of the Chinese or of

wandering nomads. Adolph von Schlagintweit met his end in this
way at Kashgar in 1857. The Scotsman Dalgleish's thirst for knowledge was rewarded with death. Hayward of England and Dutreuil
of France were also murdered, and in very recent times there have
been numerous men who bade farewell to civilization in Kalgan or
Paotou and set off westward, never to return.

The Silk Road was not merely a track. The little-known epic of
the imperial highway, as the Chinese called this international thoroughfare, was a tale of lonely hostelries built of unhewn stone and
clay, inns erected out of camel dung, small forts garrisoned to protect passing traffic, marching troops, mounted messengers, courageous pilgrims. Consignments of water for convoys traveling through
the most arid stretches of desert, interpreters, customs posts and
tollgates—all these belonged to the saga of the Road. Oxcarts trundled
painfully through the sand. Traffic on the road included donkeys,
horses, camels, dispatch riders and mounted couriers. Mile after mile,
day after day, month after month, year after year, they passed by
at a pace and in an age far removed from the split-second timing of
our own.

The Silk Road was so long that people at one end of the world
scarcely knew what the places at the other end looked like. Who
can say whether the words of Paul and Barnabas did not travel from
Antioch to China along this road in the early centuries of our era?
The noble ruins of Palmyra, the Aramaic Tadmor and royal seat
of Queen Zenobia, who for a brief time ruled a world empire, still
reveal traces of Far Eastern influence. Farther on, the road led from
Ctesiphon, chief residence first of the Parthian kings and then of
the Sassanides, to Ecbatana, now called Hamadan. This was the
capital of Media, with a fortified citadel dominating the whole city
and pillared palaces with roofs of cedar and cypress wood on a hill
below it. The Achaemenides and Parthians who made it their summer residence were so rich that they faced the woodwork of their
buildings with gold and silver foil. Rhages, the Elamite town mentioned in the Book of Tobias, is now called Rei. Situated to the
south of Teheran, it enjoys magnificent weather in springtime, and
one can well understand why the Parthian kings chose to spend
the months of March, April and May there. Passing through Bactra,
caravans stopped to do business in gold, for gold from Bactra was
as much in demand in antiquity as silk from China. Eventually, they

reached Kashgar in Chinese Turkestan, situated nearly five thousand feet above sea level in a loess oasis watered by the Red River, or Qyzyl Su. From there it was only a few days' journey across the 13,000-foot Terek Pass to the legendary town of Ferghana. If plenty of snow had accumulated in the mountains during winter, the thaw provided sufficient water for irrigation purposes. On the other hand, a cold summer high up in the Pamirs sometimes delayed the thaw, and the blazing summer heat down in Kashgar brought great hardships in its train.

Vast clouds of sand come racing westward from the wastes of Takla Makan, obscuring the Kashgar oasis under a vast curtain of dust for more than two hundred days in every year. Pan Chao, the famous Chinese warrior of the first century A.D., lies buried in a temple there. In the second century A.D. wine passed through the oasis on its way to China. And it was via Kashgar that Buddhism reached the Far East. The bearers of the new world religion, the Yue Chi, also introduced China to the peach and pear. Genghis Khan, conqueror of Asia, must have visited Kashgar in the year 1219, and in 1275 Marco Polo gazed in wonder at the fertility and bustling commercial activity of the oasis. Earthquakes usually occur in maritime regions, but reports of earthquakes here in the heart of Asia during historical times have been handed down by word of mouth from generation to generation. Passing Khotan, 4,600 feet above sea level in the Tarim Basin, the caravans journey on to Tun-huang, the oasis famous for its cave temples. A northern route leads through Turfan, where numerous ruined sites have been excavated fifty feet below sea level in the Uigurian district.

Digging in Chinese Turkestan between 1905 and 1907, Albert Grünwedel, the celebrated German Indologist, brought to light archaeological treasures which included Buddhist cave temples and sculptures. Among his other discoveries were the remains of fine and obviously very costly silken garments and silk-faced hats. Silk was once an outward and visible sign of rank and splendor in the monasteries of central Asia, more than fifteen hundred miles from Peking.

At Turfan, Grünwedel reported, the blazing sun made any form of activity extremely arduous between June and mid-August; at Quarasahr there was the additional annoyance of mosquitoes; and in Qyzyl there were storms and earthquakes. None of the mural

paintings in the cave temples had survived intact, sculpted figures
had been destroyed and inscriptions scratched out. With endless
patience, he removed many of the splendid old paintings from the
walls, listed the separate fragments, packed them up and sent them
off by caravan. Tracings and drawings had to be made so that the
pictures could be reassembled later. In winter severe cold froze
India ink to the brush, even when mixed with alcohol. Work was
made doubly laborious by flying sand, which got into brushes and
pens, decomposed ink and ruined paints. "Even when one had succeeded in mixing the main color a cloud of sand could fly in and
change everything." Goatherds had been using the cave temples as
overnight shelters for centuries, and their campfires had blackened
the walls. Other caves were blocked by drifting sand and had to
be cleared one by one. No one who saw the splendid pictures in,
say, the Museum of Ethnology at Berlin would guess how much
physical hardship and privation they had caused in far-off Turkestan,
but no one, equally, would fail to realize that the oases along the
Silk Road represent an impressive and awe-inspiring composite of
the great civilizations of Asia.

Berlin's Museum of Ethnology sent a total of four expeditions
to central Asia. The first, under the leadership of Professor Grünwedel, went to Turfan and worked there from November 1902
until March 1903. This venture produced forty-six cases, each weighing over eighty pounds and containing dismantled mural paintings,
sculptures and other objects. A second expedition under Albert von
Le Coq lasted from September 1904 until December 1905 and
carried out research at the oasis of Turfan and in the Momul district.
The material results were very substantial. A hundred and three
cases each weighing between 200 and 350 pounds were sent back to
Germany by slow and devious caravan routes. The third expedition
of 1905–07 was conducted jointly by Grünwedel and Le Coq and
worked in the oases of Kutsha, Karashahr, Turfan and Komul. A
hundred and twenty-eight cases weighing between 150 and 175
pounds were removed. The fourth and final expedition, which took
place between January 1913 and the end of February 1914, was
again led by Le Coq and produced 160 cases also weighing between
150 and 175 pounds.

Vast numbers of treasures were removed. (One cannot say stolen,
for the mural paintings, reliefs and sculptures were falling to pieces

in their original abode.) The plaster walls with their Buddhist murals were regarded as an abomination by Mohammedans, and whenever a Moslem saw one of these pictures he did his best to obliterate Buddha's features. Apart from that, the powdered loess that had piled up in the ruins over the centuries and now covered the smashed and trampled statues was a valuable manure, so the oasis dwellers made a practice of digging it up and carrying it away.

Grünwedel complained bitterly about the Turks, who smashed heads of Buddha, dug out the eyes with pickaxes and demolished or defaced frescoes. "The peasants carry off the frescoes as manure, knock down walls so that they can drive carts in and out more easily and comb the ruins for firewood, scraps of leather, jewelry and valuables. At Idikuchari, incidentally, the latter seem to have been pretty well exhausted. The unfortunate thing is that one cannot stop them from doing it, for the area is too large and accessible from every direction, and control is impossible. The arrival of a European sets them all scurrying off to find something they can sell. They go on grubbing about for some time after the European leaves, but treasure hunting on a grand scale eventually ceases and the peasants once more set about their demolition work for utilitarian purposes."

We have already mentioned the successes of the French scholar Paul Pelliot and the explorations undertaken on behalf of the Indian Government by the British geographer and philologist Sir Aurel Stein. Professor Albert von Le Coq, a director of the State Museum of Ethnology in Berlin, wrote in 1926: "Since the exploration of the ruins of Nineveh by Sir Austen Layard, no other enterprise has been carried out whose results are comparable in importance with these expeditions to central Asia." In fact, they revealed something quite new. Instead of a "Turkish" country, as the name Turkestan implies, explorers discovered that the Silk Road was occupied until the middle of the eighth century by people of Indo-European origin such as Iranians, Indians and even Europeans. Of the numerous manuscripts found along the route some were in unfamiliar tongues and had to be deciphered, translated and scientifically evaluated by experts in London, Paris and Berlin. Authorities on Indo-European and Turkish had to study and decipher no less than seventeen different languages written in twenty-four different sorts of script. Many of the Sanskrit manuscripts revealed new and important facts about Buddhism. Quantities of liturgical works composed in Syrian for the Nestorian-Syrian church were also found. Many other manuscripts of Nestorian-Christian content were written in the language of Sogdiana.

Finally, in a waterless area near the Turfan oasis the German expeditions discovered a major portion of the Manichaean literature, which had hitherto been regarded as permanently lost. The texts, which were beautifully handwritten on excellent paper in inks of various colors, gave some entirely new details of this unique religion. Also found were sheets from books which had belonged to the Manichaean religious community. Composed in Middle Persian and other Indian dialects, though mainly in the script of Sogdiana, and adorned with miniatures of startling beauty, they were subsequently translated by Professor F. W. K. Müller of Germany. The principal importance of these Manichaean texts lies in the fact that almost all other examples of Manichaean literature fell prey to Christian hatred or Mohammedan religious zeal.

Between Tun-huang and Sian, capital of the Chinese province of Shensi, the Silk Road becomes a single track. Anyone who reached that rectangular walled metropolis by way of it had, as the great Swedish explorer Sven Hedin declared, a world of unforgettable experiences behind him.

The imperial highway, as the Chinese used to call the Silk Road, cut a gigantic cross section through the ancient world. It ran from the seething plains of China, through the oases of the edge of the Gobi desert, through the barren wastes between Tun-huang and Lou Lan—still the desolate habitat of the wild camel—and through the fairy-tale cities of the Medes until it came, finally, to the metropolitan cities of the ancient civilizations of Babylon and Tyre. The Silk Road has yielded up one secret after another. On March 28, 1900, Sven Hedin found the ruined city of Lou Lan in the vicinity of the former bed of Lake Lop Nor.

A year later, there came to light in a house built of mud bricks a heap of rubble containing rags, sheep's bones, the remains of fish and, among these, a few hundred sheets of manuscript and 42 wooden sticks, all covered with Chinese characters. Sven Hedin's rubbish dump was a veritable treasure trove. The fragmentary manuscripts, some of which actually mentioned the name Lou Lan, had been left behind by a Chinese garrison stationed there between A.D. 265 and 313. The results of research into Lou Lan by Hedin and his successors were not published until 1920, by which time Hedin was dead. However, he had already recognized the value of these finds. "The documentary fragments would set the seal on my painstaking investigations. They would tell when the lake—the Lop Nor—existed, what people lived there, what parts of central Asia they were in contact with and what name their country bore. A country which had been, as it were, swallowed up by the earth's surface, a people whose history long ago passed into oblivion and whose destiny no chronicles relate—all these things would see the light of day. I was confronted with a past which I was to bring to life once more."

The carved woodwork of Lou Lan betrayed Hellenistic and Gandharan influence and so testified to indirect links with west and south. The paper documents, which had crumbled into small pieces, displayed wonderfully clear and legible Chinese characters when reassembled. While digging in the cemetery at Lou Lan, Aurel Stein unearthed human bodies whose clothing and facial expression had survived intact. The ruins of a Buddhist temple yielded some small but superb wood carvings, figures, ornaments, models of a stupa, spoons and a child's mattock. Other discoveries included coins pierced with rectangular holes, a red ring stone portraying Hermes, the remains of a woolen carpet with a marvelously lifelike head of Buddha, and pieces of finely patterned silk.

Aurel Stein's excavation of another burial place at Astana, nearly twenty miles southwest of the Turfan oasis, brought to light sculptures of the eighth century which are among the finest extant pieces dating from China's greatest artistic period, the T'ang dynasty. These funerary gifts comprised small human figures, camels, brightly painted horses, demons' heads, horsemen in gay clothing and splendid figurative paintings on silk.

Throughout the length of the Silk Road, hundreds of textual fragments were unearthed dealing with the Prajnaparamita, or Mahayana philosophy of the period. There were also tenth-century Tibetan texts on military subjects, medical treatises, commercial records and a surprising number of texts on horse doctoring.

In the golden days of the Silk Road, the only things that traveled along it from one side of the world to the other were luxuries. Jade, for instance, was not originally discovered in China but reached the Far East by way of the Silk Road. Spiritual treasures such as

Buddhism and the Manichaeism of the West met in the oases along the Silk Road and mutually enriched one another.

International trade in mass-produced articles and consumer goods is a development of the nineteenth century, a manifestation of an age which has forgotten the true meaning of luxury. In Asia, wealth and objects of real value had an almost magical significance. The Silk Road lived, worked, and made its influence felt. As they passed along it, the great thoughts of mankind changed their complexion and the Indian Buddha acquired the almond-shaped eyes of China. Pilgrims reinterpreted the sacred texts and Christian ideas were introduced into Buddhism by travelers from Europe. And all the time the natural magic of the widest and most desolate landscape in the world played its part.

Today the Silk Road has reached its nadir. Its pulsing life is stilled, its trade a thing of the past. Uncertainty, the specter of frontiers, appalling poverty and universal mistrust are doing their best to wipe it from the face of the earth. And yet, stubbornly impervious to change, it still winds its serpentine way through the heart of Asia. Wars were always continuous in the countries and empires through which the Silk Road passed, but they did not prevent peaceful traffic in things of material and spiritual value from flowing along it without interruption from East to West and from West to East.

Has the sound of caravan bells been silenced forever? Personally, I shall never forget the images conjured up by memories of my travels in Asia: the shrill song of the sandstorm, the driving snow of winter blizzards, the encounters with solitary men on foot or in carts, the fur-clad Mongol horsemen, the soft-footed progress of the camel caravans, their beasts' haughty profiles silhouetted starkly against the bright infinity of the Asian sky, the tinkle of bell harness on horses' necks, the remote, mud-walled, brown and yellow towns and, sometimes, the breathless hush of the desert.

THE TREASURE OF THE OXUS

The discovery of any remarkable treasure or hoard naturally arouses speculation as to the persons who may have concealed it, and the occasion on which the deposit was made. Archaeological curiosity in such cases is rarely satisfied, and when attempts are made to reconstruct the history, too great a strain is often placed upon the imagination.

–O. M. DALTON, *The Treasure of the Oxus*,
p. 17, London, 1926

THE world has produced large nations and empires which have bequeathed us very few relics of their material culture. In some cases they have been engulfed by sand, in others the civilizations involved are so hard to define that we are frequently ignorant of what does or does not belong to them, and in still others luxury articles and objects of a utilitarian or religious nature lie scattered over vast areas, either buried beneath the surface of steppes or submerged by rivers and lakes. The things which have been dug up are exceeded a millionfold by those which are still harbored by the soil.

About a century ago a hoard was discovered which shed significant light on the intimate secrets of tribes whose religions and daily life still present numerous problems. Archaeological research has not concerned itself until recently with the valuable objects, sometimes of solid gold, which were once owned by tribes whose domain extended from the Middle East, through the whole of Asia, to the borders of China, and which were carried by them on their interminable wanderings. Some of them remain unidentified and many more have been scattered to the four winds. The equestrian civilizations of the Middle East, southern Russia and central Asia were for a long time the neglected children of art-historical research, yet their utensils and works of art are among the rarest, most fascinating and least easily comprehended examples of early craftsmanship.

Since the "Treasure of the Oxus" was found in the former Persian satrapy of Bactria and since it probably dates from the fifth and fourth centuries B.C., a glance at the Achaemenian era of Persian history would not be inappropriate.

The centuries before and after 1000 B.C. were a period of great migrations. The West and East "Indo-European" speaking tribes dispersed the people of the pre-classical civilizations. Indo-European tribes migrated into Greece and the territories of the Old Italians, while the East Indo-European or Indo-Iranian Medes and Persians dispersed the former inhabitants of the Near and Middle East and gained supremacy there. The word Aryan is derived from the Sanskrit *arya* and is a term originally applied to the principal tribe of the Indo-Iranian speaking branch of the Indo-European speaking family. The use of this expression in the racial sense, combined with the sort of value-judgments espoused by Houston S. Chamberlain and preached with such catastrophic results by National Socialism, is completely unscientific.

Repeated attempts have been made to determine the site of the Indo-Iranians' original home. They may have come from the great steppes of central Asia, or from the wide plains of southern Russia, or even from the shores of the Baltic. Old legends tell of a land called Aryanem-Vaejo and of interminable migrations by nomadic tribes into Persia and India by way of Bokhara and Samarkand.

The Persian empire, one of the great political edifices in world history, was built upon the ruins of the supremacy of the Indo-Iranian people whom we call the Medes. Ecbatana, now the oasis of Hamadan, was the seat of Cyaxares, most prominent of the Median kings. Not a single written sentence, not a stone memorial or work of art supplies us with information about the ancient Medes, but we know that in company with their Persian cousins they occupied the southwestern portion of modern Iran north of the Persian Gulf. The Persians' capital was Susa and their royal house that of the Achaemenides, named after Achaemenes, who ruled circa 700–675 B.C.

The Persian empire literally owed its existence to a dream. In the year 585 B.C. the Median king Astyages succeeded to the throne of his father Cyaxares. Because interpreters of dreams predicted at Ecbatana that the child of his daughter Mandane would one day rule the whole of Media, Astyages devised what he believed to be an extremely cunning plan. Unfortunately, overingenious plans of this sort usually go awry. Astyages was determined at all costs to keep a future ruler of the world under his thumb. Any Mede of noble birth was a potential usurper, so instead of giving his daughter to a Mede, who might prove dangerous, Astyages decide to offer Mandane's hand to a prince from a vassal state, reflecting that he would be able to get rid of the potentially dangerous offspring of such a marriage without undue difficulty.

The Medes of this period did not have a very high opinion of the Persians, who were a small tribe, so Astyages selected the Persian prince Cambyses as his daughter's consort. When Mandane presented the Persian with a son named Cyrus, Astyages bade his chancellor Harpagus to kill the child without delay. The commands of such implacable tyrants as Astyages were always carried out— though not necessarily to the letter. Harpagus carried off young Cyrus to the highlands, but instead of killing him he handed him over to a cowherd. We shall not relate in detail how the whole of Media fell into the hands of the boy who was brought up in the wind-swept highlands by a herdsman, or how the Median empire became a Persian empire. Suffice it to say that Cyrus was a prince of the Achaemenian clan and that the world supremacy of that great and renowned dynasty began with him.

Susa now became the Persian capital, but Cyrus built a second and equally important stronghold at Parsagarda, or "Camp of the Persians." This fortress, which was known to the Greeks as Pasargadae, is the site of Cyrus' tomb. The great king conquered first Ecbatana, then the whole of Media, then Lydia and its famous capital Sardis, and finally Caria, Lycia and Ionia. Cyrus' principal foes were the courageous Saka tribes or Scythians, a mysterious and still largely unidentified people of whom we shall hear more. Bactria, Margiana and Sogdiana became Persian provinces. In the year 539 B.C. Cyrus marched into Babylon, acclaimed by the whole of the East, and by so doing transformed Persia into the largest political structure in pre-Roman antiquity.

Cyrus died in battle. Under pressure from Scythian tribes, the related tribe of the Massagetae had moved westward and was pouring down from the steppes of southern Russia. It was while combating this menace that the great Achaemenid fell in battle in the summer of 530 B.C.

Under Cyrus' son Cambyses the Persian empire was extended to the Nile. Then, after a period of revolution and counterrevolution, the throne passed to Darius, the king who was defeated by the Greeks at Marathon in 490 B.C. Being bred in the spirit of classical

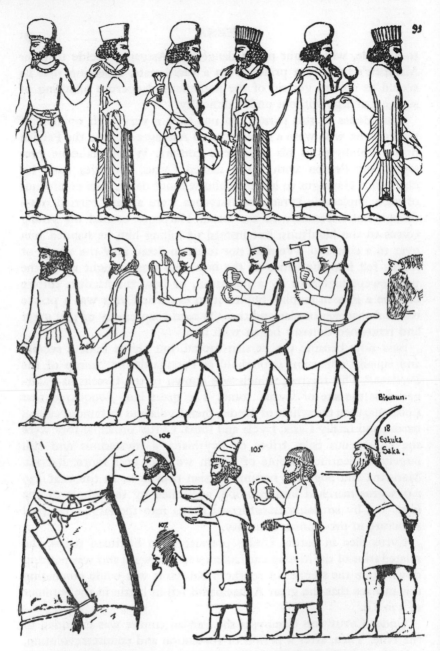

This frieze from a corridor in the Hall of Xerxes at Persepolis shows Syrians, Bactrians and Scythians presenting gifts to the Great King. The royal seat of Persepolis lies northeast of Shiraz in Persia.

antiquity, we only know Darius in the hour of defeat and have never given him due credit for his enduring achievements in the East. Darius did great things for the Persian empire. He, too, fought against the Scythians far north of the Danube. He founded the city of Persepolis and died during preparations for a vast expedition against Greece which he hoped would wipe out the Persian defeat at Marathon. In 520 B.C. he had a record of his achievements carved into the rock face at Behistun, high above the road and thus beyond the reach of would-be desecrators. The mighty Achaemenid also built himself an eternal resting place in the steep rock face at Naksh-i-Rustam, not far from Persepolis, where the burial chambers of Darius the Great and his successors can still be seen to this day.

Darius' successor, Xerxes, was the Ahasuerus of the Book of Esther in the Old Testament, the king who ruled at Susa and made Queen Esther his consort. Xerxes was defeated by the Greeks at Salamis and Plataea, and his armies were finally crushed on the Mycale Peninsula. As a result, Persia was banished to Asia for all time and never became a European power. Under Xerxes' successors, internal feuds and dissensions reduced the immense Persian empire to political impotence and laid it low in a welter of blood and misery. Seen from the West, Alexander's victories over the Persians were a gigantic spectacle, but in reality they were only the final demolition of what had already collapsed.

The southern shores of the Aral Sea are broken by the estuary of the Amu Darya, which rises in the southern Pamirs, threads its way through the mountainous country south of Bokhara and debouches into the Turanian plain, where it becomes a river of steppe and desert. For some hundreds of miles it forms the frontier between Afghanistan and southern Russia and divides Turkmenistan from Uzbekistan. The river's course runs through the former sites of age-old civilizations such as the vanished realm of Chorasmia and the ancient land of Bactria. Since the Amu Darya is identical with the renowned Oxus of ancient history, it is obvious that its waters still conceal thousands of undisclosed secrets. Modern research has indicated that in ancient times the Oxus flowed from the Aral Sea, along a watercourse now completely choked with silt, into the Caspian.

One evening in May 1880 a British political officer named F. C. Burton, who also acted as Resident in Seh Baba, three days' journey from Kabul, the capital of Afghanistan, was sitting in his police station in the Tezin Valley. It was nine o'clock, and Captain Burton was just resigning himself to a night as uneventful as all the other lonely nights when a Moslem burst into his camp and raised the alarm.

Apparently, three Mohammedan merchants from Bokhara had been traveling along the road from Kabul to Peshawar. They were in high spirits and, suspecting no danger, had unwisely left their caravans and ridden on ahead. The three worthy Moslems plied their trade between Khiva, Samarkand and India, sometimes taking their caravans as far as Amritsar. Their intention had been, as usual, to buy up large quantities of tea, silk and other goods in northwest India and dispose of them in the bazaars along the route between Afghanistan and southern Russia. On this occasion, however, they had taken no money with them on their journey to Peshawar, for the very good reason that Abd-er-Rahman, later Amir of Afghanistan, used to station himself at Kunduz in order to search passing caravans and confiscate the large sums of money needed to maintain his army. Instead of money, therefore, the three Moslems had been carrying articles of value unobtrusively sewn into leather wallets.

Suddenly they were attacked by bandits, who carried them, their servants and merchandise off into the hills. Crossing the Tesinka Kothal, the brigands and their prisoners made for the Karkatcha Range, where they halted in some lonely caves to examine their booty at leisure and divide it.

The man who had stumbled into Captain Burton's camp was one of the Mohammedans' retainers, who had escaped from his guards. Taking only two soldiers with him, Burton at once set off in the darkness. When, toward midnight, he came upon the bandits and took them by surprise, he found they had quarreled among themselves and four of them lay wounded on the ground. The merchants sat huddled together, not daring to move, and remnants of their valuables lay scattered about the cave.

Burton negotiated with the bandits and persuaded them to hand over the major part of their loot, but he had scarcely left when he was warned that they were planning to ambush him and recover it. Hearing this, he lay low and did not return to his little police station until six o'clock the following morning. He then sent someone to inform the bandits that he would muster a force and go after them if they did not surrender the rest of their spoils, and was rewarded by the return of a further batch. Having recovered three-quarters of their property, the merchants continued their journey to Peshawar. The three Moslems told Burton that they had acquired most of the contents of their leather wallets at Kabadian. Kabadian or Kahndian may have been one of the ancient townships which were buried by the Oxus. It appeared that the local inhabitants used to go digging for hidden treasure and that they sometimes found gold and valuables in the ruins of the vanished town, but the exact site of Kabadian could not be elicited. It may conceivably have been the place known as Kuad, a small town situated not on the Oxus but on its tributary the Kafirnigan.

Be that as it may, the Mohammedan merchants had certainly invested in some buried treasure and taken it to India with them as a medium of payment instead of money. The total value of the original treasure was 80,000 rupees, an enormous sum of money in 1880, of which 52,000 rupees were recovered when the remaining pieces were sold in Rawalpindi.

We lose sight of the Oxus hoard for a time, but it eventually came into the hands of General Sir Alexander Cunningham, whose collections were later acquired by Sir Augustus Wollaston Franks. Today, its adventurous career at an end, the treasure reposes in the British Museum.

The traders of northwest India who specialized in antiquities of this type sometimes commissioned reproductions of ancient bracelets, bowls, cylinders and animal figures in gold because they knew that Western archaeologists were interested in them. Franks immediately recognized that several original pieces had been imitated in gold, but he managed to acquire the originals as well, and it at once became apparent how much finer the authentic pieces were than the imitations. For all their skill, the goldsmiths of Rawalpindi had been unequal to the task of imitating silver and bronze antiques in gold with sufficient perfection to disguise the fraud. It should, however, be mentioned that the hoard did include some magnificent originals in gold.

Among other items in the Treasure of the Oxus were 1,500 coins from the Persian satrapies, tetradrachmas from Athens, pieces from Acanthus and Macedon, about two hundred gold pieces bearing the name of Alexander the Great and coins struck by Seleucus Nicator,

Antiochus I, II and III, Diodotus and Euthydemus. These coins ranged in period between the fifth and second centuries B.C., but since it was not known if they were originally found with the other articles and were unearthed at the same spot and in the same layer, they were no help in determining the date of the entire hoard. Comparative research has indicated that the Treasure of the Oxus belongs to the Achaemenian period in Persian history, that is to say, that it dates from the sixth to fifth centuries B.C., when the Persian throne was occupied by King Cyrus II, Darius I, Xerxes I and their successors.

There is still no clue as to who actually concealed the treasure. General Cunningham suggested that 2,000 years ago the valuables had belonged to an old Bactrian family and that they were hastily buried by a member of that family when Bactria was threatened by internal unrest or foreign aggression. As the sole party to the secret, he may have meant to return and retrieve his cache, but this was destined never to be. If the coins actually formed part of the hoard, the last owner must have been alive in 209 B.C., for the most recent coins date from the reign of Euthydemus.

We know that Alexander the Great captured the royal treasuries at Susa, Persepolis and Pasargadae, together with their immensely valuable contents, and that these treasures were later dispersed among his successors. It is quite possible, therefore, that a Bactrian family may have acquired a valuable nest egg of this sort.

The Treasure of the Oxus contains many objects which are related to early Scythian finds made in western Siberia, so the Scytho-Siberian works of art in the Oxus hoard represent a link between the goldsmith's art of Persia under the Achaemenides and the arts and crafts of western Siberia.

Most of the items in the hoard are of religious significance. Among these are gold bowls and jugs, cult statuettes of gold and silver, dishes portraying Ahura-Mazda, signet rings engraved with goddesses, lotus blossoms and birds, Persian kings at sacrifice, a fish beaten out of gold leaf (an ancient embodiment of magical or religious ideas), chariot horses, sun symbols, gold plaquettes bearing the figures of bearded men wearing cloaks, crowns and earrings, and others depicting a Median invention: the first long trousers in world history!

The religion to which most of these articles were dedicated was

founded by Zarathustra, who lived circa 600 B.C. Zarathustra, known
to the Greeks as Zoroaster and to the Persians as Zardusht, was probably born in Bactria, that is to say in the eastern region of Persia
where the Treasure of the Oxus was discovered. Latest research puts
the year of Zarathustra's birth at 630 B.C. His disciples incorporated
doctrines and commandments in the "sacred book" which came to
be called the Zend-Avesta, meaning roughly "Interpretation and
Texts." The original work was unfortunately burned when Alexander the Great destroyed the palace at Persepolis, and only one
volume and a few fragments are still extant. However, the surviving
gathas of the Avesta preserve the hymns and meditations of the
prophet in their original purity.

The deeper we probe, the more clearly Zarathustra emerges as one
of the greatest preachers of divine truth and religious perception.
Zarathustra believed implicitly in a single supreme god. It is true that
the old gods of the Indo-Europeans were also invisible and that the
Indo-Europeans of ancient India probably made no images in human
or animal shape, but when Zarathustra started to teach he railed
against the fact that men were worshiping not only large numbers
of gods but animals as well. His wrath did not confine itself to these
"heathen" practices but extended to the Magi, the priests who controlled the sacrifice, liturgy and half the daily life of Media from
their religious center at Raga, not far from modern Teheran.

Zarathustra alone was responsible for introducing the Persians to
the idea of a single, all-embracing, invisible god. He attacked the cult
of Mithras and the sanguinary hecatombs associated with it. For
Zarathustra, the universe was divided into two hostile camps ruled
by two hostile, elemental beings, Ahura-Mazda the good spirit and
Ahriman the spirit of evil, forces that have been competing for
mastery of the world since all eternity. Ahriman, the Indo-European
Devil, was endowed with creative power, which showed that Zarathustra was well aware of the perilous ambiguity and diversity of
evil and of the highly active and sometimes, even, creative nature of
the powers of darkness.

Man is, however, free to support the side of his choice, and it was
in order to help him and set him on the right path that Ahura-
Mazda made his teachings known through Zarathustra. Three days
after his death a man comes before the supreme tribunal, which con-
demns the evil and godless to perpetual torment and grants im-

mortality of the soul to the righteous. Zarathustra's doctrine is fundamentally hopeful because it implies that the spirit of goodness will some day triumph and that mankind will be redeemed.

The teachings of Zarathustra had been in circulation for some two hundred years before they were embraced by Darius I. But, although the latter proclaimed the Zoroastrian faith as the national religion of Persia, the common people still clung to their ancient beliefs and the Magi stubbornly resisted extinction.

Persia's art was fructified partly by Zoroastrianism and partly by the ancient civilizations of Mesopotamia, the Hittites, the Egyptians and the Greeks. The British curator O. M. Dalton, who wrote an important work on the Treasure of the Oxus, pointed out that Persian art served no apprenticeship but sprang abruptly into being when the Achaemenides seized power.

Nevertheless, it cannot be denied that the architects and sculptors of Naksh-i-Rustam, Persepolis and Susa and the artists of this often savage world of horsemen also achieved something imperishable on a smaller scale; nor can it be asserted that their art, sometimes strangely close to us and animated by the perpetual inspiration of a great religion, is doomed to oblivion.

THE SCYTHIANS

It is only within the last hundred years or so that Southern Russia has been definitely added to Europe. Before that time Asiatic tribes have been more at home in it than European.

—ELLIS H. MINNS, *Scythians and Greeks,*
p. 1, Cambridge, 1913

"TAKING into account all the characteristics of man, the Scythians occupy first place only in one respect. Though I admire nothing else in them, they surpass all other peoples in the single fact that none who attacks them escapes, and if they do not wish to be found no one can lay hands on them."

Herodotus had with his own eyes seen the Scythian homeland, which lay by the Black Sea in what is now the Ukraine. The famous pre-Christian traveler and "father of history," who was born in 485 B.C., had visited the ancient Greek colony of Olbia, now the town of Nikolaev in the Black Sea estuary of the river Bug, and had even traveled up the Borysthenes. The Borysthenes of antiquity was the Dnieper of modern times, and ran through the heart of the Scythian domain. Seldom has an eyewitness explored and described anything of comparable importance, for the Scythians were a mysterious people who first emerged as a recognizable force in world history about 700 B.C. and made their final exit about 200 B.C.

What sort of people the Scythians were, where they came from and what relationship they bore to other races are all questions that still remain in doubt. The Scythians had no writing of their own and left behind no written documents of any kind. It is seldom realized how quickly people without written traditions lapse into oblivion and to what extent their real importance is overshadowed by much smaller races with a more substantial literature to bequeath. By about A.D. 400 the life, deeds and renown of the Scythians had faded so completely that they became lost to contemporary view and lay in their graves until only a century ago before being brought to life once more. Not until the present has it dawned on us that the Scythians' customs, material culture and whole way of life made them one of the more fascinating peoples to have walked the earth.

The great speculation surrounding the Scythians is due partly to the fact that the ancient term "Scythian" was not a racial designation and had no purely ethnological meaning. Herodotus saw the Scythians as a fluctuating political force. There is, however, a second early source of information about the Scythians. This was no less a person than Hippocrates of Cos, a contemporary of Socrates and the most celebrated of all Greek physicians, who was more interested in the Scythians' geographical location and the way in which they were affected by their natural environment.

The Greeks called the Scythians Scythae, a name first mentioned by the poet Hesiod in the eighth century B.C. The Scythians' own name for themselves was Scoloti, and the Persians referred to them as Sacae. The origin of the name is unknown, but it may have been derived from the Indo-European word *sequ*, meaning "pursue." Again, the Greeks' Scythae may have been a modification of the Hebrew name Ashkenaz. Genesis: x, 3, tells us that Ashkenaz was a grandson of Noah, and according to Jeremiah the people that bore this name lived somewhere in the region of Armenia. The difficulty of interpreting even the Scythians' name and the manifold problems raised by it are illustrated by the fact that the Jews of later times used Ashkenaz as a name for what is today Germany.

The Scythians were at once many nations and one nation, visible and invisible. They appeared, only to vanish once more. All references to them sound typically Asiatic, but the writers of classical antiquity used the term Scythian to cover all the barbarian inhabitants of what is now Russia, and in the fifth century B.C. it was employed as a generic term for the peoples of European Russia. When Alexander the Great brought back news of similar tribes in Asia the term was extended to Asiatic tribes as well. It is clear from a sentence in his *Histories* (IV, lxxxi) that Herodotus distinguished between genuine Scythians and the various Scythian tribes: "I found it impossible to determine the Scythians' numbers. I was given very diverse estimates of the size of their population, being told sometimes that it was very large and then again that there were very few genuine Scythians."

One approach to the problem may be to concentrate on Hippocrates' description of what the Scythians looked like. In his work on *Airs, Waters and Places* he reported that they were plump and fleshy, sluggish and flabby, with fat bellies and no visible joints.

The Greek physician attributed this to their not being swaddled as babies and to their habit of not walking if they could ride. They had a reddish complexion "because of the great cold in their country" and their obesity rendered them unprolific.

This description does not match the very precise details given by Herodotus. Why could no one attack these fat men unscathed? Besides, Herodotus paints the Scythians as tent-dwelling nomads and mounted archers. If they really were the most skillful horsemen in ancient history, as many accounts would have us believe, they could hardly have been plump and flabby.

Hippocrates ascribes their physical condition to their uniform way of life. The men always traveled on horseback, the women in carts. The country was perpetually cold and misty. The Scythians' reddish or reddish-brown complexion might well have applied to the Tatars. We know, for instance, that Kublai Khan, who ruled the Mongol empire in 1260, had a red and white complexion. Marco Polo tells us that Genghis Khan, who brought the whole of central Asia from China to the Oxus under Mongol domination, was a source of surprise to himself because he was brown-complexioned whereas most members of his family had reddish hair and blue eyes. The Mongol prince Batu, who subjugated Russia and devastated Poland, Silesia and Hungary between 1235 and 1246, was said to have had a reddish face. The Flemish Franciscan traveler de Ruysbroeck, who undertook a mission to the Mongol emperor's court at Karakorum between 1253 and 1255 at the behest of Pope Innocent IV and Louis IX of France, mentioned the reddish complexion of Batu Khan in his report, which was written in Latin. It is probable, however, that the vital sentence should be translated as follows: "His face was entirely covered with red patches." I myself have seen Tatars in the Volga estuary whose complexion appeared gray or olive-green, though it should be remembered that complexion and pigmentation can change in the course of centuries and that continuous interbreeding must have taken place in the past seven hundred years.

Hippocrates tells us that Scythians were very easygoing, and once more attributes this to the time they spent on horseback. His remarks are limited to the ruling class, however, for the lower orders were evidently not so devoid of temperament. In his *Natural History* Pliny includes the Massagetae among the tribes of Asiatic

The Black Sea

Russia. He tells us that each man had a woman of his own but shared her with his fellow tribesmen. This was a practice among the Massagetae, however, not the Scythians. Marco Polo reports that the Tatars, who were often identified with the Scythians, regarded marital infidelity as a vice and thought it thoroughly reprehensible (I, xlvii). We do not know whether the Scythians were monogamous or polygamous. In most Scythian graves the women who were obliged to keep men company in death were buried in the same pit, but some distance apart. The only instances where women who had shared death with their menfolk were buried in the same coffin are the Scythian graves of Pazyryk, east of the upper reaches of the Ob. Tamara Talbot Rice takes this as an indication that wives and not concubines were involved. Although women occupied a very subordinate position among the Scythians, the killing of women after their husbands' death should be regarded not as a mark of humiliation but as a signal honor.

Among the Nile-Hamitic tribes of East Africa, and notably the

Nandi, it was customary for a man who retired to his hut with another man's wife to stick his spear into the ground in front of the entrance. Herodotus describes a similar custom among the Massagetae, who used to hang their quivers up outside their covered wagons when they wanted to spend an undisturbed siesta with another woman.

For all that, it seems doubtful that such tent-to-tent dalliance took place among the Scythians. The polygamous Asiatic tribes who keep their womenfolk in subjection insist that they remain in purdah with the other women and make themselves available to their own husbands and no one else.

Many similarities have been reported between the ancient Scythians and the Russians, probably because the Russians adopted a number of cultural assets from the Tatars and because intermarriage between Tatars and Russians went on for centuries. The apparent resemblance between Russians and Scythians probably depends, therefore, on Tatar intermediaries. The Russians borrowed a great deal from the nomadic tribes of their vast territories, notably via the Cossacks. The latter, in particular, borrowed extensively from their traditional foes in matters of horsemanship and dress. Many Russian expressions for articles of clothing are of Tatar origin. When Herodotus records that the Argippaei, who wore Scythian clothing, had flat noses and large chins (IV, xxiii), he corroborates information about central Asia given by travelers of the seventeenth century, who say much the same about the Tatars. Many of the Crimean Tatars, too, are squat men with broad faces, small eyes and a tendency toward plumpness.

Like the Tatars, the nomadic Scythians never planted crops, tilled the soil or built houses, but carried their dwellings with them on horse-drawn carts. These abodes were rectangular constructions like large boxes, woven out of osiers and covered with black felt rubbed with tallow or sheep's milk as a protection against rain. Marco Polo reports the same thing of the Tatars and supplies the additional information that they lived exclusively on meat and milk and never stayed long in any one place because they were always on the move in search of fresh pasturage.

Linguistic research has done little to solve the problem of the Scythians' origin. Many authorities assume that they were of Mongol extraction, others that they were of Iranian or generally Indo-

European stock. Speaking in Moscow in 1887, Professor V. T. Miller suggested that the Scythic language was related to Iranian but strongly influenced by the Uralo-Altaic tongues. Professor T. I. Mishenko, the Russian translator of Herodotus, espoused a similar theory, and the British scholar Ellis H. Minns, who wrote an extremely useful work on the Scythians and Greeks in 1913, also recognized the presence in Scythic of Iranian elements and Mongol influence.

Since we are unable to distinguish the Scythians from the other ancient peoples of southern Russia either from historical sources, linguistic attributes or ethnological characteristics, our sole remaining hope of identifying them lies in anthropology. In fact, the famous burial mounds or kurgans of southern Russia, eastern Europe and western Siberia have yielded human remains which indubitably belonged to Scythians. Were the skulls all wide or all narrow, anthropologists would be able to form conclusions about their racial identity, but we are unfortunately confronted by yet another riddle. For instance, five skulls dating from the fourth century B.C. were found in the famous grave at Chertomlyk in the valley of the Dnieper. Describing the find, K. E. von Baer stated that two were wide, two narrow, and one average. It is well known that at every stage in history there have been nations whose ruling class belonged to one racial type while the lower orders belonged to another, but in this case archaeologists were unable to tell which were the masters and which the servants. After years of research, the Russian authority Prince Bobrinskoy wrote that some of the skeletal remains found in Scythian graves revealed Mongol characteristics while others were purely European. It is now generally accepted that the Scythians were of Iranian stock and, as such, belonged to the Indo-European race. It is also clear that they all spoke the same language, probably an Iranian dialect.

Even though there is no more scientifically reliable method of defining the Scythians' racial type, one avenue of approach still remains open to us: their culture. When General Melgunov opened the first Scythian graves in southern Russia in 1763, and men like Clarke, Pallas, Dubois de Montpéreux, Sumarokov and many others followed his example by uncovering more and more of these mysterious burial mounds of 2,500 years ago, the outlines of Scythian culture began to re-emerge in the wide steppes of southern

Russia. One extraordinarily fortunate discovery was made in the year 1865 by Wilhelm Radloff at Katanda in the southern Altai, where the largest grave of all was found in an enormous cemetery. Born at Berlin in 1837, Radloff was a student of Turkology and had been traveling in Russia since 1858 in his capacity as Inspector of Tatar Schools. His discoveries made it clear that Scythian graves were also be to found in the southern Altai, over 1,600 miles from the sites on the Dnieper, Don and Kuban. Radloff had chanced upon some graves that were so well protected by a thick layer of ice that both occupants and clothing had remained well preserved for more than 2,000 years. Radloff gazed in wonder at the funerary gifts, the fine pieces of bronze, the strangely garbed bodies and the colorful Scythian way of life to which they had belonged, once consigned to oblivion but now recalled from the dead. Sadly enough, when the ice melted and nature's most efficient preservative flowed away, part of the find disintegrated before it could be saved.

Finally, in the Pazyryk Valley in the Altai, the Russian archaeologist S. I. Rudenko came upon about forty graves which had also been so well protected by the layers of ice which clothe the soil of Siberia that the art, life and history of the people of the Eurasian steppes appeared in an entirely new light.

The Scythian race has been resurrected from the many burial mounds that have been laid bare. Let us watch their mounted archers ride by once more, enter the presence of their kings and tribal chieftains, peer into the graves where they were buried with horses and huge retinues, examine their superbly ornamented goldsmith's work, learn to know their gods, beasts and sacrifices, hear of the dangerous life their soothsayers led so long ago.

COMPANY FOR THE KING

Having rubbed and washed their heads, they deal with their bodies as follows. Leaning three poles together, they pull sheets of felt over them, tie them up tightly and throw red-hot stones into a tub within the poles and sheets. Now hemp grows in their country. The Scythians take the seeds of this hemp, slip beneath the felt sheets and scatter the seeds on the glowing stones, thus producing smoke and diffusing steam better than in any Hellenic steam-bath. And the Scythians roar with pleasure in their sweat-house.

—HERODOTUS, IV, lxxiii and lxxv

ABOUT 1200 B.C. Russia was invaded by a strange people known as the Cimmerians, who were described by the earliest Greek writers as "a people by the ocean in the extreme west, wrapped in darkness and mist." We do not know the true identity of Homer's "ne'er sunlit neighbors of Okeanos close to the entrance of Hades." At all events, they were not a Scythian people, nor under any circumstances should they be confused with the Cimbri of Germany. In about 1000 B.C. the historical Cimmerians lived around the Strait of Kerch, known in the ancient world as the Cimmerian Bosporus. Because Europe and Asia are always treated as two distinct entities by Western historians, the long but coherent chain of events that stretches from the Pacific and across the whole of Asia and Europe does not enter into our calculations. One event has always given rise to the next, a reciprocal action not confined to the Balkans and central Europe but also embracing the widely separated areas of China, central Asia, Russia, Greece and Rome. Enough has been dug up in recent years between the Dnieper and Yenisey, the Urals and the Ordos desert to justify the compiling of a general history of Eurasia. History must continually be rewritten because the present explains and reveals so much about the past. Sometimes an interval of many hundreds of years has to elapse before the effects and, consequently, the true significance of an historical event can be assessed.

The interaction of Asiatic peoples and the migrations into Europe caused by their mutual impingement have promoted a new attitude toward history. What happened in China did, in fact, have very considerable effects on central Europe. This form of reciprocal action is destined to exercise a profound influence on the future course of European history, too. One has only to think of China's unresolved relationship with Outer Mongolia!

The decline of the Roman Empire, the eruption of Germanic tribes into western Europe, the migration of Slavic tribes into central and southern Europe, the Renaissance, the revival of western Europe's interest in classical antiquity and, finally, the voyages that led to the discovery of the New World—behind all these gigantic upheavals lurked the hordes of central Asia, as the American Sinologist Montgomery McGovern so rightly pointed out in 1939.

Emperor Hsüan Wang, who ruled China between 827 and 781 B.C., in this sense "made" European history. During the time of the Chou dynasty to which he belonged, the north and northwest of China was invaded by the seminomadic Hsiung-nu. The Chinese emperor marched against the invading Hsiung-nu, defeated them in the region of the modern provinces of Shansi and northern Shensi, and pursued his dangerous adversaries into the mountains from which they had been making their mounted forays into the fertile plains of China.

By withdrawing to more westerly grazing lands the Hsiung-nu exerted pressure on other nomads and so sparked off a series of migrations which ran through central Asia until they impinged on the Massagetae, who lived in the area between the Caspian and the Aral Sea. In their quest for fresh grazing land for their horses, these powerful nomads, who according to Strabo used to kill off the old men of their tribe in order to preserve their mobility, attacked the Scythians. The Scythians, who may originally have roamed east Turkestan, turned on the East Cimmerians. The tribes of the endless Asiatic steppes may also have been set in motion in this way, as Ellsworth Huntington and Tamara Talbot Rice suggest, due to a great drought about 800 B.C. In the ensuing wars between the Cimmerians and the Scythians the latter proved victorious.

The secret of the Scythian success lay in the way their hordes charged, hit the enemy hard and then withdrew at lightning speed. The Scythians pushed on farther westward, migrated into southern Russia and settled there between 722 and 705 B.C., partly as nomads and partly as sedentary communities.

This was when the true history of the Scythians began. They

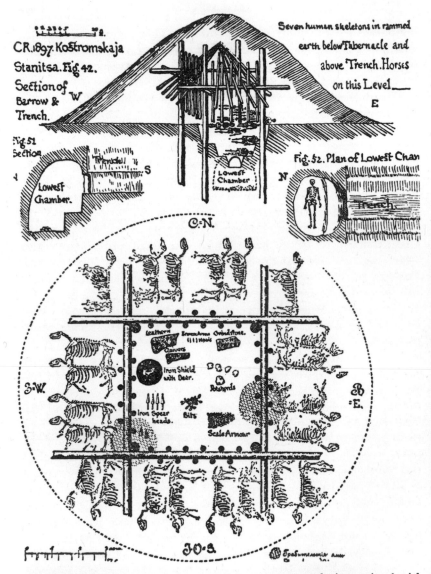

CR.1897. Kostromskaja Stanitsa. Fig 42. Section of Barrow & Trench.

Seven human skeletons in rammed earth below Tabernacle and above Trench. Horses on this Level

W   E

Fig. 51 Section

Lowest Chamber.

Lowest Chamber

Trench

S   N

Fig. 52. Plan of Lowest Chamber

Trench

C. N.

Leather

Iron Arms Grindstone

Heads

Quivers

Iron Shield with Deer.

Potsherds

Iron Spear heads.

Bits

Scale Armour

S. W.

O. E.

The Russian archaeologist Weselowski dug up an extremely interesting burial mound at Kostromskaya in the Kuban region. This diagrammatic illustration of it shows how a kurgan was arranged. In the lowest chamber lay the dead chieftain, and above him were buried the thirteen or more people who accompanied him into death. Around the rectangle of the actual grave were found the skeletons of twenty-two horses. The famous golden stag on the iron shield was also discovered in this grave.

must have been genuinely dangerous opponents in war, because in the year 512 B.C. they succeeded in repelling an invasion by the Persian king Darius and in 325 B.C. they annihilated an expeditionary force under the command of Alexander's general Zopyrion. They were not driven out of the Balkans and the eastern half of central Europe by the up-and-coming Celts until after 300 B.C., but were eventually crushed in southern Russia by the Sarmatians. Perhaps their once tough and battle-hardened way of life had been vitiated by a superabundance of slaves, spoils and riches.

Their downfall may, on the other hand, have been due to their womenfolk, who were completely subordinate to their husbands. During the long treks on which thousands of slave girls accompanied the Scythian columns, the Scythians were obviously unable to treat their own wives any differently from their concubines. Thus, both wives and slave girls rode in carts the whole time, with the result that in the long run their health suffered in the way mentioned by Hippocrates.

The people who ultimately defeated the Scythians, the Sarmatians, had womenfolk of quite another caliber. Sarmatian women took part in war, rode about freely and won such a reputation for strength and independence that they supplied a basis and pattern for the Amazon stories of antiquity. According to legend, the Amazons were warlike women whose name was derived from the Greek expression "breastless," because, if we are to believe Hippocrates, they amputated their right breast to help them string bows more easily. This derivation is probably erroneous, and it is more likely that the name is related to *maza*, which is the Circassian expression for "moon" and would denote an association with a moon cult. The Scythians called the Sarmatian Amazons "Oiorpata," from *oior* (man) and *pata* (kill). Amazons are said to have lived on the eastern and southern shores of the Black Sea and in the Caucasus, notably in the area of Trebizond, now the port of Trabzon in northeast Anatolia.

When referring to Scythians, the Greeks always meant nomads. According to Herodotus there were also "agricultural Scythians," "royal Scythians" and "plow Scythians" in the Ukraine, but these were probably tribes who merely plundered the earlier residents of the black-earth district and disposed of their surplus production of grain to the Greeks on the Black Sea coast, bartering it for vessels and metalwork of Greek manufacture. Herodotus himself tells us that, having always been tent nomads and mounted archers, the Scythians generally supported themselves by cattle breeding rather than agriculture and that they owned horse-drawn dwellings rather than towns and fortresses. Their homeland, a vast area of plains, was rich in grass and well irrigated by the many wide rivers that flowed through it. The Scythians had inexhaustible reserves of pasturage for their cattle, although, as the knowledgeable Herodotus added darkly, grass was a sovereign cause of galls.

We learn of gods with strange names, of the supreme god Pappaeus and his consort Apia, of their son Oetosyrus, of a Scythian Aphrodite named Artimpasa and a Scythian Neptune called Thamiasadas. The Scythians had no idols, altars or temples, and Herodotus stated that the only altars and effigies they had ever possessed were dedicated to one particular god who was the equivalent of Ares.

The Scythians did, however, sacrifice to their gods. Having tied the forelegs of the sacrificial beast together, the man in charge tugged at the rope so that the animal fell over. Then, calling upon his god, he threw a noose around its neck and garroted it by inserting a stick in the noose and twisting it to form a tourniquet. The meat was cooked on the spot. Since the nomadic Scythians inhabited plains which were "dreadfully deficient in wood," they are reported to have devised an interesting expedient. Having skinned the sacrificial beast and removed the bones, they boiled the meat in a caldron—if they owned one—apparently using the bones as fuel for their fire. If they had no caldron they threw all the meat into the animal's stomach, added water, and lit a fire of bones beneath it. "Bones burn wonderfully," writes Herodotus, "and the animal's stomach can hold the meat cut off the bones tolerably well. Thus the ox has to cook itself, as does every sacrificial beast." Horses were an especially favored form of sacrifice among the Scythians, who used to throw out the first cuts from meat and entrails to the accompaniment of special rites.

Sacrifice varied only in the case of Ares. Wherever the Scythians pitched camp they built a shrine to him out of bundles of brushwood heaped up to form a tall tower. At its summit, in front of the sacred image of Ares, they placed an ancient iron sword to which they sacrificed horses and other grazing animals. They did not stop there, however. Of all the prisoners taken during the Scythians' never-ending wars, one in every hundred was sacrificed. Pouring wine on their heads, the Scythians slaughtered them over a vessel and poured the blood on the sword. Then they cut off their victims' right arms and hurled them into the air, leaving them to lie where they fell. Herodotus stresses that pigs were never sacrificed and that the Scythians neither kept them nor ate their meat.

The Scythians' warlike customs tended to be extremely gruesome. When a Scythian had killed a man he drank his blood and brought his enemy's head to the king; only then could he share in the spoils of war. The victor hung his opponent's scalp on the reins of his charger "as a towel" and "flaunted it," as Herodotus puts it. The man who had most scalps enjoyed the highest reputation. The Scythians also made capes out of their victims' skin or stuffed them and led them about on horseback. Many of the customs of these savage tribesmen are too disgusting to mention here, but there is no doubt that they used to cover their deadliest enemies' skulls with leather or, if they were wealthy enough, gold leaf, and use them as drinking vessels.

Family disputes were apparently settled in just as gruesome a manner. When the king had delivered judgment on the case, the victor treated the skulls of his kinsmen "according to ancient custom." Then, inviting guests to join him, he placed the "drinking vessels" before them and related how he had got even with his kinsmen for insulting him. "And that is what they call heroic virtue," adds Herodotus.

Once a year each chieftain filled a large mixing bowl with wine. Any Scythian who had slain at least one enemy was permitted to drink from it, but the "inglorious ones" were not even allowed to watch. Not to own a scalp was a mark of disgrace, but those who had scalped a large number of enemies were always poured two cups of wine.

The Scythians evidently had shamans, though it is not clear whether their necromancers were only soothsayers or had wider functions. They used to collect large bundles of osiers, lay them on the ground and jumble them together. Then, picking up each twig in turn, they interpreted its meaning and returned it to the pile. When one bout of soothsaying was completed the whole process began again. Herodotus also mentions the Scythian clairvoyants or *enares*. The latter expression was the Greek equivalent of an unknown Scythic word meaning men whose virility was on the wane. These effeminate individuals used to forecast the future from pieces of lime bark.

The wise men or magicians played an important role in the community, especially if the king fell sick, for on such occasions the most eminent of them were summoned to give their advice. They announced that such and such a Scythian had committed perjury before the king's hearth, and gave the guilty party's name. Important oaths were always taken standing before the royal hearth. Even though the Scythians were a nomadic people, the picture of their kings seated on the throne before the circular fireplace is strangely reminiscent of the Mycenaean culture and of Nestor in his palace at Pylos.

A man who had been charged with perjury was seized and dragged before the assembly. The soothsayers then explained how the signs had convinced them that the accused had forsworn himself before the royal hearth. When the accused had denied the charge and protested violently—as he usually did—the king called in another three magicians. If they also came to the conclusion that the prisoner was guilty of perjury, the unfortunate man was summarily decapitated and the first three soothsayers shared his personal effects between them.

The process was not devoid of danger even for the Scythian sages. If the second committee of three pronounced the accused man innocent, a succession of soothsayers was called in. Unlike modern courts, the Scythians did not rely on the judgment of one or two experts alone. If the majority found the accused not guilty the first three soothsayers were themselves executed in a far from pleasant manner. Bound hand and foot and gagged, they were placed in carts loaded with brushwood and harnessed to oxen. The brushwood was set on fire, the oxen galloped off, and the carts raced eerily across the plain like huge flaring torches. "Many oxen are burned with the soothsayers," Herodotus remarks cheerfully, "but many of them escape with a singeing when the shaft burns through." (By "them" he means, of course, the oxen.) When the king condemned a man to death all the male members of his extensive clan suffered a like fate, only girls and women being exempt.

Since Herodotus personally visited the Borysthenes and traveled through the countryside around the Dnieper where the Scythians used to live, his account of the burial of Scythian kings is worthy of credence. An enormous rectangular pit was dug, and the king's corpse was embalmed by removing his entrails and stuffing him with shredded spices, frankincense, celery and dill.

The Scythians cut off a piece of their ear as a small token of loyalty, shaved their skull, slashed their arms, scratched their brow and nose and drove an arrow through their left hand. Thus prepared, they transported their dead king on a cart to a neighboring clan and demanded the same visible manifestations of loyalty. When these were forthcoming, the horrid procession moved on to the next tribe, and so on until all the dead king's subjects had demonstrated their fidelity to him in this simple but heartfelt manner. On reaching the burial place, the mourners placed the corpse on a mat and stuck spears into the ground on either side. Poles were laid across these and covered with wickerwork. At least one of the king's wives was strangled as a funerary offering, as were his cupbearer, cook, stable master, body servant and herald. A suitably impressive number of horses was also placed in the king's grave. All these sacrifices were "buried in the ample space remaining in the grave," together with votive offerings and gold bowls. Then, when the tomb was ready to be closed, everyone joined in building a mound above it, competing with one another in their efforts to make it as tall and massive as possible.

Even that did not end the respects paid to the dead king. After a year had elapsed the rest of his most favored young retainers had the great honor and good fortune to be strangled and so follow their former master into death. These privileged persons were not, however, allowed to exceed fifty in number. Fifty of the finest horses were eviscerated, cleaned, stuffed with chaff and sewn together again. Peculiar catafalques were then erected. The dead horses were suspended on poles complete with bridle, bit and reins. Each of the fifty slaughtered youths was placed upon a horse and the gruesome cortege took up its station around the tumulus. Only then did the Scythians leave their king in peace, consoling themselves with the thought that they had to some extent alleviated his loneliness.

Anyone who thinks that the Greek historian's descriptions of a period already three hundred years in the past were invented or fabricated by a fertile imagination can be disabused by archaeology. The Scythian graves of Russia and the finds made in those amazing cemeteries have confirmed much of what Herodotus wrote.

KINGS, CONCUBINES AND HORSES

The account of Scythian funerals given by Herodotus agrees so well with the archaeological data, as summarized in the survey of the principal Scythian tombs of South Russia, that the two sources of information may be used to supplement one another.

—ELLIS H. MINNS, *Scythians and Greeks,*
p. 87, Cambridge, 1913

DESCRIBING the funerals of Turko-Tatar chieftains in the year 1300, Marco Polo said that they were carried to a mountain and there buried. "Listen to this strange story," wrote the Venetian explorer. "When they carry the corpse of a ruler to its burial they kill all the people who pass the funeral procession on the way, crying 'Go and serve your master in the next world!' The same applies to horses, for when their ruler dies they slaughter all his best chargers so that they shall be at his disposal in the world hereafter. I tell you this as a true fact: that when Mangu Khan died more than twenty thousand people who chanced to meet his funeral procession were slain." At the death of Genghis Khan, twoscore pretty girls had to accompany the emperor into his tomb. In 1260, after visiting the court of the Mongol prince at Karakorum, Wilhelm de Ruysbroeck reported: "They erect a large burial mound over their dead and on it place an effigy of the dead man with a drinking cup in its hand and its face toward the east. I saw the freshly dug grave of a prince for whom they had hung sixteen horsehides on tall scaffolds, four for each quarter of the earth. They had also placed meat and drink in his grave, yet they declared that he had been baptized a Christian."

The Arab author Ibn Batuta, who traveled widely in western and central Asia, as well as in India, China, Sumatra and North and East Africa in the middle of the fourteenth century, described the obsequies of a khan who had fallen in battle. The dead man was laid on a handsome couch in a large grave. All his weapons and all his gold and silver household utensils were buried with him, as were four female slaves and six of his favorite mamelukes bearing a number of drinking vessels. They were entombed, and the earth was heaped above them to form a tall mound. Then four horses were slaughtered and hung on the mound in precisely the manner described by Herodotus 1,800 years earlier. The kinsmen of the khan were likewise killed and buried with their gold and silver vessels. Three horsehides were hung on the doors of ten of his relatives' tombs and one each on the remainder. This happened in the Chinese province of Shensi.

An inscription found at Orkhon and dated August 1, 732, is extremely informative. It is the earliest written tradition in the Turkish language and was composed by Jolygh Tigin as a memorial to Bilgä or Pitkia, Khan of the Turks. The inscription runs:

My father, the Khan, died on the thirty-sixth day of the tenth month of the Year of the Dog. On the thirty-seventh day of the fifth month of the Year of the Pig I decreed his obsequies. Lisün tai Sängün came to me at the head of five hundred men. They brought a huge quantity of perfume, gold and silver. They brought musk for the funeral and sandalwood. All these mourners had cut off their hair and clipped their ears. They gave up their best horses, their black sables and blue squirrels without number.

We also know that the Huns mutilated themselves at the death of Attila, and that this custom persisted among the Turkish tribes of central Asia until the nineteenth century. The practice of sacrificing horses to a dead man as funerary gifts is recorded among the Avars, the Magyars, the ancient Bulgarians and the Cumans, an extinct Turkish people who became completely Magyarized during the eighteenth century. Stuffed horses were also presented to the dead by the Yakuts, the Voguls, the Ostyaks and the Chuvashes. Among the Kirghizes a horse is dedicated to the dead man at his funeral but not sacrificed until the first anniversary of his death. It is also known that the Chinese give their dead a horse of wood, cardboard or paper which is carried in the funeral procession and burned at the burial.

Archaeological finds, too, have supplied astonishing confirmation of what Herodotus wrote about the Scythians. For the last seventy years or so, the Russians have taken the lead in unearthing *kurgans*, a Tatar expression for a burial mound which has been adopted into the Russian language. The Scythian kurgan graves cover a huge area. Tombs of this nature have been found as far afield as the Black Sea coast, the Kuban district, the lower reaches of the Volga, the Urals, the Don, the Dnieper, the Bug, Rumania, Hungary, Bulgaria, Vettersfelde in Brandenburg, the Altai Range and Minusinsk, on the river Yenisey in West Siberia. All these Scythian graves came into being between the sixth and third centuries B.C.

The contents of such a tomb were published in 1912 and 1913 by the Russian archaeologist N. J. Weselowski, who excavated the Solocha kurgan in the valley of the Dnieper. In an undisturbed side grave there, he found the Scythian prince, his head pointing eastward, complete with all his weapons and finery. At his feet lay an iron dagger with a bone handle, together with three hundred pieces of sheet gold beaten into different shapes and bearing punched decoration. The grave also yielded a gold neckband, five gold bracelets and an eighteen-inch iron sword with a gold-plated hilt and scabbard. To the right of the dead man's head lay a coat of iron mail. His helmet and a golden comb illustrating Scythians in battle had fallen off during his stay in the tomb. The comb is one of the finest pieces of antique goldsmith's work to have been found in south Russia. There were also a second sword, six silver vessels adorned with Scythian scenes, a wooden vessel plated with gold, a gold bowl, and on it a *goryt* containing 180 arrows. This piece of equipment, a case designed to hold both bow *and* arrows, was used by Scythians, Saka and Persians. Near the north wall of the burial chamber lay the skeleton of a man who had been given to the dead prince as a servant. He, too, was equipped for the next world with a short sword, iron mail, three spears and some arrows. Only the iron spear points and bronze arrowheads were found, the wooden shafts having completely disintegrated. Close by was a burial chamber containing five horses.

Excellent reviews of the fascinating discoveries made in the kurgans of Russia, Hungary, Rumania and Bulgaria were compiled by the late Professor M. Rostovzev of Yale in 1931 and by Ellis H. Minns in the year 1913.

Russian archaeologists have classified the kurgan finds under the following headings: the Kuban group, the Taman group (named after the Taman Peninsula), the Crimean group, the Dnieper steppe group, and the kurgans of the Kiev area, Poltava, the Don, the

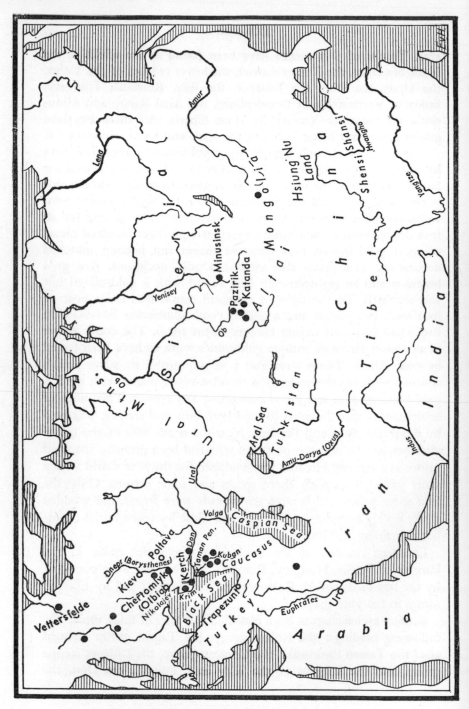

Central Asia

Volga and the Urals. Hundreds if not thousands of such kurgans have been unearthed.

From these graves have emerged a people who can properly be described as Scythians, together with a culture whose Scythian elements can easily be distinguished from the Persian, Greek, Mesopotamian and other influences which are also in evidence. A great and unique cultural domain extending to the borders of China has been discovered, and Eurasia's diverse but individual style of animal portrayal has become an accepted feature of cultural history.

The sites of Scythian culture disclose an art richer in gold than that of almost anywhere else on the globe. Even Mycenae, "rich in gold," as Homer described it, was surpassed by the Scythians. Gold could only have been amassed in such quantities by regular and systematic prospecting and mining. In fact, the principal sources of the precious metal were the Urals and the Altai.

We shall never know how many undiscovered treasures lie beneath the Siberian steppes and the black earth of the Ukraine. Thousands of graves were rifled by the Russians in the eighteenth century, but the treasures on display in The Hermitage at Leningrad are impressive enough in themselves.

The custom of burying horses with the dead and of stationing a prince's chargers protectively around the four sides of his tent-shaped tomb of wood or stone was first devised by the Scythians and died out—on this scale, at least—when they themselves became extinct.

For a long time Scythian art remained incomprehensible. It is so rich, so personal, so "modern," so "impressionistic," that it defies any form of classification. Taking its themes almost invariably from life, it shows us complete animals, separate limbs, animals' heads, animals' feet, stylized animal figures with subtle modifications, gaping jaws, a kneeling stag, horses, mythical beasts, animals fighting—all depicted with a wealth of ornamentation. It is a very expressive art, yet there is always an element of naïveté in it. Wherever we look, we are confronted by the ornamental contortions and convolutions of animals in gold, silver, bronze, iron, wood and even stone.

In 1903, near the river Kelermes in the Kuban area, D. Schulz excavated a kurgan which had been partially looted by thieves but still contained the untouched body of the prince. He wore a bronze helmet adorned with a gold band and a diadem of rosettes, flowers and hawks. The grave contained a large number of other valuable finds.

In 1904 Schulz opened up another mound in which a man and a woman were buried together. Both had been interred with a veritable treasure trove of gold and silver, diadems, mirrors and other works of art.

In two other kurgans the Russian archaeologist Weselowski found the bones of human beings and horses, and in one west wall the skeletons of ten more horses. In another spot in the same grave twelve horses' skeletons were unearthed complete with harness. The harness of one of these beasts was decorated in solid gold and comprised a headpiece, cheekpieces, gold-plated girths and a whip with a handle wound around with spiral strips of the same metal. 1898 saw the exploration of a cemetery in the Kuban group of kurgans near the Ulskiy Aul. One of the kurgans there was fifty feet high. It is uncertain whether the horses were slaughtered or buried alive, but a platform discovered at the summit of the kurgan carried the remains of more than fifty beasts. The complexity of the wooden structure indicated that sacrifice was accompanied by equally complex rituals. A total of more than 360 horses was found in this kurgan.

An amazingly wide range of harness was found in the Kuban group of kurgans. Ironwork trappings ended in massive birds' and griffins' heads, and other ornamentation included lions, rams, stags, hares, a mountain antelope and a female elk. Bronze bridlepieces ornamented with expressive animal figures, collars adorned with bulls' heads, superbly encrusted headpieces—all these were found buried with Scythian princes. Archaeologists have even found bells and fragments of iron that belonged to the original hearses. In one grave in the Yelizavetovskaya and Marinskaya Stanziya group of kurgans a corridor which must once have been revetted with wood was found to contain two hearses, each harnessed to six beasts. One of them has survived almost intact. The front of the wooden bodywork was adorned with bone knobs, the four wheels were faced with iron, the shaft was of wood, and the horses were wearing full harness, including iron bridles and copper trappings.

One kurgan with walls more than fifty feet long contained a

group of five female skeletons wearing bracelets, rings and ear pendants. These women were facing eastward, but two more were found facing to the west. Although no human sacrifice on the scale of the graves of Ur has been discovered, almost all Scythian chieftains were accompanied into death by their wives, slave women or concubines.

Probably the richest grave of all is situated at Chertomlyk in the Dnieper area, where the ground told a dramatic story. Having dug a shaft into the interior of the huge and complex kurgan, thieves had piled their loot in the corners of one of its burial chambers, ready for removal, when the roof collapsed at the point where the shaft entered the chamber. One of the grave robbers was trapped and entombed, surrounded by priceless treasures, in the grave where archaeologists eventually found him.

It is fortunate that this tomb was never stripped completely, for it contained the finest known examples of Scythian art, among them the remains of spears, iron knives, traces of a carpet, gold plates and gold bands once used to adorn clothing. The garments had been hung on iron hooks set into the roof and walls of the tomb so that the dead could don them in the world hereafter. Although the clothes had disintegrated, the ornaments were still there.

The people in this grave were richly decked with gold and silver, finely ornamented plaquettes, rings and earrings, bracelets and spiral gold necklaces. On either side of one woman's skull were found heavy earrings, and on her head twenty-nine gold plates shaped like flowers, twenty rosettes and seven buds. The head and upper part of the body had been draped in a purple veil decorated with fifty-seven rectangular pieces of gold on which could be seen the figures of a seated woman with a mirror and a male Scythian standing before her. Lavishly buried queens were also discovered in the graves of Kul Oba in the Crimea and of Karagodinashk, south of the Kuban estuary. Lying near one of the Chertomlyk ladies was a bronze mirror with an ivory handle on which traces of a blue material could be discerned. Beside her lay a man with bangles of iron and bronze and a knife with an ivory hilt, and not far away were some spear points. (Knives were always placed near the left hand.) This warrior had probably been buried with his queen to guard her in the world to come.

The same burial chamber yielded the famous Chertomlyk vase, a masterpiece of the first rank, even when compared with the finest vessels produced by any other civilization. Professor Adolf Furtwängler, the archaeologist from Freiburg, attributed it to the end of the fifth century, but it is probably of more recent date. The vase is 27½ inches high. Beneath its neck is an interesting frieze depicting a young filly being broken in. The reins and the men's lassos were made of silver wire which originally protruded from the relief but had fallen off in the course of centuries, leaving only the ends visible in the figures' hands. The horses depicted are of two different breeds, and the Scythian horsebreakers are modeled with such masterly technique that every article of their clothing can be clearly discerned.

Another vase, found four miles west of Kerch at Kul Oba, was made of electrum, or gold and silver alloy. Its wide band of relief depicts, among other things, a Scythian dentist at work and a man removing the bandages from an obviously broken leg. Here, too, the Scythian mode of dress is discernible in detail.

The most recent finds come from the Altai Range, from the sources of the Ob and from the Pazyryk kurgans in the valley of the Ulagan, which is 5,200 feet high at that point. Some of the kurgans unearthed there between 1927 and 1949 were as much as 200 feet in diameter, and were built of rocks and boulders, some of which weighed two or three tons. Franz Hančar, who has studied the Russian discoveries made there, tells of enormous shafts, of buried horses, of a huge larchwood sarcophagus sixteen feet long and three feet high, and of well preserved bodies with virtually undamaged skin which bore artistic and clearly visible designs tattooed on their arms, legs, backs and chests. The frozen ground had preserved wood, leather, felt, furs, silk and even human bodies in a remarkably good condition, though whether the lords of Pazyryk were genuine Scythians or belonged to a related tribe is not entirely clear.

In 1959 I. M. Zamatorin attempted to date the Pazyryk kurgans by comparing the annual rings in pieces of wood found in the various burial chambers, but came to no definite conclusion. On the other hand, the finds made in some of the Pazyryk tombs made it possible to verify certain passages in Herodotus whose accuracy had previously been in doubt because his reports had not hitherto been confirmed by archaeology. Rarely has archaeology supplied so detailed an attestation of the truth and reliability of a 2,400-year-old account.

The kurgans have revealed the Scythians' whole colorful, hazardous, barbarous but artistic way of life just as Herodotus described it. After lying buried for 1,700 years, a civilization has re-emerged which may well lead us back to the earliest roots of the Slavic race.

KING SOLOMON'S FURNACES

We find it significant that at the very end of the account in I Kings 9 of Solomon's manifold building activities throughout Palestine, there is narrated in some detail the story of the construction of a fleet of ships for him at Ezion-geber, which, manned by Phoenician sailors, sailed to Ophir for gold. For some reason or other, the author of this account failed to mention that Solomon exported copper and iron ingots and finished products on these ships in exchange for the gold and other products obtainable in Ophir, and also failed to mention that shortly before, or shortly after, or at the same time as the ships were being constructed, the port-city and industrial town of Ezion-geber I was being built.

—Nelson Glueck, *The Second Campaign at Tell el-Kheleifeh*, Bulletin of the American School of Oriental Research, No. 75, 1939, pp. 16 and 17

HISTORIANS a hundred or two hundred years hence will understand far better than we do the mysterious interrelationship of all historical occurrences, for research is constantly disclosing new links in the infinite chain of events that not only binds nation to nation and continent to continent but appears to encircle the entire globe.

Israel's greatest king, David, who ruled circa 1000–960 B.C. and was renowned as a singer, psalmist and musician, also found time to destroy Philistine supremacy, install the Ark of the Covenant in Jerusalem and usher in a golden age in Jewish history. He was a gifted politician and statesman, and it seems probable that he modeled the internal organization of his realm on that of Egypt. After winning a succession of victories, David found himself king of Jerusalem, king of the lands of Israel and Judah, king of Ammon, ruler of the provinces of Aram (Damascus) and Edom and lord of the vassal kingdom of Moab. But only David's forceful personality held this intricate political structure together. Finding a worthy successor to a genius is always a problem, and in this respect David failed, just as Augustus was to do later when he abandoned the Roman Empire to the not-so-tender mercies of Tiberius.

David's firstborn son Amnon was murdered by Absolom, who

tried, even during his father's lifetime, to usurp the throne by force. The aging king was forced to give ground before his son's army and withdraw to Mahanaim in the east of Jordan. Somewhere there, "in the wood of Ephraim," the decisive battle took place, and Absolom was defeated and killed while escaping. Adonia was now David's eldest son, but a clique of hostile courtiers succeeded in alienating the elderly king from his new heir. Foremost among the women in David's life was the celebrated Bathsheba, whose beauty so captivated him that he took her for himself and arranged that her husband, Uriah the Hittite, should be killed. As the mother of Solomon, Bathsheba began to play an important part in court intrigues. Working in concert with the court prophet, Nathan, she managed to persuade David to make her son heir to the throne. Solomon was, in fact, publicly proclaimed king at Jerusalem.

Like David, Solomon was one of the most interesting figures in world history, though his genius lay perhaps more in the intellectual and creative sphere than in the realm of statesmanship. He retained the respect of his subjects but did not augment it, perhaps because he was not fond of war. No one could have hoped to surpass David, and Solomon's reign heralded the eventual downfall of the empire built by his father. Nevertheless, Bathsheba and the palace intrigues did give mankind the Wise King, the king of the Proverbs and the author of the Song of Solomon. Oriental tradition saw in Solomon the ideal picture of a wise and powerful ruler whose very name, Shelemoh, meant "man of peace" in Hebrew.

King Solomon extended his frontier defenses, maintained far-ranging diplomatic relations, tried to guarantee the continued existence of his empire by shrewd marriages, and encouraged royal pomp and splendor. His harem included many foreign women, among them an Egyptian princess who was probably the daughter of one of the Pharaohs of the 21st Dynasty. All this entailed heavy expenditure which could not be met from the scanty natural resources of his own dominions. That was the sole reason why such an uncanny judge of human nature, such a connoisseur of human weakness, such a seeker after wisdom, should have gone to such lengths in his quest for wealth. His bold and profitable business ventures did, in fact, amass him incalculable riches.

The king's staggeringly luxurious way of life is described in I Kings: x, which tells how the Queen of Sheba journeyed to

Jerusalem with a huge retinue because she had heard of Solomon's
wisdom and his fabulous wealth. She herself had brought camel
caravans laden with a great quantity of gold, precious stones and
spices. In an attempt to find out if Solomon really was the wise man
of whom the whole world was talking, she set him a number of
riddles which she had rehearsed beforehand. The record is unambiguous: "And Solomon told her all her questions: there was
not any thing hid from the king, which he told her not." The queen
was overwhelmed by Solomon's splendor, his mien and intelligence.
The palace, the tableware, the residences of his courtiers and
servants, their manners and dress, the magnificent burnt offerings—
all these filled her with amazement. "Howbeit I believed not the
words, until I came, and mine eyes had seen it: and, behold, the
half was not told unto me: thy wisdom and prosperity exceedeth
the fame which I had heard. . . . And she gave the king an hundred
and twenty talents of gold, and of spices very great store, and
precious stones: there came no more such abundance of spices as
these which the queen of Sheba gave to king Solomon."

The queen was not, however, the first person to introduce gold
into Jerusalem, for the Bible relates that the city had long been a
repository of immense wealth. Where did King Solomon acquire his
vast treasures and his gold?

Two passages in the Old Testament shed light on this. I Kings:
ix-x and II Chronicles: viii-ix both mention that Solomon used
Phoenician sailors or Phoenician ships to reach Ophir via the Red
Sea and bring back immense quantities of gold. The round trip
apparently took three years. Solomon was backed in these ventures
by Hiram, the Phoenician king of Tyre, with whom he maintained
friendly relations as his father David had done before him. The only
difference between the two accounts is that in I Kings Hiram only
supplied Solomon with sailors whereas in II Chronicles he dispatched the whole fleet on its voyage to Ophir.

The expedition's point of departure is clearly stated in the Bible.
The voyage began "in Ezion-geber, which is beside Elath, on the
shore of the Red Sea, in the land of Edom." Ezion-geber was a
seaport at the erstwhile northern end of the Gulf of Aqaba, now
twenty-eight miles from the sea.

Are these accounts legend or reality? We received the answer
to that question a few years ago.

Between the months of March and May, 1938, the American
School of Oriental Research at Jerusalem began to excavate Tell
el-Kheleifeh. The reports of this undertaking which the leader of
the party, Nelson Glueck, was soon able to publish exceeded everyone's wildest imaginings. The Americans proved virtually beyond
question that they had discovered the Ezion-geber of the Bible.
The ruins of a whole town were brought to light from beneath the
desert sand. King Solomon's harbor had been found.

The shore had always been flat and sandy, but the small barks
of 3,000 years ago required such a coastline because they were
drawn up onto the beach. The Americans made a further discovery:
a whole system of smelting furnaces. Occupying the most important quarter of the town, the skillfully constructed smelting
works revealed how high a standard Solomon's architects and
technicians had attained. Taking advantage of the winds that blow
incessantly from the direction of the gulf, the builders had erected
their furnaces so that the air passed through vents and fanned the
flames to produce great heat.

In the course of time, structural alterations were carried out.
The air channels were sealed and hand bellows installed in their
place. Copper fumes and intense heat had turned the furnace walls
green, and the stone had become so hard that even after thirty
centuries and the effects of excavation many of the walls still
stood intact. The furnaces were fed with charcoal obtained from the
palm forests in the neighborhood.

Three years of digging made it increasingly clear to the Americans
that only slaves could have worked in this fiery hell. The smoke and
dangerous vapors combined with the local climate would have
precluded anyone's spending a substantial length of time in the
vicinity of the furnaces voluntarily. Slaves must have died like
flies there. As an illustration of the local conditions, Nelson Glueck
reported that by the end of the third year the members of his party
had reached the limit of their physical endurance. On one occasion
such severe sandstorms raged over Tell el-Kheleifeh that for ten
solid days visibility never exceeded thirty yards. The rooms on the
northern side of the site, which had taken three years to clear, were
once more choked with sand.

Officers of the guard and merchants presumably lived some
distance from the furnaces and smelting works, while the slaves

who had to bear the brunt of the work were lodged inside a stoutly built brick wall between three and four feet thick, where they were kept under surveillance by relays of guards and soldiers. Because of the risk of an insurrection in the heart of the inferno and also because of possible outside attack, Ezion-geber had been transformed into a strong fortress and dominated the intersection of the land and sea routes between Arabia, Sinai and Greater Palestine. This function is fulfilled today by the Jordanian fortress of Aqaba, a far less important place.

Diggings have revealed that ore was transported to Ezion-geber to be smelted and processed, and that it was a thriving center of metalwork. Ships, too, were built at Ezion-geber and dispatched to all parts of the known world. Caravans visited the town from Sinai, Egypt, Judah and Arabia. The town's most active period was the tenth century B.C., which included the reign of Solomon (965–926).

Having worked for years on this fascinating Biblical site with a distinguished team of collaborators, Glueck asserted cautiously that, as far as he knew, there was only one man with the energy, wealth and farsightedness to plan and carry out the construction of an industrial center like Ezion-geber, which in its first and greatest period was a highly complex and specialized installation. That man was King Solomon. He alone of his contemporaries would have had the ability, vision and drive to build such an important industrial town and seaport so far from Jerusalem. At Ezion-geber, Solomon was able to smelt, refine and process the ore which he obtained from his large copper and iron mines in the Arabah Valley. He exported finished products by sea and land and bartered them for the spices, ivory, precious woods and gold of Arabia and Africa. As Glueck pointed out, the wise ruler of Israel was a copper baron, a shipping magnate, a merchant prince and a great architect all in one. Yet he was at once the bane and blessing of his country, for with the growth of his might and wealth he developed an autocratic attitude and ruthlessly rode roughshod over his people's democratic traditions. Solomon's great network of enterprises stretched from the Phoenician ports of Spain to Arabia, Syria and the east coast of Africa, but the town of Ezion-geber was one of the greatest of all his achievements.

We know the port from which Solomon's fleets set sail in their quest for gold, but what was their destination?

The location of Ophir has stimulated the imagination of many generations, and a huge literature has been devoted to the subject. The legendary region or city has been sought—and found in the imagination—on all five continents.

Augustus Keane suggested in *The Gold of Ophir*, a book published in London in 1901, that Ophir was situated in the Arabian district of Dofar. R. F. Burton assumed that Ophir was identical with the Land of Midian on the Gulf of Aqaba, though if it was so close at hand one wonders why there should have been any need for a fleet. In 1844 Christian Lassen wrote in Germany that Ophir was to be found in the Indus area because a tribe called the Abhira lived there. Ophir has also been identified with Africa, but this must be a fallacy because Africa first got its name in Roman times from the Afri, a North African tribe. R. Mewes suggested Ophir was to be found in Peru because II Chronicles:iii speaks of the "gold of Parvaim." The Jewish historian Flavius Josephus suggested in the first century A.D. that Ophir lay somewhere in India, while Alexander von Humboldt regards Ophir as a general geographical term, not a particular place or region. The man who pioneered the decipherment of Babylonian cuneiform script, Jules Oppert, espoused a similar theory.

Because the Old Testament informs us that ships came back from Ophir laden with gold, silver, ivory, apes and peacocks, people have tried to identify its location from these animate and inanimate articles of merchandise. Richard Hennig points out that the Hebrew word for apes, *kophim*, was borrowed from the Sanskrit *kapi* and that peacocks, too, could only have been of Indian origin. On the other hand, the Hebrew word *thukkiyim* was interpreted as parrots or guinea fowl by the French scholar Quatremère and by Karl Mauch as ostriches. The Coptic name for India, Sophir, is another etymological pointer in the direction of India.

There has been commercial activity between India and the east coast of Africa since time immemorial, so it is not surprising that ancient Indian names sometimes reappear on the other side of the Indian Ocean. For example, there is a Sofala Coast in West Malabar and a Sofala Coast in Mozambique. It is an interesting fact that Columbus, too, was preoccupied with the discovery of Ophir and that he intended to reach it on his voyage to the west. "The splendor and power of the gold of Ophir are incalculable. Whoever possesses that gold achieves on earth whatsoever he desires," said the Genoese explorer.

In approaching this problem we should reflect that gold is produced in only two areas in the western half of the Indian Ocean: India, and the country behind Mozambique, i.e. Southern Rhodesia.

India has gold mines at Mysore, Madras and Hyderabad, but in India Solomon would have had to fight for his gold because no native prince would have surrendered it without a struggle. Besides, Richard Hennig has rightly pointed out that throughout history India has always used much more gold than she could produce herself—hence her traditional nickname "the Grave of Gold."

We are left with the hinterland of the Sofala Coast in southeast Africa. There in Southern Rhodesia, west of Mozambique and more than six hundred miles from the sea, lie the richest goldfields in the southern half of Africa. The theory that Ophir should be sought in south Africa was first broached by Karl Mauch and Karl Peters. There is no need to assume that the Israelites maintained mines of their own so far from home or that the Phoenicians ever penetrated into the richest gold areas. The natives would undoubtedly have transported sufficient gold from the interior to the coast if it had been worth their while.

This does not, however, explain how Solomon came into possession of the gold. Professor Hennig believed that the Israelites obtained gold from the southeast regions of Africa not by trade or from colonial mines but, as so often in the history of gold, by war and piracy. He added that one need only think of the Spaniards' infiltration into Mexico under Cortez and into Peru under Pizarro. This would explain why the Phoenicians voluntarily took members of another race, the Israelites, with them on their expeditions. The Phoenicians had never been efficient soldiers, Hennig asserted, and would not have fought successfully on their own. Thus, in order to carry out their projected raids, they sought help from a battle-seasoned and militarily powerful race like the Israelites.

This theory seems artificial. In the first place, one cannot assume that King Solomon only undertook one gold expedition to Ophir. The Bible implies that several voyages were made and that each of them lasted three years. One raid every three years? History provides scarcely any instance where a distant people was attacked on such a long-term basis, and the hypothetical raids undertaken

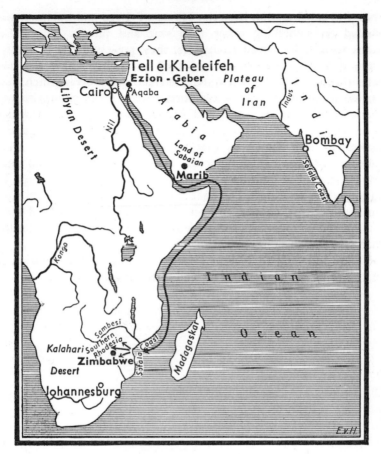

Zimbabwe, Southern Rhodesia

in collaboration with the Phoenicians would certainly not have gone according to plan each time. Hennig's assertion that the Phoenicians were inefficient soldiers and never represented a political force is flatly contradicted by the historical fact of the Punic Wars, Hannibal's heroic feats and the defense of Carthage. The Semitic Carthaginians defended their metropolis with a bravery unsurpassed by any race before or since. We know that the Phoenicians were not only first-rate seamen, brilliant diplomats and shrewd businessmen, but also excellent fighters.

No, the collaboration between Hiram of Tyre and Solomon was founded on something other than war and piracy. The Phoenicians were experienced navigators, they possessed the best ships in the contemporary world, and they invariably knew the best routes through little-known waters, navigational secrets which they guarded jealously. Their contribution to the great enterprise was experience of the sea, ships and crews. King Solomon provided something quite different; namely, trade goods. Since the American excavations have shown us that Ezion-geber boasted what were probably the largest smelting works in the ancient world and since King Solomon had built up a thriving metalwork industry there, he had something to export. Ships set sail from Ezion-geber laden with iron and, perhaps, copper, and on reaching Ophir exchanged these much-prized commodities for gold, slaves, apes, ivory, peacocks and other rare merchandise.

We are indebted to Nelson Glueck for finding this solution in the course of his excavations at Tell el-Kheleifeh.

IN QUEST OF OPHIR

The ruins of the Great Zimbabwe, as it is sometimes called to distinguish it from any others, are very imposing. They are not so extensive as those north of Inyanga, nor so beautiful as those of the Insiza district, but it is undeniable that they have a massive grandeur all their own. There are three distinct, though connected, groups of buildings, viz. the "Elliptical Temple," the "Valley Ruins," and the "Acropolis."

—David Randall-MacIver, *Medieval Rhodesia,*
p. 61, London, 1906

WE NOW come to one of the most mysterious chapters in the history of Black Africa. Étienne Marc Quatremère, A. H. Heeren and the German geologist Karl Mauch have all ascribed the gold-fields of Ophir to this area and assumed that the source of Solomon's gold was Mashonaland in Southern Rhodesia.

The theory of a "Southern Rhodesian Ophir" has not yet been proved, but it is noteworthy that the Arab traveler Ibn Batuta, who was born at Tangier in 1304, referred to the country behind the Sofala Coast under the name Yoûfi. Professor Richard Hennig, a German who devoted a lifetime to the study of geography and natural science, pointed out that Yoûfi sounds very much like Ophir. The passage of Ibn Batuta runs: "From Yoûfi they bring gold dust to Sofala."

The ruins of Zimbabwe were discovered by Adam Renders in the year 1868. Being a hunter, Renders did not attach any great importance to his find, and it soon relapsed into oblivion. On September 5, 1871, the German geologist Karl Mauch examined the ruins more thoroughly, and at once realized that these strange stone buildings in the southern part of Southern Rhodesia were not merely the remains of African kraals of fairly recent date. His discovery came to be associated with Ophir, and when, at the turn of the century, a belief sprang up that Zimbabwe was the original site of King Solomon's Mines, Mashonaland and Matabeleland became the scene of a sort of gold rush. People began to mine gold from places which had been worked in ancient times and where relics of smelting equipment still survived. It was thought that a "Phoenician gold-

287

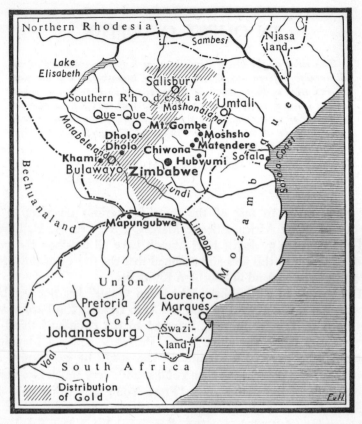

Zimbabwe

mining town" had been found in the Zimbabwe ruins, and gold-hungry adventurers rifled and destroyed many of the precious old ruins and mining installations.

Zimbabwe is a Bantu name, probably compounded of *zimba* ("houses") and *mabgi* ("stones"). By about the turn of the century, Zimbabwe had become well known through the work of the English traveler and archaeologist J. T. Bent, but the theory that its ruins were the remains of an ancient Phoenician colony or that they had been erected in pre-Christian times by members of an advanced Mediterranean civilization was not exactly beneficial to renewed archaeological attempts to determine their true origin and

[88] Buddhist altar in Cave 111a at Tun-huang, excavated by Paul Pelliot, the celebrated French archaeologist and authority on central Asia.

[89] Silver rhyton, evolved from the simple drinking horn. The vessel was held above the drinker's head and tilted so that the wine spurted into his mouth from the beak of the mythical beast without touching his lips. Present-day Georgians have inherited this custom from Persia of the ancient steppe culture of southern Russia.

[90] This solid gold jug, which formed part of the so-called Oxus Hoard, dates from the 5th century B.C. and is only 5 inches high. It is an example of the great metallic culture that once extended from Persia to the south of Russia.

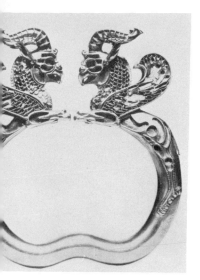

[91] A golden armband from the hoard found in the dried-up bed of the river Oxus. The winged monsters betray Assyrian and Babylonian influence, but in this particular form are genuinely Persian. The beauty of this piece of jewelry and the uncommonly delicate workmanship suggest that it was once worn by a woman of the royal household.

[92] This racing chariot drawn by a team of four horses is one of the finest pieces in the Oxus Hoard. Made of solid gold, it reproduces details of harness, wheels and even the clothing of the drivers. Vehicles like this were used by the Persian king Darius, defeated by the Greeks at Marathon in 490 B.C.

[93] This bronze stag (6½ inches high) is a typical example of the kurgan art of
Minusinsk, which is situated in the forest-steppe region in the upper reaches of the
Yenisey. The beast is standing on a bell-shaped rattle with a ring on which cords
could be hung.

[94] Scythian art traveled as far east as Mongolia. This piece of woven carpet, which had remained miraculously preserved, was found in the grave of a Mongol prince at Noin Ula in Mongolia and dates from the 1st century A.D. The portrayal of the griffin attacking the elk is a fine example of later Siberian-Scythian art.

[95] This wooden coffin was dug up at Basadur, Siberia, in 1950, complete with its original occupant. The manner in which the tiger was carved into the wood, as well as the presence in the grave of eighteen horses and other finds, indicate that the dead man was the chieftain of a Scythian-like people.

[96 and 97] This vase of silver-bearing gold ore is 5.5 inches high and reposes in the Hermitage Museum at Leningrad. It was found in Kul Oba. The frieze depicts a Scythian "dentist" at work on a tooth and treatment being administered to a man with a broken leg. It is noticeable that the Scythians resembled early Russians both in physiognomy and dress.

[98] A monolith on the "acropolis" of Zimbabwe. These unhewn stone buildings were probably erected during the Middle Ages by an as yet unidentified African people, perhaps a Bantu tribe.

[99] The "acropolis" was approached by a steep and narrow flight of steps running between towering crags. The unknown designers of this fortress built their citadel into the living rock.

[100] The famous soapstone bird discovered in the Zimbabwe ruins by R. N. Hall on July 27, 1903. It has since become the national emblem of Southern Rhodesia. This supreme example of Zimbabwe art is now in Bulawayo Museum, Southern Rhodesia.

[101] The so-called "acropolis" of Zimbabwe was virtually impregnable. This is the west wall of the massive fortress.

precise date. The British archaeologist R. N. Hall defended the Phoenician theory with sound and detailed scientific arguments. He had personally carried out diggings in Zimbabwe and several other ruined sites in Southern Rhodesia with good results. It is still hard to resist the cogency and descriptive power of the works which he published in 1902 and 1907, but when the Egyptologist David Randall-MacIver subjected the ruins of Southern Rhodesia to further scrutiny he formed new conclusions which were completely at odds with all the arguments and "evidence" previously adduced.

In MacIver's opinion, Zimbabwe was purely African in origin and built far later than had been supposed hitherto. It came into being toward the close of the Middle Ages and continued to flourish until about the fifteenth century. Having examined seven sites, MacIver reported he had nowhere found any object dating from earlier than the fourteenth or fifteenth century A.D. He was equally unable to discover any non-African features in the architecture of Zimbabwe or any trace of European or Oriental style. The famous "Elliptical Building," the "Acropolis," the "Valley Ruins," the fortifications, cult sites and living quarters—indeed, the whole metropolis —were completely African in character. Unfortunately, there are no inscriptions of any kind at Zimbabwe, whose master builders were evidently unfamiliar with the art of writing. In addition, however, to articles of African make, MacIver found works of art and utensils which had been imported from India and the Far East. In fact, it was because these articles were embedded in layers of rubble and their date of manufacture was known from other sources that MacIver was able to attribute the building of the entire city to the medieval centuries.

If MacIver did not succeed in solving the riddle of Zimbabwe in every detail, he did at least write finis to the supposition that it belonged to a pre-Christian Mediterranean culture.

In the year 1929 the British archaeologist Dr. Gertrude Caton-Thompson carried out further excavations at Zimbabwe and other ruined sites. She confirmed MacIver's findings and established even more precise dates for the miraculous buildings of Southern Rhodesia.

No less than five hundred ruined sites lie scattered between the rivers Zambezi and Limpopo. It is both interesting and important to note that in general these buildings were not situated in the

direct vicinity of goldfields. Caton-Thompson inferred from this
that they were not associated with the exploitation of mineral
deposits. In her opinion, the massive ruins were not mining towns
but relics of urban development carried out by the advanced Bantu
tribes of central Africa. Nevertheless, there seems to be a strong
possibility that Zimbabwe itself was an important distribution center
for gold, for on what else could the power and wealth of this
Southern Rhodesian metropolis have been founded?

Al-Masudi, an Arab writer who visited Africa in A.D. 916 or 917,
declared that Zimbabwe had been founded by a people from
Abyssinia, that it had been in existence for some generations and was
already a powerful kingdom in his day. To quote his actual words:
"It is a land that produces gold in quantity and other marvels as
well." It thus seems that the modern Ba Roswi and Ba Venda tribes
may be regarded as the direct descendants of the builders of Zimbabwe. The numerous necklaces of Indian and Malayan manufacture found there enabled the fantastic buildings to be dated with
even greater accuracy. Caton-Thompson thinks that Zimbabwe and
certain other towns flourished between the eighth and tenth centuries
A.D. and may even have done so since the beginning of the Middle
Ages.

The district is extremely rich in granite, a material which lies
readily available in the immediate vicinity of the numerous building sites. This natural granite could be removed in slabs and needed
scarcely any dressing.

The diggings undertaken by Hall, Randall-MacIver and Caton-
Thompson have not yielded a very rich harvest from the quantita-
tive aspect, but they include iron arrowheads and spear points, axes,
large quantities of bronze wire, principally in the form of ankle
rings, gold wire, soapstone bowls, rings, necklaces, soapstone and
earthenware flywheels for spinning contrivances, battle-axes, iron
swords, phalli, bone tubes and jugs for water or beer. The celebrated
pillars surmounted by a soapstone bird are of particular interest,
and a likeness of the bird has since become the national emblem of
Southern Rhodesia.

$\rightarrow$

This British archaeologist's ground plan of Zimbabwe shows (*top right*) an
elliptical building presumed to be a temple and (*top left*) the acropolis hill
surmounted by its citadel.

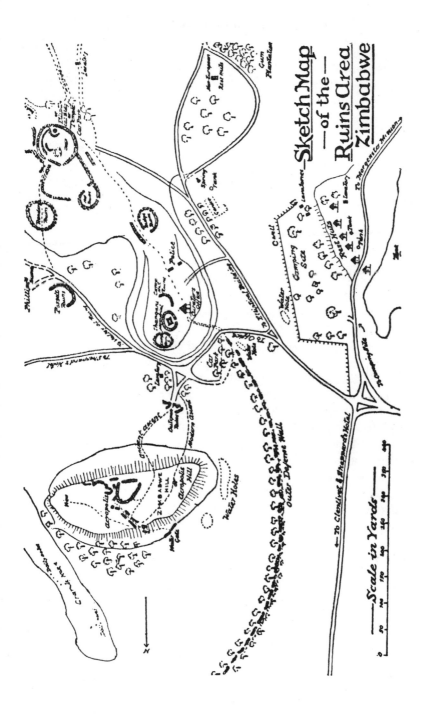

Sketch Map
— of the —
Ruins Area
Zimbabwe

Scale in Yards

The place is still shrouded in mystery. Even the purpose of the large "elliptical building" is unknown, though many scholars regard is as a temple. The monoliths in this co-called Temple of Zimbabwe, which are about thirteen feet high and taper roughly to a point, were probably connected with the phallus cult which is still such a feature of the area.

It is likely that the mysterious culture of Zimbabwe did not originate from one source but was the outcome of many varied influences. G. A. Wainwright thinks that a people from southern Abyssinia, perhaps the Galla, migrated to Southern Rhodesia long before A.D. 900 and that it was they who were responsible for the megaliths of the Zimbabwe civilization. The racial identity of the Galla aristocracy probably became submerged in the neighboring Bantu population. Since the phallus cult happens to play an important role in southern Abyssinia and the abundance of phallus finds in Southern Rhodesia indicates that the phallus cult was equally important in the Zimbabwe culture, we cannot overlook this obvious link.

When the first Europeans made their way into the southern half of Africa 450 years ago, they found themselves in a living museum representing many different cultural epochs. Post-Stone-Age cultures are, as we know, divided into the Bronze Age and Iron Age. The bushmen were still living in the Stone Age. The Hottentots were already using bronze and copper but were unfamiliar with iron. The Bantu of the east coast, on the other hand, manufactured implements out of iron and had already entered the Iron Age. Indeed, iron was already known in Southern Rhodesia before the buildings of the Zimbabwe culture came into being. We are thus confronted by a unique cultural transition from stone to iron. Africa south of the Sahara was isolated from the ancient world during the fourth, third and second millennia B.C. Only this can explain why many tribes in the southern part of Africa never passed through a Bronze Age. In Rhodesia the Iron Age followed directly on the heels of the Stone Age without, as in North Africa and almost everywhere else in the ancient world, going through the inter-mediate phases of development known as the Copper and Bronze Ages.

Iron probably reached the regions of Africa south of the Sahara from the countries of the Mediterranean as early as the tenth century, but by what routes? The Zimbabwe culture, in so far as it has been excavated, belongs to the Iron Age but has also yielded articles of bronze. Why has nothing earlier been found? Why are there no traces of Solomon's ore consignments? These questions have not as yet been answered.

Although there has been a tendency to stress the purely African features of the ruins in Southern Rhodesia ever since 1906, when reaction set in against the first wild assumptions about mysterious Phoenician colonists, traces of former cultural contact between the Mediterranean world and South Africa are now being brought to light. G. Mathew, for instance, has cited archaeological evidence indicating that there were very ancient pre-Islamic links between southern Arabia and the east coast of South Africa. It is not beyond the bounds of possibility that the people of Sheba landed there and penetrated into Southern Rhodesia, which transports the theory of a sea route from Tell el-Kheleifeh (formerly Ezion-geber) through the Red Sea, via the land of Sheba and down to the Sofala coast, from the realm of legend to that of reality. Roger Summers, a distinguished student of South African archaeology and culture, says in this connection that small pieces of evidence are coming to light here and there which link Africa with the fringe of the ancient world.

Research into the Zimbabwe culture has not yet produced a definite answer to the Ophir enigma, but everything indicates that, manned by Phoenician crews, King Solomon's ships did, in fact, explore the coasts of southeast Africa. We know now that Solomon's fleet came back from Ophir laden with vast quantities of gold. We know, too, from the American excavations of Ezion-geber at Tell el-Kheleifeh, that King Solomon refined iron and copper in the smelting furnaces unearthed there, commodities which possessed great value as trade goods throughout the contemporary world and particularly in the southern half of Africa.

Nevertheless, the secret of Ophir remains unsolved, perhaps because ships leave no perceptible traces of their passage.

THE BRONZES OF BENIN

The ivory carvings and, above all, the bronzes of Benin surpass anything that Black Africa has produced in the realm of art. The purpose of many of these objects remains a mystery, though leading authorities on the culture of Yoruba and Benin have solved many of the secrets of those unusual civilizations by hard work and exhaustive digging. The finest pieces from Benin now repose in the Museum of Ethnology, Berlin, in the British Museum, and at Lagos.

ON THE west coast of Africa at the point where its waist is pinched in by the Gulf of Guinea, lies Nigeria, melting pot of many African tribes and races and a country of some forty million inhabitants. Among them are the Ibo, the Hausa, the Fulbe and the Yoruba, each numbering about four millions.

Nigeria is not known to the world for its political history or economic resources, yet its culture is far more interesting to the modern world than that of many other far more important nations. The city and culture of Benin have occupied a prominent place in the history of art ever since 1897, when the British opened up the kingdom of the same name in the marshes of the Niger delta by force of arms, and especially since the ethnologist and explorer Leo Frobenius virtually revolutionized our knowledge of the Negro civilizations in 1911. Benin is not only a city but a region that includes the lands west of the Niger delta and around the Benin River, a country inhabited by Negroes of Sudanese stock who founded Great Benin, a once powerful and greatly feared kingdom and one of the most culturally advanced districts in West Africa. Leo Frobenius even thought that in Benin he had found the heirs and descendants of the lost continent of Atlantis.

The Benin coast was first explored by the Portugese in 1472, and during the eighteenth and early nineteenth centuries became one of the chief centers of the slave trade. Between the time of its discovery by the Portuguese and the British expedition of 1897, Europe almost lost sight of the Negro kingdom, and for four centuries no precise details of its ancient civilization emerged. In 1897, however, an event occurred which was to destroy Benin's autonomy. The British Acting Consul-General for the Niger Coast Protectorate, J. R. Phillips, set out on an expedition to Benin and was unwise enough to approach the capital just as a memorial service, complete with ancestor-cult sacrifice, was being held in honor of the reigning king's late father. Phillips was murdered in the bush before he could enter the city.

The British immediately dispatched a punitive force, and the already tottering monarchy was completely destroyed. With that, Europe gained its first glimpse of the cultural history and the bloodthirsty but far from primitive religious practices of the mysterious kingdom of Benin. The British caused a sensation by bringing back bronzes of such artistic merit that experts racked their brains as to which European, Egyptian or Islamic artists could have been responsible for them.

The bronzes of Benin attracted the attention they did because they represented a unique exception among the sculptures produced by other African Negro races. To those endowed with a Western sense of form they appeared more intelligible and less alien than the Negro art of the rest of the Dark Continent.

We now know that the Yoruba, a tribal group of Sudanese stock who live northwest of Benin, had cities of more than 100,000 inhabitants before the first European colonizers arrived on the scene, and that they were not only skilled hoe-farmers and breeders of small livestock but also traders on an extensive scale. Their highly developed handicrafts, cotton weaving, dyeing, pottery, and bronze- and brass-founding techniques spread beyond the borders of their own territory.

Ancient Yoruba colonies still exist in Dahomey and Togo, and the ruling class of Dahomey, the Fon, inherited great artistic gifts from sources that are hard to ascertain. Yoruba was, in fact, the mother country of the kingdom of Benin, and Benin not only owed its existence to Yoruba colonists but inherited from them rudiments of its remarkable art.

Africa was for thousands of years the principal center of the slave trade, and the Yoruba colonies of which Benin was one were founded due to the desire to establish loading points for human merchandise. Between the years 1486 and 1641, it is recorded that 1,389,000 slaves were exported from Angola alone. On the average, Brazil received shipments of 10,000 slaves each year from 1580 to 1680. Between 1783 and 1793, no less than 900 trips were made from

Liverpool by vessels carrying 300,000 slaves to a value of 15 million pounds sterling.

In an Africa accustomed to the idea of slavery this was no more than a natural development, for, as Basil Davidson recently emphasized, it is only a small step from the ownership of slaves to their exportation.

The chief center of Yoruba art was Ile-Ife, religious capital, cultural center and seat of the spiritual head of all the Yoruba. Ile-Ife, which lies about fifty miles from Ibadan in Nigeria, means "land of the origin" and has a present population of 50,000. The only surviving works of art of the "Ife period" are made either of stone, quartz, granite, bronze or baked clay, because wood carvings have fallen prey to the climate in the course of centuries. Yoruba sculptures found during the past twenty years occupy a unique position in the art of Africa as a whole. In 1938 and 1939 some splendid works of art were unearthed in the palace precincts of the Oni of Ife, most of them sculptures in brass. Brass varies from red to pale gold in color according to the proportion of copper employed. In this case the alloy was 20 percent zinc. So amazingly lifelike in every detail is one bronze male figure from Tada on the Niger and so subtle and expressive are the Negroid faces of the Ife finds that experts are continually searching for signs of extraneous influence.

Foreign artists may well have taught in the foundries at the court of the Benin kings, and the Yoruba pantheon of 401 deities is reminiscent of the angelic communities of early Christianity, but it is hard to say whether the Graeco-Christian art of late antiquity or the art of the Middle Ages played any part there. Eckart von Sydow, an outstanding student of primitive art, and especially of African sculpture, believes that Benin's works of art were in some way influenced during the Middle Ages by the traffic that passed along the long caravan routes running through the Sudan from north to south and from east to west. From the purely technical aspect, the brassworks of ancient Benin will stand comparison with the finest European examples, for the works of art in bronze and brass that came from the hands of these native artists were nothing short of masterpieces. Yet the inexplicable, incomprehensible problem of interrelationship remains. None of the numerous metal plaques or other surviving works in bronze came from the hand of a European artist. They are all completely African in style and composition, even though they far surpass all other African examples of plastic art. This opinion was shared by the distinguished German ethnologist Felix von Luschan and by Professor Josef Marquart of Berlin, whose comprehensive work on the Benin collections was published at Leyden in 1913. The art as a whole is characterized by the unusual proportions of the statues, the short legs, the schematic treatment of physiognomy, the partial neglect of hands and feet, the painstaking emphasis on details of jewelry, clothing and weapons and, last but not least, the predilection for full-face portrayals.

It is very difficult to divide Benin art into periods because its inhabitants had no form of writing and used sculpture to express all their vital impulses, all their desires and aspirations, all their religious ideas. Bernhard Struck of Heidelberg has, however, distinguished five periods in the cultural history of Benin. They range from 1140 to 1887 and cover the sixteenth and seventeenth centuries, which represented the golden age of Benin art. Certain clues are afforded by the strange bronze plaques, some of which depict Europeans whose clothing, hats and weapons belong to the years between 1530 and 1585. Except in this respect, the bronze plaques have defied all attempts at interpretation. They are between twelve and twenty inches long. Even the most fragile and prominent portions of the figures are hollow. The natives have no recollection of their original purpose, but at one time they were affixed to the posts that supported the roof of the royal palace, as the nail holes in them indicate. Although this does not explain why such infinite pains were taken with their manufacture, they have preserved the rich and varied life of the people of Benin in so grandiose a manner that they compensate to some extent for our lack of written records.

We have been left a description of Benin by a Dutchman who painted a vivid picture of the splendor of its royal court in the seventeenth century. He reported that the city was a very large place with broad streets and neat houses whose verandas were swept clean by slaves. Inside the royal palace were rectangular courtyards surrounded by galleries. The king kept horses in well-appointed stables, and the warriors and nobility were devoted to him.

The king has very many slaves and slave women. One often sees the slave women carrying water and yams, also palm oil. This is said to be for the king's wives. The king has many wives and holds two processions, a year, on each of which occasions he parades his power and wealth and finery, accompanied by all his wives—more than six hundred in number. The noblemen also have numerous wives, some of them eighty and others ninety or more. No man of rank is so poor as to own less than ten or twelve wives. Thus, more women are to be found here than men.

According to native tradition, King Overami Eduboa, who was deposed by the British in 1897, was the twenty-second member of his line. The tenth king, whose name was Esige Osawe, prided himself on having been born a "white man." Before he died he sent emissaries across the "great water" to the land of the whites, bearing gifts and an invitation to the whites to visit him in Africa, but in vain. They settled in Gwatto and carried on trade there. Apparently, they were accompanied by a man called Ahammangiwa or Mohammangiwa ("Elephant-Mohammed"). This Moslem was a brass founder, perhaps a member of the Hausa tribe. He traveled to Benin and brought the artists there fresh inspiration with his portrayals of Europeans and new styles of ornamentation. He stayed with the king for a long time and had "many wives but no children." The king apprenticed numerous young men to him. "We can still produce metalwork," the Benin people said later, "but we cannot make it as he made it because he and all his pupils are dead." Professor Josef Marquart of Berlin, who tried to solve the riddle of Benin's artistic origins, thought that the story of Ahammangiwa could have stemmed from an obscure recollection of the first attempts at conversion by the Portuguese, and that the "many wives" may have been nuns belonging to a mission led by Ahammangiwa himself. There is in existence a fine ivory cup made by an ivory carver from Sierra Leone which may point to the presence of a Catholic mission in West Africa as early as this. The cup, together with elephant tusks bearing skillfully carved reliefs, is now in the National Museum of Ethnology in Holland.

We do not know if the plaques and their figurative reliefs derived any inspiration from European brass-founding technique, but we do know that Mohammangiwa was alive during the reign of the *oba* (king) named Esige Osawe; that is to say, at the time when the Portuguese navigator João Afonso de Aveiro first discovered Benin.

It is hard to ascertain whether the Yoruba art of Ife, which represented the cultural progenitor of Benin, was very much more ancient than the art of Benin itself. Sculpture and foundry technique probably reached their prime at Ife between the twelfth and four-teenth centuries. Under the last autonomous ruler of Benin, Oba Overami, brass founding was prohibited for some unknown reason, which was why the British were surprised to see such magnificent bronzes nailed up in huts. After the conquest of 1897, when the king was deposed and Benin City went up in flames, talented native artists began to ply their craft once more. Their artistic impulses and abilities live on today, although their art itself has declined under the impact of industrialization.

The British scholar Bernard Fagg has demonstrated the existence of an interesting relationship between the ancient Nok culture, which produced tools of iron as well as stone, and the art of later Nigerian tribes. In 1956 Fagg published details of a life-size terra-cotta head dug up in the south of Zária Province (northern Nigeria) in 1954. This find owes its importance to the fact that it dates from pre-Christian times and that its finely detailed hair, superbly modeled eyes and animated, expressive mouth are reminiscent of the finest pieces from Ife and Benin. The Nok culture has not yet been dated precisely, but it probably flourished in the first century B.C. Fagg points out that the sculpture's hair resembles the hair styles affected by the modern Kachichiri and Numana tribes who live about thirty miles from Nok, so the first beginnings of Benin art may well be rooted far more deeply in the past than we have hitherto supposed.

What lay behind the expressive busts of queens, the figures, heads and countless other objects? The chief impetus and source of Benin's art was the ancestor cult. That was the soil in which the bronze art of Benin thrived and the foundation on which its royal families built their religion. Altars to fathers and forefathers, groups of kings and their retinues, groups dominated by queen mothers, bronze heads, cockerels, carved elephants' tusks—all these belonged to the ancestor cult.

For all that, ancestor worship was not as highly spiritualized here as in many of the civilizations of the Far East. The relationship between living and dead was intended to bring practical advantages. The head of the family shook rattles, pounded the floor, rang bells and called loudly upon the spirits of his ancestors, who entered the central head on the altar and gave ear to the family's prayers. During prayer, pieces of cola nut were crumbled. Taking these in his mouth, the priest chewed them and spat them onto the rattles, thereby giving the signal for sacrifice. The main sacrificial beast was the panther, which was dedicated to the soul of the king of Benin during his lifetime. Sacrifice was heralded by a sword ritual performed by headmen. After a cockerel, a goat and a cow had been slaughtered, food was placed before the rattles and the altar, and the proceedings were consummated by a feast in which the whole family shared.

With the advent of Western civilization the old spirit of Negro art declined, the tribes' links with their ancestors fell asunder, ancient tribal traditions waned and native artists began to manufacture curios for the benefit of foreign collectors. The missing element in these new arts and crafts has been neatly defined by William B. Fagg, who says that a comparison between the traditional art of a tribe and the art produced for tourists discloses something much more important than mere external changes in form. To him, the missing element is the vital force that once provided tribal life with its basis of existence and philosophical world of ideas.

That this vital force existed, that it breathed life into inanimate bronze and gave birth to sculpture of such unique beauty and astounding naturalism was due alone to the spirit and faith of the people of Benin.

RIVER OF A THOUSAND EYES

The civilizations of the Sepik district, whose magnificence is due in particular to their religion and art, are regrettably on the verge of extinction. In an outwardly almost untouched-seeming country the natives' ancient and traditional way of life has largely disappeared or is rapidly disintegrating.... All these changes are attributable to contact with modern civilization. Confronted by the superiority manifest in it, the natives lost their inward and often their outward stability as well. That is why their cultures are dying.

—ALFRED BÜHLER, *Sepik*, p. 23,
Stuttgart-Berne-Vienna, 1958

LARGER than all the five continents put together, the Pacific Ocean is encircled by a chain of volcanoes, both active and extinct. It is the most recently formed portion of the globe, and its birth pangs and the concomitant appearance and disappearance, advance and withdrawal of its islands and shores are far from complete. Between Hawaii and New Zealand, New Guinea and Easter Island, thirty thousand islets project from the gleaming, glittering waters of the South Seas.

The present inhabitants of the South Pacific migrated to their oceanic world from Asiatic countries and islands in times beyond our ken. Wave after wave of migrant peoples sailed across the sea to find a watery grave in the blue depths of the Pacific or land on some hospitable shore and make their home there.

The vast expanse of the Pacific contains three worlds, the Polynesian, the Micronesian and the Melanesian, each of which is very different in character. Their common features are illiteracy, lack of metals and the other raw materials, and the creeping death which has been continuously eroding the native population of all three areas —the Maoris of New Zealand and a few other tribes excepted—ever since the advent of the European.

Polynesia is a Greek word formation meaning "place of many islands." The enormous triangle bounded by Hawaii, New Zealand and Easter Island could contain whole continents—Australia four times over, the United States and Canada three times over—yet the thousands of islands within that area are inhabited by only 1,100,000 people, of which only 100,000 are genuine Polynesians.

The Polynesians have preserved a remembrance of their eastward migrations from Hawaiki, the legendary land of their forefathers. Samoa and Tonga were their first main settlements, and they reached the Society Islands about the eighth century A.D. From their base at Raiatea, the political and religious center of Polynesia, they then populated the eastern Pacific as far as Easter Island. The first Polynesians sailed off into the Pacific at about the time of Christ's birth or three or four centuries earlier. According to the latest radiocarbon tests, the Polynesians settled in Hawaii during the early centuries of our era, perhaps between A.D. 100 and 200.

Where did the Polynesians come from?

We do not know exactly, but we must assume that they came from Indonesia. While the Polynesian language is more closely related to Malay, it shows evidence of the influence of the Indonesian tongue. Since Sanskrit arrived in Indonesia from India circa A.D. 350 and since the Polynesian languages contain no Sanskrit, the Polynesians must have left their Indonesian home sometime before A.D. 350. However, their main migrations took place in the eleventh, twelfth and thirteenth centuries A.D., New Zealand being populated by migrants from the Society and Cook islands about 1350. These voyages across the world's largest sheet of water in frail outriggers and catamarans with triangular woven sails were among history's greatest feats of daring, even though our only record of them is preserved in the traditions, myths and songs of the island peoples.

Bold hypotheses and venturesome theories exercising the fascination over modern humanity that they do, people have been asserting for decades that the Polynesians came from South America. This pet fable has not yet gained favor with most scientists, however, because ancient traditions, ethnological facts and anthropological characteristics all tend to prove that the Polynesian migrations originated in the west. "It is one of the best established findings of ethnological research that this island world was populated from the west, from Asia. An eastern origin, i.e., from the American continent, is out of the question." So says Herbert Tischner, a leading authority on the tribes of the South Seas, and modern science in general shares his view.

Micronesia, the "place of small islands," comprises 1,458 islands,

most of them minute, and is inhabited by a total population of
170,000. The islands are composed mainly of calcareous coral and
the great majority are atolls. Only 97,000 Micronesians still live in
the Marianas, the Palau Islands, the Carolines, the Marshall Group,
Nauru and the Gilbert Islands. These Micronesians with their peculiar Old Mongol admixture are doomed, like so many primitive
peoples, to become extinct without ever having been adequately
studied. We have only to remember the Tasmanians, the Fuegian
Indians and others.

The name Melanesia is compounded of the Greek words *melas*
("black") and *nesos* ("island"). Structurally speaking, the region
belongs to Australia and used in very ancient times, before the intervening land masses sank beneath the sea, to form the outer rim of
Australia. Situated in the southwest Pacific, Melanesia includes the
world's second largest island, New Guinea, the Bismarck Archipelago, the Solomon Islands, Santa Cruz, the New Hebrides and New
Caledonia.

Anyone familiar with the islands of the Pacific and their inhabitants
knows that the Polynesians are distinguished by their tall and sturdy
build, their pale brown complexion and the long, smooth black hair
which they share with their Japanese cousins and the Chinese. The
Polynesians do not have naturally curly hair, and this immediately
sets them apart from the crinkly-headed Melanesians. The Micronesians include both very light-skinned and dark-skinned people,
though they are not so dark as many Melanesians, some of whom are
completely black. The Solomon Islanders are examples of the latter
type of Melanesian.

Melanesia was the first group to be inhabited, which is why it is
the site of the most rudimentary cultures. Parts of the island of
New Guinea, for instance, form one of the last great open-air
cultural and ethnological museums in the world. New Guinea is a
fascinating place, and the district around the river Sepik has produced
what are probably the finest works of art in the entire Pacific area.

The riddle of New Guinea begins with its population. There are
tall, dolichocephalic people, there are short, pygmoid people, there
are some other groups related to the aboriginals of Australia and
Tasmania, and there are natives who either resemble the Melanesian
type or are genuine Melanesians. Almost all the coastal tribes of
New Guinea are Melanesian, as opposed to the shorter, Papuan-speak-

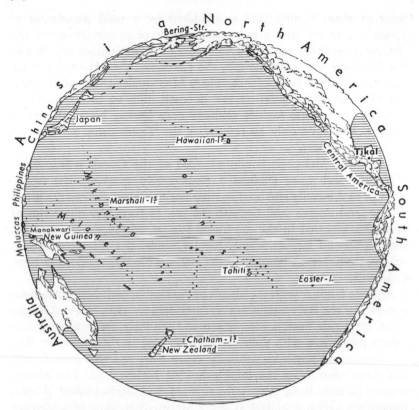

ing tribes of the interior. The people are largely Negroid, dark-skinned and curly-headed, but there are also some tribes in New Guinea who appear to be related to the Mongoloid races. Linguistically, the oldest tribes belong to the Papuan group.

These dark-skinned but heterogeneous tribes speak an extraordinary number of languages. The central mountain range forming the island's backbone is about 1,250 miles long and includes peaks of up to 16,000 feet, some of which carry glaciers despite their proximity to the equator. The whole island is segmented by a maze of mountain ranges and isolated mountainous features, which is why its inhabitants, separated as they are by huge forests, rivers and escarpments, have retained their confusion of languages. It is the same with their culture. When white men first landed on New Guinea the natives had no metal of any kind. This situation persists in many parts of the island, so some of the inhabitants of New Guinea are still, in fact, living in the Stone Age.

Culturally, on the other hand, they are amazingly advanced, as we at once realize if only we succeed in divesting ourselves of the standards accepted in Europe and the West. This is, of course, exceedingly difficult. We are so firmly rooted in our Christian notions of morality that we regard cannibalism, for example, as the *ne plus ultra* of savagery. Yet in New Guinea and other Melanesian islands it was the focal point of magical rites, possessed the most exalted spiritual significance, and was, viewed in terms of the Melanesian world, a symptom of advanced culture.

The island's principal river, the Sepik, rises in the central mountain chain. It is about as long as the Rhine but its volume is infinitely greater because of the torrential tropical downpours that feed it. The gateway to the island's interior, it weaves its serpentine way through the northern plains to the sea in a series of wide curves and intricate convolutions. When the German astronomer Carl Schrader traveled upstream in 1886 and 1887, the natives greeted him with such hostility that he had to abandon his expedition before reaching the river's highest navigable point. He was followed by the ethnologists Poech, Dorsay and Friederici and, finally, in 1908, by the Hamburg South Seas Expedition, which brought back an extremely valuable collection of ethnological data.

Even at that time, the Western world was amazed at the artistic sense of the "savages" of the Sepik. Their superb clay vessels, beautiful carvings and magnificent domestic architecture all aroused great admiration. But New Guinea was and still is an explorer's nightmare. This is due to the very nature of the country, to its swamps and tropical rain forests, to its warm and humid climate, to the difficulty of obtaining food supplies in the interior, to the natives' determination to persevere in their own way of life rather than adopt that of the West (a resistance which has been slow to yield), and to a thousand other obstacles which have for decades worn down the morale, endurance and physique of so many scientists and their companions.

To see the splendid utensils and cult objects of the Sepik culture in a museum is to recognize the strength of the spiritual impetus that engendered them.

This spiritual force stemmed from the idea that the world of the supernatural, the spirit world, is more important and exercises a more decisive influence on mankind than the mundane aspect of existence. Like almost all primitive peoples, the tribes of New Guinea are unable to account for occurrences such as natural disasters, sickness, death or bad harvests in scientific terms. Instead, they seek the cause of these events in the supernatural, thus securing a means of intervening in nature, of warding off mischief and disaster and, perhaps, even of erecting a prophylactic barrier against them. To the New Guineans, everything in their natural environment is animate. There is no thing, no living creature, which is not instinct with soul or vital force. This belief in the ubiquity of souls or animism, so called from *anima*, the Latin word for "soul," implies that animals, human beings, plants and lifeless objects are all invested with a power that must be contacted and utilized, never offended or provoked. It is a deeply religious faith because it senses the divine, sacred and supersensual element in all natural phenomena.

Life-force and souls are at their strongest in human beings. When a man dies, this magical force only becomes intensified, so the dead are not only held in awe but offered sacrifice as a token of love and respect.

Thus, the Papuan world is filled with ancestral spirits—material objects included—because all that man owns or makes owes its existence to his ancestors. Articles of daily use, material objects of every kind, customs and cults all derive from our ancestors, and every thing and every contrivance inherits something of its creator's soul. If a man's ancestors are ill-disposed toward him, for instance, they can ensure that he is never blessed with offspring.

In order to gain the favor of the dead, the living must provide their souls with a dwelling place. The best abode for the soul of a dead man is, of course, his own head. Since the skull is endowed with magic powers and is the least perishable part of the human body, the dead are exhumed after a certain length of time, their skulls cleaned and their original features reproduced in clay.

Nowhere in the entire South Pacific area is this done with such artistry as in the valley of the Sepik. Clay is skillfully molded over the skull, the eye sockets inlaid with cowrie shells, and human hair affixed. One more thing: because the most important events in the life of the deceased were the cult ceremonies which he attended and the battles he fought, the face is painted exactly as it was on those occasions. This done, the soul's abode is complete.

Ancestral skulls are arranged on finely carved and decorated boards and placed in the large "spirit houses" where tribesmen meet to conduct memorial ceremonies for their ancestors. If the skulls of the departed are not available their place is taken by wooden figures designed to accommodate their souls.

It was this belief in a spiritual force residing in the human head which fostered cannibalism and head-hunting, because it implied that if life-force really dwells in a skull it can be acquired from people outside the family circle. All one needs is a head. Hence the New Guineans' raids on neighboring tribes and their villages, a practice unknown in any part of the Pacific area except Melanesia.

Anyone who acquires a man's head acquires his name as well, and it is essential to know the name of one's victim because of the power inherent in it. A name obtained in this way can be given to a child, thereby endowing it with the positive spiritual strength of its original owner. That is why head-hunters try to trick their victim into revealing his name before killing him.

Paul Wirz, who collected some very interesting material during his lengthy explorations of the Indian Archipelago and New Guinea, has given us a verbatim account of his conversation with a head-hunter.

"In the middle of the night we surrounded the settlement which we had reconnoitered the previous day and challenged the sleeping inhabitants to fight. Five of them fell into our hands. I killed this one," said the man, proffering an armbone with flesh still adhering to it. "Rawi was his name. He was still a young man. My brother Monai held him fast while I asked what his name was. He screamed as though spitted, but it did him no good. I cut off his head with my bamboo knife. The man poked his tongue out like this," continued the narrator with a dreadful grimace, and then hurried off to his hut. After a while he reappeared and laid the freshly painted trophy with its long, plaited hair-extensions at my feet. "You can have it for your child, if it has no name yet, as long as you give me two axes, ten knives and ten packets of tobacco. Take note of his name," he screeched at me. "Rawi! Rawi! That was what the man was called."

The powers and forces inherent in every human being are described in Melanesian as *mana*. Codrington first identified this term

among the Solomon Islanders, but it is an idea prevalent throughout
the Pacific area that the magical power inherent in animals, human
beings and material objects can be exploited by certain behavior. The
more important a man is, the more vital force or *mana* he contains.
In the view of many tribes in the Melanesian area, *mana* can be
obtained by eating human flesh. And since the flesh of a chieftain
possesses more spiritual energy than that of a common mortal, people
of superior rank have for centuries been hunted down with particular
zeal.

Far from being a cultural nadir, cannibalism is scarcely ever
present in the rudimentary stages of a civilization. On the contrary,
it is at its strongest and most widespread in Polynesia, whose oceanic
culture is of a peculiarly high standard. In Polynesia, as in Melanesia,
both men and women were numbered among its victims, and in the
former area the victims might include members of a man's own tribe
and family. The chieftain was the first and sometimes the only person to partake of human flesh. Prisoners were occasionally fattened
before being devoured.

A chieftain's illness, the consecration of a spirit house, the launching of a boat, the termination of a war, an initiation ceremony—any
one of these things could occasion the eating of human flesh. Tischner
says that the old Viti Islanders of the Fiji group were reputed to be
the most inveterate cannibals in the South Seas. While some of their
chiefs abhorred the practice, many prominent headmen disposed of
a large number of victims in their time. The hero Ra Unreundre, for
instance, was supposed to have devoured nine hundred men, and in
Viti there were even special forks and plates for use at cannibalistic
repasts.

Walter Behrmann, former Professor of Geography at Berlin
University and one of the first to explore the Sepik area, stressed
that any assessment of the natives' way of life should be based on
how *they* imagine the world, not on our own conception of it. New
Guinea is badly off for meat, he pointed out, and has no large mam-
mals apart from pigs and dogs. "Imagine, therefore, that someone
has slain in battle an opponent who, in the eyes of the islanders, is
indistinguishable from an animal. Seen in this light, it seems almost
natural to devour one's enemy, for human beings are not vegetarians
and need meat to eat. This is how cannibalism should be regarded—
though not, of course, condoned." Behrmann's theory that human

beings were killed in New Guinea for lack of meat does not, however, accord with the general view. The motives underlying cannibalism seem in every case to be of a religious rather than carnivorous nature, as can be inferred from the fact that at one feast in New Guinea, cannibalism prevailed even though between four and five hundred pigs were slaughtered for the occasion.

Thus we discover in the interior of New Guinea a secluded culture characterized by head-hunting and cannibalism, by the most beautiful masks in the South Seas, by colorful and skillfully composed articles of adornment and by carvings and paintings unexcelled in any other part of the Pacific. Spirit-crocodiles, tapering masks, figureheads for the prows of dugout canoes, amazingly impressive spirit or *tambaran* houses—all these have a spiritual, indeed a religious, significance.

The island's art—and particularly that of the Sepik people—invariably emphasizes the eyes, whether framed by the painting on skulls, or staring from a white or black ground on masks, or peering from shields, or looking down from the gables or houses, or set into the prows of dugouts. Wherever a surface has to be filled, the eye motif almost always predominates. If one pair of eyes is not enough for the purpose, additional pairs are painted in. One reason why these eyes impress themselves on the beholder is that all curves and ornamentation serve to frame and stress them. Even the tall gable of the spirit house becomes transformed into a face. In the assembly hall within lives the *tambaran* or spirit. It is his eyes that peer watchfully from beneath the overhanging eaves of the palm-leaf roof, protecting the tribe and shielding it against evil influences.

It seems possible, even probable, that there are links between the T'ao-t'ieh of the Shang people of ancient China and the eye motif of New Guinea. The bronze vessels with their T'ao-t'ieh masks were used in ancestor-worship rituals. Perhaps the T'ao-t'ieh of China evolved from some ancient skull cult (compare the skulls found at Chou-k'ou-tien near Peking), just as the eye motif of New Guinea is associated with the painting of ancestral skulls.

No Western exponent of abstract art can compete with the color sense of the people of the Sepik culture. The ineffably beautiful color compositions embodied by the natives of the central Sepik area in their masks, painted spirit houses, cult figures and carvings have formed a vast and inexhaustible reservoir of inspiration for the abstract artists of the West. The people of the Sepik used colors of astonishing delicacy and almost disconcerting loveliness in their miraculous works of art.

The Sepik River area and the highland regions of Washkuk and Maprik are, as Alfred Bühler, the eminent authority on New Guinea, declared, true centers of advanced art. But although the inhabitants of New Guinea defended themselves against European colonization more staunchly than other primitive peoples, cultural infiltration by the West spelled the downfall of their religious centers and forced the *mana* which they had transformed into reality to give way before the ruthless god known as Western technique.

All art springs from religion. In New Guinea, art was never more than a handmaiden of spiritual ideas and a purveyor of spiritual strength. Here, even more clearly than in other ancient civilizations, we can see how genuine art is derived from the supersensual and how, as soon as modern civilization topples the sublime edifice of the mind, the soul and spiritual energy, the people that built it are doomed to extinction.

MEN OF MAIZE

*The purpose of research in every field, as Lawrence Housman
said, is to set back the frontier of darkness. With so many frontiers
of darkness, even in the study of man, why choose Maya civilization? To that, I think, the answer must be that Maya civilization
not only produced geniuses, but produced them in an atmosphere
which to us seems incredible. One can never assume the obvious
when dealing with the Maya, who excelled in the impractical but
failed in the practical.*

—J. E. S. Thompson, *The Rise and Fall of
Maya Civilization*, p. 13, Norman, 1954

THE Polynesians must be ranked among the great seafaring peoples
of the world, rivaled in ancient times only by the Phoenicians. The
island-studded waters of the Indo-Pacific area tempted venturesome
spirits to undertake ocean voyages far earlier there than in the
Atlantic. The Melanesians, too, made some notable journeys by sea.
We know, for instance, that the natives of Manokwari, just below
the equator, sailed from west New Guinea to Ternate in the Moluc-
cas, a distance of five hundred miles. The inhabitants of New Guinea
used to navigate their largest river, the Sepik, in dugouts more than
ninety feet long, but they also made extensive trips along the coast.
The Polynesians explored the watery wastes of the Pacific on rafts
and in outriggers, journeying across the ocean in their puny craft
for as long as five months on a single voyage, during which time they
survived on a sparse diet of fish and rainwater. If a storm proved
too much for a boat it was deliberately swamped to ease the strain
on the lashings, and the crew had to survive in the angry sea.

The Polynesians did not confine themselves to island-hopping, but
traversed deep-sea areas where no land was visible in any direction
for weeks at a time. It has been proved that they frequently made
journeys of up to 5,000 nautical miles—roughly the distance between
Tahiti and Hawaii. They had a wide knowledge of reefs, shallows,
currents, swells and winds, and their knowledge of astronomy was
so highly developed that they could calculate how far currents had
carried them off course. The Marshall Islanders were probably the
first to devise charts containing precise navigational instructions.
Their well-constructed outriggers were so swift and maneuverable

that Tischner described European explorers' ships as "clumsy, slow and awkward" by comparison.

The inhabitants of the lonely Chatham Islands in the South Pacific probably reached New Zealand on rafts. It should be noted that these Moriori only had rafts constructed of bundles of New Zealand flax held together by a boxlike wooden frame. Although New Zealand is only 250 miles from the Chatham group, it was quite an achievement to cover the distance in such frail craft. On the other hand, the Polynesians' catamarans or double canoes were often 90 to 120 feet long and could carry two or three hundred men. The Melanesians and Micronesians were also building large ocean-going vessels of this sort long before the discoveries of Fernão de Magalhães, Francis Drake and Captain Cook. Nearly all the seaborne migrations undertaken by these island peoples followed an eastward course. No American tribe ever migrated into the Pacific. The tribes of South America certainly possessed rafts with sails and centerboards, but these were used exclusively for coastal work. Alexander von Humboldt saw vessels of this type on the Ecuadorian coast. They were rafts constructed of balsa, the lightest wood in the world, and were equipped with primitive sails and bamboo huts.

It was Adalbert von Chamisso, once a page to the Queen of Prussia and later an author and scientist, who first theorized that the languages of the Micronesians and Polynesians were related to the Malay languages (as opposed to the American). Chamisso, who sailed around the world in the Russian brig *Rurig* between 1815 and 1818 and made a special study of the languages of Malaya and the South Pacific, identified twenty-two grammatical systems in the Philippines alone. Recent comparisons between the sculptures of Tiahuanaco on the southern shores of Lake Titicaca in Bolivia and the stone figures on Easter Island will not withstand serious scientific scrutiny. There are huge monoliths in both places which resemble each other to a considerable degree, but that is about all. The Polynesian dialect of Easter Island originated in the Malayan Archipelago, not in the Americas. An Easter Islander can communicate quite adequately with a Maori from New Zealand or a Polynesian from Mangareva, but the language and culture of the American Indians are entirely alien to him. Hans Plischke wrote in 1957, "The origin of Polynesian culture is to be found only in southeast Asia, not in America."

Abundant evidence supports the west-east theory. Countless

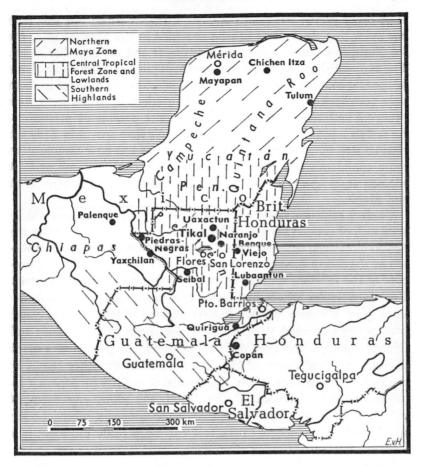

groups of tribes continued to migrate for thousands of years across
the Bering Strait from northeast Asia to America. But these earliest
inhabitants did not belong to the Mongol race but were Europeo-
Caucasian in type. They were followed at about the close of the
Ice Age by the Lagoa Santa race, first identified by the Danish
archaeologist Lund. Mongol migrations did not take place until
much later, perhaps not before 2000 B.C. Even so, the Mongoloid
tribes may not all have come by way of Siberia, and may, even at
that date, have been capable of traversing the Pacific. These Mongol
latecomers were responsible for the hint of Mongol blood perceptible

in so many North and South American Indian tribes, but this does not mean that the Indians can be classified in the Mongol race, for the Europeo-Caucasian element is stronger and considerably older. The early inhabitants of America remained pure-blooded descendants of the Old World for several millennia, whereas the Mongol in them only goes back four thousand years. Migrations by tribes from Asia occurred and continued to occur in remote periods of prehistory. As research progresses, so the date of man's first arrival in America retreats step by step into the past, so that we can now assume with some confidence that man first set foot on American soil at least 100,000 years ago, as I tried to demonstrate in my book *Man, God and Magic*.

There is evidence, albeit it is controversial and by no means widely accepted, of contact between China and Central America during the period circa 2000 B.C.–A.D. 1000. Certain symbols on bronze cult vessels of the Shang dynasty of the second millennium B.C. are reminiscent of the religious symbolism of pre-Columbian Central America. There are similar echoes in painted Peruvian pottery and cloth designs. The Viennese scholar Robert Heine-Geldern has for years been trying to unearth pre-Christian associations between China and Central America, and cites the step pyramid, the parasol as a mark of rank, the significance of the figure 4 and many other things as evidence. Nevertheless, when the Spaniards arrived in America its inhabitants were ignorant of the wheel, the plow, any form of vehicle, the potter's wheel, glass, stringed instruments, wheat, barley and rice. If late influences of the sort envisaged really did exist, it is hard to explain the absence of such important cultural assets.

Before the Spaniards' arrival there were no beasts of burden of any kind save the llama in Peru and no domestic animals except the dog. The theory that plow, wheel and cart were not adopted in America because its inhabitants owned no draft animals will not, however, hold water. The Americanist Hans Dietrich Disselhoff retorts with some logic that human beings would have expended less energy by pulling carts than by carrying heavy loads on their backs. On the other hand, Disselhoff does mention a relief from Yucatán in Mexico and a similar one from Amaravati in southern India whose iconographic resemblance is astounding. The numerous features common to the world of religious ideas on both sides of the Pacific, in the Asiatic and the ancient American civilizations, can hardly be mere accident.

The Mayas' Adam was "made of maize," a grain which they regarded as a gift of the gods and held in religious awe. We do not know for certain if maize and gourds originated in the Peruvian highlands or in the Mayas' homeland, although it is attested in Central America some eight hundred years before it is in Peru, but maize, beans and gourds were staple items of nourishment in Central America and were grown there by its culturally advanced peoples. During his Tamaulipas expedition, R. S. MacNeish discovered Mexican maize 4,500 years old in the La Perra Cave. Sylvanus G. Morley of the Carnegie Foundation stated that years of intimate contact with the modern Mayas had convinced him that even today 75 percent of their thoughts revolved around the subject of maize.

The English word for gourds, "squash," is of Indian origin. Cotton, too, was developed in the advanced civilizations of Central America. America has fifty species of agave, the plant from which most of the Mexicans' national drinks are manufactured, e.g. their highly intoxicating pulque, which is fermented in gourds. The agave was widely used by the Mayas, who were the first people to manufacture sisal from it. The Mayas were probably also the discoverers of cocoa. The words cocoa and chocolate come from Aztec, it is true, but their origin is the Mayan name *chacau haa*.

Cocoa beans were used throughout Central America as money, and J. E. S. Thompson hit upon the interesting notion that it was the Mayas' habit of using large quantities of beans as a medium of exchange which accustomed them to thinking in huge numbers.

Of all the peoples in the world, the Mayas probably evolved the most remarkable civilization, much of which seems baffling, contradictory and inexplicable, and almost all of which strikes one as alien. The Mayas produced geniuses whose names we shall never know but whose astute brains exploited intelligence, energy and physical exertion in the service of extraordinary projects. Yet obvious and essential things, things which people in every other part of the world discovered at an early date, remained a closed book to them. They hauled and carried loads like animals, harnessed to them by a headband, because the idea of the wheel never occurred to them. They constructed the most magnificent buildings in Central America, buildings for priests and gods, architectural creations

which necessitated an enormous expenditure of effort but had no
bearing on daily life. They could calculate in millions, yet they were
incapable of weighing a few pounds of fruit.

The Mayan area is divided into three zones. The northern zone
embraces the Yucatán Peninsula, the major part of Campeche and
the district of Quintana Roo. The heart of the central zone is the
Petén district of Guatemala and includes adjoining areas of Mexico
and British Honduras. The southern zone comprises the Guatemalan
highlands and parts of El Salvador.

It is strange, as is almost everything in the Mayas' vanished way
of life, that it was the central zone which evolved the most advanced
civilization. The lowlands are swathed in vast tropical forests containing giant trees which reach a height of over 150 feet, towering
mahogany trees, Spanish cedars, ceiba or God trees (once sacred to
the Mayas), innumerable species of palms, and the sapodilla, which
during the rainy season supplies the thick milky juice that forms
the basis of chewing gum. The hundreds of *chicleros* who roam the
tropical forests collecting chicle sap have very often been responsible
for directing archaeologists' attention to ruined sites. Today, the
area is almost uninhabited, and Flores, the capital of the Petén
Department, is a small township of only 4,000 inhabitants lost in the
vastness of the surrounding forest.

It was in the central zone that the oldest and most important Mayan
cities such as Tikal, Uaxactún, Copán, Palenque and Piedras Negras
once flourished. Many other former towns could be listed, and
others still remain to be wrested from the embrace of a forest which
twines its giant fingers around palaces, pyramids and terraces, runs
riot across open ground and erodes the stones of former cities, hiding them forever from view.

Mayan civilization and the Mayas' way of life depended principally on agriculture. When they needed land they burned down a
patch of forest, harvested two or three crops and abandoned their
fields as soon as they became unproductive, leaving the forest to
reclaim it once more. It is incomprehensible that Mayan culture
should have attained its zenith in an area which is not only con-
spicuously lacking in natural resources but possesses only a thin
layer of cultivable soil. The Mayas' sole implements were made of
wood and stone, and their only additional aid was fire. Year after
year they waged a laborious battle against the all-devouring forest,

yet it was here that they built their cities, evolved their complex religious cults and wrested their food from the reluctant soil. In his *Study of History*, Arnold Toynbee claims to supply an explanation of their behavior by suggesting that the conditions under which the most advanced cultures evolve must be neither too difficult nor too favorable. This explanation does not tell us much, for the highest cultures generally grew up in fertile river valleys, i.e. under extremely favorable conditions. But, even if harsh conditions are regarded as a prerequisite of cultural development, Thompson demurs that living conditions in the lowland jungle were so arduous that it is scarcely conceivable that Mayan civilization evolved there at all.

In the Guatemalan highlands south of the central zone the climate is much kinder and never displays extremes of heat or cold. Wheat, sugar cane and beans flourish there today, just as the main crops of the Mayan period were maize, melons, sweet potatoes and cocoa. The area also yielded obsidian for stone knives and spear points, and toward the close of the Mayan period gold was washed from the rivers. Above all, the northwest highlands of Guatemala formed the great hunting grounds where the Mayas trapped quetzals, the trogons from whose long tail feathers and red or yellow belly feathers they made their celebrated articles of adornment. The quetzal ultimately became the national emblem of Guatemala.

Despite the wealth of the Mayas' southern territories, the highland never gave birth to such remarkable cultural achievements as the central lowlands. On the contrary, sculpture and architecture were far inferior in what was materially the richest area. Why this should have been so, and whether the frequent earthquakes exercised a prejudicial effect, we do not know, but it is a remarkable fact that not a single pillar bearing hieroglyphic inscriptions has so far been discovered in the highland regions of the south.

Pillars or steles played a very important role in Mayan culture. These monoliths with their surfeit of inscriptions can be regarded as chronological records, for they were used to define sections of the calendar. In addition, the steles carried rows of sacred symbols, reliefs depicting priest-princes, scenes portraying prisoners and slaves (especially at Tikal) and, later, whole groups of figures. The Mayas attempted to heighten the effect of their reliefs by painting them, so the steles must once have glowed with color. Figures are normally carved in profile, and the pillars vary between six and twelve feet in height.

One stele in Quirigua, dating from the year A.D. 731, is over thirty-two feet high. One hundred and three steles have been counted at Calakmul. Tikal boasts 86 steles of which 65 bear no hieroglyphs, though the tropical rains may have washed them off. In the year A.D. 790, during the period when Mayan culture was at its zenith, nineteen steles of this type were erected at various places in the Mayas' domain. Steles were probably dedicated at fixed intervals, and the stele cult must have enjoyed great significance in a culture which combined astronomy with religion in such a unique manner.

The Mayan cities served as cult centers for religious ceremonies, but they were also administrative and commercial centers. Not much, however, is discernible of the everyday life of the townsmen and peasants who once walked their streets.

At the summit of the pyramids in Mayan cities were temples with exceedingly thick walls. No one could have lived in these stone buildings. They had no doors, no windows, no smoke vents, and they were damp and ill-lit. The only light came from narrow door-ways, so the priests must have performed their rites either in semi-darkness or complete gloom.

Unlike those of Egypt, Mayan pyramids were not burial places but cult buildings. The traces of burial which have been found beneath the floors of many of them are probably the remains of human sacrifices or chieftains' families.

The very fact that Mayan pyramids were not tombs added to the sensational nature of a discovery made in 1952. In 1950, a grave had been found inside the Temple of Inscriptions at Palenque in Chiapas State, Mexico. A hidden flight of stairs led down through the floor of the temple, which stood on the upper platform of the pyramid, into the heart of the substructure. Archaeologists cleared first forty-six steps, then two horizontal air shafts which emerged into the open air, and finally a second flight of thirteen steps. These led into a tunnel whose builders had rendered it impassable with clay and stones. Alberto Ruz, an archaeologist employed by Mexico's National Institute of Anthropology and History, uncovered eight further steps during the 1952 digging season and came upon a passage whose central section had been blocked by a thick wall. Near the end of the vault Ruz found a stone kist containing sacrificial offer-

ings such as pottery, shells and jade pearls. At about the middle of
the pyramid's foundations lay another stone kist together with the
skeletons of five young men and a woman. These six people were
probably members of a prince's retinue who had been killed so that
they could serve their master in the world hereafter. Removing
another stone slab, Ruz found himself in a vaulted chamber 75 feet
beneath the floor of the temple at the pyramid's summit. On the
walls were nine stucco reliefs of gods, probably the nine gods of
the underworld. The vault contained a massive stone sarcophagus
with a superbly ornamented lid weighing five tons. Hieroglyphs on
the sarcophagus revealed that the burial had taken place about A.D.
700, and inside lay the skeleton of a Mayan prince, richly adorned
with jade and other jewelry. One pear-shaped pearl was almost one
and a quarter inches long!

In 1953, when the pyramid had not yet surrendered its secret,
Professor E. Noguera wrote: "Perhaps the foundation on which the
relief-covered slab rests will prove to be a large stone kist in which
a person of superior rank lies buried." The Mexican scholar was
right. For the first time, archaeologists discovered a Central American
pyramid which had also served as a royal tomb.

However, there is no doubt that the burial chamber was built
before the pyramid and probably during the prince's lifetime, so
even this remarkable discovery has done nothing to shake the theory
that Mayan pyramids are temples rather than tombs.

CITIES IN THE JUNGLE

*The Maya monuments are the Sphinxes of America. While I
was in Copán I was irresistibly drawn each day to these great
sculptures, which exercise an almost hypnotic effect. Contemplat-
ing them, one becomes absorbed without knowing why or coming
any closer to a solution.*

—E. P. Dieseldorff, *Art and Religion
of the Maya Peoples,* Vol. II, p. 1,
Berlin, 1931

THE Mayas, especially those of Yucatán, are among the broadest-
featured people in the world. They augment their bullet-headedness
by deliberately distorting the shape of their skulls, an artificial process which the inhabitants of ancient Teotihuacán also regarded as
enhancing physical beauty and effected by fitting a wooden frame
around the heads of young children. The Mayas' descendants in
Yucatán and Guatemala resemble portrayals of the ancient Mayas
so strongly that we can form a good idea of their ancestors' original
appearance. They were generally shorter than Europeans and broader
in the shoulders and chest. They had longer arms and smaller hands
and feet. Their teeth must always have been good, but they filed
their eyeteeth to a point. The modern Mayas also have good teeth.
Morley mentions that 50 percent of them remain completely free of
dental decay until the age of twenty, whereas in the United States
90 percent of all children require dental treatment before the age of
fourteen. Smooth hair ranging in color from dark brown to black,
dark brown eyes and, often, decidedly hooked noses are the main
characteristics of this copper-colored and far from unattractive
race.

In addition, the Mayas retain the so-called Mongol patch, a dis-
coloration in the region of the sacrum common to all Mongoloid
peoples until the age of ten. It is much the same with the Japanese.
Ninety-nine percent of all one-year-old Japanese children have a
distinct blue patch on the sacrum which completely disappears by
the time they reach ten. A similar sacral patch is found among
Malays, Eskimos and most American Indians.

On the average, Mayan girls marry at sixteen and young men at
twenty-one. Diego de Landa (1524–1579), the celebrated church-

[102] A particularly fine example of Benin art, this bronze depicts a native—perhaps the king—on horseback. The plaque is now in the Museum of Ethnology, Berlin.

[103] One of the famous bronze plaques of Benin. The inhabitants of Nigeria have long since forgotten what their original significance was—let alone whom or what they portray. There is a possibility that they were used in religious ceremonies.

[104] This wooden figure from Cokwe in Angola shows how African artists used to modify the proportions of limbs to lend emphasis to weapons and head ornaments. In this particular case it is evident that the artist wished to stress the frontal view of his subject.

→

[105] The people of Benin used to wear hunting masks while stalking game. This wood and leather mask comes from Loko, Nigeria.

→

[106] The Hausa are a race of mixed Arab and Negro blood numbering about 4 million, of which 3½ million live in northern Nigeria. This leather flask effectively kept liquids cold.

→

[107] Wooden drum from Calabar, a provincial town situated on the estuary of the Cross River in southern Nigeria. It is a particularly fine example of the Benin wood-carver's art.

[108] A mask from Balumbo in Gabon. Like Nigeria, the coast of Gabon lies on the Gulf of Guinea. African artists no longer produce masks as handsome and impressive as this.

[109] In order to preserve a relative's life-force after death, the natives of New Guinea cut his head off and coat it with a layer of clay which they model so as to re-create the dead man's facial expression. The head is then painted in the style traditionally adopted by ancestors for cult purposes of war, and the eye sockets are inlaid with cowrie shells.

[110] The Mayan city of Chichén-Itzá was founded in the sixth century A.D. Here one can see a step-pyramid capped by a massive temple.

[111] The ruins of this once mighty temple are to be found at Uxmal in Yucatán. This so-called "nunnery," dating from the tenth century A.D., is here photographed from a pyramid.

[112] This sculpture of a god was found behind a pyramid at Copán. The step at the god's feet is carved with Mayan hieroglyphics.

[113] A sacrificial Mayan altar at Copán. The relief shows a group of sitting priests, identifiable by their headdress.

[114] A handsome stele at Copán. Round altars are to be seen on each side of the stele. Copán, the "Athens of the New World," was the center of Mayan astronomy.

[115] The "Temple of the Giant Jaguar" at Tikal, Guatemala, was discovered in the jungle by an American expedition from the University of Pennsylvania. This temple is one of the finest examples of Mayan architecture; the interior has to a large extent been restored.

man whose history of Yucatán, published in 1560, is a veritable treasury of ancient Mayan customs, related that girls used to marry at the age of twenty but now (in his day) married between the ages of twelve and fourteen. A Franciscan monk, Landa arrived in Yucatán a few years after the Spanish conquest. We owe much of our information about the Mayas to the fact that he was subsequently brought to trial in Spain for having exceeded his authority in the New World and defended himself against the allegation by writing an apologia while in prison.

Human beings are complex creatures. Even the sketchiest description of them must include a long list of items. The Mayas are strong family men. They are equable, not particularly inventive, and unperturbed by the idea of death. Their keen powers of observation and retentive memory are such that one can properly describe them as intelligent. Several authorities have called the Mayas superstitious, and the same applies to their latter-day descendants, though people who devote the majority of their thoughts and actions to a god or gods might equally be called religious. The Mayas certainly *were* religious, but their character exhibits a marked streak of fatalism, probably inherited from remote epochs when, in order to provide the gods with sacrifice, human beings had their hearts torn out or were drowned—men, women and children alike—in sacred pools, or, later still, were crucified.

The Mayas are a thrifty but remarkably honest people. There are no thieves in a land where doors and windows are unknown. Like all American Indian tribes, they have a regrettable tendency toward drunkenness, but their womenfolk keep their houses extremely tidy, they are generous and hospitable, and murderers and beggars do not exist. One conspicuous trait is their extraordinary personal cleanliness. Like the Japanese, they bathe each night and morning.

Landa, who is painted sometimes as a saint and sometimes as a ruthless persecutor of the Indians, declared that the women of Yucatán were generally better-looking than the women of Spain. They were not white but had a yellowish-brown complexion occasioned by exposure to the sun and their habit of bathing frequently in the open air. Their breasts were bare and their bodies tattooed above the waistline with finer and more elegant designs than those of their menfolk. They perfumed and anointed themselves with red resin and wore their hair long or built it into elaborate coiffures.

Mothers took great care to see that their daughters looked after their hair. Little girls wore three or four spiky plaits like small horns, a style which Landa found extremely charming. Women usually dressed in the *manta*, a sacklike garment open at each side. Landa noted with resignation that they were good-natured and proud—and rightly so, "for before they became acquainted with our nation, a circumstance bewailed by their old men, they were wondrously chaste." Captain Alonso López de Avila, he wrote, once captured a Mayan girl of great beauty and charm, but his blandishments were in vain. The young woman had sworn to be faithful to her husband and preferred to die rather than yield, so the Spaniards had her torn to pieces by dogs.

Mayan girls carried chastity to extremes. They always turned their backs on men, even when they were offering them something to drink. Encountering a man on a path, they stepped aside to let him pass. Their ambition was to have many children, to which end they prayed fervently to the gods and made sacrifice. Landa described the women as sensible, courteous, very friendly to those that understood them, and extraordinarily generous. They were pious, too, and sacrificed cloth, food and drink in token of their devotion to the gods.

The Mayas believed in the immortality of the soul. In fact, said Landa, "They believed in it more firmly than many other races." They also knew that the soul was destined to another and better life once it had left the body.

The ancestors of the Mayas reached their new home sometime between 2000 and 1000 B.C. J. E. Thompson thinks that they wrested supremacy from the indigenous inhabitants of the area and so constituted a superior caste. After about five hundred years new tribes arrived who were numerically stronger than the existing inhabitants. They probably came from Asia, bringing with them a knowledge of pottery, spinning and weaving, and probably a vague knowledge of agriculture as well, although they did not introduce any seeds from the old continent. The last migrants, who arrived at about the time of Christ's birth, may have transmitted certain religious ideas from their Asiatic home, e.g. the celestial dragon and the four corners of the world. These are only suppositions, however, for the Mayas' actual place of origin remains shrouded in mystery.

Mayan history is divided into three periods: the formative period (circa 500 B.C.–A.D. 325), the classical period (325–800) which reached its zenith between 625 and 800, and the period of decline (800–925). After that came the Mexican conquests of 975–1200 and finally a period during which Mayan culture enjoyed a brief renaissance.

Important inventions are attributed to the peoples of Central America. Although it is not always known precisely which American tribe first implemented this or that new idea, many inventions undoubtedly stem from the Mayas, as, for instance, the manufacture of rubber, rubber balls, rubber soles for sandals, impregnated rainproof capes, "Maya blue" (extracted from the mineral clay known as beidellite), indigo, a purple obtained from shellfish, a type of mechanical artillery catapult and "live wasps' nests" for use as ammunition against the enemy. The Mayas also cultivated a very large number of wild plants and were accomplished naturalists. They were excellent road builders, too, even though the Incas surpassed them in that respect. For example, one of their roads ran for over sixty miles from the town of Cobá in Quintana Roo to Yaxuná, a few miles from Chichén Itzá. The road, which is about thirty feet wide, was enclosed on either side by primitive stone walls and had a well-laid foundation of mortar. In marshy areas it ran along a raised embankment, and just outside Cobá it was supported by a platform. One very interesting discovery made on the Cobá–Yaxuná road was a limestone roller about fifteen feet wide and five tons in weight. The roller, which had broken into two pieces, must have required a team of fifteen men to propel it. We even know that the road was built from east to west, i.e. from Cobá to Yaxuná. Mayan roads, which were mainly designed to carry processions, must have made enormous demands on a people who had no carts or beasts of burden. They also presupposed considerable engineering skill. How the Mayan engineers managed to cut their way through the dense rain forest so unerringly that they arrived directly at their intended destination is a still unsolved mystery.

Architecturally, the Mayas probably excelled all other ancient American civilizations, Aztec and Inca included. Copán in Honduras was the Mayas' main scientific center. This was where their finest astronomers worked and probably where the 200-day calendar was first introduced. It was also the place where a temple was dedicated to the planet Venus, where the dates of solar eclipses were calculated, and where, on the steps of Temple 26, the longest extant Mayan inscription was found, a series of approximately one thousand hieroglyphs. The "Athens of the New World," as Copán has justly been called, boasted a so-called acropolis, numerous pyramids, terraces, temples, altars and steles, a large open square and a court for the ball games which the Mayas regarded as a form of religious ceremony. The ball-game court at Copán, with its crenellations, stone parrots and sunbirds, was one of the handsomest in the whole Mayan area.

Chichén Itzá, a sort of Mecca, first reached its prime under the Mexican rulers of the eleventh, twelfth and thirteenth centuries. The pyramid temples there were resplendent with pillars portraying the famous feathered serpents of Central America. There, as at Piedras Negras, a finely appointed steam bath was discovered. Chichén Itzá had seven ball-game courts. The natural rubber ball had to pass through one or other of the stone rings set into the walls of the court, the main difficulty being that the critical stroke could not be delivered except with the elbow, wrist or hip. The trick came off so seldom that legend has it that when it did, all the spectators had to hand over their clothes and jewelry to the winner. To evade this obligation, witnesses of a successful attempt hurriedly left the scene, usually followed by the winner's friends, who ran after them to exact payment.

Thrones were found in the great colonnades of Chichén Itzá. These colonnades enclosed the so-called "courtyard of a thousand pillars," a huge open plaza which may have been the ancient city's market place. The large circular building known as the Observatory or, because of its snail-like shape, the Caracol, is over fifty feet high and towers above two massive rectangular terraces. The numerous sacrificial offerings found in the sacred springs of Chichén Itzá included jewelry, jade, incense, and the remains of about fifty victims of drowning, eight of them women.

The cities of Palenque, Yaxchilán and Piedras Negras likewise represent a peak of achitecture unequaled elsewhere in ancient America. As Morley rightly says, the stucco works of Palenque are unsurpassed by any other examples in the Mayan area. The limestone reliefs there are so finely carved and so wonderfully composed that they merit comparison with the finest reliefs of ancient Egypt. The splendid terraces and pyramids, the temples, stairways, corridors, subterranean galleries and altars, the remarkable artistic ability, wealth and power of Palenque have overwhelmed not only the Spaniards, whose first glimpse it was of the ancient Mayan empire, but every visitor since the year 1553. Frans Blom, the Danish archaeologist, wrote in 1923 that "one's first visit to Palenque is immeasurably impressive, and when one has spent a while there the ruined city becomes a sort of obsession."

The four superb and richly ornamented temples at Yaxchilán are renowned for their twelve carved lintels, two of which bear sculpted reliefs of outstanding beauty. The wall sculptures of Piedras Negras, dating from A.D. 761 and chiseled in limestone, are among America's finest pre-Columbian works of art.

At Piedras Negras the Mayas observed and celebrated the end of their *hotuns* or 1,800-day periods with particular reverence. Each of the twenty-two hotun periods between A.D. 608 and 810 was solemnly commemorated by the erection of a monument adorned with pictures in relief, and all twenty-two of these have survived.

Mayan astronomy was not only a science but also a means of influencing the future. Inconceivable as it may sound, Mayan priests working with no more equipment than the naked eye succeeded in determining the orbital period of Venus. The astronomers of Copán tried to reconcile the calendar year of 365 days with the true tropical year of 365.24 days and established the duration of the solar year as early as A.D. 700. The Mayas invented and used the figure nought two hundred years before any nation in Europe. Instead of arranging their numbers with the smallest units on the right, they inscribed them vertically. They had calculated the mythical beginning of their calendar to be 3113 B.C., but their chronological system did not come into use until the fourth or third century B.C.

It is interesting to pursue an idea expounded by Sylvanus G. Morley, a man who devoted his life to a study of the Mayas. On his long journey through prehistory and history, Morley argued, man has surmounted five obstacles: first he mastered fire, then he discovered agriculture, then he domesticated wild animals, then he devised tools of metal, and finally he discovered the principle of the wheel.

The Mayas had mastered fire and learned how to sow and reap in an area inimical to agriculture. They had, it is true, domesticated the wild turkey and knew how to keep bees, but apart from the dog they possessed not a single domestic, farm or draft animal of any kind. They owned no metal implements and the principle of the wheel was unknown to them. Of the five obstacles, therefore, they had surmounted only two, whereas the Egyptians, Chaldeans, Babylonians, Assyrians, Persians, Chinese, Phoenicians, Etruscans, Greeks and Romans were endowed with all five prerequisites of civilization.

In order to assess the status of Mayan culture correctly and draw the appropriate conclusions we must go far back into the history of mankind, to the neolithic age in which the Mayas, with their stone tools, really lived. Comparing the Mayas' many achievements with the prehistoric civilizations of the Old World, we can say without hesitation that no Stone-Age people attained such cultural heights as the ancient Mayas of Central America.

TIKAL, THE ENIGMA

Day after day we work among the bared temples and monuments, extending trenches, tunnels, and pits through floors and stairways, recording in notebooks and on film the often perplexing intricacies of construction, demolition, and rebuilding. The tens of thousands of potsherds and other objects recovered each season become laboratory objects, to be catalogued and studied. All of this work continues with the expectation that the time-sequence of related construction, artifacts, sculpture, and inscriptions, as well as site mapping and important studies of environment, will collectively produce answers.

—WILLIAM R. COE, *Tikal 1959, Expedition 1959,*
Vol. I, No. 4, p. 7

THE British expert J. E. S. Thompson estimates that in A.D. 800 the total population of the Mayan area was between two and three million. In contrast to so many extinct or slowly dying primitive races, the descendants of the Mayas still survive in considerable numbers and are in no danger of dying out. Fifty years ago Karl Sapper put the Mayan-speaking population at about 1,250,000.

In all, fifteen Mayan languages and dialects are still in use, and two more became defunct a relatively short time ago. These languages are divided into two groups, highland and lowland, all the remainder being classified as dialects of one group or the other. Oddly enough, Mayan is not related to any other language in Mexico or Central America as a whole.

Of all American peoples, only the Mayas devised a form of writing and used it. Their hieroglyphs can be seen on steles, on altars, on the walls of ball-game courts, on steps, on wall facings, on posts of wood and stone, on door frames. They are scratched on stucco and jade jewelry, painted on vessels and inscribed in books. There are two types, one head-shaped and the other symbolic. Most Mayan glyphs are still undeciphered because no "Rosetta stone" has been found in the Mayan area and obviously no Mayan text exists beside a parallel translation in another language. Yet we know the Mayas' hieroglyphic script was used to record the passage of time, list the names and attributes of reigning gods and note down the findings and observations of priest-astronomers.

The Mayas left behind whole books, the "paper" for which was provided by a species of wild fig whose fiber was steeped in rubber and coated with a layer of chalk. The Mayas' volumes were folding books rather like early Chinese manuscripts. However, so many Mayan texts were destroyed because of the religious fanaticism of the Spaniards that only three are still in existence: the oldest and most valuable, the Codex Dresden, devoted principally to astro-

Mayan hieroglyphs symbolizing twenty days. It is noticeable that some days were expressed by symbols of similar shape.

nomical notes; the Codex Madrid, a horoscopic catalogue used for priestly prophecies; and the Codex Paris, listing rites associated with individual dates of the calendar. The books contain colored pictures of gods and mythical occurrences, series of numerals, and hieroglyphs, all executed with a very fine brush.

About a third of the hieroglyphs can now be read. Everything so far deciphered relates to the calendar, the cardinal points of the compass, astronomical events, deities and religious rites. Fortunately, all the numerals have been identified. The study of Mayan glyphs is far from simple, however, because one glyph often possesses several meanings. The Mayan numerals from o to 19 are simply heads in profile, each with a different face. This strange arithmetical system is unique, but the hieroglyphs representing the nineteen Mayan months are just as unusual. A figure seen in profile with its knees drawn up presumably denotes a dead body. The symbols expressing the nominal forms of gods are normally human heads. Other hieroglyphs take the form of hands, snails, birds' heads, lizards and sacrificial offerings of many kinds. It was a very considerable task to decipher these enigmatic symbols, and the men who accomplished it deserve the highest praise. They include the Germans Paul Schellhas, Ernst Förstemann, Eduard Seler and, more recently, Thomas Barthel and Günter Zimmermann, the Americans J. T. Goodman, C. P. Bowditch and Cyrus Thomas, and in very recent years Morley and the British scholars Spinden and Thompson. Altogether they have succeeded in deciphering a third of the hieroglyphs —at least in general purport. Morley's five-volume work on the inscriptions of Petén is a scientific achievement of the first order.

What is the earliest authenticated date in Mayan culture? For a long time, the oldest datable object bearing Mayan hieroglyphs was the famous Passion Plate, a piece of jade measuring 21.59 by 7.62 centimeters and found in 1864 near the Caribbean port of Puerto Barrios in Guatemala. When deciphered, its date proved to be A.D. 320. This plaque so greatly resembled pictures of prisoners on monuments in the Mayan city of Tikal that Morley came to the conclusion that the piece was originally made there. Tikal stands in the north of central Petén and is the largest of all the Mayas' sacred temple precincts.

Another date identified by Morley came to light on May 5, 1916, on a stele in Uaxactún known to archaeologists as 9. (Numbers like these are based on the sequence in which steles were found at the various archaeological sites.) Uaxactún, which is only ten miles north of Tikal, was founded by people from that great cultural center, and must, therefore, have existed at least since the year A.D. 328.

Tikal, the largest and probably the most interesting of all Mayan cities, is currently being excavated by archaeologists from the

Mayan hieroglyphs for months. The year was divided into the nineteen periods whose names are given here.

University of Pennsylvania. It is now generally accepted that Tikal originated in the early phase of Mayan civilization.

As a religious center, Tikal was not only the largest Mayan city. It also boasted the tallest pyramids, fascinating edifices of which all are over 125 feet high and the largest reaches a height of 230 feet. Their massive proportions are emphasized by their slim lines and steeply sloping sides. Two large step pyramids of this type rise on either side of the rectangular ceremonial courtyard, their numerous terraces crowned by temples with very thick walls. These sacred shrines contain the gloomy cult chambers typical of the whole Mayan area, as well as some walled-up platforms which may have been altars used by Mayan priests.

The priests performed their duties garbed in great splendor. Their jade jewelry, the quetzal feathers in their headdresses, the comings and goings through doorless entrances surmounted by superbly carved wooden lintels, the clouds of incense and the atmosphere of intense religious fervor—all this must have made a deep impression on the people assembled in the courtyard below or on the terraces of the pyramid itself. It should be remembered that Mayan festivals were preceded by long periods of fasting. Priests, novices and perhaps officials, too, gathered in the twilight of the narrow stone chambers to fast in preparation for the feast day. Water was brought to them by servants, and perhaps also by their wives and mothers, none of whom was permitted to enter the temple itself. They merely put down the priests' scanty rations and withdrew, leaving the inmates to watch and wait in solitude.

The Mayas' religious life was compounded of endless hours and days of fasting, of sacred fires, of blood drawn from tongue and ears, of sacrifice and the burning of copal incense. They were searching for God, as men have always done throughout the history of civilization. All material considerations were subordinated to their spiritual endeavors, to their building, their suffering, their fasting, their yearning and their quest for the divine. Anyone who stands at dusk among the ruins of these splendid buildings will sense something of their sanctity and nearness to God.

On the south side of Tikal's main plaza are some multichambered buildings whose purpose, though often debated, has not yet been ascertained. Were they palaces? Were they monasteries? Were they merely assembly rooms? Tikal is still a book with many uncut pages.

Tikal has water reservoirs, paved streets, pyramids with and without buildings on their platforms, sixteen temples on the northern acropolis, and innumerable steles. Under the leadership of Edwin M. Shook, who has already dug successfully at Uaxactún, Kaminaljuyú and Mayapán, excavations sponsored jointly by the University of Pennsylvania and the Guatemalan Government have been revealing the Mayas' most important city in ever greater detail. In 1959 William R. Coe, one of the outstanding authorities on the Mayas, declared that Tikal was a unique manifestation of Mayan culture, a summit of achievement unequaled elsewhere in the New World. Largely cut off by the hot and steamy rain forest, Tikal constituted a vast study in human development. Some might yearn to reach Mars and discover what has evolved outside the earth, Coe wrote, but he and his colleagues preferred to remain in Tikal and discover how and why the American Indians had met the challenge of their environment, how they built their tall temples, how they managed to think in terms of five million Mayan years, how they survived for perhaps two thousand years and then fell silent, leaving behind the tangible legacy of sculptures, hieroglyphs, potsherds and building layers which are now providing material for the endless tasks of compilation and measurement.

During the diggings of 1958, a temple was uncovered. This consisted of three chambers, each with one central doorway. When American archaeologists gave orders to clear the six feet of rubble in the innermost chamber, workmen came upon Stele 26. Because the stele still bore traces of red paint, the whole building was christened the Temple of the Red Stele. A fine example of early classical Mayan architecture, it had been deliberately and violently destroyed at some undetermined point in time, after which priests had apparently tried to appease the gods with sacrificial offerings, for their cult fires had blackened the plaster of the altar. How long the temple survived after that we do not know, but it was eventually subjected to fresh devastation. The altar was partially ripped out and the finely chiseled, red-painted portrayals of marine sacrifices and pieces of coral and stone were destroyed. In the floor of the chambers the Americans found circular cavities filled with huge quantities of sponges, coral, seaweed, fishbones and other strange objects of marine origin, together with some finely carved pieces of obsidian. It is hard to account for these peculiar sacrificial gifts. Many of the finds came from the far-off Pacific coast, while others came from the Atlantic. It remains incomprehensible that products of the sea should have been sacrificed at all, for sacrificial offerings of this type have been found nowhere else in the Mayan area.

Probably the most important discovery of all was made by the University of Pennsylvania archaeologists in 1959. Just over two hundred yards from the great plaza of Tikal there was found a broken stele which represented the earliest datable Mayan monument so far discovered in the lowland jungle of Guatemala. Linton Satterthwaite, Mary Ricketson and Benedicta Levine identified the date of this stele, which bears the number 29, as July 6, 292. Although this is our earliest authenticated date, Mayan culture naturally goes back much farther into the past, and there we are groping in the dark.

Another unsolved mystery is when and why Mayan culture met its end. Why should cult places which evidently made such enormous demands on the Mayas' material and human resources have been abandoned? What storm had broken over their heads?

All authorities on the Mayas have tried to fathom why they disappeared so suddenly at the height of their powers and why all building, scientific research and religious observance came to such an abrupt halt. It was long thought that the Mayas relinquished their cities in the central region and migrated, some to Yucatán in the north and some to the Guatemalan highlands in the south, but this cannot be correct because during the classical period all three zones flourished concurrently, not one after the other. Many theories have been put forward to explain the abandonment of the Mayan cities. Perhaps their particular kind of plowless agriculture eventually proved too much of a drain on the population's energy. Their method of burning down patches of forest, cultivating the soil for a year or two and then giving up their fields and moving to a neighboring area to begin all over again may, in the long run, have struck them as too laborious and wasteful.

Malaria, yellow fever and hookworm have all been held responsible for the abandonment of the Mayan cities, but marsh fever and jungle fever, a virus disease, seem to have been bequeathed to the New World by the Spaniards and probably did not exist there before their arrival. The same applies to hookworm, reputed to have caused the deaths of so many Egyptian Pharaohs.

Everything would be explained if the Mayas had abandoned their holy places gradually and if their culture had declined by easy stages. We know, however, that many Mayan cities were abandoned virtually overnight. The city of Uaxactún, for instance, was abruptly depopulated before many of its buildings could be completed.

Copán ceased to erect hieroglyphic monuments in A.D. 800. At Quiriguá, Piedras Negras and Etzna, life faded in 810. Tila fell silent in 830, and the last steles were erected at Tikal and Seibal in 869. Uaxactún, Xultún, Xamantún and Chichén Itzá flourished only until 889. Probably the last date recorded by the Mayas is on a stele found at San Lorenzo in the vicinity of La Muñeca. It corresponds to our year A.D. 928.

Life died away in the great religious centers like the fading tones of a bell, leaving them silent and deserted, but we know that many of them showed renewed signs of life in the sixteenth century and that the Copán area became quite densely populated. People were still living in the central region at the time of the Spanish conquistadors, though far fewer of them than eight hundred years previously. The rain-forest civilization declined so abruptly that even war cannot be held responsible for it. Furthermore, except in Tikal, very few traces of wanton destruction have been found.

Thompson thinks that the Mayan territories fell prey not to foreign domination but to something far more dangerous; namely, foreign ideas. It is possible that there were widespread insurrections by the peasants against the priestly caste. For once the religious faith of the Mayan people waned, their culture, like every culture that forfeits its faith, was doomed to perish. Without faith the peasants would have been reluctant to contribute their labor or make material sacrifices. Egypt and the Renaissance bear testimony that the largest and most sublime works of man were the fruit not of coercion but religious faith. The priestly ruling class may have been massacred or hounded from one city to the next, leaving peasant chieftains and shamans to take its place. Building, the erection of steles and architecture in general came to a standstill, and the tropical forest crept into courtyards, up steps, across terraces and onto the roofs of buildings.

The sudden abandonment of a residential area measuring 375 by

125 miles and containing dozens of large, thriving religious centers would seem to defy any form of explanation, especially as it occurred at a period when Mayan culture showed few if any signs of debility. The German Americanist Franz Termer has, however, pointed to one possibility which is at least worthy of consideration. In a religious state, spontaneous abandonment of the homeland might have taken place at the behest of the gods. Seen in this light, an exodus instigated by the gods and supervised by the priests who implemented their will becomes conceivable.

The great exodus of the ninth century is probably the most out-standing of the many mysteries surrounding this mysterious people. Yet wherever we probe the civilization of the rain forest we find ourselves confronted by unanswered questions. We do not know what secrets lie hidden behind the Mayan inscriptions that have not yet been deciphered; we have little inkling of the Mayas' political system; we are ignorant of whether the rain-forest region was welded into a unified kingdom or consisted of city-states; we have only a minimum of information on the Mayas' daily life, despite the magnificent work done by Thompson, Morley, Shook and so many others; we cannot plumb the basic concepts of the Mayan religion; we know virtually nothing of the Mayas' origins or ultimate destiny; and we can find nothing truly comparable with their language.

Mutely, the massive buildings of these highly gifted people return the beholder's gaze; mutely, their holy places molder and decay beneath the onslaught of the all-devouring jungle.

"BEHOLD, ALL THINGS ARE BECOME NEW"
(II Corinthians: v, 17)

It is very doubtful whether man's artistic capabilities are actually any higher today than they were in late prehistoric times, though the number of motifs, techniques, and media available to him now is, of course, immeasurably greater.

—WILLIAM FOXWELL ALBRIGHT, *From the Stone Age to Christianity*, pp. 127-8, Baltimore, 1946

WHAT does the twilight, the deliquescence, the often tragic finale of all civilizations, mean?

It is never more than an apparent withdrawal, an ebbing of something which, at another time and often in another place, is destined in some mysterious and unfathomable way to flare up once more. Nothing in the world vanishes forever. The downfall of a civilization is not a natural phenomenon. No form of life ever dies without the acquiescence of man and without a voluntarily engendered cause. All theories which allege that the course of events is determined by laws of nature or history, all "cyclical fluctuations" and "wave" theories of history ultimately break down because the future is molded by the ideas, decisions and actions of living men, by their works and achievements both past and present. The existence of human freedom is one of the most difficult things in the world to understand. All great civilizations have spiritually enriched one another since time immemorial, but the longer a civilization remains isolated and the longer it lives exclusively in its own individual way, the more specialized it becomes and the less easily reconciled with another. It is always the most highly specialized civilizations that run the greatest risk of extinction. The principle is borne out in reverse by man, who has a good chance of outliving the animals of the world because he is the least specialized of all creatures. Civilizations which have become unadaptable, isolated and imprisoned in a straitjacket of rigid formulas and habits, are as susceptible to external or internal shocks as a delicate piece of machinery. External occurrences such as natural catastrophes, epidemics, economic fluctuations and invasions do not necessarily spell the doom of a civilization. It will not die until it abandons its faith and ideals.

A grandiose picture of this process is given in Genesis. First comes the "corruption" of the earth, and then a vast inundation that wipes out men and the works of their hands. Something must have happened to the faith of the antediluvian inhabitants of the world, because for some reason they abandoned their god or gods. It is no accident that natural catastrophe as a consequence of the abandonment of exalted ideals is a theme common to the traditions of many different races. The legend of the Great Flood recurs in Babylonia, Assyria and Syria, in Egypt and Greece, in Australia and China, in the South Pacific and among the tribes all over America. The story of the Flood has itself been seized upon as evidence that cultural assets are interchangeable and that ideas which originate in one place are borrowed by others and disseminated throughout the world. If the cataclysm has any basis in fact—as we must infer from the frequency and precision with which details recur in different descriptions of it—the ubiquitous nature of the tradition must be attributable to its basic truth. To account for the existence of parallel and identical thoughts by citing the homogeneity of the human mind throughout the world—in fact, to espouse the theory of "basic ideas"—is a pastime too often indulged in. The Flood does not fit into this theory, its only universal characteristic being a realization of the fundamental truth embodied in it.

As we have seen when reviewing various civilizations, foreign invasion can often be equated with the overwhelming of a weaker faith by a stronger. So it was with Jericho, whose Biblical walls collapsed between 1375 and 1300 B.C., a city built 8,000 years before the birth of Christ at a time when man was ignorant of pottery, the earliest fortress ever to be unearthed.

The realization that the strength of every civilization and its greatest art were each born of a marriage between the natural and the supernatural is perhaps the ultimate realization reached by any sensitive person who stands before the ruins of ancient temples, or gazes at tablets thousands of years old, or responds to the entreaty crystallized in stone by the world's most compelling works of art. All that is enduring, great and artistic has been engendered by the strongest of all man's impulses, not by his craving for house and hearth, food and clothing, but by his far more imperious urge for the things of the spirit and thus for eternal life. A. V. Kidder, an American scholar who devoted his life to a study of the Mayas and to archaeological research in the southwestern areas of the United States, asserted with justification that at every stage in its history the human race has sacrificed almost everything for the sake of culture.

Wherever human strength has proved unequal to the task in hand it has been supplemented by faith, religion and ideals of the most exalted kind. One can feel this almost tangibly in the hallowed precincts of Nara in Japan, in the Chinese rock temples of Lung Men, Yün Kang and Tun-huang, in the caves of Lu Lan and Qyzil, on the "spirit road" near Nanking with its gigantic beasts and tutelary figures, in the celestial temples of Peking. One can sense it in the great stupas of India, in the frescoes of Ajanta, in the reliefs at Borobudur in Java, in the sphinxes and royal tombs of Egypt and the pyramids of the Mayas. It is not mere chance that the period at which Greece attained its greatest prime, 470–400 B.C., coincided with the lifetime of Socrates, spiritual father of Western philosophy as a whole.

The less well-known, more obscure civilizations also provide us with instances where the motivating force behind achievements of great magnitude has been man's quest for something beyond the limits of his experience. What, for example, was the Hypogeum at Hal Saflieni in Malta? This immense subterranean vault bears witness to a faith that literally moved mountains in its endeavor to realize the highest of human ideals. Avebury, Stonehenge and the other vast buildings of the megalithic period were also holy places. Even the riddle of the menhirs must be solved in religious terms because they were invested with religio-magical significance. The statuettes commissioned by the citizens of Mari, who lived on the middle reaches of the Euphrates in 3000 B.C., also served as a link with the gods, as, hands folded in prayer, they watched and waited for tokens of divine favor. The unique figurines produced by the bronze culture of Sardinia between 2,500 and 3,000 years ago were also born of religious faith and destined for the service of the gods, as were the bronze figures of the Benin culture, whose purpose was to grace altars and serve God and ancestral spirits. Only the fervent belief of the Gandharans and the Indians of Mathura, who collaborated with Hellenistic sculptors, could have bequeathed the effigy of Buddha to central Asia and the whole of the Far East.

The Silk Road, that gigantic cross section of all the religions of Asia, owed its existence in no small measure to the missionary spirit, for its endless expanse was worn by the sandals and caravans of Manichaeans, Buddhists, Mohammedans and Christians.

The bell tolls for an advanced civilization as soon as images are removed from altars and works of art find their way into museums and the drawing rooms of worthy but unbelieving citizens. Such is the funeral procession of all the world's civilizations.

There is something inexplicable about products of human handiwork in which the author of the original motivating force is no longer identifiable. That is why we have attempted to explore some of these problems, even though so many must necessarily remain obscure. For instance, we do not know why the Bronze-Age culture of China sprang into being about 4,000 years ago and immediately reached a peak of perfection without revealing a hint of its origins or background. We have no idea what the people of the megalithic civilizations of western Europe actually looked like; or how long the Mayas took to evolve their system of chronology and their hieroglyphs; or why the palace of Knossos in Crete, testimony to an extremely high degree of culture, collapsed in ruins in 1400 B.C.; or whether Nestor, Agamemnon, Odysseus and Telemachus could read; or who were the Indo-European inhabitants of Troy; or what was the real secret of the Delphic Omphalos; or why the bronze caldrons of Dodone fell silent; or exactly where on the coast of southwest Spain the city of Tartessus once stood; or exactly who the Cimmerians were; or who was the chief deity of the Shang period; or how the moon-being known as T'ao-t'ieh originated; or what the marks on the rocks of Las Palmas and Hierro in the Canary Islands mean; or who inhabited the islands before the Guanches arrived.

Races die out, towns and villages lie buried, and many written traditions elude interpretation. All that remain are stones and layers of rubble, ruined buildings, myths and legends. Yet the times that produced them were not necessarily poor and devoid of culture. Where information is plentiful it throws a period into sharp relief, but the study of less well-known and intelligible civilizations is of particular importance because it sheds light on obscure intermediate periods which are just as much a part of us and our past and have played an equal part in making us what we are.

Inaccessible and mysterous civilizations arouse especial interest because all history, both visible and invisible, and all civilizations, both buried and unearthed, live on in us. Our restless urge to lay bare the hidden, strange and baffling features of the past is born of a feeling that all civilizations are part of us and that we should like —quite instinctively—to track down an unknown quantity in ourselves.

It is because the future lends itself so imperfectly to accurate prediction that historians, archaeologists and ethnologists attempt to cull information from the past and project it into the future. Equally, it is because all theories, all hypothetical cultural cycles and all assumptions of historical recurrence are based on natural laws and not on the human spirit that they fail so dismally. Despite all our research and accumulated knowledge, the past has become a bloodless thing. Not to re-examine it continually is to lose sight of the glowing embers of former civilizations and thus fall like scorched moths from an ever-burning flame that escapes our comprehension.

But forebodings about the future are born of fear, and this fear springs from the seldom-voiced but dawning realization that purely material progress, in so far as it bears no relation to life as a whole and ceases to serve any ends but those of destruction, lies like a deathtrap in the path of all living civilizations. It is because our era senses this that there is so much skepticism, so much pessimism, so much insecurity and so much heedless abuse of time.

Where superficial control of nature is concerned, man presses forward indefatigably and without pause, yet his character, morals and intelligence show no perceptible signs of improvement. Belief in intellectual progress and the idea of spiritual evolution are merely naïve offspring of the technical and scientific marvels of our age. Outward progress is counterbalanced by a lack of inward development, for the spritual life of modern man, his relationship to his fellows and the spiritual and moral qualities of the individual are all in a process of retrogression. Our age is epitomized not by atomic science but by the fact that religious values are losing their force, that modern man is afflicted by a strange sense of guilt, and that the spiritual basis essential to works of art simply does not exist.

Gone are the days of hospitality in the grand manner, the sort of hospitality practiced by all the world's so-called primitive peoples and by the advanced civilizations of the past; silent are the voices that once saluted the passing stranger; forgotten is the obligation to help those in need, shelter travelers and show magnanimity to the vanquished. The great days of divine sacrifice, oracles, religious architecture, preservation of the dead and a belief in resurrection seem gone beyond recall. We are no better than we were.

In A.D. 58, Paul foresaw a different kind of world. He regarded judgment according to material and fleshly standards as a thing of the past, and thought that henceforth the victory of man's spiritual side was assured. Addressed to the Corinthians from Macedonia, the most personal of all his letters included the words: "Behold, all things are become new."

BIBLIOGRAPHY

The Walls of Jericho

ALBRIGHT, W. F.: From the Stone Age to Christianity, Baltimore 1946. – GARSTANG, J.: Jericho: City and Necropolis, Annals of Archaeology and Anthropology, Liverpool 1932, Vol. 19, p. 3 sq., p. 35 sq.; 1933, Vol. 20, p. 3 sq.; 1934–35, Vol. 21–22, p. 99 sq., p. 143 sq.; 1936–37, Vol. 23–24, p. 67 sq., p. 35 sq. – KENYON, K. M.: Excavations at Jericho, Palestine Exploration Quarterly, 1953, pp. 81–95. Jericho, Oldest Walled Town, Archaeology 1954, Vol. 7, pp. 2–8. Digging up Jericho, London 1957. Earliest Jericho, Antiquity 1959, Vol. 33, No. 129.

Good Living in Ugarit
The World's First Alphabet

DUSSAUD, R.: Les Découvertes de Ras Shamra [Ugarit], Paris 1937. – SCHAEFFER, C. F. A.: Ugaritica, Paris 1939, tome 3. Le Palais Royal d'Ugarit, Mission de Ras Shamra, Paris 1955, tomes 3, 4. – VIROLLEAUD, C.: The Gods of Phoenicia, Antiquity 1931, Vol. 5, pp. 405–414. La déesse Anat-Astarté dans les poèmes de Ras-Shamra, Paris 1937.

Tyre and Sidon

AUTRAN, C.: Phéniciens, Paris 1920. – CONTENAU, G.: Mission Achéologique à Sidon, Paris 1921. – POIDEBARD, A.: Un grand port disparu Tyr, Paris 1939. – POIDEBARD, A. and LAUFFRAY, J.: Sidon, Beyrouth 1951.

Queen of the Seas

CINTAS, P.: Contribution à l'étude de l'expansion Carthaginoise au Maroc, 1947. La Céramique Punique, Tunis 1950. Fouilles à Utique, Karthago, Vol. 2 and 5. – EHRENBERG, V.: Karthago, Leipzig 1927. – FREND, W. H. C.: The Donatist Church, Oxford 1952. – GARCIA Y BELLIDO, A.: Fenicios y Carthagineses en Occidente, Madrid 1942. Phönizische und griechische Kolonisation im westlichen Mittelmeer, Karthago, Historia Mundi, München 1954, Bd. 3. – GAUCKLER, P.: Nécropoles Puniques de Carthage, Paris 1925. – GSELL, S.: Histoire ancienne de l'Afrique du Nord, Paris 1928, I–VIII. – HARDEN, D. B.: The topography of Punic Carthage, Greece and Rome, 1939, Vol. IX, No. 25. – LAPEYRE, G. and PELLEGRIN, A.: Carthage Punique, Paris 1942. – MELTZER, O.: Geschichte der Karthager, Berlin 1879, Bd. 1; 1896, Bd. 2; Kahrstedt, U.: 1913, Bd. 3. – PICARD, G.: Le Monde de Carthage, Paris 1956. – VOGT, J.: Rom und Karthago, Leipzig 1943. – WARMINGTON, B. H.: Carthage, London 1960.

The Silent Stones of Malta

BRADLEY, R. N.: Malta and the Mediterranean Race, London 1912. – BREA, L. B.: Malta and the Mediterranean, Antiquity 1960, Vol. 34, No. 134, p. 132. – BUXTON, L. H. D.: The Ethnology of Malta and Gozo, Journal Royal Anthrop. Inst. 1922, Vol. III, p. 164 sq. – CESCHI, C.: Architettura dei templi megalitici di Malta, Rome 1939. – GJERSTAD, E.: Studies on Prehistoric Cyprus, Uppsala Universitets Årsskrift 1926, Stockholm 1926. – LEOPOLD, H. M. R.: Malta, Ex Oriente Lux, Leiden 1943, pp. 341–344. MURRAY, M. A.: Excavations in Malta, London 1923,

Part I, II, III. – PEET, T. E.: The Prehistoric Period in Malta, Papers of the British School at Rome, London 1910, Vol. V, p. 141 sq. – UGOLINI, L. M.: Malta 1934. Malta Antica, Vol. 1–5. – ZAMMIT, T.: Prehistoric Malta, The Tarxien Temples, London 1930. The Prehistoric Remains of the Maltese Islands, Antiquity 1930, p. 55 sq.

Their Faith Moved Mountains
The Megaliths of Morbihan

BAGGE, A. and KAELAS, L.: Die Funde aus Dolmen und Ganggräbern in Schonen, Schweden I und II, Stockholm 1950 und 1952. – DANIEL, G. E.: The Dual Nature of the Megalithic Colonisation of Prehistoric Europe, Proceedings of the Prehistoric Society, 1941, Vol. VII. The Prehistoric Chamber Tombs of England and Wales, Cambridge 1950. The Megalith Builders of Western Europe, London 1958. – FORDE, C. D.: The Early Cultures of Atlantic Europe, American Anthropologist, 1930, Vol. 32. – GARCIA, L. P.: Los Sepulcros Megalíticos Catalanes y la Cultura Pirenáica, Barcelona 1950. – HAWKES, C. F. C.: The Prehistoric Foundations of Europe, 1940. – KIRCHNER, H.: Die Menhire in Mitteleuropa und der Menhirgedanke, Akademie der Wissenschaften und der Literatur, Wiesbaden, 1955. – LEISNER, G. and V.: Die Megalithgräber der Iberischen Halbinsel, Madrider Forschungen, Bd. 1, Berlin 1956 und 1959. – MONMARCHÉ, G.: Bretagne [La France illustrée], Paris 1950. – NORDMAN, C. A.: The Megalithic Culture of Northern Europe, Finska Fornminnesföreningens Tidskrift, 1935, Vol. 39. – PÉQUART, M. and S.-J., LE ROUZIC, Z.: Corpus des Signes Gravés des Monuments Mégalithiques du Morbihan, Paris 1927. – PIGGOTT, S.: Recent Work at Stonehenge, Antiquity 1954, Vol. 28, No. 112, p. 221. – RÖDER, J.: Pfahl und Menhir, Studien zur westeuropäischen Altertumskunde, Neuwied 1949.

Mari, the Wonder City

DOSSIN, G.: Les archives épistolaires du Palais de Mari, Syria XIX, 1938, pp. 105–126. Les archives économiques de Mari, Syria XX, 1939, pp 97–113. Inscriptions de fondation provenante de Mari, Syria XXI, 1940, pp. 152–169. Correspondance de Šamši-Addu, Archives Royales de Mari, Paris 1950, tome I, and Paris 1951, tome 4. – JEAN, C. F.: Lettres Diverses, Archives Royales de Mari, Paris 1950, tome 2. – KÜPPER, I. R.: Correspondance de Kibri-Dagan, Archives Royales de Mari, Paris 1950, tome 3. – PARROT, A.: Le Temple d'Ishtar, Mission Archéologique de Mari, Paris 1956, tome I. Le Palais, Mission Archéologique de Mari, Architecture, Paris 1958, Peintures murales, Paris 1958, Documents et Monuments, Paris 1959. – SODEN, W. VON: Das altbabylonische Briefarchiv von Mari, Die Welt des Orients, Göttingen 1948, p. 187 sq.

Island of 8,000 Towers
A Pre-Christian Madonna

DESSY, N.: I Bronzetti Nuragici, Milano 1957. – KUHN, A.: La posizione del Sardo fra le lingue Romanze, Atti del V Convegno internazionale di Studi Sardi, Cagliari 1954. – LILLIU, G.: Il Nuraghe di Barumini e la stratigrafia Nuragica, Studi Sardi XII–XIII, Sassari 1, 1955. I Nuraghi della Sardegna, Realtà Nuova, 9, 1956. Illustrated London News, March 8, 1958, p. 388 sq. The Nuraghi of Sardinia, Antiquity, Vol. 33, March 1959, No. 129, p. 32 sq. The Proto-Castles of Sardinia, Scientific American 1959, Vol. 201, No. 6. Primi Scavi del Villaggio Talaiotico di ses Païsses [Arta, Maiorca], Rome 1960. – Pais, E.: Storia della Sardegna e della Corsica, Vol. i, ii, Rome 1923. – Pittau, M.: Studi Sardi di linguistica e storia, Pisa 1958. – Raspi, R. C.: La Sardegna Nuragica, Cagliari 1955. Il Volto della Sardegna, Cagliari 1956. – Steinitzer, A.: Die vergessene Insel, Gotha 1924. – Zervos, C.: La civilisation de la Sardaigne, Paris 1954.

Linear B
Life in the Mycenaean Age

Bennett, E. L. jun.: The Pylos Tablets: texts of the inscriptions found 1939–54, Princeton UP. for University of Cincinnati, 1955. – Blegen, C. W.: Excavations at Pylos, Amer. J. Archaeol. 1952 and 1953, Vol. 57 and 58. The Palace of Nestor excavations of 1954, Amer. J. Archaeol. 59. – Chadwick, J.: The Decipherment of Linear B, Cambridge 1958. – Chantraine, P.: Le déchiffrement de l'écriture Linear B à Cnossos et à Pylos, Revue de Philologie 29, 11–33. – Cook, J. M.: The cult of Agamemnon at Mycenae, Geras, Athen 1953, pp. 112–118. – Evans, A. J.: Scripta Minoa, The Hieroglyphic and Primitive Linear Classes, Vol. 1, Oxford 1909. The Palace of Minos, Oxford 1935. – Fimmen, D.: Zeit und Dauer der kretisch-mykenischen Kultur, Leipzig und Berlin 1909. – Glotz, G.: La civilisation égéenne [L'évolution de l'humanité], Paris 1923. – Kantor, H. J.: The Aegean and the Orient in the Second Millennium b.c., The Archaeological Institute of America, Monograph Number 1, Bloomington, Ind., 1947. – Marinatos, S.: Zur Entzifferung der mykenischen Schrift, Minos [Revista de Filologia Egea], Salamanca 1956, Vol. iv, p. 11 sq. – Nilsson, M. P.: The Minoan-Mycenaean Religion and its Survival in Greek Religion, Lund 1950. – Severyns, A.: Grèce et Proche-Orient avant Homère, Bruxelles 1960. – Snijder, G. A. S.: Kretische Kunst, Versuch einer Deutung, Berlin 1936. – Ventris, M. and Chadwick, J.: Documents in Mycenaean Greek, Cambridge 1956.

The Cult of Apollo
The Delphic Oracle
The Pythia Replies

Amandry, P.: Dédicaces Delphiques, Bulletin de Correspondance Hellénique 1940 à 1941, Paris 1942, lxiv–lxv, p. 60 sq. La mantique apollinienne à Delphes, Essai sur le fonctionnement de l'Oracle, Paris 1950. – Bourguet, E.: Les Ruines de Delphes. – Bousauet, J.: Delphes comptes du quatrième siècle, Bulletin de Correspondance Hellénique, lxvi–lxvii, 1942–1943, Paris 1944, p. 84 sq. – Coste-Messelière, P. de la: Les Trésors de Delphes, Paris 1950. Au Musée de Delphes, 1936. – Courby, F.: Fouilles de Delphes, Vol. ii. – Festugière, A. J.: La Révélation d'Hermès Trismégiste, Paris 1954. – Finley, J. H.: Thucydides, Cambridge 1947. – Flacelière, R.: Le fonctionnement de l'Oracle de Delphes, Annales de l'Ecole des Hautes Etudes de Gand, Gand 1938, tome ii, p. 69 sq. – Heinevetter, F.: Würfel- und Buchstabenorakel in Griechenland und Kleinasien, Breslau 1912. – Holland: The Mantic Mechanism at Delphi, Amer. J. Archaeol. 37, 1933, p. 201 sq. – Nilsson, M. P.: Geschichte der griechischen Religion, Handbuch der Altertumswissenschaft, 5. Abt., 2. Teil, 1. Bd., München 1955. – Oppé, A. P.: The

Chasm at Delphi, JHS, XXIV, 1904, p. 214 sq. – PARKE, H. W.: The Delphic Oracle, Oxford 1939. – PATZER, H.: Gnomon, Bd. 27, 1955, Heft 3, p. 1 sq. – PERSSON, A. W.: Die Exegeten und Delphi, Lund Universitets Årsskrift, Lund und Leipzig 1918. – POULSEN, F.: Delphi, 1920. – SCHNEIDER, C.: Gnomon, Bd. 27, 1955, Heft 3, p. 167 und Bd. 27, 1955, Heft 1, p. 21. – SCHOBER, F.: Delphoi, Realenzyklopädie der klassischen Altertumswissenschaft, Supplementband V, 1931, p. 62 sq.

Olympias, Zeus and Alexander
Latest News of Dodona

BÜRCHNER, L.: Dokimion bibliographikon ton peri tes Epeiru kata tus neoterus chronus demosieuthenton, Epeirotika Chronika 1, 1926, pp. 7–38. – CENTLIVRES, M.-C. and EICHE, H.: in: Reallexikon für Antike und Christentum, Stuttgart 1959, pp. 746–763. – COOK, A. B.: Zeus, Jupiter and the oak, in: The Classical Review, Vol. XVII, London 1903, April, p. 174 sq.; June 1903, p. 268 sq.; November 1903, p. 403 sq.; Vol. XVIII, London 1904, February, p. 75 sq.; July 1904, p. 325 sq.; October 1904, p. 361 sq. – DETERING, A.: Die Bedeutung der Eiche seit der Vorzeit, Leipzig 1939. – DYGGVE, E.: Dodonaeiske Problemer, in: Poulsen, F.: Arkaeologiske og Kunsthistoriske Afhandlinger, Kopenhagen 1941. – EVANGELIDES, D. E.: He anaskaphe tes Dodones, Praktika tes Archaiologikes Etaireias, Athens 1952, pp. 279–325. Anaskaphe en Dodone, Praktika tes Archaiologikes Etaireias, Athens 1954, pp. 188–193. – JACOBSOHN, H.: Dodona, Zeitschrift für vergleichende Sprachforschung auf dem Gebiete der indogermanischen Sprachen, Göttingen 1928, pp. 35–37. – NILSSON, P. M.: Zeus Naios in Dodona, in: Geschichte der griechischen Religion, Bd. 1, München 1955, pp. 425–427. – PRELLER: in: Real-Encyclopädie der klassischen Altertumswissenschaft, Stuttgart 1842, pp. 1190–1195. – WARDE FOWLER, W.: in: Archiv für Religionswissenschaft, Leipzig und Berlin 1913, pp. 317–320. – WENIGER, L.: Altgriechischer Baumkultus, Leipzig 1919.

Altantis, Fact or Fiction?
City Beneath the Sands
The Civilization of Tartessus

ALY, W.: Strabons Geographica in 17 Büchern; Text, Übersetzung und erläuternde Anmerkungen, Bonn 1957, Bd. 4. – AVIENUS: Avieni Ora Martima, Periplus Massiliensis saec. VL. A. C. edidit A. Schulten, Barcinone-Berolini 1922. – BACO OF VERULAM, F.: Nova Atlantis, London 1638. – BAILLY, J. S.: Lettres sur l'Atlantide de Platon et l'ancienne histoire de l'Asie, London 1779. – BÄR, F. C.: Essai sur les Atlantiques, Paris 1762. – BARTOLI: Essai sur l'explication historique donnée par Platon de sa République et de son Atlantide, Paris 1780. – BLANCO FREIJEIRO, A.: El vaso de Valdegamas [Don Benito, Badajoz] y ostras vasos de Bronce del mediodia Español, Consejo Superior de investigaciones científicas, Instituto de Arqveologia y prehistoria «Rodrigo Caro», Madrid 1953. Orientalia [Estudio de objetos y orientalizantes en la peninsula], Consejo Superior de investigaciones científicas, Instituto Español de Arqveologia y prehistoria «Rodrigo Caro», Madrid 1956. – BLANCO DE TORRECILLAS, C.: El tesoro del cortijo de «Evora», Archivo Español de Arqveologia, 32, 1959. – BONSOR, G.: Tartesse, New York 1922. Tartessos, Excavaciones del cerro del Trigo, Junta Superior de excavaciones y Antiguedades, Núm. 5 de 1927, Madrid 1928. – BORI DE ST-

VINCENT: Essai sur les îles fortunées et l'atlantique Atlantide, Paris 1803. –
BOSCH-GIMPERA, P.: Fragen der Chronologie der phönizischen Kolonisation in
Spanien, Klio, Bd. 22, 1928, pp. 345–368. Etnologia de la Peninsula ibérica, Barce-
lona 1932. – CADET: Mémoires sur les jaspes et autres pierres précieuses de l'île de
Corse, Bastia, 1785. – CHRIST, W.: Avien und die Ora maritima, Leipzig 1865. –
CONWAY, R. S.: Italy in the Etruscan Age, A. The Etruscans, The Cambridge
Ancient History, Vol. IV, pp. 383–432. – DIODORUS SICULUS: V, 35, 36. – DONNELLY,
I.: Atlantis, the antediluvian world, London 1882. – FROBENIUS, L.: Und Afrika
sprach, Leipzig 1911. – GAFFAREL, P.: La mer des Sargasses, Paris 1872, p. 600. –
GARCIA Y BELLIDO, A.: La Dama de Elche, Consejo Superior de investigaciones
científicas, Instituto Diego Velázquez, Madrid 1943. Phönizische und griechische
Kolonisation im westlichen Mittelmeer, Historia Mundi, Bd. 3, pp. 328–356. –
GOMARA, F. L. DE: Historia de las Indias, Saragossa 1553. – HENNIG, R.: Von
rätselhaften Ländern, München 1925. Das Rätsel der Atlantis, Meereskunde, 14.
Jahrgang, Berlin 1925, Heft 161. Die Erreichung der Azorengruppe durch die
Karthager, Archäologischer Anzeiger, Beiblatt zum Jahrbuch des Deutschen
Archäologischen Instituts, Bd. 42, 1927, pp. 12–19. – HUMBOLDT, A. VON: Veu des
Cordillères, Paris 1810. – HERRMANN, A.: An den Ufern einer versandeten Meer-
esbucht, Die Woche, Jahrgang 33, 1931, Nr. 35. Unsere Ahnen und Atlantis,
Berlin 1934. – JESSEN, O.: Südwest-Andalusien, Petermanns Mitteilungen, Er-
gänzungsband 40, Heft 186, 1924. Tartessos-Atlantis, Zeitschrift der Gesellschaft
für Erdkunde, Berlin 1925, p. 184. Zur geographischen Seite der Tartessos-Frage,
Jahrbuch des Deutschen Archäologischen Instituts, Bd. 40, 1925, pp. 346–355. –
KIRCHMAIER, G. C.: Exercitatio de Platonis Atlantide, Wittenberg 1685. –
KNÖTEL, A. F. R.: Atlantis und das Volk der Atlanten, Leipzig 1893. –
KRÜMMEL, O.: Die nordatlantische Sargassosee, Petermanns Mitteilungen, 1891,
p. 129 – KUKAHN, E. and BLANKO, A.: El tesoro de «El Carambolo», Archivo
Español de Arqveologia 32, 1959. – LAMMERER: Gedanken zum Tartessos-Prob-
lem, Jahrbuch des Deutschen Archäologischen Instituts, Bd. 40, 1925, pp. 356–364.
– MEYER, E.: Tartessos, in: Geschichte des Altertums, Bd. 2, 2. Abteilung Stuttgart und Berlin 1931, pp. 94–105. – OPPERT, G.: Tharshish und Ophir, Zeitschrift
für Ethnologie, Berlin 1902, Bd. 35, p. 50 and 212 – PEMAN, C.: El Pasaje Tartés-
sico de Avieno, Consejo Superior de investigaciones científicas, Instituto Diego
Velázquez, Madrid 1941. – PLATON: Timaeus-Critias, Collection des Universités
de France, Paris 1956. – PLONGEON, A. LE: Sacred mysteries among the Mayas
and the Quichas, 11 500 years ago, New York 1886. – REDSLOB, G. M.: Thule, die
phönizischen Handelswege nach dem Norden, insbesondere nach dem Bern-
steinlande, Leipzig 1855. – RUDBECK, O.: Atlantica, Upsala 1675. – SAAVEDRA Y
PÉREZ DE MECA: Mastia y Tarteso, y los pueblos litorales del sud-este de España
en la Antigüedad, Murcia 1929. – SCHULTEN, A.: Forschungen nach Tartessos,
Jahrbuch des Deutschen Archäologischen Instituts, 1923, 1924, Bd. 38, 39, Beiblatt I, II, 1–10 und Bd. 40, 1925, pp. 342–345. Forschungen nach Tartessos,
Archäologischer Anzeiger, Beiblatt zum Jahrbuch des Deutschen Archäologischen Instituts, Bd. 42, 1927, pp. 12–19. Die Etrusker in Spanien, Klio, Bd. 23,
1929, pp. 365–432. Tartessos, Hamburg 1950. – SCHULTEN, A. and JESSEN, O.:
Tartessos und anderes Topographische aus Spanien, Jahrbuch des Deutschen
Archäologischen Instituts, Bd. 37, 1922, Beiblatt I, II, pp. 18–55. – STRABO: III, 1,

6; 2, 14; 1, 9. – WIRTH, H.: Das Geheimnis Arktis-Atlantis, Die Woche, Jahrgang 33, 1931, Nr. 35.

The Guanches

BROWN: Madeira, Canary Islands and Azores, London 1903. – DE CAMPOS, C. M.: Canarias en la Brecha, Las Palmas de Gran Canaria, 1953. Las Vírgenes Canarias, in: Revista de Estudios Políticos, Vol. 81, May-June, Madrid 1955, pp. 83–132. – DELGADO, J. A.: Excavaciones Arqueológicas en Tenerife [Canarias], Nr. 14, Madrid 1947. – GLAS, G.: The History of the Discovery and Conquest of the Canary Islands, London 1764. – GSELL, S.: Histoire Ancienne de l'Afrique du Nord, tome VIII, Paris 1928, p. 296 sq. – JUBA MAURITANUS: in: Fragmenta historicorum Graecorum, Vol. 3, Paris 1849. – PARKER-WEBB, P. and BERTHELOT, S.: Histoire naturelle des Iles Canaries, tome II, Paris 1839. – PLINIUS SECUNDUS, GAIUS: Naturalis Historia, VI, 37. – SHOR, J. and F.: Spain's "Fortunate Isles," the Canaries, in: The National Geographic Magazine, June 1955, Washington, pp. 485–522. – TORRIANI, L.: Die Kanarischen Inseln und ihre Urbewohner, in: Quellen und Forschungen zur Geschichte der Geographie und Völkerkunde, Bd. 6, Leipzig 1940. – WARMINGTON, E. H.: The Ancient Explorers, London 1929, p. 52 sq.

The Mask of T'ao-t'ieh

D'ARDENNE DE TIZAC, H.: Les Animaux dans L'Art Chinois, Les Arts de l'Asie, Paris 1922. – BUSHELL, S. W.: Chinese Art, London 1914. – ECKE, G.: Frühe chinesische Bronzen aus der Sammlung Oskar Trautmann, herausgegeben von Gustav Ecke, Peking 1939. – HAJEK, L.: Chinesische Kunst in tschechoslowakischen Museen, Prag 1954. – HENTZE, C.: Frühchinesische Bronzen und Kultdarstellungen, Antwerpen 1937. – KOOP, A. J.: Early Chinese Bronzes, London 1924. – SAMMLER: Sammlung Lochow, Chinesische Bronzen, herausgegeben von Sammler, Peking 1944. – TCH'OU TO-YI, M.: Bronzes Antiques de la Chine, Paris-Bruxelles 1924. – WHITE, W. C.: Bronze Culture of Ancient China, Toronto 1956.

A Man Named Siddhartha

BASHAM, A. L.: The Wonder that was India, London 1954. – FOUCHER, A.: La Vie du Bouddha, Paris 1949. Les Vies Antérieures du Bouddha, Paris 1955. – GLASENAPP, H. VON: Buddha, Geschichte und Legende, 1950. – KERN, M.: Das Licht des Ostens, Stuttgart-Berlin-Leipzig 1922. – OLDENBERG, H.: Buddha, 1923. – RENOU, L. and FELLIOZAT, J.: L'Inde classique, Paris 1947 and 1953. – THOMAS, E. J.: The Life of Buddha, London 1927. – WALDSCHMIDT, E.: Die Legende vom Leben des Buddha, 1929.

Gandhara and the Buddha Image

ADAM, L.: Buddhastatuen-Ursprung und Formen der Buddhagestalt, Stuttgart 1925. – BUCHTHAL, H.: The Western Aspects of Gandhara Sculpture, Proceedings of the British Academy, London 1945, pp. 151–176. – BUSSAGLI, M.: L'irrigidimento formale nei bassorilievi del Gandhara in rapporto all'estetica indiana, in: Archeologia Classica, Vol. V, 1953, pp. 66–83. Osservazioni sulla persistenza delle forme ellenistiche nell'arte del Gandhara, in: Rivista dell'Istituto Nazionale di

Archeologia e Storia dell'Arte, N.S. anni v–vi, 1956–57, p. 149. L'Arte del Gand-hara in Pakistan e i suoi incontri con l'Arte dell'Asia Centrale, Rome 1958. – DEYDIER, H.: Contribution à l'Etude de l'Art du Gandhara, Paris 1950. – FOUCHER, A.: L'Art Gréco-Bouddhique du Gandhara, Paris, tome I 1905, tome II 1918. – FOUCHER, A. and BAZIN-FOUCHER, E.: La Vieille Route de l'Inde de Bactres à Taxila, Paris 1942 – GHIRSHMAN: Journal Asiatique, Nr. 234, 1943–1945, pp. 59–71. Mémoires de la Délégation Archéologique Française en Afghanistan, XII, 1946, pp. 99–108. – HARGREAVES, H.: The Buddha Story in Stone, Calcutta 1914. – INGHOLT, H. and LYONS, I.: Gandharan Art in Pakistan, New York 1957. – KEMPERS, B.: Die Begegnung der griechisch-römischen Kunst mit dem indischen Kulturkreis, Handbuch der Archäologie, II, München 1954. – MARSHALL, Sir J.: Taxila, 3 Vols., Cambridge 1951. The Buddhist Art of Gandhara, Cambridge 1960. – MONNERET DE VILLARD, U.: Le monete dei Kushana e l'impero romano, in: Orientalia, Vol. 17, 1948, pp. 205–245. – NARAIN, A. K.: The Indo-Greeks, Oxford 1957. – ROWLAND, B.: Gandhara, Rome and Mathura. The Early Relief Style, in: Archives of the Chinese Art Society of America, Vol. X, 1956, pp. 8–17. – SALMONY, A.: Notes on a Stone Sculpture from Gandhara, in: Artibus Asiae, XVII, 1954, pp. 29–99. – SCHLUMBERGER, D.: Le temple de Surkh Kotal en Bactriane, I, II, III, in· Journal Asiatique, 1952, pp. 433–453; 1954, pp. 161–205 and pp. 269–279. – SOPER, A. C.: Aspects of Light Symbolism in Gandharan Sculp-ture, in: Artibus Asiae XII, 1949, pp. 252–283 and 314–330; XIII, 1950, pp. 63–85. The Roman Style in Gandhara, American Journal of Archaeology, 1951, Vol. 55, pp. 301–319. – WALDSCHMIDT, E.: Gandhara, Kutscha, Turfan, Leipzig 1925. Die Entwicklungsgeschichte des Buddhabildes in Indien, Ostasiatische Zeitschrift 1930, pp. 265–277. – WHEELER, Sir M.: Rome beyond the Imperial Frontiers, London 1954.

The Cave Temples of Tun-huang

CHAVANNES, E.: Les Documents Chinois découverts par A. Stein, Oxford 1913. – GILES, L.: Dated Chinese MSS in the Stein Collection, Bulletin of the School of Oriental Studies, London 1933–46. Six Centuries at Tun-huang, London 1944. – MASPERO, H.: Les Documents de la troisième expédition de Sir A. Stein, 1953. – PELLIOT, P.: Les Grottes de Tun-huang, Paris 1920–24. Les Fresques de Touen-Houang et les Fresques de M. Eumorfopoulos, Revue des Arts Asiatiques v., 1928, p. 143 and 193. – STEIN, A.: Ruins of Desert Cathay, 2, London 1912. A Catalogue of Paintings recovered from Tun-huang, London 1931.

The Silk Road

LE COQ, A. VON: Auf Hellas Spuren in Ost-Turkistan, Leipzig 1926. – FUCHS, W.: Huei-ch'ao's Pilgerreise durch Nordwest-Indien und Zentral-Asien um 726, Berlin 1939. – GRÜNWEDEL, A.: Bericht über archäologische Arbeiten in Idiku-tschari und Umgebung im Winter 1902–1903, Abh. d. Akad. d. Wiss., München 1906. Altbuddhistische Kultstätten in Chinesisch-Turkistan, Berlin 1912. – HEDIN, S.: Sidenvägen, Stockholm 1936. – HERRMANN, A.: Die alten Seidenstrassen zwischen China und Syrien, 1910. Lou-lan, Leipzig 1931. – MARSHALL, Sir J.: A Guide to Taxila, Calcutta 1921. Taxila, Vol. 1–3, Cambridge 1951. – STEIN, M. A.: A Journey of Geographical and Archaeological Exploration in Chinese Turk-

estan, The Geographical Journal, December 1902. – YULE, Sir H.: Cathay and
the Way thither, new edition, revised by H. Cordier, Vol. 1–4, London 1915.

The Treasure of the Oxus

ALCOCK, A. W. et al.: Report on the Natural History Results of the Pamir
Boundary Commission, Calcutta 1898. – BARTOLD, V. V.: Istorija Turkestana,
Taschkent 1922. – COBBOLD, R. P.: Innermost Asia, London 1900. – CURZON, G.
N.: The Pamirs and the Source of the Oxus, The Geographical Journal, Vol.
VIII, London 1896, pp. 15–54, 97–119, 239–264. – DALTON, O. M.: The Treasure
of the Oxus with other Examples of early Oriental Metal-Work, London 1926. –
Fox, R.: People of the Steppes, London 1925. – GRIESBACH, C. L.: Geological
Field Notes, No. 3, Afghan Boundary Commission, 1885. – KROPOTKIN, P.: The
Old Beds of the Amu-Daria, The Geographical Journal, Vol. XII, London
1898, pp. 306–310. – MITCHELL, R.: The Regions of the Upper Oxus, Proceed-
ings of the Royal Geographical Society, Vol. VI, London 1884, pp. 489–512. –
REGEL, A.: Journey in Karateghin and Darwaz, Proceedings of the Royal
Geographical Society, Vol. IV, London 1882, pp. 412–417. In: Izvestija Imp.
Russkago Geografitscheskago Obschtschestva, Vol. XIII, St. Petersburg 1882. –
YATE, C. E.: Northern Afghanistan, London 1888.

The Scythians
Company for the King
Kings, Concubines and Horses

BOROVKA, G.: Scythian Art, London 1928. – CLEMEN, C.: Einige religionsgeschicht-
lich wichtige skythische Denkmäler, Festschrift zum sechzigsten Geburstag von
Paul Clemen, Bonn 1926. – FRYE, R. N.: Treasures of the Hermitage Museum,
Archaeology, 1958, Vol. II, pp. 105–110. – GIMBUTAS, M.: Timber-Graves in
Southern Russia, A Pre-Scythian Culture, Expedition 1961, Vol. 3, pp. 14–22. –
GINTERS, W.: Das Schwert der Skythen und Sarmaten in Südrußland, Berlin
1928. – GRJAZNOV, M. P.: Pervyj Pazyrykskij kurgan, Leningrad 1950. – HANČAR,
F.: Altai-Skythen und Schamanismus, Ethnologica, Actes du IVe Congrès in-
ternational des Sciences Anthropologiques et Ethnologiques, tome III, 1956,
p. 183 sq. Aus dem Arbeitsbereich der sowjetischen Ur- und Frühgeschichte,
Saeculum, Jahrgang 1961, Bd. II, Heft 1, 2, pp. 83–85. – HARMATTA, J.: Studies
on the History of the Sarmatians, Budapest 1950. – HERODOTUS: History,
Book 4. – JUNGE, J.: Saka-Studien, Leipzig 1939. – KRETSCHMER, P.: Zum Balkan-
Skythischen, Glotta Bd. 24, 1935, pp. 1–56. – MAKARENKO, N.: La civilisation
des Scythes et Hallstatt, Eurasia Septentrionalis Antiqua, Helsinki 1930, Vol. 5,
pp. 22–48. – McGOVERN, W. M.: The Early Empires of Central Asia, Chapel Hill
1939. – MINNS, E. H.: Scythians and Greeks, Cambridge 1913. – NIEDERLE, L.:
Manuel de l'antiquité slave, tome 2, Paris 1926. – ROSTOWZEW, M.: Skythien und
der Bosporus, Bd. 1, Berlin 1931. – RUDENKO, S. I.: Gornoaltajskie nachodki i
Skify, Moskau-Leningrad 1952. Kultura naselenija gornogo Altaja v skifskoe
vremja, Moskau-Leningrad 1953. – SALMONY, A.: Sino-Siberian Art, in the Collection of C. T. Loo, Paris 1933. – TALBOT RICE, T.: The Scythians, London
1957. – TALLGREN, A. M.: Zum Ursprungsgebiet des sogenannten skythischen

Tierstils, Acta Archaeologica, Bd. 4, pp. 258–264. – VAMBERY, H.: Reise in Mittelasien, Leipzig 1865.

King Solomon's Furnaces
In Quest of Ophir

CATON-THOMPSON, G.: The Zimbabwe Culture, Oxford 1931. – DAVIDSON, B.: The Lost Cities of Africa, Boston-Toronto 1959. – GLUECK, N.: The First Campaign at Tell el-Kheleifeh [Ezion-geber], Bulletin of the American Schools of Oriental Research, No. 71, 1938, pp. 3–18. The Second Campaign at Tell el-Kheleifeh, Bulletin of the American Schools of Oriental Research, No. 75, 1939, pp. 8–22. The Third Season of Excavation at Tell el-Kheleifeh, Bulletin of the American Schools of Oriental Research, No. 79, 1940, pp. 2–18. – HALL, R. N.: Great Zimbabwe, London 1907. – HALL, R. N. and NEAL, W. G.: The Ancient Ruins of Rhodesia, London 1902. – HENNIG, R.: Von rätselhaften Ländern, München 1925, p. 65 sq. – J. L. M.: The Rhodesia Ruins, Mediaeval Rhodesia by David Rendall MacIver [Review], The Geographical Journal, Vol. 28, 1906, pp. 68–70. – MACIVER, D. R.: Mediaeval Rhodesia, London 1906. – NOTH, M.: Geschichte Israels, Göttingen 1954, p. 187 sq. – SALZBERGER, G.: Die Salomo-Sage in der semitischen Literatur, Berlin 1907. – SUMMERS, R.: Possible Influences of the Iron Age in Southern Africa, South African Journal of Science, Vol. 52, 1955, pp. 43–46. – WAINWRIGHT, G. A.: The Founders of the Zimbabwe Civilization, Man, No. 80, 1949, pp. 62–66. – WHITE, F.: Notes on the Great Zimbabwe Elliptical Ruin, Journal of the Anthropological Institute, Vol. 35, 1905, pp. 39–47.

The Bronzes of Benin

BLAKE, J. W.: Europeans in West-Africa 1450–1560, Vol. I and II, London 1942. – BRADBURY, R. E.: Benin, London 1957. – BRYANT, A. T.: Olden Times in Zululand and Natal, London 1929. – BURNS, Sir A.: History of Nigeria, London 1951. – CORBEAU, J.: L'empire du Bénin, Lyon 1950. – DIKE, K. O.: Trade and Politics in the Niger Delta 1830–1885, Oxford 1956. – DITTEL, P.: Die Besiedlung Südnigeriens von den Anfängen bis zur britischen Kolonisation, Wissenschaftliche Veröffentlichungen des Deutschen Museums für Länderkunde zu Leipzig, Leipzig 1936, p. 71 sq. – EGHAREVBA, J.: Some stories of ancient Benin, Lagos 1951. The city of Benin, 1952. – ELISOFON, E. and FAGG, W.: The Sculpture of Africa, London 1958. – FAGG, W.: On the Nature of African Art. Memoirs and Proc. of the Manchester Lit. and Phil. Soc., 1953. The Study of African Art. Allen Memorial Museum Bulletin XIII, No. 2, 1955–1956. A Life-Size Terracotta Head from Nok, Man 1956, Vol. 55, p. 89. – FAGG, W. P. and FORMAN, W. and B.: Afro-Portuguese Ivories, London 1959. – FORDE, D.: The Yoruba-Speaking Peoples of South-Western Nigeria, Ethnographic Survey of Africa, London 1951. – FORDE, D. and JONES, G. I.: The Ibo and Ibibio-Speaking Peoples of South-Eastern Nigeria, Ethnographic Survey of Africa, London, New York, Toronto 1950. – FORMAN, W. and DARK, Ph.: Die Kunst von Benin, Prag 1960. – FORMAN, W. and FAGG, W.: Vergessene Negerkunst. Afro-portugiesisches Elfenbein, Prag 1959. – GLÜCK, J. F.: Die Kunst Neger-Afrikas, Kleine Kunstgeschichte der Vorzeit und der Naturvölker, Stuttgart

1956. – GOODWIN, A. J. H.: Metal Working among the early Hottentots, The South African Archaeological Bulletin, Vol. XI, 1956, p. 47. – HAILEY, L.: An African Survey, London 1938. – JEFFREYS, M. D. W.: The origin of the Benin bronzes, Afr. Stud., 1951, pp. 87–91. – LUSCHAN, F. v.: Die Altertümer von Benin, 3 Bände, Berlin 1919. – MARQUART, J.: Die Beninsammlung des Reichs-museums für Völkerkunde in Leiden, Leiden 1913. – MEEK, C. K.: The North-ern Tribes of Nigeria, Vol. I, London 1925. – SMITH, H. F. C.: The Benin study, J. hist. Soc. Nigeria 1956, I. Dec., pp. 60–61. – SUMMERS, R.: Possible Influences of the Iron Age in Southern Africa, South African Journal of Science, Vol. 52, 1955, p. 43 sq. – SYDOW, E. VON: Ancient and modern art in Benin city, Africa, 11, Jan. 1938. Kunst und Kulte von Benin, Atlantis, 10. Jahrgang, 1938, p. 53. Afrikanische Plastik, herausgegeben von G. Kutscher, Berlin 1954. – TALBOT, P. E.: Peoples of South Nigeria, Vol. 1–4, Oxford 1926. – TONG, R.: The ancient city of Benin, Corona, 3, Jan. 1951, pp. 30–32. Figures in Ebony, London 1958. – UGHULU, E.: Short history of [Esan] islan-Benin, Lagos 1950.

River of a Thousand Eyes

BEAVER, W. N.: Unexplored New Guinea. London 1920. – BEHRMANN, W.: Der Sepik und sein Stromgebiet, Mitteilungen aus den deutschen Schutzgebieten, Ergänzungsheft Nr. 12, Berlin 1917. Im Stromgebiet des Sepik, Berlin 1922. – BÜHLER, A. and GARDI, R.: Sepik, Bern, Stuttgart, Wien 1958. – CHAMPION, I. F.: Across New Guinea from the Fly to the Sepik, London 1932. – DETZNER, H.: Ergebnisse von Reisen in Neu Guinea, 1914–1918. – TISCHNER, H.: Kulturen der Südsee, Hamburg 1958. – WICHMANN, A.: Nova Guinea, Vol. I 1909; Vol. II, 1, 1910; Vol II, 2 1912; Vol. III 1907; Vol. IV 1917, Leiden. – WIRZ, P.: Im Herzen von Neuguinea, Zürich 1925. Dämonen und Wilde in Neuguinea, Stuttgart, 1928.

Men of Maize
Cities in the Jungle
Tikal, the Enigma

COE, W. R.: Two carved lintels from Tikal, Archaeology, Vol. 11, Nr. 2, 1958, p. 75 sq. Tikal 1959, Expedition 1959, Vol. 1, p. 7 sq. – DIESELDORFF, E. P.: Kunst und Religion der Mayavölker, Berlin 1926, Bd. 1; 1931, Bd. 2; 1933, Bd. 3. – DISSELHOFF, H. D.: Geschichte der altamerikanischen Kulturen, München 1953. – GANN, T.: Maya Cities, London 1927. – JOYCE, T. A.: Mexican Achaeology, 1914. – KELEMEN, P.: Mediaeval American Art, New York 1956. – LENTZ, F. J.: Aus dem Hochlande der Maya, Stuttgart 1930. – MacNEISH, R. S.: Ancient Maize and Mexico, Archaeology, 1955, Vol. 8, p. 108 sq. – MALER, T.: Explora-tions in the Department of Peten Guatemala, Cambridge, Mass., 1911. – MORLEY, S. G.: An Introduction to the Study of the Maya Hieroglyphs, Washington 1915. The Inscriptions of Petén, Vol. 1–5, Washington 1937–38. The Ancient Maya, London 1946. The Ancient Maya, 3rd edition, Stanford 1956. – PLISCHKE, H.: Vom Ursprung der polynesischen Kultur, Saeculum, Bd. 8, 1957, pp. 404–408. – SAPPER, K.: In den Vulcangebieten Mittelamerikas und Westindiens, Stuttgart 1905. Mittelamerikanische Reisen und Studien, Braunschweig 1902. – SCHROEDER, A. H.: Ball Courts and Ball Games of Middle America and Arizona, Archaeology, Vol. 8, 1955, pp. 156–161. – SELER, E.: Gesammelte Abhandlungen zur amerikanischen

Sprach- und Altertumskunde, Bd. 1, 1902, Bd. 2, 1904, Bd. 3, 1908, Berlin. –
SELER-SACHS, C.: Auf alten Wegen in Mexico und Guatemala, Stuttgart 1925. –
SHOOK, E. M.: The Temple of the Red Stela, Expedition 1958, Vol. 1, p. 27 sq.
Tikal Stela 29, Expedition 1960, Vol. 2, p. 29 sq. – TERMER, F.: Die Maya-
forschung, Nova Acta Leopoldina, Bd. 15, Nr. 105, Leipzig 1952. – THOMP-
SON, J. E. S.: The Rise and Fall of Maya Civilization, Norman 1954. – TISCHNER,
H. and KRICKEBERG, W.: Australien/Amerika, Die große Völkerkunde, herg. v.
Hugo A. Bernatzik, Leipzig 1939, p. 187 sq. – TISCHNER, H.: Südsee, Völker-
kunde, Fischer Lexikon, Frankfurt a. M. 1959. Kulturen der Südsee, Hamburg
1958. – TOZZER, A. M.: A preliminary study of the prehistoric ruins of Tikal,
Guatemala. A report of the Peabody Museum Expedition 1909–1910, Cambridge
1911. Landa's Relación de las Cosas de Yucatan, Papers of the Peabody Museum
of American Archaeology, Vol. 18, Cambridge, Mass. 1941. – TRIMBORN, H.:
Indianische Welt in geschichtlicher Schau, Iserlohn 1948. – ZIMMERMANN, G.:
Kurze Formen- und Begriffssystematik der Hieroglyphen der Mayahandschrif-
ten, Hamburg, 1953. Die Hieroglyphen der Mayahandschriften, Universität
Hamburg, Abhandlungen aus dem Gebiet der Auslandskunde, Bd. 62, Reihe B,
Hamburg 1956.

SOURCES OF ILLUSTRATIONS

SOURCES OF ILLUSTRATIONS

1 Male head from Jericho. Photo: Garstang
2 Skull sculpture from Jericho. Photo: Kathleen Kenyon
3 Building in Jericho. Photo: Kathleen Kenyon
4 Human skulls, Jericho. Photo: British Museum
5 The oldest house in the world, Jericho. Photo: Kathleen Kenyon
6 Canaanite goddess, Ugarit. Photo: Musée du Louvre
7 Copper statuette, Ugarit. Photo: Service des Antiquités, Paris
8 The harbor of Ugarit. Photo: 39e Escadr. aér. du Levant
9 Bronze statuette of the god Baal, Ugarit. Photo: Musée du Louvre
10 Clay tablet from the central archives of Ugarit. Photo: Service des Antiquités, Paris
11 Clay vessels, Ugarit. Photo: Service des Antiquités, Paris
12 Fragment from an ivory plaque. Photo: Service des Antiquités, Paris
13 Phoenician man, terra-cotta figurine from Byblos. Photo: Maurice Dunand
14 Neck of a Phoenician vase, Byblos. Photo: Maurice Dunand
15 Punic gravestone. Photo: Rauchwetter
16 Statue of a Carthaginian noblewoman. Photo: Rauchwetter
17 Ceramic head from Carthage. Photo: Rauchwetter
18 Three heads sculptured in glass, Carthage. Photo: Rauchwetter
19 The Hypogeum, Malta. Photo: Luigi Ugolini
20 The "Sleeping Woman of Malta." Photo: Luigi Ugolini
21 Terra-cotta head, Malta. Photo: Luigi Ugolini
22 Excavations at Hal Tarxien. Photo: Luigi Ugolini
23 Overall plan of the temple at Hal Tarxien. Sketch: Luigi Ugolini
24 Remains of megalithic graves in Portugal. Photo: Archives
25 "Tholos da Fariosa," Portugal. Photo: Archives
26 Stonehenge. Photo: Camera Press, London
27 Passage grave, Schonen. Photo: Archives
28 Mural painting in the palace of Mari. Photo: Mission Archéologique de Mari
29 A fertility goddess, Mari. Photo: Mission Archéologique de Mari
30 City administrator of Mari. Photo: Mission Archéologique de Mari
31 Clay bathtubs, Mari. Photo: Mission Archéologique de Mari
32 The interior of a nuraghe, Sardinia. Photo: Christian Zervos
33 A typical nuraghe, Sardinia. Photo: Enit, Roma
34 Ruins of houses of the Barumini fortress. Photo: Enit, Roma
35 Weeping goddess, Sardinia. Photo: Christian Zervos
36 Bronze statuette of an archer. Photo: Christian Zervos
37 Priestess of the nuraghe culture. Photo: Christian Zervos
38 Nuraghe bronze sculpture. Photo: Christian Zervos
39 Gold death mask, Mycenae. Photo: Professor Hirmer
40 Gold mask from Shaft Grave IV, Mycenae. Photo: Professor Hirmer
41 Gold rhyton in the shape of a lion's head, Mycenae. Photo: Professor Hirmer
42 Head of a bull vaulter, Knossos. Photo: Professor Hirmer

INDEX